PUBLICATIONS ON THE NEAR EAST

PUBLICATIONS ON THE NEAR EAST

Poetry's Voice, Society's Song: Ottoman Lyric Poetry by Walter G. Andrews

The Remaking of Istanbul: Portrait of an Ottoman City in the Nineteenth Century by Zeynep Çelik

The Tragedy of Sohráb and Rostám from the Persian National Epic, the Shahname of Abol-Qasem Ferdowsi, translated by Jerome W. Clinton

The Jews in Modern Egypt, 1914–1952 by Gudrun Krämer

Izmir and the Levantine World, 1550–1650 by Daniel Goffman

Medieval Agriculture and Islamic Science: The Almanac of a Yemeni Sultan by Daniel Martin Varisco

Rethinking Modernity and National Identity in Turkey, edited by Sibel Bozdoğan and Reşat Kasaba

Slavery and Abolition in the Ottoman Middle East by Ehud R. Toledano

Britons in the Ottoman Empire, 1642–1660 by Daniel Goffman

Popular Preaching and Religious Authority in the Medieval Islamic Near East by Jonathan P. Berkey

The Transformation of Islamic Art during the Sunni Revival by Yasser Tabbaa

Shiraz in the Age of Hafez: The Glory of a Medieval Persian City by John Limbert

The Martyrs of Karbala: Shi'i Symbols and Rituals in Modern Iran by Kamran Scot Aghaie

Ottoman Lyric Poetry: An Anthology, Expanded Edition, edited and translated by Walter G. Andrews, Najaat Black, and Mehmet Kalpaklı

Party Building in the Modern Middle East: The Origins of Competitive and Coercive Rule by Michele Penner Angrist

Everyday Life and Consumer Culture in Eighteenth-Century Damascus by James Grehan

The City's Pleasures: Istanbul in the Eighteenth Century by Shirine Hamadeh

Reading Orientalism: Said and the Unsaid by Daniel Martin Varisco

The Merchant Houses of Mocha: Trade and Architecture in an Indian Ocean Port by Nancy Um

Tribes and Empire on the Margins of Nineteenth-Century Iran by Arash Khazeni

Tribes & Empire on the Margins of Nineteenth-Century Iran

Arash Khazeni

UNIVERSITY OF WASHINGTON PRESS
Seattle & London

Printed in the United States of America
Design by Thomas Eykemans
12 11 10 09 5 4 3 2 1

UNIVERSITY OF WASHINGTON PRESS
PO Box 50096, Seattle, WA 98145 USA
www.washington.edu/uwpress

The paper used in this publication is acid-free and 90 percent recycled from at least 50 percent post-consumer waste. It meets the minimum requirements of American National Standard for Information Sciences—Permanence of Paper for Printed Library Materials, ANSI Z39.48–1984.∞

LIBRARY OF CONGRESS CATALOGING-IN-PUBLICATION DATA

Khazeni, Arash.
Tribes and empire on the margins of nineteenth-century Iran / Arash Khazeni.
p. cm. — (Publications on the Near East)
Includes bibliographical references and index.
ISBN 978-0-295-98994-5 (hbk. : alk. paper)
ISBN 978-0-295-98995-2 (pbk. : alk. paper)
1. Bakhtiari (Iranian people)—Government relations—History—19th century. 2. Bakhtiari (Iranian people)—Social conditions—19th century. 3. Zagros Mountains Region (Iran and Iraq)—History—19th century. 4. Isfahan Region (Iran)—History—19th century. 5. Iran—History—Qajar dynasty, 1794–1925. 6. Iran—Politics and government—19th century. 7. Tribes—Iran—History—19th century. 8. Imperialism—Social aspects—Iran—History—19th century. 9. Land settlement—Iran—History—19th century. 10. Iran—Ethnic relations—History—19th century. I. Title.
DS269.B3K48 2009 323.11891'59—dc22
2009033962

CONTENTS

To Dana

ACKNOWLEDGMENTS

IN WRITING THIS BOOK, I have accumulated a long list of debts. The Department of History at Yale University provided me with a nurturing environment in which to study and write about the past. I am particularly grateful to Abbas Amanat for accepting me as his student and training me in Safavid and Qajar history. Professor Amanat's encyclopedic knowledge of early modern and modern Iran, his creative approach to the craft of history, and his generosity with his students have made a lasting impression on me. John Demos was involved in this work from the start, and I am grateful to him for his help on a subject so far from his own field. His insights into writing history and narrative have been invaluable to me. This book emerged from the Agrarian Studies Program at Yale and is one version of the story of "the modern transformation of the countryside of the world." I thank James C. Scott for his friendship and for showing me ways to approach and recover the often hidden history of people who move around. Special thanks also go to Kay Mansfield in Agrarian Studies for her gracious and unwavering support.

I was fortunate to receive helpful comments from friends and colleagues, including John Gurney, Houri Berberian, Mohamad Tavakoli-Targhi, Vanessa Martin, Houchang Chehabi, Janet Afary, Ali Gheissari, Magnus Bernhardsson, Mridu Rai, David Yaghoubian, Nikki Keddie, Rudi Matthee, and Sebouh Aslanian, who read versions and drafts. In New Haven, I found friendship and encouragement among a collegial cohort, including Farzin Vejdani, Thomas McDow, Jennifer Boittin, Jonathan Padwe, Adriane Lentz-Smith, and Christian Lentz. At the Claremont Colleges, I have benefited immensely from the support of colleagues, including Pardis Mahdavi, Lara Deeb, Diana Selig, Jonathan Petropoulos, Edward Haley, David Yoo, Arthur Rosenbaum, Bassam Frangieh, Marie-Denise Shelton, Fazia Aitel, Bonnie Snortum, Marc Massoud, Asuman Aksoy, Shahriar Shahriari, Zayn Kassam, and Dru Gladney. Among my students at the Claremont Colleges, special thanks are due to Lila Nazemian, Daniel Yousef Tehrani, Joshua Schneider, Sophie Sung, Keara Duggan, and Jemel Derbali.

I received institutional support to conduct the research for this book from various corners at Yale, including the Department of History, the Council on Middle East Studies, the Center for International and Area Studies, and the Howard Lamar Center for the Study of Frontiers and Borders. These fellowships allowed me to conduct archival research in Iran and the United Kingdom, as well as in collections in the United States. The librarians and archivists of the Iranian National Archives (Sazman-i Asnad-i Milli), Iranian National Library (Kitabkhana-yi Milli), University of Isfahan, British National Archives, University of London–School of Oriental and African Studies, India Office Library, British Petroleum Archives, Firestone Library at Princeton University, Widener Library at Harvard University, and the UCLA Special Collections were all extremely helpful. I am particularly indebted to Kiyanush Kiyani Haft-Lang for his help and generosity during my visits to the National Archives in Tehran. Among friends and scholars in Iran, I thank ʿAbd al-Mihdi Raja'i, Elham Malekzada, Sekandar Amanallahi, Sayyid Farid Qasimi, and Kavih Bayat. I am also grateful to Nikki Keddie for bringing to my attention the Isabella Bird photograph album held in Special Collections at ucla. I thank Sylvester Segura and Ben Royas for all their work in drawing the maps. I also acknowledge the subvention offered by Claremont McKenna College toward the production of maps and photographs.

Michael Duckworth, Beth Fuget, Marilyn Trueblood, and Thomas Eykemans at the University of Washington Press graciously saw the manuscript through to publication. I also wish to thank two anonymous readers for reviewing the manuscript and Linda Rabben for editing it. Chapter 3 was presented at a conference, "Of Mediums and Motored Ways: The Social Lives of Transit Networks," at the University of Washington in May 2005. I thank Lisa Mitchell, Lynn Thomas, Rudolph Mrazek, and other conference participants for their comments on the chapter. An earlier and much different version of chapter 5 appeared in the Duke University journal *Comparative Studies of South Asia, Africa, and the Middle East.*

I thank my mother, Farah, for her patience and for all the long hours spent discussing the history of Iran with me. My deepest gratitude is reserved for Layla, Aiden, and Dana—my own beloved tribe. I could not have made it through this book if not for them and I hope that in some ways it makes up for the times when I was away.

ABBREVIATIONS OF ARCHIVES, COLLECTIONS, AND TEXTS

BNA/FO British National Archives, London

BP British Petroleum Archives, University of Warwick, Coventry, UK

CAM Cambridge University, Manuscripts and Archives, Cambridge, UK

CHI University of Chicago, Regenstein Library, Middle East Collection, Chicago

HAR Harvard University, Widener Library Archives, Cambridge, MA

ICHO Iranian Cultural Heritage Organization (Sazman-i Mir'at-i Farhangi), Tehran

INA National Archives of Iran (Sazman-i Asnad-i Milli), Tehran

IOR British Library, India Office Records, London

ISFA University of Isfahan Archives, (Kitabkhana-yi Markazi), Isfahan

JRGS *Journal of the Royal Geographical Society*

KL *Khuzistan va Luristan dar ʿAsr-i Nasiri, Khanlar Mirza Ihtisham al-Dawla*

MB *Mir'at al-Buldan, Muhammad Hasan Khan Iʿtimad al-Saltana*

NLI National Library of Iran (Kitabkhana-yi Milli), Tehran

NT *Nasikh al-Tavarikh*, Mirza Muhammad Taqi Lisan al-Mulk Sipihr

PRGS *Proceedings of the Royal Geographical Society*

PRI Princeton University, Firestone Library, Near East Collection, Princeton, NJ

RSN *Rawzat al-Safa-yi Nasiri*, Riza Quli Khan Hidayat

SK *Safarnama-yi Khuzistan*, ʿAbd al-Ghaffar Najm al-Mulk

SOAS School of Oriental and African Studies Archives, London

TB *Tarikh-i Bakhtiyari*, Sardar Asʿad and Lisan al-Saltana Sipihr

TM *Tarikh-i Muntazam-i Nasiri*, Muhammad Hasan Khan I'timad al-Saltana

UCLA University of California, Los Angeles, Special Collections, Los Angeles

A NOTE ON TRANSLITERATION

THE PERSIAN TRANSLITERATION used in this book follows the Library of Congress system without the diacritical marks. Exceptions are the names of places and people, such as Herat and Shahsevan, which are spelled in their common form, and terms such as *tayafa*, which are spelled without the *h*. In quoting from older European sources, I have reproduced the language and spellings used in the texts. Dates are given in the Common Era Calendar, except in cases where there is a reason to include the Islamic *hijri* calendar. All Persian translations in the text are my own, except for those otherwise credited in the notes.

TRIBES AND EMPIRE ON THE MARGINS OF NINETEENTH-CENTURY IRAN

INTRODUCTION

THIS BOOK is about tribe and state interactions on the periphery of Qajar Iran. It explores the history of the Bakhtiyari tribal confederacy of the Zagros Mountains during the long nineteenth century, when the balance between the center and the periphery in Iran was forever transformed. Drawing upon nineteenth-century chronicles, tribal histories, ethnographies, and manuscripts, the following pages examine imperial projects to develop the wildlands and settle pastoral nomadic tribes in Qajar Iran. After tracing the rise of the Bakhtiyari during the early nineteenth century in the mountainous periphery of the city of Isfahan, the narrative turns to examining the role of road building, oil exploration, and the Constitutional Revolution in the waning of tribal power and independence in Qajar Iran.

The following pages approach the history of nineteenth-century Iran from its edge—in this case the Bakhtiyari tents and the Zagros Mountains—and place tribal history at the heart of a tale about empire and assimilation. Such an account of Qajar Iran has rarely been attempted. With some exceptions, most of the literature on the period has emphasized the political and cultural center. This study, by contrast, is concerned with the nomadic and seminomadic tribes on the periphery. It asks the question, how was the balance between the state and the tribes, the center and the periphery, transformed in nineteenth-century Iran? In the Qajar period (1785–1925) the nature of tribe and state interactions was altered and the autonomy of pastoral societies was compromised through imperial projects that opened the land and assimilated indigenous subjects into "the guarded domains of Iran." The tribes did not remain passive, however, in the imperial transformation of environment and society. These projects of empire in the hinterlands of Iran were always mediated through encounters, accommodation, and engagement with the tribal periphery.

Tribes and Empire

In the early nineteenth century approximately half of Iran's population was nomadic.[1] These pastoral nomadic societies were politically organized into tribes (*il; tayafa; 'ashayir; qabila*) and claimed extensive land for their seasonal pastures (*yaylaq; qishlaq*). The tribes possessed customary grazing rights and migration routes (*il rah*) and were governed by an array of local rulers, including the paramount chieftains of the confederation (*ilkhan; ilbayg*), the hereditary tribal chieftains (*khan*), the headmen of the subtribes and clans (*kadkhuda; kalantar*), the "white beards" and camp elders (*rish safid*).[2] By necessity the Qajar state treated the tribes as semi-autonomous political units and delegated responsibility for taxation and conscription in the tribal areas to the khans and headmen. For this purpose the khans often received land grants (*tuyul*), and this policy allowed for indirect administration of tribal territories.[3] The state ruled the periphery indirectly, and no sustained policy aimed to settle Iran's tribal populations permanently. The tribes gave nominal allegiance to the early Qajars, offering military service and paying light taxes while retaining substantial autonomy beyond the pale of permanent state domination. Although the tribes were subject to the state's traditional policies of control, including punitive military expeditions and forced migrations, powerful tribal confederacies flourished on the margins of the empire.

In the frontiers and hinterlands of Qajar Iran, tribal populations were semi-independent and beyond the reach of state authority. The tribes of the borderlands included the Turkmen, the Baluch, the Kurds, and the Shahsevan. Although geographically on the margins, these groups had longstanding interactions with the cities of the Iranian plateau and their culture. They lived within the boundaries of Iran, but all except the Shahsevan remained Sunni, unlike the majority of the Persian population. During the Qajar period the Yamut, Guklan, Tekke, Salor, and Ersari Turkmen tribes, among others, inhabited the northeastern provinces of Astarabad and Khurasan in the steppes known as the Turkmen Sahra. The Baluch, an Indo-Iranian tribe, lived in the eastern province of Sistan, the Makran highlands, and the borderlands with India and Afghanistan. The Kurds were concentrated in the Zagros Mountains, on the edge of the Ottoman Empire and Iraq, in western Iran near the city of Kirmanshah. The Turkish Shahsevan confederacy inhabited the northwestern frontier in the vicinity of Dasht-i Mughan.

The tribes in the hinterland included the Qashqa'i and the Bakhtiyari confederacies in the south. The Qashqa'i, a confederation of Turkic-speaking

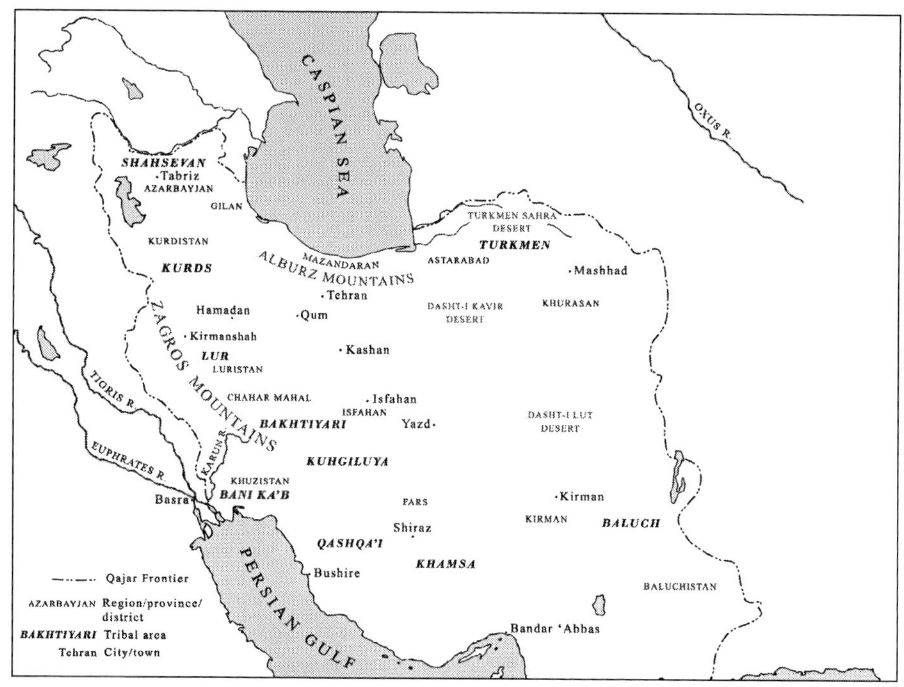

Tribes in Nineteenth-Century Iran

tribes, had their encampments and grazed their flocks in the southern province of Fars, near the provincial capital of Shiraz. The Bakhtiyari, the tribes that are the focus of this study, migrated between the highest peaks of the Zagros Mountains west of Isfahan and the plains of Khuzistan. Since the tenth century CE the tribal groups on the periphery of Iran had periodically established powerful dynasties, moving “from the tent to the throne.”[4] The Qajar dynasty was the last of these traditional tribal states to rule in Iran. By the late nineteenth century, pastoral nomadic subjects and tribal confederacies were confronted by a modern state that was “the enemy of people who move around.”[5]

Anthropology and the Tribes of Iran

Previous scholarship on tribal societies in Iran has paved the way for this book. Tribalism in Iran is a subject that has in the past generated much scholarly interest, particularly among anthropologists. In the first half of the twentieth century, ethnographies by Iranian scholars appeared on several of the tribes in Iran, and beginning in the 1960s Western anthropologists and social scientists began conducting research on Iran's major tribal populations.[6] Scholars such as Fredrik Barth, Lois Beck, Jean-Pierre Digard, Gene Garthwaite, William Irons, Brian Spooner, Pierre Oberling, and Richard Tapper produced a series of new ethnographies on various tribes on the Iranian periphery.[7] *Nomads of South Persia: The Basseri Tribe of the Khamseh Confederacy* (1961), by Fredrik Barth, was a groundbreaking study of pastoral adaptation to the natural environment. Barth's ethnography of the Basseri began by describing the elementary units of tent, clan, tribe, and confederation, moving on to examine economic, political, and demographic aspects of pastoral ecology in the southern Iranian province of Fars. In *Nomads of South Persia*, Barth presented a groundbreaking work that heralded a new literature on pastoral nomadic groups in the Middle East.[8] Following Barth a number of new anthropological studies appeared on the Qashqa'i, the Bakhtiyari, the Shahsevan, and other tribes in Iran.

In the early 1980s, two important monographs on the Bakhtiyari tribes appeared: an ethnography by Jean Pierre Digard and a history by Gene Garthwaite. Digard's *Techniques des nomads baxtiyari d'Iran* (1981) and other articles take segmentary lineage theory as their point of departure. In contrast to Barth's image of the kinship-based and egalitarian Basseri tribe of Fars, Digard found the various segments of the Bakhtiyari tribes to be unequal in power and lodged in a significant social hierarchy. *Techniques des nomads baxtiyari* provided a Marxist analysis of the Bakhtiyari, with emphasis on the division of labor, modes of production, and unequal access to resources among the tribes. Land and its distribution, he suggested, resulted in the establishment of centralizing structures and the division of classes among the Bakhtiyari.[9] Digard, however, did not account for history, leaving the written sources for the study of the Bakhtiyari practically untouched. Garthwaite's *Khans and Shahs: A Documentary Analysis of the Bakhtiyari in Iran* (1983) helped to recover a great deal of the Bakhtiyari's textual history.[10] Garthwaite's monograph also included an appendix with an array of unpublished manuscripts, for which he provides translations. The most notable among these documents is the "notebook" *(kitabchich)* of the late nineteenth-century chieftain Husayn Quli Khan. *Khans and Shahs* offers a thorough history of the Bakhtiyari, focusing on the relations between tribal chiefs and the Iranian state from the Safavid dynasty (1501–1722) to the Islamic Revolution. Garthwaite's pioneering ethnohistory of the Bakhtiyari khans opened the way for the further study of the social, political, and cultural history of tribes in Iran.

A more recent attempt at writing tribal history appeared in Tapper's *Frontier Nomads of Iran* (1997). Tapper's ambitious ethnohistory of the Shahsevan tribes of northwestern Iran is noteworthy for combining evidence from fieldwork and historical research. At the intersection of history and anthropology, Tapper's *Frontier Nomads* brought together ethnographic findings with the use of European and Persian primary sources to trace the origins and history of the Shahsevan.[11] But much more work remains to be done in bringing textual sources to bear on tribal history. The time also seems ripe to depart from the rather dry and insular discussions of the definition of tribe, tribal history, and tribal identity that predominate the existing literature. The language of social science has often left little room for actual narratives of the social and cultural history of tribes in Iran to emerge. In particular, there is a need for new conceptual approaches to tribe and state interactions in the nineteenth century based upon a full reading of the rich array of available Persian and European textual sources.

While there has been a marked decline in Western scholarly interest in the tribes over the last two decades, partly a result of the nationalist historiography prevalent in the field of Iranian Studies, in the Islamic Republic, scholars have been active in producing numerous ethnographies and histories of the Bakhtiyari, Buyr Ahmad, Lur, Qashqa'i, Kurd, Shahsevan, and Turkmen tribes.[12] This literature, in addition to the volumes of Persian primary materials being published, suggests the lasting significance of scholarship on ethnicity and tribes in Iran.

Center and Periphery in Qajar Historiography

This book is an attempt to write the history of nineteenth-century Iran "from the edge." It seeks to de-center a historiography that has emphasized the urban, political, and religious elite, silencing the indigenous subjects of Qajar Iran in the historical narrative. In studies of early modern Iran, particularly the times of dynastic instability during the eighteenth century, exchanges between the center and the periphery, the state and the tribes, have been explored in studies of the Safavid, Afshar, and Zand dynasties by Laurence Lockhart, Ann Lambton, John Perry, and most recently, Kathryn Babayan in her magisterial history of "the waning of the Qizilbash," *Mystics, Monarchs and Messiahs: Cultural Landscapes of Early Modern Iran* (2002).[13] Having shaken off the dust of the turbulent eighteenth century, scholars of the Qajar period have been reluctant to leave the shelter of the new capital of Tehran and been mainly preoccupied with the political center, the world of the shahs, the court, the ministers, and the high ulama. The question of the tribal and ethnic diffuseness of the

Qajar polity thus remains absent in accounts of the transformation of the state in nineteenth-century Iran. Most of these existing studies have been political histories mainly interested in the structure and operation of the central government.[14] Despite this historiographical trend, there have appeared traces of tribal history in the Qajar period in works by Lambton, Gavin Hambly, Nikki Keddie, Abbas Amanat, and Afsaneh Najmabadi.[15] With the recent work of Vanessa Martin and Heidi Walcher, among others, the Qajar periphery has taken center stage.[16]

Drawing upon archives in Istanbul and elsewhere, scholars working on the Ottoman Empire have developed a rich literature of regional and provincial history. These works have included social and economic studies of the Ottoman Empire with some documentary based histories of the tribes.[17] A considerable body of work has also burgeoned of late on the history of the Ottoman provinces. The works of Julia Clancy-Smith on the Maghrib, Beshara Doumani on Palestine, Dina Rizk Khoury on Mosul, and Eugene Rogan on Transjordan, among others, have depicted the different parts of the Ottoman realm in more vivid detail.[18] This book contributes to this literature about the periphery of Islamic empires by examining the transformation and assimilation of a tribal hinterland in nineteenth-century Iran.

By presenting a history of the Qajar periphery and the indigenous subjects of the empire, this research also seeks to complement the growing number of histories of the Middle East "from below" in the tradition of E. P. Thompson and others.[19] One tends to forget that a vast number of Qajar subjects were nomads and semi-nomads, since most written sources were left behind by settled populations and townsmen.[20] If read critically, however, these sources offer views of encounters between the Qajar state and the tribes on the margins of Iran. Tribe and state interactions in nineteenth-century Iran were marked by negotiation and a constant give and take. As Rudi Matthee has noted in *The Politics of Trade in Safavid Iran* (1999), state authority in Iran was "the outcome of bargaining processes in which central power and domination confronted local clout and peripheral recalcitrance."[21] There was a certain balance between centralization and decentralization, between centripetal and centrifugal elements throughout the empire. The tribal periphery lay beyond the geographical reach of the central government, which could only extend its authority over the periphery through the tribal khans and their subjects. Imperial chronicles and tribal histories from the Qajar period convey these compromises between the state and the tribes.

In southwestern Iran, the nature of the Zagros Mountain range formed a

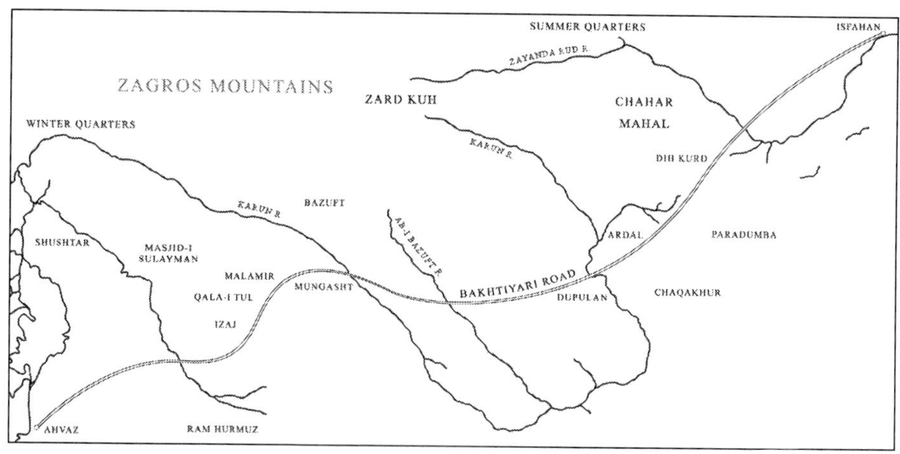

Isfahan and the Bakhtiyari Hinterland

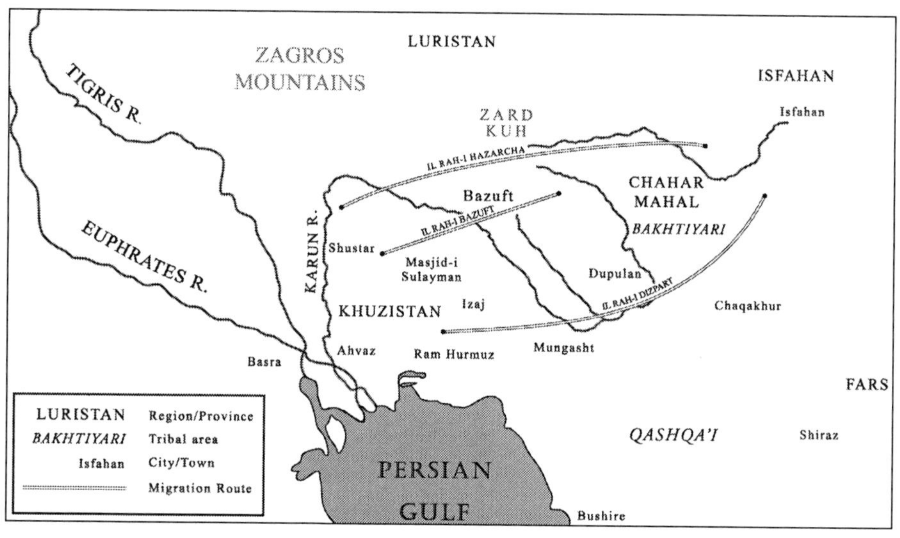

Bakhtiyari Tribal Migration Routes

physical barrier to state intrusion. Throughout the nineteenth century, the presence of the state in the mountains to the west of Isfahan was mediated through contacts with the Bakhtiyari tribal confederacy. This pattern of accommodation between the center and the periphery, between imperial rule and tribal autonomy continued even amidst the British Empire's inroads into the Zagros Mountains during the late nineteenth century. British imperial projects, by necessity, had to be mediated through the Bakhtiyari khans and their tribal subjects, who held considerable power in the mountainous territory between the Karun River and Isfahan. The volumes of British archival materials on the Bakhtiyari, ranging from consular reports to surveys and agreements, attest to the persistence of this negotiation between empire and tribes in the Zagros. At the same time, they chronicle the opening of the Bakhtiyari Land (Khak-i Bakhtiyari) and the beginnings of centralizing processes that transformed this mountainous periphery of Qajar Iran. They are records and narratives of the nineteenth-century imperial transformation of the natural world and the ecologies of indigenous subjects.

Domesticating Wildlands

By the late nineteenth century, a different conception toward the limits of the natural world had slowly emerged in parts of Qajar Iran. These changes were based on encounters between imperialism and nature. The development of powerful centralizing modern empires equipped with methods of scientifically exploring, surveying, and mapping the ends of the earth led to changes in the ways the environment was constructed and used. During the nineteenth century, European and Islamic empires were actively engaged in efforts at the representation, control, and settlement of wildlands and the domestication of indigenous populations. Printed maps, ethnographies, and travel narratives represented the transformation of natural environments. As John Richards noted in *The Unending Frontier* (2003): "Accumulating scientific insights and technical advances stimulated an appetite for intervention in the natural world. . . . The ultimate civilizing mission became that of exploring, comprehending, and controlling the wild places of the earth."[22]

The classification of the mountains, plains, deserts, rivers, oceans, flora, fauna, and peoples of the earth varied from place to place and entailed the mediation of environment and society wherever it occurred. In other words, legibility came about through the interactions between empire and the spaces it sought to tame. This point has been elucidated in Timothy Mitchell's *Rule of Experts* (2002). In Mitchell's provocative study, the interconnected histories of irrigation projects on the Nile River, the spread of contagious diseases, and the onset of war and famine in twentieth-century Egypt are woven together in a critique of the relation between science and nature. Scientific plans and projects, Mitchell suggests, were created in combination "with what is called nature and the material world."[23] What is more, the very notion of "taming the mighty elements of nature" were constructed and manufactured. In reference to the building of the Great Dam at Aswan, Mitchell writes, in "the distinction between nature and science, between masonry and symbol, between the river to be tamed and the expertise that later claimed to have tamed it, one can locate any number of episodes, elements, and forces that disrupt the effect created by the final artifact. Engineering the dam was a messy, uncertain, conflict-ridden, and haphazard project."[24]

The present study of the opening of tribal territories in nineteenth-century Iran also suggests the uncertainties that attended imperial projects in the Middle East. It stops short, however, of claiming that nature was simply an artifact produced or manufactured by projects of empire. This book does not approach nature as an "effect" or "outcome" of the scientific changes taking place.[25] The settlement, domestication, and reclamation of natural environments were among the most salient changes taking place in late Qajar Iran. The transformation of natural environments was not only imagined, it was quite tangible and real, radically altering the ecologies of the mountains, deserts, and marshes. The premodern Islamic state in Iran, itself rising from tribal origins, had allowed for the autonomy of pastoral nomadic societies and ethnic groups. During the nineteenth century, however, the Qajar state consolidated its power and managed to diminish, without completely destroying, the autonomy of the tribes. British projects of exploration, meanwhile, opened tribal territories to commercial traffic and state expansion, contributing to the dissolution of the power and independence of tribal confederacies such as the Bakhtiyari of the Zagros Mountains. State building, imperialism, and integration into the world economy altered environment and society on the distant margins of nineteenth-century Iran.

By the mid-nineteenth century, modern imperial projects initiated by foreign concessions had reached the interior and hinterlands of the country. The accumulation of geographical and ethnographic knowledge in the form of printed texts allowed for the control of environment and society. With the advent of the telegraph in the 1850s the provinces were more firmly linked to the Qajar capital in Tehran and beyond. The infamous Reuter Concession of 1872 promised the modern development of the environment and its resources through the building of railways, canals, and mines. The navigation of the Karun River, which flowed parallel to the Tigris and Euphrates, allowed the river to be opened to international trade in 1888, facilitating commerce, communication, and the expansion of the world economy into the interior of Iran. Likewise, the building of the Bakhtiyari or Lynch Road through the

Zagros Mountains in the 1890s enabled the extension of commercial traffic and imperialism through the remote territories and seasonal quarters of pastoral nomadic tribes. These nineteenth-century imperial missions in the Zagros Mountains came to a culmination with the British exploration for oil in the late Qajar period. Altogether, they constituted an unprecedented attempt to control natural environments and their resources in the area. What is more, nineteenth-century imperial projects and the expansion of the world economy contributed to the dissolution and waning of the pastoral economy of Qajar Iran. The effect of these transformations, as Marx claimed in the mid-nineteenth century, was the alienation of humans from nature: "All fixed, fast-frozen relations, with their train of ancient and venerable prejudices and opinion are swept away. . . . All that is solid melts into air."[26] The march of scientific progress and the world economy dissolved and remade the material basis of relations between societies and environments.

Chronicles, Ethnographies, and Tribal Histories

There exist an array of textual sources for approaching the history of imperial transformations on the periphery of nineteenth-century Iran. This book is based on a reading of imperial records found in archival collections in Iran and the United Kingdom, as well as nineteenth-century printed sources, texts, and editions. These include Persian imperial chronicles and geographical gazetteers, tribal histories and genealogies, manuscripts and ethnographic literature that shed light on tribe and state interactions in Iran during the long nineteenth century. Although I have visited the Bakhtiyari in their summer quarters and traveled through the Zagros Mountains, the following research is rooted in texts from the Qajar period.

Persian chronicles remain untapped sources for the history of tribes and cultural difference in Qajar Iran. Previous scholars have mined chronicles for the study of the court, the political and religious elite, and the structure of the central government. However, nineteenth-century Persian histories also reveal an awareness of the tribal and ethnic difference that flourished throughout the empire. Qajar chronicles, including *Rawzat al-Safa-yi Nasiri*, by Riza Quli Khan Hidayat, *Nasikh al-Tavarikh*, by Mirza Muhammad Taqi Lisan al-Mulk Sipihr, *Mir'at al-Buldan* and *Tarikh-i Muntazam-i Nasiri*, by Muhammad Hasan Khan I'timad al-Saltana, as well as local histories such as *Farsnama-yi Nasiri*, to name just a few examples, contain a range of information on the tribes of Qajar Iran.[27]

The most useful Qajar era text for the purpose of this book has been *Tarikh-i Bakhtiyari* (History of the Bakhtiyari), a tribal history and perhaps the first ethnography in the Persian language. The text was a collaborative project by ʿAli Quli Khan Sardar Asʿad and ʿAbd al-Husayn Lisan al-Saltana Sipihr, among others, written between 1909 and 1911. In 1909 Lisan al-Saltana Sipihr wrote the following words of introduction to this history of the Bakhtiyari tribes:

> In the name of Allah, the benevolent, the merciful. The one that gave the history of those who have passed for the people who have come and made the news of the ancestors written for their descendants . . . for memoirs are the best maxims (*andarz*) of life. This humble servant ʿAbd al-Husayn Lisan al-Saltana, "the king of historians" [*malik al-muvarrikhin*], in this year 1909/1327 Hijri, which is the third year of the Iranian Constitutional Revolution, is writing the history and geography of the Bakhtiyari by the order of the matchless minister, the prudent and wise land-conquering *amir*, the possessor of the sword and the pen, the protector of the land of Fars and Daylam, the protector of Iran and its people, the excellent Hajji ʿAli Quli Khan, the Minister of War, the son of the late Husayn Quli Khan Ilkhani Bakhtiyari. Thanks to God, I was able of achieve this great service and now it passes before your view. I named this work *Tarikh-i Bakhtiyari* [*History of the Bakhtiyari*] so that as long as the world lasts, the name of this lineage will remain.[28]

The original manuscript of *Tarikh-i Bakhtiyari* consists of about 600 lithographed pages, with some of the text consisting of quotations from passages in official Persian chronicles and translations of sections from nineteenth-century Western ethnographies. Other portions of *Tarikh-i Bakhtiyari* consist of original material and are devoted to the oral histories and geographical lore of the tribes, including references to Bakhtiyari organization, administration, and customs. The *Tarikh-i Bakhtiyari* provides a view of Qajar Iran from its edge. It chronicles the tribes' repeated interactions with the central government during the nineteenth century and the major role they played in the restoration of the constitution in the capital of Tehran.

Archival materials and collections at the Iranian National Archives, the Iranian National Library, the University of Isfahan Archives, the British National Archives, the British Petroleum Archives, the India Office Library, Cambridge

University, the University of London–School of Oriental and African Studies, Harvard University, Princeton University, the University of Chicago, and the University of California have been consulted in this study.

The Iranian National Archives holds a range of documents related to the Bakhtiyari tribes in the Qajar period, including correspondence, surveys, and reports from provincial authorities and agents. At the National Library in Tehran and the Archives of the University of Isfahan, I consulted Qajar-era newsletters and gazetteers that provided urban perspectives on the tribes in Iran. These included *Ruznama-yi Vaqa'i'-yi Ittifaqiya*, *Farhang-i Isfahan*, *Ruznama-yi Dawlat-i 'Alliya-yi Iran*, *Surayya*, *Kashkul*, *Habl al-Matin*, *Mulla Nasr al-Din*, *Jahad-i Akbar*, *Isfahan*, *Anjuman Muqaddas-i Isfahan*, and *Zayanda Rud*, among others.

This book also draws upon a variety of European sources, including manuscripts from the British National Archives, the British Library, the School of Oriental and African Studies, and the British Petroleum Archives. In addition to these, the writings of several nineteenth-century Western travelers and ethnographers have been used. The limitations of these genres of European writing about the "East" have been suggested in Edward Said's groundbreaking critique of Orientalism and the unreliability of Western literature on the Islamic world.[29] On the subject of tribes in nineteenth-century Iran, however, European sources contain invaluable information and cannot be cast aside. But they must be carefully selected and "read against the grain," in the subaltern sense of the phrase. These materials reveal the accommodation and bargaining that lay at the foundations of tribe-state interactions.

Based on this array of Persian and European sources, this book is organized in five chapters. The first chapter, "On the Periphery of Nineteenth-Century Iran," explores interactions between the Bakhtiyari tribes and the early Qajar state in the late eighteenth and early nineteenth centuries. While the Bakhtiyari offered military service to the state, paid taxes, and were vulnerable to Qajar military expeditions, they retained substantial autonomy and were beyond the pale of permanent state domination. Chapter 2, "The City of Isfahan and Its Hinterland," traces the complex ties between the provincial capital of Isfahan and its mountainous tribal periphery between the 1860s and 1880s. In those decades, the Bakhtiyari tribal confederacy was unified and reached the peak of its power under the charismatic chieftain Husayn Quli Khan, allowing for indirect rule over the tribes to be established through ties of kinship and contacts with the provincial government of Isfahan. Chapter 3, "A Road through the Mountains," examines the planning and construction of a commercial road through the rugged Bakhtiyari Mountains by the British during the 1890s and its effects upon the local tribal population. Moving through very difficult terrain, the road was described by the British as an effort to civilize and pave over the roughness of nineteenth-century Iran. Chapter 4, "In the Fields of Oil," delves into the social and cultural history of oil exploration in the Bakhtiyari tribal territory. It recounts the early history of the Anglo-Persian Oil Company and the commercial exploitation of natural resources in the Zagros Mountains. The book closes with Chapter 5, "The Bakhtiyari Tribes in the Iranian Constitutional Revolution," which considers the decisive participation of the Bakhtiyari tribes in the Constitutional Revolution of 1906–11 and their integration into the politics and language of the Iranian homeland.

The narrative presents a view of state building, imperialism, and territorial assimilation on the tribal periphery of nineteenth-century Iran. Set in the wildlands on the margins of Isfahan, it examines the efforts of the Qajar dynasty to expand settlement, to collect taxes, and to maintain nominal state order among the Bakhtiyari tribes as the British Empire made commercial inroads into their once inaccessible mountains. British imperial projects, such as the accumulation of geographic and ethnographic knowledge, the building of roads, and the exploration for oil, diminished the power and independence of the Bakhtiyari tribes. These nineteenth-century projects assimilated the pastoral nomadic tribes on the peripheries of Qajar Iran into a wider imperial territory and the world economy.

1

ON THE PERIPHERY OF NINETEENTH-CENTURY IRAN

IN THE SPRING OF 1809, the soldiers of Fath 'Ali Shah Qajar (1797–1834) mounted a military expedition against Asad Khan Bakhtiyarvand in the lofty peaks of the Zagros Mountains. According to the mid-nineteenth-century Persian chronicle *Nasikh al-Tavarikh*, Asad Khan was known as the "lion killer" (*shir kush*), and according to legend he once killed a lion with a single blow of his sword.[1] For nearly a decade the daring khan had brazenly rejected the word of the shah, robbed caravans on the road, and withheld taxes from the government. Although the shah's troops surrounded the Bakhtiyarvand near the snow-capped summit of Zard Kuh, the tribes scaled the rugged cliffs and made their escape over difficult passes to impenetrable fortresses in the mountains.

The flight of Asad Khan and the Bakhtiyarvand epitomized the tribal autonomy encountered on the periphery of nineteenth-century Iran. Various pastoral nomadic tribes (*ilyat*), including the Baluch, Kurd, Lur, Bakhtiyari, Qashqa'i, Arab, and Turkmen, were virtually free from state authority on the edges of the empire.[2] Because of the inaccessibility of the terrain and the local power of the tribes, the Qajars found it difficult if not futile to try to assimilate them, and the empire contained a heterogeneous population. Like its predecessors the Safavids and the Afshars, the Qajar dynasty saw no alternative but to rule pastoral nomads as tribal confederacies with considerable political and cultural autonomy on the imperial periphery. The maxim of the fourteenth-century Muslim scholar Ibn Khaldun in *The Muqaddimah* still held true:

> A dynasty rarely establishes itself firmly in lands with many different tribes and groups. This is because of differences in opinions and desires. Behind each opinion and desire, there is a group feeling

defending it. At any time, therefore, there is much opposition to dynasty and rebellion against it, even if the dynasty possesses group feeling, because each group feeling under the control of the ruling dynasty thinks that it has in itself enough strength and power.[3]

Likewise in early modern Iran the central state perennially struggled to control the dissident and powerful tribes on the margins of the empire.

This chapter explores the history of tribalism on the periphery of nineteenth-century Iran by examining the interactions between the Bakhtiyari tribal confederacy of the Zagros Mountains and the ruling Qajar dynasty. It details the nature of Qajar state control over the pastoral nomadic subjects and the tribal margins of Iran. At the end of the day the tribes in nineteenth-century Iran were beyond the pale of the state. Although the Bakhtiyari gave nominal submission to the Qajars, the presence of the state was scarcely felt in their mountainous territory. Itself of tribal origins, the Qajar dynasty kept loose and indirect control over the tribes through the intermediary chieftains or khans.[4] By offering military service and paying light taxes to the central government, the Bakhtiyari ensured their autonomous status in the Zagros Mountains of southwestern Iran. The central state's limited control over the periphery was further revealed by instances of tribal resistance, mobility and flight.

Nineteenth-century Persian chronicles, gazetteers, and histories depict the autonomy of the tribes in early Qajar Iran. Although state-centric in perspective, nineteenth-century Persian chronicles, such as Mirza Muhammad Taqi Lisan al-Mulk Sipihr's *Nasikh al-Tavarikh* and Riza Quli Khan Hidayat's *Rawzat al-Safa-yi Nasiri* convey a deep awareness of tribal and cultural difference in Iran.[5] This is also true of other state sources, including Muhammad Hasan Khan I'timad al-Saltana's geographical dictionary *Mir'at al-Buldan* and official history *Tarikh-i Muntazam-i Nasiri*, Muhammad Taqi Khan Hakim's chronicle *Ganj-i Danish*, Mirza Hasan Fasa'i's geographical history of Fars Province *Farsnama-yi Nasiri*, Mirza Abu al-Hasan Sani' al-Mulk Ghaffari's illustrated gazetteer *Ruznama-yi Dawlat-i 'Alliya-yi Iran*, and Iran's first newspaper, *Ruznama-yi Vaqa'i'-yi Ittifaqiya*.[6] These texts reveal the attitude of state authorities toward the tribes. Focused on portraying the monarchical glory of the Qajars and their dauntless campaigns against rebellious pastoral nomads, official chronicles seek to sanction and legitimize the state and its expansion through the writing of official history. Chronicles tend to highlight outbreaks of tribal violence and the government's efforts to control them, with the Qajar nobility emerging as benevolent princes and kings subduing tribal insurrections throughout the country. However, Persian chronicles also praise the bravery, resilience, and independence of the Bakhtiyari in their rugged mountain territory on the distant edge of the guarded domains of Iran (*mamalik-i mahrusa-yi Iran*).

By mid-nineteenth-century estimates the Bakhtiyari tribal confederacy numbered between 28,000 and 51,000 tents, or approximately 140,000 to 256,000 individuals.[7] In Qajar chronicles, the Bakhtiyari tribes appear as rebellious nomads perpetually in need of being kept in line by the state. They are labeled as rebels (*yaghi*), robbers (*rahzanan*), and ruffians (*awbash*), instigators of mountain uprisings (*tuqiyan, shararat*), and nomads prone to plundering and looting (*gharat kardan*) in and around the provincial capital of Isfahan.[8] Despite their slanted outlook, however, Qajar chronicles provide views of the edges of Iran, the Zagros Mountains, and the black tents of the Bakhtiyari tribes. Nineteenth-century Persian chronicles and geographical texts suggest the Qajar's awareness of ethnic or tribal difference among the peoples of Iran, as well as the limitations of rule from the center.

These nineteenth-century historical and geographical narratives have yet to be mined for the history of the tribes in the Qajar period. Although several ethnographies have appeared on the Khamseh, the Bakhtiyari, the Qashqa'i, and the Shahsevan, among others, there has yet to be a study devoted to the tribes in the Qajar period based on the range of existing Persian and European sources. Nineteenth-century Persian imperial chronicles and histories have been cursorily explored and most often dismissed as biased and not pertinent to the pressing questions of social science. According to Tapper:

> The available source material for such a social history is mostly written from a distance by outsiders and views the tribes with hostility or some other bias. For example, the information on the tribes that can be gleaned from sources such as Persian court chronicles, manuals, and local histories, and from European agents' and travelers' reports, largely concerns such matters as taxation, military contingents, disturbances and measures taken to quell them, and inaccurate lists of major tribal groups, numbers and leaders. Economic and social organization are treated superficially if at all, and even for the last two centuries their basic features must be inferred circumstantially or deduced from later, more comparative studies.[9]

State chronicles and gazetteers, however, are essential sources for the study of the imperial periphery, as recently suggested by anthropologists and historians working in other areas of Asian studies.[10] Read "against the grain" these texts can reveal a great deal about the nature of tribe and state interactions in early modern Iran. In the case of the Bakhtiyari, the genre of chronicles and historical gazetteers allows us to approach and piece together the "montane" autonomy that existed within the Qajar realm, offering views of spaces of refuge and retreat from imperial state authority.[11]

This chapter revisits the genre of Qajar chronicles (*tavarikh*) and reads them ethnographically to explore the tension between tribal autonomy and imperial sovereignty in nineteenth-century Iran. Following a brief analysis of the origins and formation of the Bakhtiyari tribal federation from the sixteenth through the eighteenth centuries, it explores the complex exchanges between the tribes and the state during the early Qajar period.

The Bakhtiyari Tribal Confederacy in the Safavid Age

According to tribal history the Bakhtiyari tribes of the Zagros Mountains were descendants of the ancient Persians, and the ruined monuments of the past were found in the tribes' lowland winter quarters (*qishlaq*). The authors of the tribal history, *Tarikh-i Bakhtiyari*, traced their lineage back to the descendants of Elam, an ancient language and kingdom in southwestern Iran that thrived as early as 2200 BCE. Close to the Bakhtiyari tribal stronghold of Malamir could be found the ruins of the Elamite capital of Susa, as well as the nearby rock reliefs and cuneiform inscriptions in the caves of Shikaft-i Sulayman and on the cliffs of Kul-i Farah. In one passage 'Ali Quli Khan Sardar As'ad writes of the Bakhtiyari's cultural continuities with the seemingly distant Persian past:

> The native tongue of the Bakhtiyari is Old Persian (*Farsi-yi Qadim*), broken by Kurdish. The customs and culture of the Bakhtiyari people are the ancient customs of Iran. Bakhtiyari women still wear the costumes of the Sasanian period, resembling the clothes of Zoroastrian women.[12]

Elsewhere in *Tarikh-i Bakhtiyari* the Lurs are traced to the land and people of Elam: "Elam is Luristan. . . . It may be said for certain that since times of old and the beginning of civilization, this country has been the pastures and campgrounds of the Lurs."[13]

Yet there is little Bakhtiyari history to speak of before the Safavid period. Medieval geographers described the peoples of the Zagros but made no mention of the Bakhtiyari, referring instead to Kurds and Lurs. The Persian historian Abu Ja'far al-Tabari was among the first to write of the "Kurds" in his *History of Prophets and Kings*. The tenth-century author Mas'udi listed the Lurriya tribes as Kurds. According to the medieval geographer Ibn Hawqal, "Lur was a prosperous country with a mountain climate attached to the provinces of Khuzistsan and Jabal . . . the great majority of the population is Kurd."[14] This view was later confirmed by al-Yaqut's geographical dictionary, written in the Mongol period. It mentions the Lur as a "Kurd tribe living in the mountains between Khuzistan and Isfahan"—the land known as *bilad al-Lur*.[15] In *Sharafnama-yi Tarikh-i Mufassal-i Kurdistan*, Amir Sharaf Khan Bidlisi counts the Bakhtiyari as among the 400 Kurdish clans that migrated from Syria (*bilad al-sham*) to Jabal and Khuzistan around the beginning of the twelfth century, coming to be known as Lur-i Buzurg. Among these tribes were the Bakhtiyari, the Astaraki, the Javaniki (Janiki), the Gutvand, the Jaki, the Liravi, the Mamasani, and two Arab tribes called the 'Akili and the Hashimi.[16] The fourteenth-century geographer Hamdallah Mustawfi called their territory Jabal, Arabic for "mountains," and mentioned the snow-covered peak of Zard Kuh, the source of the Dujayl (Karun) River, which flowed through Khuzistan, and Zayanda Rud, which flowed into Isfahan.[17]

During the sixteenth century, as the Safavids moved the capital of Iran from the northwestern cities of Tabriz and Qazvin further south to the more centrally located Isfahan, the state came into proximity with the Zagros Mountains, home to the largest concentration of pastoral nomadic tribes in Iran.[18] Safavid chronicles and administrative manuals contain scattered references to the Bakhtiyari.[19] These sources chronicle the Safavids' penetration of the Zagros Mountains and contact with the "Bakhtiyari Lurs," whom they sought to consolidate under tribal leadership and thus integrate into the fabric of the empire.

In the 1560s Shah Tahmasp (1524–1576) tried to bring order to the Bakhtiyari tribes and assert state control over them. He first granted the title of *sardar* (commander) to Tajmir, a chief of the Astaraki clan, whom he held to be the most powerful khan among the Bakhtiyari Lurs. But following Tajmir's failure to collect taxes and establish order among the tribes, the shah had him executed and gave the office to Jahangir, a Bakhtiyari khan put in charge of supplying the Safavids with 10,000 mules yearly. This seems to have established the taxation of the Bakhtiyari and might have been the time when the

Haft Lang and Chahar Lang branches were created.[20] As some of the tribes of the Great Lur, including those of the Kuhgiluya, rebelled against taxation, the Bakhtiyari may have risen to first rank among the tribes and given their name to the tribal confederation.[21] The two administrative categories of the Haft Lang ("Seven Legs") and the Chahar Lang ("Four Legs") were further divided into four subtribes, or *tira*. According to the *Tarikh-i Bakhtiyari* the Haft Lang are a conglomeration of the Duraki, the Babadi, the Bakhtiyarvand, and the Dinaruni tribes, while the Chahar Lang are composed of the Mahmud Salih, Muku'i, Zulqi, Kiyanursi, and Mamivand tribes. In the *Tarikh-i Bakhtiyari* these are then divided into multiple clans, subtribes, and branches (*shu'ba*).[22]

Tribal history also suggests that the creation of the Haft Lang and the Chahar Lang branches occurred during the sixteenth and seventeenth centuries. These names were based originally on rates of taxation, known among the Bakhtiyari as *shakh shumari* (flock counting). The wealthier tribes of the Haft Lang, who lived on the northern banks of the Karun River, were taxed at a rate of one-and-three-quarter mules, or seven legs; the Chahar Lang, who lived on the southern banks of the Karun, were taxed at the rate of one mule, or four legs.[23]

The Bakhtiyari also contributed horsemen and footmen to the Safavid armies and fought alongside the Qizilbash in the kingdom's wars against the Ottoman Empire. In the Safavid chronicle *Tarikh-i 'Alamara-yi 'Abbasi*, Iskandar Bayg Munshi mentions the good military fortunes of Jahangir Khan and the Bakhtiyari Lurs, who fought under Khalaf Bayg in engagements against the Ottomans near Erivan in the Caucasus in 1616. In a list of the "Amirs of the Major Qizilbash Tribes and Tribes Subordinate to Them" that appears in *Tarikh-i 'Alamara-yi 'Abbasi*, the name of Jahangir Khan's brother, Khalil Khan, is listed as the governor of Lur-i Bakhtiyari. The same source, however, also suggests the perennially "rebellious behavior" of the Bakhtiyari Lurs that resulted in a punitive expedition being sent against them in 1595.[24]

Safavid policies toward the tribes underwent reorganization under Shah 'Abbas I (1588–1629). Under Shah Tahmasp there had been a thin line between tribal khans, military commanders, and provincial governors, with the periphery remaining largely under tribal control.[25] Shah 'Abbas worked to rein in pastoral nomadic populations and further increase state authority in the hinterlands and on the frontiers of the Safavid domain. He formed a nontribal corps of infantry composed of Georgian and Armenian captives converted to Islam, known as the *Tufangchi* (riflemen). He resettled tribes such as the Qajar, Afshar, and Kurds to the frontiers of the empire and initiated a more assertive

The Bakhtiyari Tribal Confederacy

HAFT LANG

- *Duraki Tayafas*
  - Zarasvand Tayafa
  - Asiwand Tayafa
  - Mawri Tayafa
  - Qand ʻAli Tayafa
  - Baba Ahmadi Tayafa
  - Arab Tayafa
  - Astaraki Tayafa
- *Dinaruni Tayafas*
  - Awrak Tayafa
- *Babadi Tayafas*
  - ʻAwli Anvar Tayafa
  - ʻAkkasha Tayafa
  - Raki Tayafa
  - Kalla Tayafa
  - Malmali Tayafa
- *Bakhtiyarvand Tayafas*
  - Bakhtiyarvand Tayafa
  - ʻAwli Jamali Tayafa
  - Janiki Sardsir Tayafa

CHAHAR LANG

- *Mahmud Salih Tayafa*
  - Kiyanursi Tayafa
  - Muku'i Tayafa
- *Zulqi Tayafa*
  - Mamivand Tayafa

Tribes and subtribes of the Bakhtiyari tribal federation, as listed in *Tarikh-i Bakhtiyari.*

state administration over the tribes. Shah ʻAbbas also showed increased interest in keeping records on his tribal subjects, as elders (*rish safidan*) were ordered to prepare lists of the lords (*amiran*) in the provinces and the tribal retinues in their service.[26] According to the Safavid administrative manual *Tadhkirat al-Muluk*, the Bakhtiyari tribes were akin to the Lurs, occupying the highlands between Isfahan and Khuzistan. The Bakhtiyari khans were counted among "the Great Amirs enjoying the title of *ʻAli-Jah*" and held the highest rank of *vali*, earning a stipend in *tumans* and *dinars* for contributing a contingent of 361 men. They were among the "amirs of the frontiers, marches, and *sarhadd*."[27]

The Safavids also made efforts to propagate a normative brand of Shiʻism among the tribes. As John Malcolm, envoy from British India to Persia in 1800, would later write, "During the reign of the Suffavean kings, the Sudder-ul-Suddor, or 'chief pontiff,' appointed a Cauzee, or judge, to every one of the principal tribes of Persia."[28] Shah 'Abbas might have fostered ties with the Bakhtiyari to compensate for the fading loyalties of the Qizilbash, in effect raising the Bakhtiyari to the status of the tribes that would contend for the Safavid throne in the eighteenth century.

With the capital of Iran moved to the central Iranian city of Isfahan, the Safavids sought to draw upon the resources of the Bakhtiyari Mountains. It has been suggested that the Safavid period, particularly the rule of Shah 'Abbas, saw the deforestation of the Bakhtiyari foothills to supply timber for the construction of Isfahan.[29] The effort to make Isfahan flourish during the late sixteenth and early seventeenth centuries led Shah 'Abbas to embark on plans to divert the headwaters of the Karun River at Kuh Rang into the Zayanda Rud, the famed river flowing through the city.[30]

According to Iskandar Bayg Munshi's *Tarikh-i 'Alamara-yi 'Abbasi* the Safavid's plan was to redirect the waters that flowed through the mountains of Luristan, where agriculture was marginal, toward the capital Isfahan via the Zayanda Rud, which was known to run dry in times of drought.[31] To this end, Shah 'Abbas appointed Mir Fazlallah Shahristani to direct the task, and although his workmen (*kar kunan*) began to work diligently on the project, they found the mountains impassable and were ultimately stopped by rocks too difficult to dig through. According to *Tarikh-i 'Alamara-yi 'Abbasi*:

> Shah 'Abbas had long had a scheme to divert the waters of the Kuh Rang, link them with the Zayanda Rud, and increase Isfahan's water supply, so the inhabitants of the city might not suffer from a shortage of water in a dry year. The extra water would also permit additional acreage to be brought under cultivation or planted with orchards. The *vazir* of Isfahan, Mir Fazlallah Shahristani, was first put in charge of the plan. The chief difficulty was that a lofty mountain massif lay between the headwaters of the Kuh Rang and those of the Zayanda Rud. Mir Fazlallah had hired miners and well diggers, who tunneled away at the rock and made as much progress as they could but finally gave up in despair. The work was abandoned.[32]

Shah 'Abbas, however, refused to give up on the project and continued to plan for a dam at Kuh Rang. He sent teams of engineers, masons, and state officials to survey the prospects of redirecting the river's flow toward his capital. In 1619, after receiving reports that the project could be completed in four to five years, the shah ordered the work to be resumed. Imam Quli Khan, the lord governor (*bayglarbayg*) of Fars, was put in charge of the tunnel mining operations, while Husayn Khan, the governor of Luristan, and Jahangir Khan Bakhtiyari, whom the shah considered the head of all the Bakhtiyari tribes, were given responsibility for the construction of the dam. According to Iskandar Bayg Munshi, thousands of Bakhtiyari tribesmen were employed and received wages for working on the Kuh Rang dam.[33] In 1620 Shah 'Abbas paid a visit to the site of the dam's construction and observed the work, encouraging the workers in their task. As recorded in *'Alamara-yi 'Abbasi*:

> The shah, who has been extremely keen on the Kurang scheme, decided this year to go in person to the site to see how work was progressing. He spent several days in the area, informing himself thoroughly on the merits and defects of the scheme, and giving his amirs working on the project lengthy instructions. Imam Quli Khan, the *bayglarbayg* of Fars; Husayn Quli Khan, governor of Luristan; Jahangir Khan Bakhtiyari; Safi Quli Khan, governor of Hamadan; and the nobles from Fars and Isfahan who were working on this project had been exerting themselves to the utmost in constructing the dam and tunneling through the mountain. Let us hope that the scheme is completed to the shah's satisfaction.[34]

But the work again proved too difficult to complete and five years turned out to be an overly optimistic goal, given that Kuh Rang was in a distant region snowed in four months of the year. Although the Kuh Rang dam project established a precedent of state penetration of the Bakhtiyari territory, it was ultimately abandoned following the death of Shah 'Abbas, not to be completed until the mid-twentieth century. The seventeenth-century traveler Adam Olearius (1603–1671) aptly summarized the failed Safavid enterprise to divert the flow of the Karun River:

> *Schach Abas* had a design to bring into the River of *Senderut* that of *Abkuren* which rises on the other side of the famed Mountain of *Demawand* [Kuh Rang]; whereas, to bring these two Rivers into the same Chanel, there was a necessity of cutting the Mountain, he employ'd, for the space of fourteen years together, above a thousand

> Pioneers at that work. And though they met with extraordinary difficulties, not only that they had to do with pure Rock, which in some places was above two hundred feet deep; but also in regard, the Mountain being cover'd with Snow for nine Months of the year, they had but three to work in, yet had the work constantly carried on with such earnestness, that all the *Chans* and Great Lords fending their Work-men thereto, upon their own charges, there was in a manner no doubt made of the successe of that great enterprize, since there remained to do but the space of two hundred paces, when *Schach Abas* died. . . . If *Aaly*, the Patron and great Saint of the *Persians*, had liv'd in that time, he might have done *Schach Abas* a very great kindness, by opening that Rock at one blow with his Sword, and so made way for the River.[35]

The area of the mountains where the work was begun in Safavid times has come to be known among the Bakhtiyari as the Kar Kunan or "workers," after those who toiled to build the dam. The Safavid's unsuccessful attempts to redirect the course of the Karun River toward Isfahan revealed the difficulties and natural obstacles confronting imperial ventures in the rugged Zagros Mountains.

Foreign observers did not fail to notice the autonomy of the tribal populations in Iran. The extension of Safavid imperial authority into the mountains of the Bakhtiyari was periodic and impermanent. Early modern travelers viewed the pastoral nomadic ecology and political independence of the tribes as intertwined. As John Chardin (1643–1713), the French jeweler who traveled through Safavid Iran in the late seventeenth century, recalled, the "shadow of Liberty" remained among the pastoral tribes on the periphery of Isfahan:

> To the East [*sic*] of *Ispahan* and near adjoining to his Territory lyes the province of *Lour-Estom*, which is held to be a part of ancient *Parthia*, extending on *Arabia's* side toward *Basra*. The peoples that Inhabit it, never mind the building of Cities, nor have any settled Abodes, but live in Tents, for the most part feeding their Flocks and their Heards [*sic*], of which they have an infinite number. They are Govern'd by a *Kaan* who is set over them by the King of *Persia* but chosen from among themselves: and for the most part all of the same Race, the Father Succeeding the Son. So that there still remains among them some shadow of Liberty; however they pay both Tribute and Tenths.

> This Province furnished *Ispahan* and the Neighbouring parts with Cattel; which is the reason that the Governor of these people is greatly respected in those parts.[36]

Other seventeenth-century travelers recorded similar, often impressionistic, descriptions of the freedom of the nomadic tribes. The British traveler John Fryer wrote the following on the subject of nomads or "husbandmen":

> Those that breed up Cattel are wandering Shepherds, and have no stated Habitation; but where they find the best Pasture they pitch their Tents, together with their Wives, Children, and Families, with all their Troops, in the fattest Vallies, living abroad far from great Towns, like the Wild *Arabs*, whose Chief, or father of the Tribe, is owned by them, and no other, he giving account to the Emperor for the Number of their Flocks, and the Annual Increase; for they are Morose and Untamed, and are enough to Worry any who fall unadvisedly among them. . . . These go clad in course Cloths underneath, above with Felts, kneaded into the form of a Coat, and are covered with Hats of the same, but their Hats are grey, bound about with a Linnen Cloth either of White, Green, or Blew.[37]

The Bakhtiyari spent their winters in the lowlands of Khuzistan and migrated into the highlands of the Upper Zagros during the summer. In the words of John Ogilby (1600–1676), the royal cosmographer to King Charles II: "The Inhabitants, who have the Mountains to the Northward of them, are forc'd by the violent heat to retire amongst them during the Summer."[38] What is more, the tribes made their subsistence on the basis of their flocks of goats and sheep, whose wool they also used to "weave both Cloth and Carpets very fine, which they sell at dear Rates."[39]

For Thomas Herbert (1606–1682), a member of Sir Dodmore Cotton's diplomatic mission of 1627–1630, there was much to be admired about the freedom and simplicity, even austerity, of pastoral nomadic life:

> A mile from this Towne we view'd threescore black Pavillions; black without; within full female beauties: the Persians call them Vloches [*ilyat*]; the Arabs, Kabilai [*qabila*]; the Turq'itans and Armenians, Taiphae; the Tartars, Hoords; the Antients, Nomades. . . . how free from unreasonable care, pale Envie, affrighting Tumult, and nasty

surfet doe these enjoy themselves; happy Conquerors! how mutually doe they accord, how joyfully satiate Nature, in what is requirable.[40]

This pastoral nomadic lifestyle in the mountains, described romantically by Herbert, ensured autonomy vis-à-vis the state. The French missionary N. Sanson counted the Bakhtiyari khan among the ten valis of the kingdom, who remained autonomous unless the shah would appoint a governor to their province:

> The *Valis* are Descendants from such Princes as have been conquer'd by the King of *Persia*, and whose Kingdom he leaves to their sole Governments. . . . These *Valis* have their places at the Council-board, and at Feasts and Publick Audiences. They are considered of as Princes, and have those Preiviledges as the King's Guests have, which is to be Pensioners and Tablers during their stay at Court.[41]

This status as a vali conferred special privileges and cultural regalia upon the Bakhtiyari khan:

> All these *Valis* are *Begueler-Beguis*, and have a right to the sounding of Twelve *Keronas*, which are a sort of long Trumpets like Speaking-Trumpets, in which they bawl aloud, mixing with their confused Cries the Harmony of Hautbois, Drums, and Tymbals, and which they are wont to play upon at Sun-setting, and Two Hours after Midnight. There's none but the *Valis* and *Kans* that can have so compleat a concert of Musick. . . . They carry 'em always with them when they Travel or Hunt.[42]

The independence of the Bakhtiyari tribes under their ruling khans was a fact that the Safavid state, with its limited power in the hinterland, had little choice but to accept. The precariousness of state power in the mountainous terrain of the Zagros was noted by the illustrious French traveler Jean de Thévenot (1633–1667):

> Their Countrey is so mountainous, and so hard to be passed, that I do not now wonder that the King of *Persia* [every time that they went to besiege *Bagdad*,] instead of taking Cannon with him, carried upon Camels metal to cast them, obliging every Trooper besides to carry

an *Oque*; for it is absolutely impossible to have Cannon drawn along these ways.[43]

Although the early-modern state could collect revenues or mount occasional military campaigns to subdue uprisings, the tribes of the Zagros Mountains were beyond permanent domination and would only "live under the protection of Lords; for notwithstanding they acknowledge them, yet they live free."[44]

During the Safavid period the Bakhtiyari became established as an autonomous tribal federation of predominantly tent-dwelling pastoral nomads, migrating seasonally between their summer quarters in the mountains of the Upper Karun and their winter quarters in the plains of Khuzistan. By the reign of Shah Sultan Husayn (1694–1722), the last Safavid shah, the state had established nominal authority over the Bakhtiyari, collecting revenues and conscripting up to 10,000 horsemen and footmen for the royal army without pay while holding two or three khans in attendance at the court to ensure the good behavior of the tribes.[45] With the fall of the Safavid dynasty in 1722 this tenuous balance between the tribal periphery and the central state seemed to all but vanish.

In the eighteenth-century Afshar chronicle *Jahangusha-yi Nadiri*, Mirza Mihdi Khan Astarabadi provided an alarming description of the country's condition after the fall of Isfahan in 1722:

> During these times, when the imperial throne of Iran was trampled under foot by enemies and fire and oppression from all directions dried the crops, the custom and rule of the kings of the tribes (*muluk-i tavayif*) prevailed while the high and the low rebelled. The tribes and the provinces were in revolt: From Qandahar to Isfahan the Ghilzai tribe, in Herat the Abdali, in Shirvan the Lezgi, in Fars the followers of an unknown man named Safi Mirza, in Kirman Said Ahmad Navada Mirza Davud, in Baluchistan Sultan Muhammad, who had gained fame under the name *Khar Savar* or the 'Mule Rider,' in Janiki 'Abbas, in Gilan Isma'il, and in Khurasan Malik Mahmud Sistani, a pretender to the throne. . . . In this manner, the Turkmen of Astarabad, who were regularly in rebellion, the Lurs (Alvar) of Bakhtiyari and Fayli, the Kurds of Ardalan, the Arabs of Haviza and Bandar became disobedient and asserted themselves—*sar kashi kardand*.[46]

The Bakhtiyari tribes were left virtually independent in the Zagros Mountains and seemed to be on the verge of gaining control of Isfahan. From the vantage of the tribal periphery the weakening of central authority following the Safavids' fall provided certain opportunities. The end of the Safavid dynasty and the dissolution of the Qizilbash opened the way for expressions of tribal power and identity in the hinterlands and on the frontiers of Iran.[47]

Much of the existing literature on the history of eighteenth-century Iran has emphasized the political center, focusing on the world of the shah, the court, and the dynastic state. The tribes and the periphery have been viewed from the perspective of the central state and framed in discussions of the "resurgence of tribalism" in the wake of the fall of the Safavid dynasty.[48] While the dynastic instability and the political turbulence of post-Safavid Iran cannot be denied, it may be worthwhile to view the implications of these times for the tribes and other peoples on the periphery, departing from the predominant state-centric narrative.

In the 1730s assertions of tribal autonomy and local rebellions were met by the military campaigns of Tahmasp Quli Khan, later to become Nadir Shah Afshar (1736–1747). After bringing the Afghan interregnum to an end the Afshar warlord set out to establish order among the tribes in the hinterlands and on the boundaries of Iran in the name of the Safavid Prince Tahmasp II, taking the title Tahmasp Quli Khan, the slave of Tahmasp. The Afshar chieftain sought to bring pastoral nomadic subjects under imperial control through punitive military campaigns, the forced migration of tribes from the Zagros to Iran's eastern frontier province of Khurasan where they were to guard the borderlands, and enlistment in the tribal armies (*lashkar*) on the march to Afghanistan and India.[49] In this manner the Afshars recruited the martial tribes of the empire into the army while removing them from their local territories where they were prone to rebellion. The state had little recourse apart from these often temporary, punitive measures. Afshar rulers saw no alternative but to appeal to the tribal khans, elders, and "white beards" to quell tribal rebellion, desertion, and flight on the periphery of the empire.

The ranks of the Afshar army consisted of a formidable body of tribal levies and irregular horsemen that constituted a prime component of the state military system. Nadir Shah selected horsemen and footmen from the different tribes in Iran and its frontiers, organizing them into tribal militias, each under the command of its own chiefs. In eighteenth-century chronicles the tribes are found serving in the cavalry (*sipah*) among the frontier warriors (*ghaziyan*), horsemen (*savaran*), and mounted attendants (*mulaziman-i rikabi*). Others served as tribal irregulars and paramilitaries (*ilchari*; *charikha-yi ilyati*). These tribal military units were under the command of their tribal heads, with each having control over his own tribe and being given titles based on the number of fighting men each commanded. The heterogeneity of Nadir Shah's army is revealed by contemporary accounts that depicted the brave deeds of Afghans, Hazaras, and Bakhtiyari in the Afshar's military campaigns.[50]

Nadir Shah had revived Iran's military through the incorporation of large numbers of tribesmen—Abdali Pashtun, Baluch, Uzbak, Bakhtiyari, Kurd—into the ranks of a moving nomadic army. In 1736, when Nadir Shah set out from Isfahan for Qandahar, he marched at the head of an army of 80,000 men, of whom the majority were cavalry, including Kurds, Turkmen, Baluchis, and Abdalis as well as a large contingent of Bakhtiyari. According to the Afshar chronicle *ʿAlamara-yi Nadiri*, the Bakhtiyari tribal retinues numbered between 21,000 and 23,000 men, and a Bakhtiyari named Mulla Adina Mustawfi won fame as the first to scale the walls of Qandahar when the city fell to Nadir Shah in 1738.[51] By 1743, when Nadir Shah reviewed his troops at Kirmanshah, he saw that they numbered 375,000 men from all over the empire.[52]

Service in the royal military did not weaken but rather reinforced the array of tribal and ethnic identifications throughout the empire. These were preserved and strengthened through the military administration, which gave selected tribal leaders state-sanctioned authority over related ethnic groups. The tribal army (*lashkar*) was composed of tribal retinues under the leadership of their khans, thus reinforcing the ethnic differences among the men of the army. Far from rooting out tribal identities the Afshar state, like the dynasties before it, relied on the structures of tribe and clan to exert its influence in the periphery.[53]

A reading of eighteenth-century Persian chronicles reveals that the Afshar's punitive measures and policies toward the tribes were a response to the centrifugal forces prevailing throughout the empire in the post-Safavid age.[54] References to the Bakhtiyari tribes in chronicles such as *Jahangusha-yi Nadiri*, by Mirza Mihdi Khan Astarabadi, Nadir Shah's secretary of the provinces (*munshi al-mamalik*), and *ʿAlamara-yi Nadiri*, by Muhammad Kazim Marvi, the minister (*vazir*) of Marv, attest to their power on the periphery of Isfahan and detail the efforts of the central government to rein them in. Although on the surface Afshar chronicles laud the military prowess of Nadir Shah in subduing the restless nomads of the empire, at a deeper level they attest to the Bakhtiyari's long-standing and entrenched autonomy in the Great Lur (Lur-i Buzurg) region of the Zagros Mountains.[55] The punitive measures of the state, including military campaigns, forced migrations, and recruitment, seemed fleeting compared to this permanent tribal independence and defiance in the mountains.

The rebelliousness of the Bakhtiyari forced Nadir Shah to order punitive campaigns against them in 1730, 1732–33, and 1736. In every instance rebellions and raids by the tribes were followed by extractive military expeditions by the Afshar state. In 1730 Nadir Shah led an expedition against the restive Bakhtiyari and recruited a thousand men from among them for his army.[56] When the Bakhtiyari rebelled again in 1732, overthrowing a local chieftain assigned to put the tribes in order (*tanzim*), Nadir Shah imprisoned thirty khans and headmen, including 'Ali Salih Haft Lang, in Isfahan and sent his couriers (*chaparan*) among the Bakhtiyari tribes to recruit horsemen for his cavalry.[57] In 1733, after his couriers met resistance from the Haft Lang, Nadir Shah personally departed from Isfahan at the head of troops and artillery on a march into the Bakhtiyari Mountains.[58] Seeking to offset the Bakhtiyari's power and influence in the Zagros and fortify the northeastern frontier province of Khurasan, Nadir ordered the relocation of 3,000 Bakhtiyari families of the Haft Lang *tayafa* to the districts of Jam and Langar, among other familiar tribes—*pahlunishin-i ilyat-i rufaqa kardand*. In 1734 some of these tribes left the road to Khurasan and fled back to the Zagros Mountains. According to Astarabadi, 24,000 tribal attachments (*mulazim-i iljari*), largely consisting of Lurs and Kurds, gathered in pursuit of the Bakhtiyari fugitives and forced their return to Khurasan.[59] Nadir Shah also released 'Ali Salih Khan and more than a dozen other headmen from captivity in Isfahan, sending them back to the Bakhtiyari to gather troops for the royal army. According to Marvi, 'Ali Salih Khan and other headmen from the Haft Lang gathered 7,000 mounted tribal attendants to join Nadir Shah, while 'Ali Mardan Khan of the Chahar Lang collected 10,000 to 12,000 famed horsemen, "*namdaran-i Bakhtiyari*," that joined the royal troops on their subsequent marches and campaigns.[60] As noted above, interactions between the Bakhtiyari tribal confederacy and the rising Afshar dynasty seemed to follow a pattern of rebellion and resistance followed by state retribution in the form of forced relocation of tribes and the recruitment of tribesmen into the army.

The most widespread Bakhtiyari uprising occurred in 1736, after Nadir Shah deposed the Safavid Prince Tahmasp II (Nadir Shah had been called the "Slave of Tahmasp" or Tahmasp Quli Khan until then) and declared himself king. The revolt was led by 'Ali Murad Khan, a young chieftain from the Mamivand tayafa of the Chahar Lang Bakhtiyari, in reaction against the Afshar claim to the throne. In effect 'Ali Murad Khan's rebellion grew to become the first

Bakhtiyari attempt to contend openly for a greater political role in the post-Safavid era. Presenting himself as the protector of the Safavid throne without claiming it outright, 'Ali Murad Khan led an uprising with the avowed goal of taking Isfahan and restoring the Safavid heir Tahmasp II to the throne. The authors of Afshar chronicles noted the bravery and cunning of 'Ali Murad Khan. Muhammad Kazim Marvi described 'Ali Murad as "a wise youth and a brave man"—*javan-i bud farzana va mardi bud mardana*.[61] Brazenly robbing the Ottoman 'Abdallah Pasha's treasury of a muleload of gold, he gathered a number of followers in the Bakhtiyari Mountains and took possession of Isfahan. 'Ali Murad Khan sought to revive the rule of the ex-Shah Tahmasp, while also carving out a kingdom for the Bakhtiyari. He was reported to have announced to the "white beards" at a Bakhtiyari tribal council: "After destroying the rule of Nadir Shah, I shall set foot in Khurasan and rescue Shah Tahmasp from his prison there; I shall then place power in his hands. Royalty is a great name, and many will rally swiftly to me. Shah Tahmasp will be content with 'Iraq and Khurasan, while I shall have Hamadan, Fars, and Kirman."[62]

With the arrival of contingents of Fayli Lurs, Ardalan Kurds, and Afghans, as well as troops from Isfahan and a mountain-climbing corps of the *jazayirchiyan* (heavy infantry armed with *jazayir* or *jazayil* rifles), the Bakhtiyari resistance dissipated and the tribesmen scattered throughout the mountains. According to Marvi, Nadir Shah's *ghaziyan* searched the mountains for 'Ali Murad Khan for two months, finally capturing the Chahar Lang khan at the fortress of Banavar, after which they blinded, tortured, and killed him.[63] Having dealt in this summary fashion with the rebellion of 'Ali Murad Khan, Nadir Shah proceeded to punish the Bakhtiyari by forcing 10,000 Chahar Lang and Haft Lang families to migrate to the district of Jam in Khurasan. Still impressed by the Bakhtiyari's martial skills and prowess, he also enlisted 4,000 more Bakhtiyari khans and tribesmen into his army for the upcoming march to Qandahar.[64]

In the *History of Persia* John Malcolm gave an account of the Bakhtiyari tribes during the rule of Nadir Shah:

> The peace of the country round Isfahan had been much disturbed by the depredations of a numerous and barbarous tribe, called Baukteearees, who inhabit the mountains that stretch from near this capital to the vicinity of Shuster. The subjugation of these plunderers had ever been deemed impossible. Their lofty and rugged mountains abound with rocks and caverns, which in times of danger serve them

> as fastnesses and dens. But Nadir showed that this fancied security, which had protected them for ages, was a mere delusion. He led his veteran soldiers to the tops of their highest mountains; parties of light troops hunted them from the cliffs and glens in which they were concealed; and in the space of one month the tribe was completely subdued. Their chief was taken prisoner and put to death; but the policy of Nadir treated those of his followers who escaped the first fury of his troops with lenity and favour: he assigned them better, but more accessible, lands than what they before possessed: he also took a number of them into his army; and this corps, by its extraordinary bravery at the siege of Candahar, confirmed the wisdom of this generous conduct.[65]

Although Nadir Shah's rule was bold and sweeping, the control he established during his brief and violent reign over the tribes might have been negligible. From a reading of contemporary imperial histories, it may be argued that Nadir Shah had to go to great lengths—and climb great heights—to establish the state's authority among the Bakhtiyari tribes. The state possessed only the most tenuous control over its pastoral nomadic subjects. Indeed the shah struggled to incorporate them into his army to direct their energies to his wars of expansion and conquest. For their part the Bakhtiyari found opportunities to assert their independence, either as "raiders" and "rebels" on the periphery of empire or as martial tribes who fought in the Afshar's wars. Following Nadir Shah's death in 1747 the Bakhtiyari deserted Khurasan and returned to the Zagros Mountains. In western Iran they rallied around the aged general, 'Ali Mardan Khan of the Chahar Lang, who in 1750 captured Isfahan and briefly established a de facto Bakhtiyari dynasty there before being ousted by his rival Karim Khan Zand.[66]

The Bakhtiyari Tribes and the Early Qajars

In the late eighteenth century Aqa Muhammad Khan Qajar (r. 1785–1797) ousted the last ruler of the Zand dynasty and overcame other claimants to the crown to establish the Qajar dynasty. Following three interregnums and nearly a century of dynastic instability, the Qajars would remain in power for nearly a century and a half.[67] The Qajar dynasty employed tribal policies similar to those of the Safavids and the Afshars before them, including the confederation, military recruitment, and forced resettlement of tribal groups. In bringing state order to the nomadic and semi-nomadic populations in the Iranian periphery, the Qajars relied upon "the kings of tribes," or *muluk-i tavayif*, as intermediaries and ruled through tribal structures. Despite the continuities in tribal policy the Qajars fell far short of nurturing the loyalty the Safavids had been able to achieve or equaling the military prowess of the Afshars. It may be said that in the Qajar period, tucked between the wars of the eighteenth century and western imperialism in the nineteenth century, the Iranian state became increasingly vexed by the autonomy of its tribal populations. Qajar era chronicles, histories, and geographical dictionaries recorded tales of the state's efforts to expand its rule over the tribal populations on the periphery of the empire. As the tribes struggled to preserve local autonomy and identity, the state attempted to exercise authority over and through the array of local princes, chieftains, and potentates.

The authors of nineteenth-century chronicles cast their royal Qajar patrons as the heirs to previous dynasties that had striven to preserve the boundaries of the empire and bring order to the frontiers and hinterlands of Iran. On the surface imperial histories recorded the outbreaks of tribal violence and rebellions, as well as the state's efforts to collect taxes and tributes from its subjects. But these instances of violence, resistance, and banditry may be read as signs of autonomy, revealing how the ethnic and cultural differences within the boundaries of Iran confronted and complicated the early Qajar state-building project.

In *Rawzat al-Safa-yi Nasiri*, a multivolume court chronicle written between 1853 and 1856 by the Persian literary historian, administrator, and poet Riza Quli Khan Hidayat (1800–1871), the tribes of Iran appear prominently; among them the Qajars reign supreme.[68] In the introduction to the text Hidayat acquaints the reader with the terminology of tribal and ethnic belonging: *il* (tribal federation), *tayafa* (clan, tribe), *qabila* (tribe, clan), *awlad* (descendents). Echoing Ibn Khaldun he further suggests that tribes were the foundation of the state (*saltanat*) and the units of social and political order on the Qajar periphery.[69] Contemporary European observers shared this view as well. The British diplomat and author James Morier took a tour from Fars province north to Tehran in 1809, describing the tribes and the role they played in the kingdom:

> The aggregate of the population of Persia is divided into tribes, part of which live in fixed habitations, and others live in tents. . . . Each tribe has its records, and can trace its genealogy to the first generation. The

> most considerable and renowned are the *Baktiar*, that spread themselves over the province of *Irauk*. . . . All the tribes pay tribute. When the king calls upon them for purposes of war, all are obliged to send a proportion of men, who are always ready at his summons. The names of every one of such men, the names of their fathers, and other particulars of their family, are all registered in the *Defter Khona* at the seat of government; and at the feast of the *Norooz*, they attend the King to inquire whether their services for the year are required. . . . Each tribe has its chief, who is always a *Khan*, and one of their own race.[70]

Another Qajar history, *Nasikh al-Tavarikh*, written by Muhammad Taqi Khan Sipihr (1792–1879) during the reign of Nasir al-Din Shah, chronicles world history through the year 1855, revealing how the Qajars outmaneuvered other tribes to move from tent to throne.[71] The histories of Muhammad Hasan Khan I'timad al-Saltana (1843–1896), Nasir al-Din Shah's translator, "dragoman in royal attendance," and minister of publications, also discuss the pastoral nomadic populations and tribal confederacies within the guarded domains of Iran. His geographical dictionary, *Mir'at al-Buldan* (Mirror of the Lands), completed in four volumes between 1876 and 1880, describes the topography, boundaries, and peoples of Iran.[72] Based on personal observations and information collected from the provinces as well as existing histories, *Mir'at al-Buldan* highlighted tribal robberies on villages and roads, disturbances in the countryside, and the inaccessible fortresses (*qal'a*; *diz*) that shielded nomads in the mountains.[73]

The chronicles recounted pivotal events in the history of the Bakhtiyari tribal confederacy, referring to Shah 'Abbas' efforts to divert the flow of the Karun toward Isfahan and the tribal uprisings of the eighteenth century.[74] In their emphasis on Bakhtiyari violence they attest to the great degree of autonomy enjoyed by the tribal confederacy on the southwestern periphery of the empire. In *Nasikh al-Tavarikh*, Sipihr decried the "long arms" (*daraz dasti*) of the Bakhtiyari and their plundering of Isfahan:

> Groups from the Bakhtiyari led an uprising and constantly harassed the craftsmen (*ahl-i san'at*) and merchants (*tujjar*) of Isfahan, confiscating their property without reason. . . . the city quarters broke out in revolt (*tuqiyan*), as merchants were tormented and their goods (*amval*) carried off. In the end no one had the power to halt the group's robberies.[75]

Such images of tribal violence, insurrection, and unrest indelibly marked the official Qajar outlook on the Bakhtiyari and other tribes.

In 1785 Aqa Muhammad Khan, the founder of the Qajar dynasty, advanced from his base in the north into the Zagros Mountains, the heart of the ancient Achaemenid and Sasanian empires and the stronghold of the Zand and Bakhtiyari tribes.[76] With the decline of the Zand and the weakening of central authority the Bakhtiyari tribes were left virtually independent and resisted Qajar authority. Royal decrees (*farman*) from the 1760s found at the National Archives in Tehran (Sazman-i Asnad-i Milli) reveal that Abdal Khan of the Haft Lang was consolidating his influence over "all the commanders" of the Bakhtiyari. One *farman*, dated 1769, reads, "Because Abdal Khan has been assigned as white beard (*rish safid*) of all the Haft Lang, when a theft or road robbery occurs among these tribes, he should retrieve the goods from the thieves and return them to the owners, with the punishment being so severe as to stop this kind of behavior."[77] In another *farman* from Karim Khan Zand, dated 1768, Abdal Khan's son Habiballah was given the title of khan and decreed a commander among the headmen of the Bakhtiyari.[78] By 1786 Abdal Khan and his clan had united the Haft Lang and Chahar Lang behind him and refused to recognize the Qajar claim to the throne.

Qajar histories chronicle the state military campaign against the Bakhtiyari in 1786. Mirza Hasan Fasa'i's geographical chronicle of southern Iran, *Fars-nama-yi Nasiri*, notes that Aqa Muhammad Khan subdued the Bakhtiyari rebels (*sar kishan*).[79] In *Rawzat al-Safa-yi Nasiri,* Riza Quli Khan Hidayat writes that a superior Qajar army suppressed the Bakhtiyari, leading them to defeat and desertion. In a play on the meaning of the word Bakhtiyari ("friends of fortune"), Hidayat wrote that in the end fortune abandoned them.[80] Aqa Muhammad Khan emerges as a ruler bringing order and security to the former Safavid capital of Isfahan and its tribal periphery.[81] The fullest account of Aqa Muhammad Khan Qajar's violent campaign in Bakhtiyari territory appears in the state chronicle *Tarikh-i Muhammadi* (also known as *Ahsan al-Tavarikh*), by Muhammad Fathallah Saravi, completed in 1797 and covering the first years of the Qajars' rise to power. Saravi began by noting that certain groups of the Bakhtiyari were threatening the city of Isfahan with chaos, violence, and sedition:

> At the establishment of the royal camp in Isfahan, the informed of the city stood in the presence of the blessed shah and gave notices that the tribes of the Bakhtiyari and the mountaineers of Farahan and Gulpay-

> gan have gathered together and, sharpening their swords of battle on the stones of sedition and magic (*fasad u fusun*), they have come to Chaman-i Ka'iz on the outskirts of Isfahan to fight.[82]

Aqa Muhammad Khan decided to confront the Bakhtiyari insurgents at the "killing fields" (*maqtal-i khish*), meeting them in battle outside Isfahan. According to Saravi the Bakhtiyari were at first undaunted by Aqa Muhammad Khan Qajar's campaign: "In the mist of the chaos (*girudar*) of battle, news arrived that nearly a thousand Bakhtiyari tribesmen were arriving as reinforcements."[83]

In Qajar imperial chronicles, however, the state always eventually prevails over the tribes—at least on the surface. Saravi reported that Aqa Muhammad Khan's troops and artillery triumphed over the Bakhtiyari:

> Once surrounded the Bakhtiyari horsemen saw their days filled with the smoke and dust of cannons and guns in a black field of war. They made a plan to save themselves and 4,000 horsemen with their eyes on the refuge, heedlessly abandoned their assignments and took flight into the mountains. The valorous commanders and protectors of the state swarmed on the enemy from different directions, putting them to death. . . . Abdal Khan Bakhtiyari and some of the other khans of that tribe who took part in the uprising were put to the sword.[84]

The uprising of the Bakhtiyari tribes earned them harsh retribution. The government soldiers committed violent atrocities upon the Bakhtiyari and punished them by seizing nearly 80,000 sheep as spoils while the tribes were forced to run to the higher elevations of the mountains. The cruelty of the Qajar troops in their plunder of the Bakhtiyari on the order of Aqa Muhammad Khan is openly related in *Tarikh-i Muhammadi*:

> The exalted shah decreed that the victorious *ghaziyan* and irregulars were free to raid (*chapaval*) the Bakhtiyari. With the royal decree the troops, who had given lives in the campaign, entered the mountains and searched them high and low, turning over every rock and taking everything they could lay their hands on. Eighty thousand flocks of sheep and livestock were taken from the Bakhtiyari to the camps of the regiments. The young beauties (*dilbaran*) of the Bakhtiyari tribes were taken as part of the plunder and the widows of the khans were turned into mourners.[85]

Although *Tarikh-i Muhammadi* commemorates the military campaigns of Aqa Muhammad Khan and his troops against the independent tribes of the Zagros, there is a detectable hint of remorse in Saravi's account of the Bakhtiyari's desperate flight into the mountains and the savage punishment the tribes were dealt.

Aqa Muhammad Shah also initiated the practice of collecting tribute from the Bakhtiyari tribes, ordering them to contribute forty mules (*qatir*) to the wedding of his nephew, the future Fath 'Ali Shah.[86] From contemporary sources we know that the Qajars continued the taxation of the Bakhtiyari along the divisions of Haft Lang and Chahar Lang. In his report, "Some Account of the I'liyats, or Wandering Tribes of Persia, obtained in the Years 1814 and 1815," Morier described the method by which the state collected revenues from the Bakhtiyari:

> The Bakhtiyari are now divided into two principal branches, the *Haft Leng* and the *Chahar Leng*, which again are subdivided into many *Tus* or Shafts. *Leng* in their dialect means foot, and the origin of the above designations, was, it is said, produced by a demand made on the tribe in ancient times for military contributions in men and horses. One part of the tribe, the *Haft Leng*, or Seven Feet, was taxed one-seventh proportion, whilst the *Chahar Leng*, or Four Feet, was taxed one-fourth. Their property was calculated by numbers of horses; thus when in one case seven feet, or one horse and three quarters, was levied, the other only contributed four feet, or one horse.[87]

Later in the nineteenth century the Bakhtiyari fell under the authority of three provincial governments, Isfahan, Luristan, and Khuzistan (Arabistan). During the tribes' spring migrations to the *yaylaq* near Zard Kuh they paid taxes to the provincial governors of Isfahan and Luristan, and in the time of their migrations to the *qishlaq*, or winter quarters in the plains, they paid taxes to the governor of Khuzistan province.[88] But it remains uncertain how successfully these taxes were collected, as observers like Morier noted that nomadic tribes (*sahra nishin*) found opportunities to elude taxation and had become adept at "secreting their cattle in the mountains."[89]

From contemporary sources, a picture of tribal autonomy in the mountains emerges. Regarding the allegiance of the Bakhtiyari to the Qajars, John Malcolm, the minister plenipotentiary from British India to the Court of Fath 'Ali Shah (r. 1797–1834), wrote:

> The Bukhteearee, and several other tribes, can hardly be said to have ever entirely submitted to the Kings of Persia. Guarded by their inaccessible mountains, these rude races continue to be ruled by their own customs, and admit of hardly any interference on the part of the officers of government in their internal jurisdiction. They consent to furnish a body of their own youth as soldiers, and to pay a small tribute, that they may obtain a share of the produce of some of the fine vallies that lie at the foot of the hills which they inhabit; and every effort is made to encourage them to occupy those plains, not merely with the view of rendering them more tangible to the laws of the country, but to prevent [by giving them an interest in the general peace and order of society,] those frequent predatory attacks which they are in the habit of making upon the more peaceable and civilized part of the population of the kingdom.[90]

Writing in 1841 Louis Dubeaux observed the authorities' "doubtful" control over the nomadic populations:

> Les tribus errantes ont une jurisprudence toute particulière. Chaque tribu a son chef, sous lequel se trouvent des Anciens, qui, pour l'ordinaire, appartiennent a la famille du chef de tribu. Ces homes sont tout à la fois le magistrats et les officiers militaires de la tribu. . . . L'authorité du rois sur les tribus est toujours fort douteuse. Les Bakhtiaris et quelques autres encore n'ont jamais été complétement soumis. Ils fournissent un corps de jeunes soldats et payent un petit tribut; là se borne tout ce que le roi de Perse peut tirer d'eux.[91]

The nomadic and semi-nomadic tribes were unreliable peoples for the early Qajar state and could merely be counted on to provide tribal retinues and pay nominal taxes.

Travelers reported that the Zagros Mountains shielded the Bakhtiyari and gave them refuge. Writing in the early nineteenth century Robert Ker Porter saw them as independent and often violent "sons of the mountain":

> In the most inaccessible parts of this stupendous range, live the Bactiari, Felly, and Mamazany tribes, or rather nations; the exhaustless bed of whose population stretches from the mountains above Kazaroon, to the immense piles in the vicinity of Kou-i-Zerd, whence they

pour their streams on errands of peace or war. . . . The milder groupes of these mountain wanderers descend from their heights in the summer months, and, under the name of Eelauts, take up a quiet residence for the season on the more fertile plains of the empire. . . . But the greater multitude of these sons of the mountain show themselves true brethren of Ishmael, and leaguing together by families and tribes, exist wholly by plunder.[92]

The Bakhtiyari tribes were cast as "hereditary spoilers" and "formidable bands" that hovered over almost every path outside the walls of Isfahan.[93] But there was little doubt regarding the greater freedom of the nomadic *ilyat* compared to their more "stationary" counterparts in the towns:

They bear the name of Eelauts. There are in Persia, tribes of Tartar and Turcoman descent; and tribes from the Bactiara mountains, who are of a race completely different from the northern hordes, and, probably, something more indigenous to the soil, than of any other wanderers. . . . Hence the people of the Persian empire appear to consist of two distinct classes: the stationary inhabitants of towns and cities; and the wandering dwellers in tents and temporary villages; for all equally acknowledge the sovereignty of the Shah, though with different degrees of deference to his authority. The Persian, immured in a city, is within grasp of every arbitrary order; the Eelaut, in his tent, may obey on the side of his stream, or disobey in the fastness of his mountains. And, perhaps, as some check to the natural proneness and facilities of these people to affect independence, has arisen the fashion of drawing of principal chiefs to court; where we find many of them mingling the refinements of the capital with their bolder habits; and delegating their authority over the tribe to the elders, or chieftains next in rank. These people, though despising settled habitation, claim a sort of prescriptive right, derived from their ancestors; and many of them pretend to certain mountain districts and tracts of pasturage, which they keep with the greatest tenacity; maintaining their ground against any encroaching tribe with all the determination of property. . . . Hence, though they wander, it is within bounds. They have a country and only change their place in it.[94]

The Bakhtiyari Mountains were depicted in nineteenth-century Persian and

European sources as wildlands inhabited by fiercely independent tribes.

Only through the khans, elders or "white beards," and headmen could the loyalty of the tribes be won.[95] Otherwise the tribes remained out of the state's reach:

> They will seldom consent to obey to any other person. . . . If a general levy of the tribe be required for the service of the sovereign, it is effected with difficulty and delay: but a call, connected with their own safety, or that of their chieftain, is promptly obeyed. On such occasions, the signal to assemble flies, to use their own phrase, "from tent to tent, from hill to hill."[96]

At best the Qajar state attempted to utilize the loyalty of tribesmen to their chieftains to govern the periphery. According to Malcolm:

> It was a love and duty, of inheritance, strengthened by the feelings of twenty generations. Though the superior in general repaid this feeling with regard and protection, I saw many instances of its being considered as much a property as the land, and the inanimate goods and chattels, which he who received it had inherited from his father. There are few countries which can boast of more examples of devoted allegiance of chiefs to their sovereign, as well as followers to their chiefs, than Persia. . . . Allegiance is the duty a child owes to its parent, for birth, nourishment, and protection. It is that which collected families owe to a chief of their tribe, who is their point of union, and consequently of their security; and in this climate it is that which chiefs and their followers owe to a sovereign, their concentrated attachment to whom is the ground of their safety and their glory as a nation.[97]

This was perhaps the ideal of Qajar statecraft. In practice, however, relations among tribes, khans, and shahs were rarely defined by such obedience. Although such loyalty toward a sovereign on the part of tribes may have occurred in the past, perhaps at certain points during the Safavid period among the Qizilbash, it was hardly to be found in early nineteenth-century Iran.

Unsettled in Qajar Persia

During Fath 'Ali Shah's rule (1797–1834) the Qajars increasingly took measures to recruit the Bakhtiyari, with their reputation as daring and brave horsemen, into the royal cavalry. In 1820 the shah commanded Amir Muhammad Qasim Khan Qavanlu to march to the Bakhtiyari region and reorganize all the Bakhtiyari tribes into new military formations. Muhammad Qasim Khan proceeded to organize the Bakhtiyari Order (Nizam-i Bakhtiyari), one of the most distinguished military corps in Iran at the time.[98] Fath ʿAli Shah retained 2,000 Bakhtiyari in his pay as disciplined soldiers (*sarbaz*) and kept many of their families settled in villages about Tehran as "hostages."[99] The Bakhtiyari subsequently fought in the wars of the crown prince ʿAbbas Mirza (1789–1833) against the Russians. According to Sipihr in *Nasikh al-Tavarikh*, 1,000 Bakhtiyari savaran were in the service of Hasan Khan Duraki, fighting in the Qajar army under ʿAbbas Mirza. In 1827, at the battle of Ganja in the Caucasus, the Bakhtiyari and other troops from the province of ʿIraq-i ʿAjam captured a strategic hill from the Russians, only to find shortly thereafter that the rest of the Qajar army, including ʿAbbas Mirza, had fled the battle.[100]

But the loyalty of the Bakhtiyari tribesmen proved difficult for the Qajar state to sustain. Indeed the tribal irregulars who fought on behalf of the state could also cause disorder on the periphery of the empire. According to Mirza Fazlallah Shirazi in *Tarikh-i Zu al-Qarnayn*, after the wars with Russia the discharged Bakhtiyari irregulars became "tramps" and "wanderers" (*avara*) on the roads and in the countryside:

> During the years when the Lur tribes of Bakhtiyari were the guardians of the fortress of ʿAbbasabad in Nakhjavan, they showed firm virtue effortlessly but Ahsan Khan Nakhjavani was not worthy of them and the mentioned fortress fell into the hands of Russia and the times became filled with strife and war. The shah punished the Bakhtiyari by discharging from his service two thousand of their tribesmen, who were the equivalent of ten thousand in the field. These servants and their clans, once kept as hostages in the capital of Tehran, were turned free. Because they no longer received earnings, they became wanderers and tramps, and without fear or apprehension, they turned to banditry and brigandage. From a hundred directions they marauded the roads. For a period of four or five years, robbing travelers and merchants became the basis of their livelihood and wealth. The prince governors in the region did not show diligence in disciplining the tribes and because the Haft Lang, Chahar Lang, and other tribes were divided between the various princes, order could not be established.[101]

Royal Cavalries at the Military Review of 'Abbas Mirza Qajar, artist unknown (Qajar Iran, c. 1815–16). State Hermitage Museum, Saint Petersburg, VR-1121.

In fact Bakhtiyari tribesmen enlisted in the private retinues of Qajar princes and provincial governors were likely to become involved in the rivalries between princes vying for power. This can be seen in the case of the large number of Bakhtiyari tribesmen recruited into the retinues of the governor of Khuzistan and Burujird, Muhammad Taqi Mirza Hisam al-Saltana.[102] According to Sipihr, the prince governor's soldiers included Haft Lang and Chahar Lang tribesmen, rendering him the "key to 'Iraq"—*kilid-i 'Iraq ast.*[103] In 1827 at Nahavand the Bakhtiyari in the service of Hisam al-Saltana clashed with 12,000 Lur tribesmen serving Mahmud Mirza, the governor (*farmanguzar*) of Luristan.[104] Again in 1830 the Bakhtiyari under Hisam al-Saltana skirmished with the Kurdish Kalhur and Zangana cavalries of Muhammad Husayn Mirza Hishmat al-Dawla, the governor of Kirmanshah.[105]

The central government could temporarily dominate the tribes on the periphery but could never permanently integrate them.[106] Even while under the authority of Qajar prince governors, the Bakhtiyari could descend into chaos and disorder. In moments of weak central authority, the tribal periphery was left virtually independent and even at times dominant over the provincial capitals. At the conclusion of Fath 'Ali Shah's long reign in 1834, the Bakhtiyari broke free from the authority of the central government and briefly took over Isfahan. In his *Book of Travel* (*Safarnama*), Riza Quli Mirza Nayib al-Ayala, who passed through Isfahan and the Bakhtiyari territory in 1835 on his way to London, described the violent tribal sorties in the provincial capital following the shah's death. Seeking to plunder Isfahan the Bakhtiyari savaran sided with Haydar Quli Mirza, the prince governor of Gulpaygan. Riza Quli Mirza recounts that shortly after the governor called for the Bakhtiyari retinues to assemble, 20,000 men from both the Haft Lang and the Chahar Lang gathered and proceeded to plunder Isfahan:

> Within three days of these speculations, Khusraw Khan Chahar Lang, one of the most famous Bakhtiyari khans, presented himself to the prince with four thousand horsemen (*savaran*) and a thousand footmen (*piyada*) under his command. After five days, Bahram Khan Busak, one of the heads (*buzurgan*) of the Haft Lang Bakhtiyari made his honorable entrance with three thousand horsemen and footmen. Everyday handfuls and handfuls of troops gathered—*har ruz fawj dasta bi dasta jam gashta*—and over a period of ten days twenty thousand soldiers gathered to march on Isfahan. They rampaged the royal house of crafts (*naqqara khana*). Haydar Quli Mirza opened the royal

coffers with the gold and the jewels pouring outside. The khans and the headmen, strong and weak, young and old, were made joyous by the emptying of such riches and by their success.[107]

But it was not long before the Haft Lang and the Chahar Lang tribes had turned against each other, with the violence spilling into the streets of Isfahan and its Maydan-i Naqsh-i Jahan, revealing the lack of state control over Bakhtiyari militias. In Riza Quli Mirza's book of travels the Bakhtiyari are cast as dangerous and restless tribesmen, ready for war and chronically on the verge of blood feuds:

> Each side gathered its people unto itself and a battle cry rang out. The *lashkar* now fired on each other and created such a melee that the smoke of guns and gunpowder blocked the light of the sun and the flash of swords appeared amidst all the smoke and flames. Ten or twelve thousand troops suddenly set upon each other, swords held for the kill, and within ten minutes, four hundred lay dead or wounded. Bahram Khan Busak was killed and his tribe defeated. Khusraw Khan's retinues removed Bahram Khan's body from the arena and pursued the Haft Lang for two *farsang*. They returned to the city having taken innumerable belongings and guns from the vanquished. The distraught prince Haydar Quli Mirza stood on the roof of a wing of his house lamenting the needless loss of so many of his men. Presently the victorious Khusraw Khan Chahar Lang returned and stated: "What need is there for them? I myself will see to it that what must be done is done." That day, as a result of that disaster, yet another occurrence brought the Prince's men to a halt, and that was the return of the tribes of Bahram Khan, who stood before their adversary, carrying the dead body of their khan and making an appeal to *qanun-i ilyat* or the tribal law of revenge.[108]

The recruitment of Bakhtiyari tribal levies by Qajar princes was a risky policy that could end in the disruption of peace and order in Isfahan and other cities.[109] Tension remained between the Bakhtiyari's allegiance and service to the Qajar state on the one hand and their penchant for local autonomy and independence on the other. This bargaining was a key feature of tribe and state interactions in Qajar Iran.[110]

Some of the tribes on the periphery recognized the state only grudgingly and came to be considered as *yaghi* or in rebellion against the central government. Asad Khan of the Bakhtiyarvand, mentioned in the opening of this chapter, epitomized this brand of tribal resistance against state authority. In the first decades of the nineteenth century Asad Khan (d.1821) of the Haft Lang came to personify the rugged Bakhtiyari's resistance in the mountains. In *Nasikh al-Tavarikh* Sipihr revealed how the chieftain had earned his name:

> This Asad Khan was a brave man (*dalir bud*), so brave that he once fought a lion and killed it with one blow from his sword. Entrenched in the mountains of the Bakhtiyari (*Kuhsar-i Bakhtiyari*) he followed the orders of no one and knew no bounds to plundering caravans. Government troops sent out against Asad Khan were captured and imprisoned.[111]

The chieftain and his tribe, the Bakhtiyarvand, proved too difficult for the Qajars to subdue. Following Aqa Muhammad Khan's death in 1797 Asad Khan refused to submit to Fath 'Ali Shah, carrying out raids as far away as the outskirts of Tehran. Because the Bakhtiyarvand and the Haft Lang also refused to pay taxes (*maliyat*), Qajar authorities labeled them *yaghi*.[112] European travelers shared this perception of the Bakhtiyarvand as a tribe of bandits who marauded and caused great alarm on the periphery of Isfahan. In writing about the Bakhtiyari, Morier made specific reference to the resistance of Asad Khan:

> If they had opportunity and assistance, it is likely that they would throw off their allegiance to Persia; and the King is so well aware of that, that he keeps many families of them in separate villages about Teheran, as hostages for the good behaviour of the rest. As it is, part of them are already looked upon as *Yaghi*, or in rebellion, and are headed by Assad Khan, one of their chiefs, who keeps all the country in a state of alarm, and even threatens Ispahan.[113]

The Bakhtiyari's allegiance to the Qajars was, as Morier saw it, nominal and fleeting, and among tribesmen such as Asad Khan it barely existed at all.

The first of Asad Khan's long string of run-ins with Qajar authorities reportedly occurred in 1804, when he was captured while hunting and brought to Tehran before Fath 'Ali Shah. According to one source the shah at first ordered that Asad Khan be forced to watch his own grave being dug and then buried alive. It was reported that the stoic Asad Khan, with his hands tied, had pushed the workmen aside, took hold of a shovel and began digging his own grave. When news of Asad Khan's bravery reached the shah he pardoned the chieftain, deciding instead to keep him in Tehran to ensure the good behavior of the Bakhtiyarvand.[114]

Asad Khan's time in the capital coincided with the French mission of 1807–9, headed by General Claude Mathieu Gardane.[115] The Qajars sought to modernize their military through French expertise, and the development of artillery (*tupkhana*) became essential to the army's modernization, which required a ready supply of coal (*zuqal*). Asad Khan and other Haft Lang chieftains captive in Tehran were ordered to return to the Bakhtiyari Mountains to mine coal.[116]

When Asad Khan reached his native mountains, however, he refused to gather workers to mine coal for the shah. News of Asad Khan's defiance reached the capital, forcing Fath ʿAli Shah Qajar to send a military expedition including Bakhtiyari cavalries under Ilyas Khan Duraki, the troops of the governor of Isfahan, and the accompanying French generals with their cannons into the Zagros Mountains against the Bakhtiyarvand. In 1809, these forces surrounded Asad Khan at a peak called Kulangchi near the summit of Zard Kuh, forcing the Bakhtiyarvand to climb the face of the mountain to make their escape.[117]

The exploits of Asad Khan and the Bakhtiyarvand in the War of Kulangchi are recounted in tribal folklore that champions the tribes' resistance against the state and stoic flight up the face of Zard Kuh. Folksongs describe how at one point Asad Khan and the Bakhtiyarvand were pushed back up the mountain and, having no other way out, were forced to kill thousands of sheep and use their corpses to fill a gap near the summit. They then climbed across, walking over the dead flocks. Despite great losses Asad Khan and the Bakhtiyarvand scaled the summit of Zard Kuh and eventually fled to their fortress at Diz-i Malikan, or "Fort of the Angels," located northeast of Shushtar.[118]

The legendary feats of Asad Khan are recalled in folklore in the Bakhtiyari dialect that narrates the wars the tribes have fought—*bayt bi an jang mibandand*.[119] Vernacular poetry provided the Bakhtiyari with a medium to recount stories about legendary figures such as Asad Khan across generations.[120] In songs such as "War of Kulangchi," Asad Khan emerges as the lord of the fortresses of Zard Kuh. These tales of kinship and war praise Asad Khan's bravery and celebrate his independence from the state ("who has ever seen my Shah Asad mine coal?"), even noting his distinctive style of riding a horse, with his shoulder slumped to the side.[121]

Following their narrow escape Asad Khan and the Bakhtiyarvand gained control of one of the impregnable fortresses in the Bakhtiyari Mountains, Diz-i Malikan, where they remained as holdouts against the state until 1813. In that year Asad Khan and his Bakhtiyarvand retinues entered the service of the Qajar Prince Muhammad ʿAli Mirza Dawlatshah (1789–1821).[122] In *Nasikh al-Tavarikh* Sipihr has left an account of the prince's expedition into the Zagros Mountains to establish Qajar dominion over the Bakhtiyari tribes:

> And in this year [1813] Prince Muhammad ʿAli Mirza made Asad Khan and the Bakhtiyari obedient. . . . At this time the king of kings entrusted the Bakhtiyari country to Prince Muhammad ʿAli Mirza, who set out with his own cavalry to put the Bakhtiyari in order, making camp at the foot of the fortress of Malikan, the steep and jagged stronghold of Asad Khan. Muhammad ʿAli Mirza dispatched his minister to the fortress to reach conciliation with Asad Khan and when he came down from the mountain, the prince spoke to him warmly and with kind words, as his troops suddenly surrounded the chieftain and forced him to surrender. The prince then pardoned Asad Khan and allowed him to return to his fortress for two days before entering into royal service.[123]

This encounter between Asad Khan Bakhtiyarvand and Prince Muhammad ʿAli Mirza reveals the often complex codes of bargaining between tribes and the state in nineteenth-century Iran. Although interactions between tribes and the state were often marked by violence, there were also instances of compromise and engagement. Following his submission Asad Khan accompanied Muhammad ʿAli Mirza to Kirmanshah, where he remained among provincial retinues until he was freed to return to the Zagros upon the prince's death in 1821.[124]

During the 1830s the Chahar Lang tribes emerged from a period of tribal wars and bloody vendettas as the most unified section of the Bakhtiyari under the leadership of Muhammad Taqi Khan of the Kiyanursi subtribe. Tracing his lineage to ʿAli Mardan Khan, the Bakhtiyari chieftain who gained command of Isfahan following the death of Nadir Shah Afshar in 1747, Muhammad Taqi Khan brought many of the Chahar Lang tribes, as well as the Bani Kaʿb Arab tribes of Ram Hurmuz and Falahiya, under his sway.[125] His success in raids and growing reputation as a warrior in the provinces became a concern of the central government, which sent a number of military campaigns against the Chahar Lang in the 1830s.

In Qajar chronicles we read that Muhammad Taqi Khan was plundering the countryside and withholding taxes from the state. In 1834, just before Fath 'Ali Shah's death, when a war of succession was going on in the south, Muhammad Taqi Khan ignored Qajar provincial authorities as he and his retinues raided from Fars to Isfahan. With their position among the Chahar Lang secured, Muhammad Taqi Khan and his following disregarded the authority of the Qajar state. Later that year he and thousands of horsemen conquered the town of Shushtar on the Karun River. In the geographical dictionary *Mir'at al-Buldan*, I'timad al-Saltana condemned Muhammad Taqi Khan and his followers as "seekers of mischief (*shararat talab*) and insurgents who plundered the road to 'Iraq," a sentiment shared by other Qajar chroniclers including Lisan al-Mulk Sipihr and Riza Quli Khan Hidayat.[126]

After establishing his control over Shushtar, Dizful, and Ram Hurmuz, Muhammad Taqi Khan moved toward Fars and collected 600,000 tumans in taxes from the tribes and inhabitants of the province. In addition, Muhammad Taqi Khan and the Chahar Lang seemed to threaten the provincial capital of Isfahan. In response Fath 'Ali Shah ordered soldiers from all over the country, including troops from the Qajar prince governors of Fars, Kirman, Luristan, and Kirmanshah, to gather in Isfahan to prepare a military expedition into Bakhtiyari territory. The shah ordered the governor of Isfahan, Muhammad Mirza Sayf al-Dawla, to lead these retinues into the Bakhtiyari Mountains, subdue the rebellious Chahar Lang, and set in order the tribal territories on the periphery of Isfahan. But perhaps as a result of rivalries between the competing princes, the expedition against the Bakhtiyari and Muhammad Taqi Khan was delayed and then abandoned following the death of Fath 'Ali Shah in 1834.[127] According to I'timad al Saltana in *Mir'at al-Buldan*, the Bakhtiyari remained the cause of insurgency, banditry, and disobedience in the regions of 'Iraq-i 'Ajam, Luristan, Khuzistan, and Fars.[128]

In the spring of 1837, the next Qajar sovereign, Muhammad Shah (1834–1848), ordered Prince Bahram Mirza to set off on a campaign against the Chahar Lang at the fortress of Mungasht. The military expedition included 5,000 horsemen and footmen as well as six cannons. Henry Creswick Rawlinson, who had trained a regiment of Kurdish troops for the shah, accompanied Bahram Mirza on his march against Muhammad Taqi Khan.[129] Following *Nawruz* in 1837 Qajar troops engaged the Chahar Lang to a standstill on the plain of Malamir on the banks of the Karun River until a truce was reached.[130] It was not until the stringent governorship of Mu'tamad al-Dawla in Isfahan during the 1840s, however, that the Qajar government captured Muhammad Taqi Khan and established the regular taxation of the Chahar Lang.

Throughout the 1840s and 1850s the Haft Lang continued to challenge Qajar tribal policies, and it seemed that Ja'far Khan Bakhtiyarvand, the son of the famed Asad Khan, was on the verge of establishing himself as the paramount khan among the Haft Lang and all of the Bakhtiyari from his position at Diz-i Malikan. His only rival among the Haft Lang chieftains was Husayn Quli Khan of the Duraki (discussed in detail in chapter 2). Hasan 'Ali Khan Afshar, an attendant of Nasir al-Din Shah Qajar (1848–1896) dispatched to Luristan in the fall of 1848 to deliver robes of honor (*khil'at*) to the rulers of the region, recorded in his travel book (*safarnama*) that the Bakhtiyari tribes were split between the two Haft Lang khans.[131] The Qajars tried to co-opt the Bakhtiyari khans into the state military structure. It was reported in 1852 that Prince Khanlar Mirza Ihtisham al-Dawla (d. 1862), the *hakim* of Luristan and Bakhtiyari between 1848 and 1860, held a retinue of 2,000 Haft Lang and Chahar Lang under the command of Ja'far Quli Khan and Husayn Quli Khan.[132] The Bakhtiyari cavalry in the retinues of Khanlar Mirza were employed in quelling tribal insurrections throughout the region, including those by other Bakhtiyari tribesmen.[133]

Orders and correspondence from the central government in Tehran to Khanlar Mirza reveal a great deal more about the difficulties Qajar provincial authorities faced in controlling the Bakhtiyari tribes. An order sent in 1849 to Khanlar Mirza from Nasir al-Din Shah's reform-minded prime minister (*Atabayg-i azam*), Mirza Taqi Khan Amir Kabir (1807–1852), suggests the obstacles preventing the pacification of the fortresses of the Bakhtiyari tribes. After praising Khanlar Mirza for keeping order on the Zagros frontier (*sarhadd*), Amir Kabir goes on to spell out the apparent limitations of Khanlar Mirza's control over the tribes and the persistence of their local independence in mountain fortresses, which the Qajar government was eager to destroy if it could. He wrote:

> In particular the rooting out and destruction of rebels (*ashrar u mufsidin*) from the Bakhtiyari tribes has not exactly been carried out and they need to be punished and civilized (*tanbi u tadib u gushmal*). For among those tribes all acts of retribution are advisable. You have given Ahmad Khan Bakhtiyari amnesty and he has promised that he will no longer make mischief and keep a retinue of horsemen, and the

> state has agreed to forgive his past crimes. But the policy of making tribes into subjects (*ra'iyati kardan*) will not be brought about by allowing them to hold on to their fortresses (*qal'a*), and I have heard that Ahmad Khan's fortress, known by the name of Duli, was a place that always teemed with the brigands and ruffians of that tribe. As the tribes become more emboldened and rebellious they may find the opportunity to return to this fortress and once again turn to banditry and violence. Given your experience and services it seems improbable that you have allowed that fortress to stand and have not destroyed it. The agreement between you and the court was to completely eradicate the means and the causes of Bakhtiyari rebellion. What is more of a cause of rebellion and insurgency than a strong fortress? Upon receiving this letter, completely destroy the mentioned fortress.[134]

Fortresses were principal features of the landscape of autonomy in the Bakhtiyari Mountains. Only reached through narrow passes and steep paths, they provided an impenetrable retreat for rebellious or outlawed khans and their retinues. As previously discussed, a number of these impregnable hill forts provided shelter to independent Bakhtiyari tribesmen fleeing from state domination, including the retinues of Asad Khan at the fortress of Malikan and those of Muhammad Taqi Khan at the fortress of Mungasht. Contemporary sources reveal that the Qajars sought to destroy them during their military expeditions into the Bakhtiyari Mountains but faced great difficulties in their attempts.[135]

Written orders from Mirza Aqa Khan Nuri, Amir Kabir's lieutenant, partner in the government, and successor as *Atabayg* following the premier's execution in 1852, also discuss Khanlar Mirza's jurisdiction over the Bakhtiyari during his governorship in Khuzistan and Luristan. In a letter dated 1852 to Chiraq 'Ali Khan, the deputy governor (*nayib al-hukuma*) of Isfahan, Nuri stressed that Khanlar Mirza needed to bring "discipline (*intizam*) to the Bakhtiyari and their affairs and establish complete order in the region under his guardianship."[136] The implication of this correspondence is, of course, the suggestion that such complete control over the Bakhtiyari tribes was wanting and had yet to be accomplished. In another of Nuri's letters he reported to Khanlar Mirza that the Bakhtiyari were carrying out raids in the southern province of Fars and the outskirts of Isfahan and urged the governor to rein in the turbulent Bakhtiyari tribes wherever they might be so that people would be safe from their "aggression and trespass."[137] Nuri closed by reminding Khanlar Mirza that the Bakhtiyari tribes were under his guardianship and that keeping them under control was an endless task that he could not afford to neglect.

Conclusion

During the early nineteenth century, the Bakhtiyari tribes of the Zagros Mountains maintained considerable autonomy on the southwestern edge of Qajar Iran. Persian chronicles and histories are rich sources for the study of the Bakhtiyari and other nomadic and semi-nomadic tribes in nineteenth-century Iran. These texts yield views of tribal territories in Iran from the perspective of the central government. Although imperial chronicles were most often concerned with tribal insurgencies and the "lawlessness" of pastoral nomadic populations, they may also be read "against the grain" as accounts of political and cultural autonomy on the margins of the empire. In the early Qajar period, tribes such as the Bakhtiyari gave nominal allegiance to the Qajars while preserving their independence in distant arid and mountainous environs.

This chapter has suggested that the Qajar dynasty ruled the periphery of Iran through accommodation and reliance upon tribal structures. The Qajars exerted limited and indirect rule over the tribes, based primarily on the collection of light taxes, the recruitment of tribal militias, and the control of tribal khans and headmen. During instances of tribal insubordination the state could mount violent military expeditions, but these were temporary measures with negligible effects on the perennial resistance of the tribes. The nomadic and semi-nomadic tribes of early Qajar Iran lived in large part beyond the reach of imperial authority.

2

THE CITY OF ISFAHAN AND ITS HINTERLAND

IN 1877 Mirza Husayn Khan Tahvildar wrote a description of the various quarters of the city of Isfahan and the trade in its bazaar. In his *Jughrafiya-yi Isfahan* (Geography of Isfahan) Tahvildar also ventured to discuss the city's environs, or *ab u hava* ("water and air").[1] Rising above the western periphery of Isfahan, he wrote, were the great ranges of the Bakhtiyari Mountains (Kuhistan-i Bakhtiyari), which gave the city its mountain air and were the source of the Zayanda Rud, which "flowed from the foot of Kuh Karun [Zard Kuh]" toward the city, watering its farmlands and running below its famed bridges.[2]

Such descriptions of Isfahan's hinterland are uncommon. The once famed capital of the Safavid dynasty has mostly been remembered for its built environment, with little said about the city's "nature." Although there is a rich body of literature on the history of Isfahan, most accounts have focused on the city's monuments, art, and architecture.[3] The rare studies of Isfahan's society, economy, and politics have perhaps understandably highlighted its urban society and culture.[4] By contrast, the relationship between Isfahan and its periphery has been little explored, until quite recently.[5] The words of Robert McC. Adams from some three decades ago about works on Isfahan in European languages still hold true:

> Too much of our data—either in contemporary accounts or surviving monuments—ignores whatever aspects of diversity there were and may embody little more than the ruling elite's self-perceptions and aspirations. . . . Looking outside the city, I am struck by how little has been said about the character of the dominance over the countryside it

presumably exercised. Are there any grounds for hoping that we shall ultimately be able to reconstruct the spatial extent and the organizational structure of the city's functional hinterlands?[6]

Drawing upon Persian sources from the Qajar period, including manuscripts from the Iranian National Archives, chronicles, and gazetteers, the following pages attempt to provide a history of the hinterland of Isfahan in the 1860s to 1880s. In particular, this chapter explores how the provincial government of Isfahan attempted to control the Bakhtiyari tribes on the margins of the city.

Hinterland is defined here as the region behind the city, a place remote from towns.[7] It encompasses the lands beyond the city's walls. In the case of nineteenth-century Isfahan, the hinterland meant the untamed mountains of the Bakhtiyari tribes. Throughout the Qajar period the Bakhtiyari remained autonomous on the periphery of Isfahan. Although they paid revenues and provided cavalry to the Qajar provincial governor, they were effectively an independent tribal federation. Between the 1860s and 1880s, however, as the Bakhtiyari were unified under Husayn Quli Khan, the *ilkhan* or paramount chieftain of the confederacy, they also became increasingly subject to the tribal policies of Mas'ud Mirza Zill al-Sultan (1850–1918), who served as the Qajar prince governor of Isfahan between 1874 and 1907. This chapter examines how the provincial capital of Isfahan functioned in the expansion of state control over the Bakhtiyari tribal confederacy during the Qajar period. The emergence of Husayn Quli Khan as the *ilkhan* of the Bakhtiyari and the governorship of Zill al-Sultan in Isfahan allowed the Qajar dynasty to extend its reach over the tribes of the Zagros Mountains during a time of heightened Western imperial and commercial presence.

The Margins of the City: Isfahan and the Bakhtiyari

In the mid-nineteenth century, Isfahan's population was approximately 70,000 to 80,000 people.[8] West of the city rose the Bakhtiyari Mountains. According to the Qajar geographical chronicle *Mir'at al-Buldan* (1876), by Muhammad Hasan Khan I'timad al-Saltana, Isfahan was "a city at the edge of the mountains"—*dar akhar-i kuhistan ast*.[9] I'timad al-Saltana noted that the Zayanda Rud carried the melted snow of the Bakhtiyari Mountainous into the city: "The water of Zayanda Rud flows down from Kuh Zard and the mountains of Lur-i Buzurg and passes by Isfahan . . . This mountain, famed as Kuh Zard, is in Luristan and in the lands of the Bakhtiyari tribes."[10]

This idea of the hinterland of Isfahan as a bounteous terrain of mountains and rivers—the reservoir of Zayanda Rud—is presented in further detail in Muhammad Mihdi ibn Muhammad Riza al-Isfahani's *Nisf-i Jahan, fi ta'rif al-Isfahan* (1870), thought to be one of the geographical sources I'timad al-Saltana used in *Mir'at al-Buldan*. Describing the mountains of Zard Kuh, Isfahani wrote of their connection to Zayanda Rud, which he held to be "the true essence, the source of cultivation (*abadi*), and the main work of nature (*tab'iyat*) in Isfahan." As he put it:

> The source of the Zayanda Rud is found in the foothills of this mountain, which lies on the frontier (*hadd-i fasil*) between the region of Isfahan and Luristan-i Bakhtiyari. Most of the mountain is covered in snow. . . . the very source of the Zayanda Rud River comes from three springs that join together in these mountains and connect with other springs from the waters of the melting snow in the region, forming a river called Chihil Chishma or the "Forty Springs." And it is this river, with waters from the mountains, the springs, and the melted snow that flows into the Zayanda Rud.[11]

The Bakhtiyari Mountains and the city of Isfahan were linked, interwoven, inseparable.

A similar account is given by Mirza Ghulam Khan Afzal al-Mulk in *Safarnama-yi Isfahan*, written in 1883 while he was in the service of Mas'ud Mirza Zill al-Sultan. Mirza Ghulam Husayn writes:

> The source (*sar chishma*) of Zayanda Rud is at the foot of Zard Kuh-i Bakhtiyari, the mountain that is the boundary between the provinces of Isfahan and Luristan. From the point of the Zayanda Rud's origin to Zard Kuh is one and a half *farsakh*. This mountain is always covered in snow . . . . These lands are the *yaylaq* of the Bakhtiyari tribes and are filled with snow-capped mountains. No one remains there in winter.[12]

In the rugged mountains behind Isfahan were the summer quarters (*yaylaq*) of the Bakhtiyari tribes, in places such as Chahar Mahal, Silakhur, Zard Kuh, Bazuft, Gulpaygan, Faraydan, Khvansar, Ganduman, Chihil Chishma, and the hills of Mungasht.[13] For the city's people these nomadic subjects inhabiting the wildlands on the edges of Isfahan were a source of uncertainty, detectable in their writings about the tribes. Revealing his sedentary perspective, Mirza Ghulam Husayn remarked that the Bakhtiyari's "houses were tents"—*khanaha-yi anha ahshami ast.*[14] According to Isfahani the mountains west of the city had flourished in the past with cultivation but "were now the abode of the Bakhtiyari, whose incursions and depredations had laid the land to waste."[15] What is certain is that their proximity ensured that the Bakhtiyari had frequent contacts with the people of Isfahan, particularly during the spring and summer months, when the tribes reached their upland pastures on the city's outskirts.

Ernst Hoeltzer, a German employee of the Indo-European Telegraph Department working on the telegraph line at Isfahan in the 1860s, remarked upon the Bakhtiyari's bold presence there in his survey, "Description of the City of Isfahan":

> One should also speak about the tribes that spend summers in the Isfahan vicinity. Every time I observe their camps, I cannot help marveling at their knack for shooting and horse riding. They gallop on their quick horses and, with their feet in the stirrups, they dive left and right under the horse's belly. After they defend themselves in such a way from enemy attacks, they return to the saddle and vanquish their enemies. They keep bullets in their mouths and often load their rifles and shoot while galloping. The Bakhtiyari tribesmen can hit a target only very quickly. If they come across a stronger force and feel resistance and threat of defeat, they immediately fall back. They start training at an early age and everybody seeing their exercises admires them.[16]

The Bakhtiyari tribes, which numbered between 28,000 and 51,000 tents according to mid-nineteenth-century accounts, maintained significant social and economic ties with Isfahan.[17] Hoeltzer reported in his survey, "Travels to the Mountains of the Persian Nomadic Tribes, the Qashqa'is and the Bakhtiyaris," that the Bakhtiyari were Lurs whose migrations to their summer quarters brought them into the vicinity of Isfahan, with the Chahar Lang encamped in the province of Faraydan and the Haft Lang encamped during summers in the province of Chahar Mahal.[18] The Bakhtiyari Mountains lie on an old caravan route between Isfahan and the Persian Gulf. During the spring and summer months in the *yaylaq*, the tribes had an established trade with Isfahan, exchanging their flocks of sheep and goats and herds of horses

Tent life, c. 1860s–1870s. From C. J. Wills, *In the Land of the Lion and Sun, or Modern Persia: Being the Experiences of Life in Persia from 1866 to 1881* (London, 1893).

and mules for goods found in the city.[19] Contemporary sources attest to the pastoral economy of the tribes and their trade with Isfahan, noting that "the great wealth of the Bakhtiyaris . . . consists in their flocks and herds."[20] The tribes traded textiles woven from their sheep's wool and supplied Isfahan with mutton during the summer months.[21] The Bakhtiyari's involvement in the horse and rug trade is chronicled in the *Tarikh-i Bakhtiyari*, which mentions that the khans were renowned for breeding Arab horses in the mountains.[22] They engaged in other traffic as well, such as supplying Khuzistan with tobacco grown in the plains of Janiki.[23] As Hoeltzer noted, the Bakhtiyari were a constant presence to be encountered on the roads on the city's outskirts, and during hard times, "when their rich pastures were completely dried up, leaving them with nothing, they plundered villagers and travelers and also fought among themselves."[24] It was also during the spring and summer, when the tribes were in the *yaylaq*, that the Bakhtiyari *ilkhan* paid the annual revenues to the Qajar government. During the 1830s the assessment for all of the Bakhtiyari tribes was 14,900 tumans.[25] By the 1880s the Bakhtiyari were paying 22,000 tumans in revenues to the provincial governor of Isfahan.[26] The

Bakhtiyari women weaving kilims, c. 1870s. Hoeltzer Collection, ICHO.

khans collected the taxes in mules according to the prosperity of the tribes and were required to pay the sum to the provincial governor of Isfahan, each mule being worth 100 tumans.[27]

Although the Bakhtiyari's subsistence was based on their flocks and herds, they also practiced seasonal cultivation to supply grains. Most of their arable lands lay in the lowland winter pastures (*qishlaq*), where every fall the tribes planted wheat and barley to be harvested in the spring. At that time the tribes left the heat of the lowlands to make their upward marches to the highland summer pastures, while a few men stayed behind to harvest and store the ripened crops.[28] A much-recited poem in the Bakhtiyari vernacular described the loneliness of these reluctant harvesters of the land:

The camps have broken up and departed, not a crow has remained
Save for the wild thyme, there is not a blade of grass
The lowland is well watered and has un-watered cultivation in abundance

If the cultivator has not sown it, what blame rests on me?
May the bread from the new wheat be poison to me.[29]

Once again in autumn, before the tribes descended from their highland pastures, crops were sown in the *yaylaq* and lay dormant under the snow until the tribes returned the following spring.

What is more, some of the Bakhtiyari tribes were in transition from *sahra nishin* ("dwellers in the desert" or pastoral nomads) to *dih nishin* ("dwellers in villages"), as suggested by changes in land tenure among the tribes in the province of Chahar Mahal, west of Isfahan in the foothills of the Zagros Mountains. Eighteenth- and nineteenth-century land deeds from the Iranian National Archives in Tehran (Sazman-i Asnad-i Milli) reveal that Bakhtiyari khans and their families were buying and selling land and water rights in the villages of Chahar Mahal.[30] Ownership and property rights became established in the area as tribal khans purchased pastures, arable plots, and villages. For instance, in a deed of land dated 1251/1835 from the village of Junaqan in the Bakhtiyari *yaylaq*, Mulla Hajji Muhammad and the family of Karbala'i Junaqani sold plots of land and the water rights to a brook to Khvaja Nizam.[31] This evidence suggests changes in the prevailing seasonal tending of the land and introduced changing practices of land use among the Bakhtiyari tribes in the Qajar period.

The settlement of certain groups of the Bakhtiyari is illustrated by other developments as well. In the 1830s many of the Chahar Lang gathered around the chieftain Muhammad Taqi Khan at the fortress of Qal'a-yi Tul and settled in the Bakhtiyari winter quarters near Janiki-yi Garmsir, Malamir, Shushtar, Ram Hurmuz, and Dizful, all well-watered towns near the Karun River. Qajar officials were disturbed by the fact that the Chahar Lang had occupied and come to control these once-arable lands. The Janiki region of Khuzistan, with its center at Malamir—the ancient Izaj of the Sassanians—was an agricultural district with a network of dams and canals (*qanat*). Qajar officials lamented that many of these canals had fallen into ruin: "The old buildings and settled communities of Malamir are gone and only tribes (*il nishin*) remain."[32] But much evidence suggests that the tribes that had moved into the area were taking to agriculture and paying taxes. The Janiki, for instance, were well known for growing rice, which reportedly was being farmed by as many as a thousand families. As the Chahar Lang tribes occupied the arable lowlands around the Karun and gathered around Muhammad Taqi Khan at Qal'a-yi Tul, pastoralists adopted sedentary ways of life.[33] By the second half of the nineteenth

Bakhtiyari in Isfahan, c. 1870s. Hoeltzer Collection, ICHO.

century, at least 5,000 Chahar Lang (*kapar nishin*—"hut dwellers") had settled in Janiki. These tribes were farming crops, including opium, and were paying 5,000 tumans in annual taxes.[34]

The Ilkhan and the Confederation of the Bakhtiyari Tribes

Throughout the nineteenth century the Bakhtiyari were described as the most formidable tribes in the Zagros Mountains west of Isfahan. State publications, such as the *Ruznama-yi Dawlat-i 'Alliya-yi Iran*, stressed the insecurity of settled populations around Isfahan during the time of the migration of the Bakhtiyari tribes and their flocks from *yaylaq* to *qishlaq* and the need "to keep the migrations under control and to keep banditry to a minimum."[35] The state also had to contend with Bakhtiyari tribal unrest, rebellions, and raids that revealed its tenuous rule over the margins of the empire. Since Nasir al-Din Shah Qajar (1848–1896) had ascended to the throne, the Haft Lang and the

Chahar Lang had separately rebelled, while the free-spirited Bakhtiyarvand brazenly rejected the word of the shah.[36] In the Zagros Mountains the writ of the Qajar state did not carry far, and the Bakhtiyari tribes held great autonomy.

In seeking to control the tribes throughout the empire, the Qajar dynasty relied upon the existing tribal structure and attempted to rule indirectly through the khans. These tribe and state relations intensified in the mid-nineteenth century, as the Russian and British empires made inroads into Qajar Iran. With its territorial integrity threatened the Qajar state became more assertive in the provincial administration of tribes. This was certainly the case in Isfahan and its periphery, where the Qajars took measures to control the independence of the Bakhtiyari. Between the 1860s and 1880s Qajar authorities relied on the rising chieftain Husayn Quli Khan to assimilate and confederate the Bakhtiyari tribes.

Husayn Quli Khan belonged to the Haft Lang, and by the mid-nineteenth century he had emerged as a khan capable of unifying the Bakhtiyari tribal confederation and serving the Qajar state. Born circa 1820 to a noble lineage of the tribe, he gained fame as a Bakhtiyari warrior striving to strengthen tribal solidarity.[37] According to tribal histories he was a powerful, charitable, and generous khan whose charisma and wisdom secured the support of his subjects. In her memoirs, the *ilkhan*'s daughter Bibi Maryam recounts how Husayn Quli Khan built ties between the tribes, particularly through the arrangement of marriages. As she recalls, one of the *ilkhan*'s policies toward the Bakhtiyari tribes was to make them his kin (*khishi namudan*). Taking wives from other tribes for himself, his clan, and his retainers (*bastagan*) or presenting daughters to the sons of other tribes, he also ordered the Bakhtiyari khans to take and give women. In the mid-nineteenth century Bakhtiyari marriages—between Bakhtiyarvand and Duraki, Babadi and Duraki, Haft Lang and Chahar Lang—contributed significantly to the confederation of the Bakhtiyari. The *ilkhan* also adhered to tribal expectations of generosity (*karam*). Bibi Maryam remembered the feasts that her father hosted in the 1870s, noting that at every meal the *ilkhan* hosted 50 guests, and at times the number of guests reached 200.[38] Husayn Quli Khan was also supported in his efforts to consolidate the Bakhtiyari by the Qajar government, which sought to establish loyalty among the tribes and absorb them into the fabric of the empire.

Husayn Quli Khan quickly emerged as the representative of the Qajar state among the Bakhtiyari tribes, charged with establishing order, recruiting troops, and collecting taxes. In 1852, for instance, 2,000 Haft Lang and Chahar Lang soldiers under the command of Husayn Quli Khan and other

Bakhtiyari headmen were enlisted in the retinues of Prince Khanlar Mirza Ihtisham al-Saltana, the governor of Khuzistan, Luristan, and Bakhtiyari.[39] In the same year Mirza Taqi Khan Amir Kabir, Nasir al-Din Shah's prime minister (*Atabayg-i azam*), ordered Husayn Quli Khan to pacify the Babadi and their headman, Musi Khan 'Akkasha, and to consolidate the Bakhtiyari tribal federation, joining together the Haft Lang and Chahar Lang tribes.[40] Over time the *ilkhan* gained the Qajar's confidence and worked to assimilate the tribes. According to Sipihr in *Nasikh al-Tavarikh*, "The whole Bakhtiyari land became free from fear and war, its people learned manners and began to seek the right path (*adab giriftand*)."[41] In the illustrated government gazetteer *Ruznama-yi Dawlat-i 'Alliya-yi Iran*, it was reported that even when a lost horse strayed into Bakhtiyari territory, the *ilkhan* returned it to the *tupkhana* in Isfahan; when a caravan was robbed outside the city, he retrieved the merchants' belongings.[42] For the Qajar central and provincial government, the *ilkhan* served as a familiar envoy in the Zagros Mountains, a chieftain with the authority to unify and tax the surrounding tribes for the state, bringing the southwestern peripheries of Iran into the Qajar sphere. By the 1860s Husayn Quli Khan had emerged over his rivals as the leading chieftain among the Bakhtiyari tribes and hence began to consolidate his control over the Haft Lang and Chahar Lang.

The Qajars appointed Husayn Quli Khan *nazim* in 1862 and *ilkhan* in 1867, thus allowing him to become the first Bakhtiyari khan officially mandated to rule over all of the Haft Lang and Chahar Lang tribes.[43] As the *ilkhan* he remained an autonomous ruler in the Zagros Mountains, charged with the responsibility of bringing order (*nazm*) to the tribes and collecting taxes (*maliyat*) on behalf of the state. In this role the *ilkhan* led a migratory administration. During winters he traveled to the plains of Khuzistan, where he governed the tribes in the *qishlaq* from his base at Malamir. In summers he moved higher into the elevations of the mountains to the *yaylaq*, where he held the fortress of Chaqakhur.[44] For nearly twenty years the *ilkhan* worked with the Qajar government, including Prime Minister Mirza 'Ali Asghar Khan Sadr Azam, to assimilate the Bakhtiyari tribes into one—*yaki kardan-i inha*.[45]

The Tribal Policies of Mas'ud Mirza Zill al-Sultan, Prince Governor of Isfahan

The Qajars' administration of the Bakhtiyari in the late nineteenth century fell under Mas'ud Mirza Zill al-Sultan, the notorious prince governor of Isfahan

Maydan-i Naqsh-i Jahan, the central square of Isfahan, showing the royal mosque, the bazaar, and 'Ali Qapu Palace. Hoeltzer Collection, ICHO.

who was the shah's eldest son and the most powerful Qajar official in the center and the south of the country.[46] Appointed governor of Isfahan in 1865, Zill al-Sultan simultaneously held the governorships of the provinces of Yazd, Khuzistan, Luristan, 'Iraq, Burujird and Bakhtiyari, Gulpaygan and Khvansar by 1881.[47] With their summer pastures on the periphery of Isfahan, the Bakhtiyari *yaqlaq* was under the provincial government of Zill al-Sultan during the spring and summer. Zill al-Sultan received taxes from the khans and enlisted a body of Bakhtiyari cavalry commanded by the *ilkhan*'s eldest son Isfandiyar Khan.[48] According to official state sources 500 Bakhtiyari horsemen (*savaran*) were among the governor's troops in Isfahan.[49]

For Zill al-Sultan and other Qajar officials stationed in Isfahan in the late nineteenth century, the Bakhtiyari Mountains marked a cultural boundary.[50] The prince governor recorded ethnographic descriptions of the Bakhtiyari Mountains and tribes in his memoirs, published as *Sarguzasht-i Mas'udi*:

This is the mountain that separates Arabistan-i Iran from Fars and

> ʿIraq, and this mountain is called by the people Zard Kuh-i Bakhtiyari. Around this mountain the Lurs and Bakhtiyari have campgrounds and settlements (*sukna*). Their *yaylaq* are on the northern slopes of the mountains (*kuhistanat*), stretching from Fars to the snowy peaks of Burujird. Each tribe (*tayafa*) has its own name, and they have never been obedient to one another.[51]

Scattered reports appeared on the Bakhtiyari tribes and the periphery of Isfahan in the pages of the official gazette of Isfahan, *Farhang* (Culture), which ran from 1879 to 1891 and was edited by Mirza Taqi Khan, the head physician (*hakimbashi*) of Zill al-Sultan. An article from a January 1881 issue of *Farhang* reflects the negative outlook and suspicions of city folk toward the tribes:

> They still are not civilized and their customs and life differ little from that of animals (*na hanuz dar taht-i qavaid-i madaniyat idara shodihand va na az rusumi tarbiyat va insaniyat, vaz-i taʿayush va imtiyaz ba hayvanat bahrimand hastand*). They are wild and uncouth tribes (*vahshi va jangali*), people of the wildlands (*marduman-i biyabani*), all of them savage robbers (*khunkhar va rahzan*).[52]

In the writings of the Qajar literati the Bakhtiyari were described as primitive tribes on the geographical and cultural margins of Isfahan.

Qajar correspondences and documents found at the Iranian National Archives reveal the precariousness of Zill al-Sultan's command over the Bakhtiyari tribes. Reports of Bakhtiyari thieves (*duzd*) robbing merchants (*tujjar*) on the road between Isfahan and Yazd, stealing sheep, and entering the cities armed with guns reveal the tribal power and lack of state authority that prevailed in the hinterland of nineteenth-century Isfahan.[53] Qajar officials worried that with the Bakhtiyari tribes creating chaos (*lijam gusikhtighi*), the peasantry (*raʿiyat*) would soon be destroyed, and there would be no way to collect taxes.[54]

A series of letters exchanged in 1879 between Zill al-Sultan and Mirza Yusuf Ashtiyani Mustawfi al-Mamalik, Iran's finance minister and acting interior minister for various provinces, detail the Bakhtiyari's forays in the environs of Isfahan. In a letter dated Shaʿban 1296 [1879], Mustawfi al-Mamalik asks the governor of Isfahan what measures his government has taken in response to an incident in which Bakhtiyari tribesmen attacked and killed Hajji Najaf Quli with clubs at Karvand-i Ab Garm. Zill al-Sultan responded by describing the

Between Isfahan and the Bakhtiyari Mountains, c. 1870s. Hoeltzer Collection, ICHO.

limits of his power and deflecting his responsibility over the Bakhtiyari: "I have no authority over them, they are not all under my government (*hukumat*), and I should not be questioned about them. Their governor (*hakim*) is Hishmat al-Dawla [of Luristan] and Husayn Quli Khan is their *ilkhani*."[55] Mustawfi al-Mamalik reminded Zill al-Sultan that Husayn Quli Khan was collecting taxes from the tribes of Luristan while claiming that he was carrying out his work as a servant of Zill al-Sultan. This had led many of the Bakhtiyari from Burujird to cry out because of the injustices of the *ilkhan—nala-yi Bakhtiyari-yi Burujird az dast-i Husayn Quli Khan bi falak-i asir rasid*. To this Zill al-Sultan responded by suggesting the difficulties involved in collecting taxes from migrating tribes such as the Bakhtiyari.[56] During the same year, it was reported in the local newsletter *Farhang* that the rebellious behavior (*sarkishi*) of the Bakhtiyari had forced Muhammad 'Ali Khan, the nayib al-hukuma of Burujird in Luristan, to keep additional cannons and troops, while the responsibility for collecting taxes from the tribes had been completely entrusted to the khans.[57]

The *ilkhan* and the governor of Isfahan maintained strained relations. The *ilkhan* visited the capital every spring, as the tribes reached the *yaylaq*, to pay the annual revenues. Zill al-Sultan made a number of hunting expeditions into the

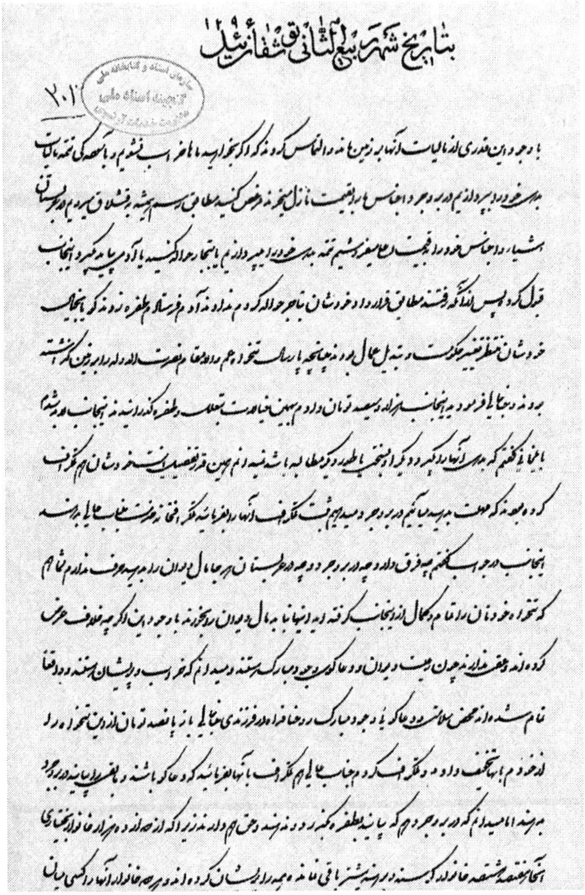

بتاریخ شهر ربیع الثانی توشقان ئیل ۱۲۹۶

۲۰۱

Letter on the difficulty of taxing the Bakhtiyari tribes, from the prince governor of Isfahan, Zill al-Sultan, to the interior minister, Mustawfi al-Mamalik, dated Rabiʿ al-Sani 1296 [1879]. INA.

Bakhtiyari territory as a guest of the *ilkhan*, giving him opportunities to survey the mountainous hinterland of Isfahan.[58] The Bakhtiyari *ilkhan*'s acquaintance with Zill al-Sultan involved him in Qajar court rivalries and intrigue. During the 1870s the *ilkhan* became involved in the power struggle between Zill al-Sultan and the prince governor of Fars Province, Farhad Mirza Muʿtamad al-Dawla.[59] Threatened by the ties between Isfahan and the Bakhtiyari, Farhad Mirza viewed the tribal confederacy as his sworn enemies.[60] Using his influence over the Qashqa'i, the most powerful tribal confederation in Fars province, if not the whole country, Farhad Mirza turned the Qashqa'i against the Bakhtiyari in a struggle for the authority to tax the lands of Falard and Khana Mirza, which lay between the two tribal territories.[61] The area became the site of repeated Qashqa'i and Bakhtiyari raids and looting in the late 1870s.[62] When Husayn Quli Khan gave refuge to 2,000 tents of Darrashuri, Kashkuli, and Farsimadan tribes that had fled from the Qashqa'i in 1878, the animosity between the two tribes brought them to the brink of open war.[63] The enmity between the two Qajar prince governors, Farhad Mirza of Fars and Zill al-Sultan of Isfahan, had disrupted relations between the major tribal federations of the south.

From the correspondence of Mustawfi al-Mamalik with both prince governors, a picture of the tribalism and provincialism in nineteenth-century Iran emerges. Various reports of discord and disorder were sent to Mustawfi al-Mamalik from Isfahan and Shiraz. The Bakhtiyari had attacked the Kazim Baygi Kashkuli, a subtribe of the Qashqa'i, and caused chaos (*harj u marj*).[64] Members of the Chahar Lang had occupied the telegraph house in Shushtar, asking for their rights and complaining that the Qashqa'i had looted their animals and sheep.[65] Qashqa'i tribesmen raided the peasants around Isfahan and created unrest. The Bakhtiyari stole herds of cows and flocks of sheep from the village of Vanak. Returning during the month of Ramazan they kidnapped two people from the village and killed a young woman.[66] Zill al-Sultan reported that Qashqa'i robbers from Fars were on the roads to and from Yazd, raiding caravans (*qafila*). While Farhad Mirza claimed that the robberies on the roads between Isfahan and Yazd were carried out by the Bakhtiyari, who were also harassing pilgrims making the *hajj* to Mecca.[67] The respective list of abuses continued.

It may have been the boldness of the Bakhtiyari *ilkhan*—at one point he reportedly wrote to Farhad Mirza in his own hand, threatening, "I'll send 5,000 horsemen against you"—that led to his demise.[68] In reaction Farhad Mirza warned Nasir al-Din Shah in a letter of the Bakhtiyari *ilkhan*'s rising prestige and reminded him that while their own ancestor, Muhammad Hasan Khan Qajar, had aspired to create a dynasty with a cavalry of merely thirty *savaran*, the Bakhtiyari *ilkhan* had thousands of horseman at his call and wrote incendiary letters to the governor of Fars in his own hand. In a letter to Mustawfi al-Mamalik Farhad Mirza warned of the growing power of the *ilkhan*: "And one thousand times I have written and a thousand more times I will write, may God help the 150-year-old Qajar dynasty from the troubles (*shar*) of this man."[69] According to Bibi Maryam, Farhad Mirza warned the shah that if he did not act soon, Qajar women would be taken on the backs of Bakhtiyari horses into the tribes' mountains—*zanha-yi Qajariya bi gardan-i asbha-yi Bakhtiyari aftada va bi kuhistan-i khudishan mibarand*.[70] Fears of tribalism and insurgency in the Zagros Mountains led Nasir al-Din Shah to seek first-hand information by sending a royal engineer to conduct a survey of the Bakhtiyari territory in 1881.

Zill al-Sultan seemed to understand that the increasing power of the Bakhtiyari confederation and its *ilkhan* were too risky a burden to bear, particularly if it meant his own fall from the shah's favor. Recognizing the bad blood between Farhad Mirza and the *ilkhan*, "two powerful servants of the state," in a letter to the Mustawfi al-Mamalik he offered to punish or even blind the *ilkhan*, if necessary.[71] Seeking to distance himself further from the *ilkhan*, he wrote to his father the shah, referring to the Bakhtiyari as "fire-burning" robbers (*duzd-i atashsuzan*) who "collect 80,000 tumans per year and pay 5,000 to the state, while every year they plunder Isfahan and Arabistan." Sensing that the tide had finally turned against the *ilkhan*, Zill al-Sultan added, "The wolf (*gurg*) cannot be asked to hold things together, for its nature is to tear them apart."[72] The governor of Isfahan's association with the Bakhtiyari *ilkhan* was nearing its end. Meanwhile, fears of tribal resistance in the Zagros Mountains, as well as the need for firsthand knowledge on the southwestern periphery of Iran, pressured Nasir al-Din Shah to seek information about the Bakhtiyari territory and surrounding regions.

The Travel Book of Najm al-Mulk

In 1881 Nasir al-Din Shah sent his royal engineer, Hajji Mirza 'Abd al-Ghaffar Najm al-Mulk, on a journey ostensibly to Mecca, but the real purpose was to complete a report on the province of Khuzistan. Najm al-Mulk's *Safarnama-yi Khuzistan* also contained a survey of the Bakhtiyari hinterland and its tribes while providing a first-hand view of the *ilkhan*'s rising authority.

Najm al-Mulk's portrayal of the power and influence of the Bakhtiyari confederation and their *ilkhan* further stoked the suspicions of the shah. The rising influence of the Bakhtiyari tribes in the Zagros Mountains increasingly became a cause of Qajar insecurity. Najm al-Mulk's travelogue painted a portrait of Khuzistan as an unsettled and ruined region, a land separate from Iran and ruled by the Bakhtiyari tribes. Describing the province he wrote that "everywhere is in ruins and unsettled—*hama ja kharab ast va qayr-i maskun*—and as long as roads are not built and villages (*abadi*) do not flourish, Khuzistan cannot be counted as a part of Iran; it is a separate land—*mulki ast juda*."[73]

Najm al-Mulk's "Book of Travels" was a product of Qajar efforts to gather information on the southwestern province of Khuzistan and included accounts of the Bakhtiyari tribal confederacy. According to him, the tribes and their flocks (*galla va rama*) had overrun Khuzistan and made the province their pasture (*jalga*). During the summer the tribes were encamped in their highland pastures, and in winter they came down into the plains. Nomads were scattered all over the province and had, in his assessment, ruined the irrigation networks and peasant communities of well-watered and arable lands. He wrote that the tribes arrived, although they had no right to be in Khuzistan—*miyayand va hal-i anka haqi nadarand.*[74] Najm al-Mulk estimated that the Bakhtiyari numbered more than 50,000 families (approximately 250,000 people) and attempted to provide the names and populations of some of the Haft Lang and Chahar Lang tribes. Moreover, he reported on the Bakhtiyari's military strength, claiming that they could assemble 100,000 men on foot and 30,000 cavalry.[75]

Najm al-Mulk's *Safarnama* alarmed the shah with its assessment of Khuzistan province and the southwestern margins of the empire. He went so far as to claim that Khuzistan was no longer under the control of the central government, writing, "in this ruined land the Bakhtiyari rule"—*dar in mulk-i kharabgah Bakhtiyari hakim ast.*[76] In Najm al-Mulk's travel book, Husayn Quli Khan emerges as a shah in his own right, with a kingdom based in the mountains between the Iranian plateau and the Mesopotamian plains. As Najm al-Mulk simply put it, "Khuzistan is the house of the *ilkhan*, and even the Arabs of the region submit to his rule."[77] Najm al-Mulk sketched the current condition of and trade on the stone-paved Bakhtiyari Road in his travelogue. The road, he wrote, had fallen into ruin along its various stages. Because few of its bridges survived, the tribes crossed rivers on foot or while floating on goatskin rafts during their migrations, causing many of their flocks to drown. Consequently supplies and trade were lacking on the road. Najm al-Mulk suggested that the road had great potential to link the well-watered lands of Khuzistan with Isfahan. By building the road, as the Atabaygs of Luristan once had, Nasir al-Din Shah could create a public work that could do wonders "for the settlement of the people"—*baray-i sukunat-i mardum.*[78] Rebuilding the road would strengthen the power of the state over the Bakhtiyari and link the province more closely to Iran—*qavat-i dawlat bar Bakhtiyari ziyad mishavad va az tarafi Khuzistan durust malhaq mishavad ba Iran.*[79]

In the *Safarnama*, Najm al-Mulk seemingly called on Nasir al-Din Shah to assert Qajar central authority over Khuzistan and its tribes. The travelogue highlighted the prevalence of pastoral nomadism in once-cultivated lands and detailed the regional power of the Bakhtiyari. By noting rising divisions between the young khans who were sons of Husayn Quli Khan and his brothers, it even suggested ways that the Qajar state could manipulate the tribes.[80] Yet Najm al-Mulk's state-centric account is belied throughout the text by the evidence he cites of the ways the Bakhtiyari tribal confederation was maintaining order in Khuzistan. For example he noted that the Bakhtiyari khans visited the governor of Khuzistan Ihtisham al-Dawla annually and presented him with 20,000 tumans as taxes in cash and kind (*naqd va jins*).[81] Elsewhere Najm al-Mulk describes Husayn Quli Khan's efforts to build bridges on the roads and paths that traversed the Bakhtiyari Mountains and recalls his surprise upon encountering sedentary Bakhtiyari tribes in Chahar Mahal and Junaqan, farming crops and weaving tribal rugs from their own sheep's wool.[82] Najm al-Mulk was even prone to ambivalent reveries on nomadic life, showing that even settled Persians accustomed to the city maintained a sense of nostalgia for the pastoral. Describing the Zagros Mountains, Najm al-Mulk recounted seeing "the black tents of the Bakhtiyari tribes everywhere" on what he praised as pasture-filled lands—*zaminha-yi chaman zar*.[83] But overall Najm al-Mulk's report had the effect of directing Nasir al-Din Shah's attention to the ascendancy of the Bakhtiyari in Khuzistan.[84]

The Death of the Ilkhan

By the 1860s the authority of the Bakhtiyari *ilkhan* in the mountainous periphery of Isfahan had become known to British merchants and travelers. In the widely read travelogue, *In the Land of the Lion and Sun*, C. J. Wills, a doctor in the service of the Indo-European Telegraph Department, romantically described the freedom and autonomy of the *ilkhan* and the Bakhtiyari tribes in the high elevations of the Zagros Mountains:

> A few hours' march brings one to the Bakhtiari country, governed by Hossein Kuli Khan, who ruled with a rod of iron the turbulent tribes of these wild men. All wanderers, they are a brave and untamed people, their customs quite different from the inhabitants of the towns, upon whom they look with contempt. They are practically independent, merely furnishing a large contingent of irregular cavalry. The illustration gives a good idea of the tent-life of the wandering tribes of Persia. The tents are very portable, impervious to rain, wind, and sun, and are woven by the women from the hair of the black goats. They are very durable. The Shah is of little authority, the whole government being vested in Hossein Kuli Khan, whose eldest son remains with the king in honourable captivity in Teheran as hostage for his father's good conduct.[85]

Bridge over the Karun at Dupulan, constructed by order of Husayn Quli Khan Ilkhan, 1890. Isabella Bird Photograph Album, UCLA Special Collections.

To open the hinterland of Isfahan to trade the British would require the cooperation of the *ilkhan* and the Bakhtiyari.

In this context the *ilkhan* opened negotiations with the British regarding the opening of a caravan road through the Bakhtiyari territory, a development that threatened the sovereignty of the shah and precipitated the *ilkhan*'s execution in the summer of 1882. The *ilkhan* had long shown an interest in roads and public works projects and had commissioned the construction of bridges, canals, and dams in the Bakhtiyari territory. He ordered the building of bridges to facilitate trade and transit and promoted the cultivation of the land.[86] British schemes for the building of the Bakhtiyari Road began in earnest in the 1870s, after George Mackenzie of Grey, Paul, and Company traveled through the Bakhtiyari Mountains to seek the opening of a southern trade route to Isfahan. Mackenzie met with the Bakhtiyari *ilkhan* while he was encamped in the winter quarters of the tribes and mentioned to him the feasibility of a Bakhtiyari mountain road that would open the hinterland of Isfahan to trade. The British merchant reported back that the Bakhtiyari were open to contacts with Europeans and prepared to accept British commercial schemes in the region.

> Their present means of subsistence, their flocks, entails on them a nomadic life, but they seem to adapt themselves readily to a more settled life, and would doubtless adopt it had they any inducement for so doing offered them. They proved themselves to be hospitable, civil and obliging when kindly spoken with, and to be free from caste prejudices. I was everywhere made welcome to sleep in their tents, and when food was brought they evinced no objection to eat out of the same dish with me, smoking the Kalian, too, at all times after me.[87]

What is more, the Bakhtiyari *ilkhan* had tentatively consented to a British road-building project and offered to guarantee the safety of caravans passing through the mountains.[88]

Reports from the early 1880s suggest, however, that the *ilkhan* might have been reconsidering the opening of the Bakhtiyari territory to British trade. In 1881 Walter Baring and Captain Henry L. Wells of the Royal Engineers completed a surveying tour of the Bakhtiyari land for the government of India and made a plane-table sketch of the road between Isfahan and the Karun. Gaining great respect for the *ilkhan*, they described him as "a fine stalwart of a man of about 60 or 62, the very picture of rude health" and noted that the chief had some 30,000 Bakhtiyari families and 3 million sheep in flocks under his command.[89] Wells reported that the *ilkhan* was having reservations about the prospect of a caravan road through the mountains, "as it would naturally weaken his now very independent position."[90] The Bakhtiyari khans were quick to remind the British of the advantages of impracticable mountain passes where "a few men could stop a host."[91]

The Qajar government settled the matter in a cruel fashion. The Bakhtiyari *ilkhan*'s growing authority and offers of cooperation with the British regarding the construction of the road may have precipitated his death and subsequent Qajar efforts to fragment the Bakhtiyari tribal confederacy. In 1882 Nasir al-Din Shah ordered Zill al-Sultan to execute the *ilkhan*, an order the prince governor carried out.[92] During the tribes' spring migration to the summer pastures, as the *ilkhan* visited Isfahan to pay the annual revenues to Zill al-Sultan, he was strangled and two of his sons, Isfandiyar Khan and 'Ali Quli Khan, were imprisoned.

The Qajars thus deprived the Bakhtiyari of their most charismatic khan, capable of preserving tribal solidarity and entering into independent negotiations with the British regarding commercial schemes in the hinterland of Isfahan. According to tribal histories the death of the *ilkhan* had implications for all of the Bakhtiyari tribes.[93] The *ilkhan*'s daughter, Bibi Maryam, recalled that when word reached the Zagros Mountains that the *ilkhan* had been killed, the Bakhtiyari tribes gathered around Chaqakhur "with black tents as far as the eyes could see."[94] Ten-thousand women cut locks of their hair that day (*gaysu buridan*), in line with Bakhtiyari custom when a highly respected person died.[95] After the death of the *ilkhan* the Bakhtiyari tribal confederacy splintered apart as the sons, brothers, and cousins of the *ilkhan* jockeyed for control of tribal leadership.[96] The arrest and captivity of the *ilkhan*'s sons added to the disintegration of the Bakhtiyari unity achieved under the *ilkhan*. Although 'Ali Quli Khan was released after one year, Isfandiyar Khan, his father's apparent successor, remained captive in Isfahan for six years.[97] By removing Isfandiyar Khan and stirring divisions within the Haft Lang, the Qajar government set out to diffuse the collective power of the Bakhtiyari khans in the mountainous hinterland of Isfahan.[98] Thereafter, Nasir al-Din Shah and Zill al-Sultan kept the Bakhtiyari "precariously under check through the juxtaposition of tribal chiefs."[99] According to tribal histories the governor of Isfahan profited from the death of the *ilkhan*, seizing much of the chieftain's property, including his personal savings of 40,000 *ashrafis*, hundreds of his horses, and the funds from his treasury (*sanduq khana*).[100]

In nurturing rivalries between the family of the *ilkhan* (Ilkhani) and those of his brothers (Hajji Ilkhani and Ilbaygi), Qajar authorities found a short-term solution to the Bakhtiyari's clout. The tribal leadership passed to the brothers of Husayn Quli Khan, with Imam Quli Khan as the new *ilkhan* and Riza Quli Khan the *ilbayg*, while Isfandiyar Khan remained in captivity as leverage over the tribes. The young Bakhityari khan was Zill al-Sultan's "jewel-bearing tree" (*darakht-i javahar*), ensuring on the one hand that the Ilkhani faction and its followers would not rebel, and on the other that the Hajji Ilkhanis would fall in line, lest he release Isfandiyar Khan to return to the Bakhtiyari Mountains, where he was revered.[101] Over the long term, however, the death of the *ilkhan* created a source of enmity between the Bakhtiyari and the Qajar dynasty that would be resolved only with the coming of the Constitutional Revolution.

Moreover, it could scarcely forestall the expansion of British trade and influence into southwestern Iran, as the Bakhtiyari territory would become the setting of British commercial projects in the late nineteenth century. British imperialism in the Zagros Mountains would alter the politics of the Qajar periphery and the indirect rule that prevailed between the state and the tribes in Iran. In the 1890s, the Bakhtiyari land would be opened to British commerce and the world economy.

Conclusion

The Bakhtiyari Mountains formed the hinterland of nineteenth-century Isfahan. During the spring and summer seasons the Bakhtiyari tribes migrated to their highland pastures on the distant outskirts of the city, engaging in trade with merchants and exchanging their flocks for goods found in the bazaars. In the mid-nineteenth century, Husayn Quli Khan of the Haft Lang branch of the Bakhtiyari emerged as the paramount chieftain or *ilkhan* of the whole of the Bakhtiyari tribes. With the support of the Qajar state and the provincial government of Isfahan, he consolidated the tribal confederacy, facilitating imperial control over the Zagros Mountains. Upon reaching the Bakhtiyari's summer quarters, the *ilkhan* paid the annual revenues from the tribes to Isfahan and showed allegiance to the Qajar dynasty. By the early 1880s, however, the Bakhtiyari *ilkhan* came to hold such sway that he rivaled the provincial governor of Isfahan in his authority. Entering into independent negotiations with British merchants concerning their commercial projects in the hinterland of Isfahan, he threatened the Qajar government, which executed him in 1882, thus fragmenting the Bakhtiyari tribal confederacy.

Despite the measures taken by the Qajar dynasty to curtail the Bakhtiyari's independence in the hinterland of Isfahan, the state could not prevent the involvement of the tribes in subsequent British commercial projects. In 1888 Nasir al-Din Shah, under pressure from the British, opened the Karun River to international navigation and trade. The navigation of the Karun promised to open the interior of the country to trade via a route that linked the Persian Gulf to Isfahan. The opening of the Karun also ensured that the Bakhtiyari hinterland would see a rise in trade and traffic as caravans made their way through the Zagros Mountains to Isfahan. The effort to open the hinterland of Isfahan to trade came to rest on the revival of the ruined Bakhtiyari Road in the 1890s.

3

A ROAD THROUGH THE MOUNTAINS

IN 1899, the Tigris and Euphrates Steam Navigation Company, a British firm operating out of Baghdad, restored an ancient stone road that crossed Iran's Zagros Mountains and passed through the territory of the powerful Bakhtiyari tribal confederacy. The impenetrable and remote mountains had once been the basis of the Bakhtiyari's autonomy, but in 1898 the Qajar government granted a concession allowing the tribal khans to sign an agreement with the Tigris and Euphrates Steam Navigation Company, commonly referred to as the Lynch Brothers firm, for the construction of a caravan road between the Karun River and Isfahan. The Bakhtiyari or Lynch Road, as it was alternately called, became a modern imperial project that revived one of the ancient trade routes of Iran, expanded British commerce and influence to the interior of the country, and signaled the opening of a tribal hinterland in Qajar Iran.

During the second half of the nineteenth century the effects of foreign concessions had begun to reach Iran's interior. With the advent of the telegraph in 1857, the provinces were more firmly connected to the Qajar capital in Tehran. The infamous Reuter Concession of 1872 gave "the exclusive and definite privilege to work, all over the Empire, the mines of coal, iron, and copper, lead, petroleum," as well as monopolies in the construction of railways and canals and the rights to the exploitation of uncultivated lands to a British subject, Julius de Reuter, for a down payment of 40,000 pounds.[1] Called "the most complete and extraordinary surrender of the entire industrial resources of a kingdom into foreign hands that has probably ever been dreamt of, much less accomplished, in history," the concession was cancelled under widespread protest, but it was followed by other foreign concessions that promised to bring modern development to Iran in the late Qajar period.[2]

As early as the late nineteenth century these imperial projects had reached the Iranian periphery and had an impact on the tribes. For the Bakhtiyari tribes of southwestern Iran changes perhaps began with the advent of the telegraph in Isfahan and the south of the country in the 1860s under the British special mission of telegraphic engineers. This was followed in 1888 by Nasir al-Din Shah Qajar's (1848–1896) opening of the Karun River, which flowed through the Bakhtiyari territory, to international trade.[3] The object of this concession, strongly urged by the British, was to facilitate commerce into the interior of Iran.[4] When the Karun was opened to international traffic the Tigris and Euphrates Steam Navigation Company, which had been running its steamships on the Tigris between Basra and Baghdad since 1862, immediately provided a steamer service in Iran, with its ship, the *Blosse Lynch*, providing a fortnightly service.[5] British officials and merchants knew quite well that for commerce to reach Isfahan and the interior, trade would have to pass through the Bakhtiyari Mountains. The building of the Bakhtiyari Road under the auspices of the Lynch Company became a British imperial project in Qajar Iran and was cast as a means of assimilating pastoral nomadic tribes.[6]

The British Government and the Lynch Company envisioned the road as a civilizing measure that would "tame" the tribes, end their migrations, and usher them into the modern world. A place is no longer "wild" after it has been paved. To the British the rebuilding of the road was seen as a precursor of commerce and communication in a nomadic hinterland. They sought the smoothness of a commercial road laid down in the mountains of Iran. The free flow of trade was the ideal, and the road was to pave the way for this kind of traffic. As the seasoned British imperialist George Curzon remarked on this "progress" in 1890, "Mule tracks must precede cart-roads; cart-roads must precede railroads."[7] The building of the Bakhtiyari Road, which first and foremost served as a speedy trade route from the Persian Gulf though the mountains to Isfahan, was also a step toward the assimilation and settlement of the Bakhtiyari tribes.

The Arduous Roads of the Bakhtiyari

Mountains comprise much of the physical geography and landscape of Iran, and the grandest of these are the Zagros, which loom over the entire western portion of the country.[8] The highland slopes and valleys of the Zagros Mountains have historically provided a sustainable environment for pastoral nomadic societies. Moreover, the inaccessibility of the mountains, with high roads that are difficult to traverse, provided pastoral nomads with political and economic autonomy *vis-à-vis* outsiders. As Fernand Braudel has written:

> The Mountains are as a rule a world apart from civilizations, which are an urban lowland achievement. Their history is to have none, to remain always on the fringes of the great waves of civilization, even the longest and most persistent, which may spread over great distances in the horizontal plane but are powerless to move vertically when faced with an obstacle of several hundred meters.[9]

Thus, into the late nineteenth century, tribal groups such as the Qashqa'is, Kurds, Lurs, and Bakhtiyari remained practically independent in the Zagros Mountains.

The Bakhtiyari Mountains were crossed by a series of tribal migration routes (*il rah*). The mountain roads of the Bakhtiyari were known for their extreme difficulty and arduous nature. To take the Bakhtiyari roads in the nineteenth century was to walk over rugged surfaces, make steep climbs and descents, ford breathtaking rivers, and traverse treacherous bridges. Buildings and caravanserais were almost nonexistent on these roads, and the black tent provided the primary shelter from the elements. Nature took its toll on the roads, and portions of the tracks were washed away every winter by rain. Outside sources that chronicle instances when travelers or the agents of the central government ventured into the Bakhtiyari Mountains note that the land was full of "arduous roads" (*sa'b al-'abur*).

In his chronicle of the mid-eighteenth century, *Jahangusha-yi Nadiri*, Mirza Mihdi Khan Astarabadi alludes to the difficulties Nadir Shah Afshar's troops had to overcome in climbing the Bakhtiyari Mountains: "If one were to speak of the difficulties faced in taking this road, one could spend till eternity describing the rockiness, the unevenness, the steep ascents and descents, as well as the perplexity and failures brought to those who venture to traverse this road."[10] European sources shared similar sentiments and called attention to the roughness and steepness of Persian roads. Such roads left wide stretches of Iran, including the Zagros Mountains, impassable to outside traffic, as travelers, merchants, and foreign armies avoided these roads at all costs. John Malcolm, an officer from British India who visited Iran in 1800 as the minister plenipotentiary to the Court of Fath 'Ali Shah Qajar (r. 1797–1834) described the character and effect of Iran's rugged roads. He wrote:

Temporary bridge (*jurra*) used by the Bakhtiyari tribes to cross over the Karun River in the Zagros Mountains. *Tarikh-i Bakhtiyari* (Tehran, 1911).

> There can hardly be said to be any roads in Persia; nor are they much required, for the use of wheel carriages has not been introduced into that kingdom. Nothing can be more rugged and difficult than the paths which have been cut over the mountains by which it is bounded and intersected. The great benefits that would be derived from good roads has often been suggested to the Persians; but they have a reluctance to adopt an improvement which they believe, and not without reason, would destroy one of those natural obstacles by which their country is defended from invasion.[11]

In a letter home to England, written in 1840, Austen Henry Layard, discussed further below, described the Bakhtiyari's roads in the following words:

> We . . . crossed the most precipitous and lofty mountains by roads which appeared scarcely practicable to the mountain goat. I could trace the line of the route by the blood from our horses' feet. Such roads—if roads the perpendicular face of a mountain can be called—nowhere else exist.[12]

Miles of bad roads rendered wide stretches of the country impassable to most outsiders. As the French traveler Dubeaux remarked: "The Persians have no idea of what we call grand routes; the reason for this is that these routes of traffic [*voies de communication*] would not be very useful in a country where one does not use wheeled vehicles. They know well the advantages that they could gain from some good roads; but they are not disposed to accept an amelioration that could facilitate the invasion of strangers."[13] Persians could live with rough roads because at the very least such conditions protected the country from invasion.

For the Bakhtiyari tribes, on the other hand, the roughness of the road was ecologically, politically, and culturally meaningful. To begin with, no alternative way was known to the tribes, and difficult roads were a fact of life for them. High mountain roads carried the Bakhtiyari from winter to summer pastures, from *qishlaq* to *yaylaq*. Overcoming the obstacles of seasonal migrations was a feat they accomplished twice annually and a hardship to which the Bakhtiyari were accustomed. They followed the grass through the mountains in search of pastures for their flocks of sheep and goats. They spent winter and early spring in the foothills of the *qishlaq* and then trekked higher into the mountains as the snow melted. Reaching the highest elevations of the *yaylaq*

Zard Kuh in the tribes' summer quarters, the tallest peak in the Bakhtiyari Mountains, viewed from the Kuh Rang spur at a pass at an elevation of 11,150 feet, with the massive and jagged Haft Tanan summit in the center of the skyline, 1890. Bird Album, UCLA.

in the summer, they remained there until autumn, when they again descended to the lowlands. There were at least three main tribal migratory routes in the Bakhtiyari territory during the nineteenth century: Dizpart, Bazuft, and Hazarcha (also called Kuh Rang).[14] The impracticability of the Bakhtiyari roads had the further effect of protecting the tribes from provincial, central, and foreign powers. Arduous roads in the mountains preserved tribal independence and vernacular culture. Climbing the same rough paths the tribes of the Great Lur were linked by the shared experience of migrations on mountain roads and passes.[15]

The nomadic life of the Bakhtiyari became a spectacle to nineteenth-century European travelers accustomed to settled life. The tribesmen's strength of will and nobility of spirit inspired travelers. Despite showing signs of admiration for Bakhtiyari honor and courage, travelers remained wary of what they perceived as tribal “wildness.” By the mid-nineteenth century, they had come to regard the opening of the Bakhtiyari Road as a modernizing measure that would bring commercial traffic into the Iranian hinterland and induce the Bakhtiyari tribes to become sedentary. With the paving of the road, the British sought to plow over the rough “‘Ali Baba paths” of the tribes.

In the Wildlands of Qajar Persia

The building of the Bakhtiyari Road was deeply connected to the geographical and ethnographic reconnaissance of British travelers and agents in the Zagros Mountains. In the early nineteenth century, Europeans increasingly journeyed to Persia, surveying its land, monuments, and peoples. Western travel books and ethnographies touched on a range of topics, including the political, focusing on the shah and his court at the capital; the archaeological, uncovering the ruins of ancient Persian empires; the geographical, mapping the terrain and topography of the country; and the cultural or ethnographic, describing the customs, peoples, and tribes of Qajar Persia.[16] Nineteenth-century British ethnographic accounts of tribes such as the Bakhtiyari were intended to convey an unknown land and people to the West. British officials and travelers set out to reveal the Bakhtiyari tribes as legible, unified, and coherent. They mapped the territory, listed the genealogies, and wrote down the histories of the tribes while collecting statistical information on tribal populations, encampments, and migratory routes.[17] In these texts, the Bakhtiyari were depicted as an autonomous tribal confederation of pastoral nomads with great sway over the southwestern edges of Iran.

On their excursions into the Bakhtiyari territory travelers followed and subsequently described the remnants of a road paved with stones leading from the valley of the ancient Achaemenid capital of Susa over the Bakhtiyari Mountains to the central Iranian Plateau. The route, known to some of the local population during the nineteenth century as Jadda-yi Atabayg, supposedly dated from the fourteenth-century Mongol lords of the province of Luristan.[18] It had fallen into disrepair and was used only as a tribal path, known as Rah-i Dizpart among Bakhtiyari pastoral nomads who followed it on their seasonal migrations.[19] Western travelers in the first half of the nineteenth century dreamed of rebuilding the road and bringing “civilization” to the Bakhtiyari Mountains. Beginning in the 1830s travelers who visited the Zagros took notice of the ruined montane route, which if restored could lead to the opening of the hinterland of Isfahan to trade. British travelers came also to view the road as a means by which the nomadic and semi-nomadic tribes could be "civilized" and incorporated into the world economy.

During the 1830s the first Western ethnographic surveys on the Bakhtiyari became available through the writings of Henry Creswicke Rawlinson (1810–1895), Baron C. A. de Bode (1810–1895), and Austen Henry Layard (1817–1894). Rawlinson, a British officer and orientalist who deciphered cuneiform in the 1840s and became known as the father of Assyriology, was the first British traveler to go into the field among the Bakhtiyari, publishing his findings in the *Journal of the Royal Geographical Society of London*.[20] Rawlinson's survey of the Bakhtiyari was largely based on information collected in the spring of 1836, when he made a long march with the Kurdish troops he had trained for Muhammad Shah Qajar (1834–1848) through the Zagros range to Khuzistan, accompanying Prince Bahram Mirza's expedition against the Chahar Lang at the fortress of Mungasht.[21] In 1841, de Bode, a secretary at the Russian Embassy, also ventured into Bakhtiyari territory, later recording his observations in *Travels in Luristan and Arabistan* (1845).[22] Another less-official ethnographer of the Bakhtiyari was Layard, who traveled as a "native" among the tribes in 1840–1841 before he excavated the ruins at Nineveh in Mesopotamia, modern-day Iraq, and wrote his well-known *Nineveh and Its Remains* (1849).[23] Layard's *Early Adventures in Persia, Susiana, and Babylonia, Including a Residence Among the Bakhtiyari and Other Wild Tribes* provided a rare view of mid-nineteenth-century Iran from its margins. Indeed, the Bakhtiyari later accepted Layard's account as part of their history, with a Persian translation of parts of Layard's travelogue included in *Tarikh-i Bakhtiyari*.[24]

In British ethnographic writing of the 1830s and 1840s, the Bakhtiyari were represented as "wild," unassimilated, and untamed. According to Rawlinson the Bakhtiyari were "the terror of the Kafilahs [caravans] . . . the most wild and barbarous of all the inhabitants of Persia."[25] De Bode wrote, "Since the remotest ages of the world, these mountains have constantly been the seat of an uncouth and warlike race of men, who set at defiance the authority of the Medes and the Persians, and in whose fastnesses, Alexander of Macedon met with such unforeseen impediments and strong opposition at the hands of the mountain clans."[26] The Bakhtiyari's racial features and costumes were cast as primitive and rough—their skin was "coarse" and "dark" from exposure to the sun, and their "black eyes looked wild and expressive."[27] The men wore a felt coat with short sleeves, a cotton shirt, wide trousers, accompanied by a "round cap" of coarse felt, and moccasins called *giva* for climbing the mountains.[28] Travelers saw the expansion of trade in the Zagros as a way to tame the nomads of Iran.

In the mountains of the Bakhtiyari, European travelers observed the ruins of a high monumental road now "only followed by the Bakhtiyari-Ilyat on foot, in their annual migrations."[29] Rawlinson and the Kurdish troops he had trained "followed the ancient high road from Susiana . . . across the great range, into Central Persia" and found it to be "the only practicable line of communication for loaded mules between Shushtar and Isfahan."[30] Rawlinson learned that the great road across the mountains was known by the name Jadda-yi Atabayg (Atabayg Road), after the thirteenth-century rulers of Luristan. Rawlinson believed, however, that the Mongol lords of Luristan had only restored an even more ancient road:

> I recognize, in this line, the route which is described by Strabo, as conducting from Gabiana (the ancient name of the district of Isfahan) through Elymais to Susiana; I believe it was by the same road that Antiochus and Mithridates were enabled to penetrate to the fire temples of Elymais; and indeed, from the stupendous character of the undertaking, and the immense labour that seems to have been bestowed on it, I am inclined to regard it was a work of the most remote antiquity.[31]

When de Bode visited the Bakhtiyari five years later he, too, was impressed by the road as a monument of public utility. He described having traveled "over several steep shoulders of the Bakhtiyari mountains by a stone pavement . . . impaired by time, and in several places scarcely passable, from the huge stones which have been disjoined by the rushing of torrents" and was impressed by the grand scheme of "carrying a stone road, worked in mosaic, across stupendous mountains, which otherwise would have remained as nature had formed them, insurmountable barriers to the traveler."[32] Early-nineteenth-century travelers praised what the road had once been and lamented its present state of disrepair. They hoped to revive the Atabayg Road and open the Bakhtiyari territory to foreign trade.

Layard also shared this view of the Bakhtiyari Road as a civilizing project and was the first to actively pursue the road's revival. He became a trusted friend of the powerful Chahar Lang chieftain, Muhammad Taqi Khan, whom he vividly and romantically portrayed as a "noble savage" and a progressive khan.[33] According to Layard the khan maintained peace and order in the mountains over which he ruled. Although he could not altogether prevent the tribes from stealing flocks and cattle, he had acquired a reputation as "generous and merciful" and remained, in Layard's words, "sincerely anxious to promote the good of his people and the prosperity of his country by maintaining peace, by securing the safety of the roads through his territories, and by opening his mountains to trade."[34] He could neither read nor write but showed interest in learning about distant lands and "was eager to induce the wild inhabitants of his mountains to engage in peaceful pursuits, and was very desirous that the country should be opened to commerce." In the inner courtyard of Qalʿa-yi Tul, where he kept his prize horses tethered, he would question Layard while surrounded by the elders and headmen of the tribes about "railways and various modern discoveries."[35] Layard also saw the ruins of the Atabayg Road and came to believe that its revival could open southwestern Iran to trade and settle its pastoral tribes. Among the ruins of the Atabayg Road Layard envisioned a development scheme that would bring about the revival of the road and the opening of the region to British trade. Between Malamir and Shushtar, and along the river Karun, he noticed the ruins of the ancient road. Although he found no inscriptions to suggest the date of its construction, like others before him he guessed it to be "one of the great highways which in the time of Darius led from the plains of Susiana to the highlands of Persia and to Persepolis."[36] The road had fallen into disrepair and was in ruins, with traffic almost impossible in certain parts. But if revived it would allow British commerce to enter the Bakhtiyari Mountains and the hinterland of Isfahan. Layard proposed that the province of Khuzistan could conduct trade with Europe and create ties with British and other foreign merchants. By improving trade and communications the Bakhtiyari khans could, with British assistance, begin the development of their tribal territory.

Layard hoped that the road would link the tribes to cities and absorb them into the world economy. In his travelogue, Layard noted the subsistence economy of the Bakhtiyari tribes:

> The Bakhtiyari had very little ready money, and what little they had they were not ready to part with. . . . They had little or no trade with the rest of Persia. Amongst themselves it was considered disgraceful "to sell bread," and as the laws of hospitality are universally recognized as obligatory upon Musulmans, no one was required to pay for the food which he might consume in a Bakhtiyari tent. They cultivated sufficient corn and rice for their immediate wants; they made their clothes and their tents out of the wool and hair produced by their flocks and herds; and the few European goods they required

were usually obtained from itinerant traders, who received produce in exchange for them.[37]

Layard sought to convince Muhammad Taqi Khan that reopening the trade route would have "the effect of introducing his people to engage in peaceful pursuits, and would enable them to obtain, from England and elsewhere, many necessaries and luxuries of which they were in need, and which would contribute greatly to their well being."[38] He wrote a report to the home government and a letter to the chamber of commerce in Bombay to suggest the utilization of the Karun trade route and became an early advocate for the construction of the Bakhtiyari Road from Ahvaz to Isfahan.

Such plans for rebuilding the Bakhtiyari Road and opening the hinterland of Isfahan to trade proved premature in the 1840s. Layard's mission coincided with a break in Anglo-Persian diplomatic relations over the Herat question and the British occupation of Kharg Island in the Gulf. Indeed this is why Layard's contemporaries and subsequent scholars considered him a British spy.[39] What is more, the close ties Layard established with the rebellious Chahar Lang chieftain Muhammad Taqi Khan and the discussions of expanding commerce via building roads through the Zagros Mountains threatened the sovereignty of the Qajars by enhancing the regional authority of the Bakhtiyari tribes. Partly out of suspicion of Layard's presence in the Zagros Mountains and concern about Bakhtiyari-British collaboration, and partly to assert the Qajar's authority over the provinces, the new governor of Isfahan, Manuchihr Khan Mu'tamad al-Dawla, pressed for the payment of 10,000 tumans taxes in arrears from the Bakhtiyari.[40] With British presence in the Bakhtiyari territory the assertive governor of Isfahan sought the capture of Muhammad Taqi Khan. In Riza Quli Khan Hidayat's words, the governor sought to cage the "mountain leopard" (*palang-i kuh*) once and for all.[41] When the chieftain refused to pay the demanded revenues, the governor of Isfahan reported to Muhammad Shah Qajar that the Bakhtiyari were *yaghi*, in rebellion against the state. As punishment the shah authorized a military expedition to occupy the Bakhtiyari Mountains in the spring of 1841, after the passes were opened.[42] As a result many of the Chahar Lang tribes became scattered. Muhammad Taqi Khan at first took refuge in the marshes of the Shatt al-Arab, the point where the Tigris and Euphrates meet the Persian Gulf, but subsequently surrendered to the governor, who denounced him as "a rebel to the Shah and ordered him to be put into chains."[43] For the early Qajars talk of building roads on the empire's tribal periphery was both unwelcome and alarming. From their perspective roads allowed foreign penetration of the "Guarded Domains of Iran." It would not be until the late nineteenth century, following the opening of the Karun River to international traffic, that British plans for opening a commercial road through the Bakhtiyari territory were again pursued.

The opening of the Karun coincided with a shift in Qajar policies toward the Bakhtiyari. In 1888, the central government dismissed Zill al-Sultan from all of his governorships in the south save Isfahan, drastically weakening his position, and ordered the release of Isfandiyar Khan from captivity. A central figure in this shift, and most likely its prime architect, was Mirza 'Ali Asghar Khan Amin al-Sultan (1858–1907), the de facto prime minister of Iran and a rival of Zill al-Sultan.[44] Believing that Isfandiyar Khan, the eldest son of Husayn Quli Khan Ilkhani, would have the most influence over the tribes, the premier and the newly appointed provincial governor of Arabistan promptly appointed him the new *ilkhan* of the Bakhtiyari.[45] Isfandiyar Khan's swift promotion brought him into conflict with the Hajji Ilkhani clan, which had been ascendant in the tribal leadership since the death of Husayn Quli Khan, and stirred unrest in the Zagros Mountains.[46] In 1890, the Qajar state restructured the tribal leadership of the Bakhtiyari, with Imam Quli Khan of the Hajji Ilkhani reinstated as the *ilkhan*, Isfandiyar Khan as the *ilbayg*, and Riza Quli Khan as the governor of Chahar Mahal. As command of the tribal federation shifted toward the younger Isfandiyar Khan, now also given the title of Samsam al-Saltana ("Sword of the State"), he became well known among the British as a progressive khan concerned with the welfare of the tribes and a possible partner in the opening of a secure caravan route from the Karun River through the Zagros Mountains to Isfahan.

British interest in the Bakhtiyari tribes and the building of the Bakhtiyari Road reached a peak in the 1890s. Searching for trade routes between the Persian Gulf and Isfahan, British merchants, officers, and travelers saw the road project as a way to extend British trade into southwestern Iran and assimilate its tribes. The prospect of opening the Bakhtiyari Mountains to Western economic penetration came to fruition at a time when the Qajar dynasty was granting foreign concessions to develop the country's resources.

Among the leading advocates of building the Bakhtiyari Road and opening southwestern Iran to British trade was George Nathaniel Curzon. Already an elected M.P. when he traveled to Iran in 1889, Curzon would become viceroy of India and be responsible for the creation of the North-West Frontier Province and the partition of Bengal. Curzon's early travels became the basis of his

The migrations and arduous river crossings of the Bakhtiyari tribes involved fording rivers (or paddling across them in goatskin rafts), as seen here on the Upper Karun with the Zard Kuh Range in the distance, 1890. Bird Album, UCLA.

ethnographic and geographical writings on West and Central Asia, the Persian Gulf, and the problem of defending India against Russia.[47] These works include *Russia in Central Asia* (1889) and *Persia and the Persian Question* (1892). The second volume of *Persia and the Persian Question* contains a survey of the Bakhtiyari and other tribes of the Zagros. Curzon sought to reveal what he saw as an unknown group of people, and to this end he catalogued the various subtribes and clans, listed their genealogies, and described their migrations. For Curzon ethnography served the purpose of Empire: the opening of Qajar Persia to British trade and influence.

Curzon understood the ecological and political bases of pastoral nomadic life in the Zagros Mountains, noting "the physical conformation" of the land and the autonomy of the tribes. He wrote:

The ruling Bakhtiyari khans of the Haft Lang and their retainers at a tribal council in Naghun, sitting around the border of a felt carpet. Seated in the front from left to right: Isfandiyar Khan (*ilbayg*), Imam Quli Khan (*ilkhan*), Khusraw Khan Sardar Zafar, and Riza Quli Khan (governor of Chahar Mahal), 1890. Bird Album, UCLA.

> In Persia . . . where great spaces are occupied by bleak mountain districts, remote from the control of government, and adapted to pastoral rather than agricultural pursuits, the immemorial prescription of the East still survives; the tribes move in compact detachments according to the period of the year, carrying with them their entire household furniture and wealth, and exchanging the lowland valleys or riverain plains, which they have occupied during the winter, for the higher and cooler crests, where life is supportable in the summer heats."[48]

Curzon wrote rather romantically of the Bakhtiyari's "undeniable virtues of character," such as their hospitality, modesty, masculinity, and most of all, liberty, which they drew from "the free breath of their native hills." Like previous travelers Curzon marveled at the Bakhtiyari horseman's martial spirit

A Bakhtiyari khan at a lion gravestone in a graveyard of young braves, 1890. Bird's caption for this photograph: "Types of the Bakhtiyari Lur, the living and the dead. . . . He is open to good influence and likes to hear of noble deeds of self-sacrifice. In imitation of the living, the dead Lur's tomb, always a rough hewn lion, invariably carries the sword, the musket, the dagger, the pouch, and the cartridge belt." Bird Album, UCLA.

and ethos: "Trained from his youth to the saddle, he is a rough-rider of the finest type, able to fire while going at full gallop . . . the finest raw material for troops."[49]

Nevertheless, he saw nomadism as an "archaic habit," the reflection of an "unsettled character," and "uncivilized."[50] The Bakhtiyari nomads were involved in "little trade" apart from supplying mutton to Isfahan during the summer months, and the rank-and-file of the tribes was "very poor" and had "next to no education."[51] The "development of the industrial and material resources of Persia" through contact with Europe, Curzon held, would bring "civilization" to the tribes.[52]

Curzon's writings and reconnaissance on tribes estimated their numbers and mapped their territories. If the British Empire were to extend its commercial activities into the region and open up southwestern Iran, it would need more precise information about the land and its inhabitants. Curzon set out to make the Bakhtiyari land "more strictly defined" and provided a topographical map of the Bakhtiyari Mountains.[53] He also compiled a statistical catalogue of the various Bakhtiyari clans and subtribes between 1836 and 1890, finding that many clans had been consolidated as a result of the ascendancy of the Haft Lang over the confederation during the late nineteenth century.[54] Social and political organization among the Bakhtiyari was local and based on tribal and clan feeling, and deference was given to the elders of the tent, the camp, the clan, and the tribe: "Obedience and loyalty were observed within these limits, but not outside them."[55] The state could collect taxes only through the tribal structure and with the aid of chieftains.

Divided between three provincial administrations the Bakhtiyari tribes were nominally responsible for contributing 22,000 tumans to the governor of Isfahan, 15,000 tumans to the governor of Khuzistan, and additional taxes to the governor of Luristan.[56] He criticized the Qajar's tribal policy of divide and conquer:

> Nowhere have the baser and more contemptible aspects of Persian government been so noticeable as here. . . . One tribe has been pitted against another tribe, one chief against another chief; and thus the animosities of individuals or communities have served the purpose while relieving the purse of the sovereign. At the same time that the tribes have been set at mutual destruction, their leaders have also been torn from their homes. . . . Simultaneously, the armament of the tribes has been discouraged; the poverty of the chieftains has brought with it a decline of the horse breeding establishments for which they were once famous; and where the Ilyats of Persia formerly constituted her armed strength on the battlefield, they are now disabled, disloyal, and broken.[57]

Curzon's writings reinforced the perception and policy that if the British sought to expand their trade into southwestern Iran, they would need to secure the cooperation of the Bakhtiyari.

One of Curzon's contemporaries, Henry Lynch of the Tigris and Euphrates Steam Navigation Company of Baghdad and later a Liberal member of the British Parliament, soon emerged as a leading advocate and potential backer of the Bakhtiyari Road project. Immediately after Nasir al-Din Shah's opening of the Karun River to international trade, Lynch Brothers, which had been connected with the navigation of the Tigris since the mid-nineteenth century, placed a steamer on the Karun and began to explore the possibility of road communications between the river and Isfahan.[58] In 1889, on the invitation of the khans of the Haft Lang, Lynch visited the Bakhtiyari summer quarters. Departing from Shushtar, Lynch traversed the Bakhtiyari Road all the way to Isfahan, observing its features firsthand. Along the way he stayed at the Bakhtiyari's fortress at Chaqakhur as the guest of Isfandiyar Khan. An account of his journey and a map of the road appeared in the *Proceedings of the Royal Geographical Society* in 1890, in the same issue of the journal as Curzon's paper regarding trade on the Karun River.

In Lynch's writings, geographical and ethnographic facts merged with an eagerness for the modern development of the land and opening of the Bakhtiyari Mountains to foreign trade. In his published report, "Across Luristan to Isfahan," Lynch made a case for "the political and commercial value of a good track or road" from the Karun through Luristan.[59] Lynch listed the various stages of the road and detailed the difficulties to be faced along the way.[60] Most notable among these obstacles was the fact that a number of steep mountain backs and ridges had to be crossed. Although considerable difficulties were known to exist on the road—the steep mountains, the lack of bridges and caravanserais, the snow that closed the route during the winter months—Lynch remained optimistic that a road could be opened to loaded mules and maintained "at small expense." Thus Lynch recommended a modest road-building scheme, proposing the construction of a route suitable merely for mule transport. Although natural obstacles would have to be overcome, Lynch held the view that the removal of a few stones and the blasting of rocks was little cost for the improvement of communications and the development of Iran as "an integral state."[61] Nature would open up with the helping hand of empire. Having come from Baghdad and "the burning plains of Mesopotamia," Lynch welcomed "the freshness of the atmosphere" in the Zagros Mountains. In the *yaylaq*, he described the khans' custom of sleeping in tents among the tribesmen, clustering "round the fort upon the green turf where the cattle graze."[62] On reaching Malamir, he saw for the first time the ruins of the Atabayg Road, of which he later wrote: "At present it only serves to mock the insignificance of modern Persia; and it is in the sculptured cave or on this noble pavement that the traveller feels the awe of a great past, contrasts it with present squalor, and draws from it refreshing hopes that what has once been grandly done may yet be done again."[63]

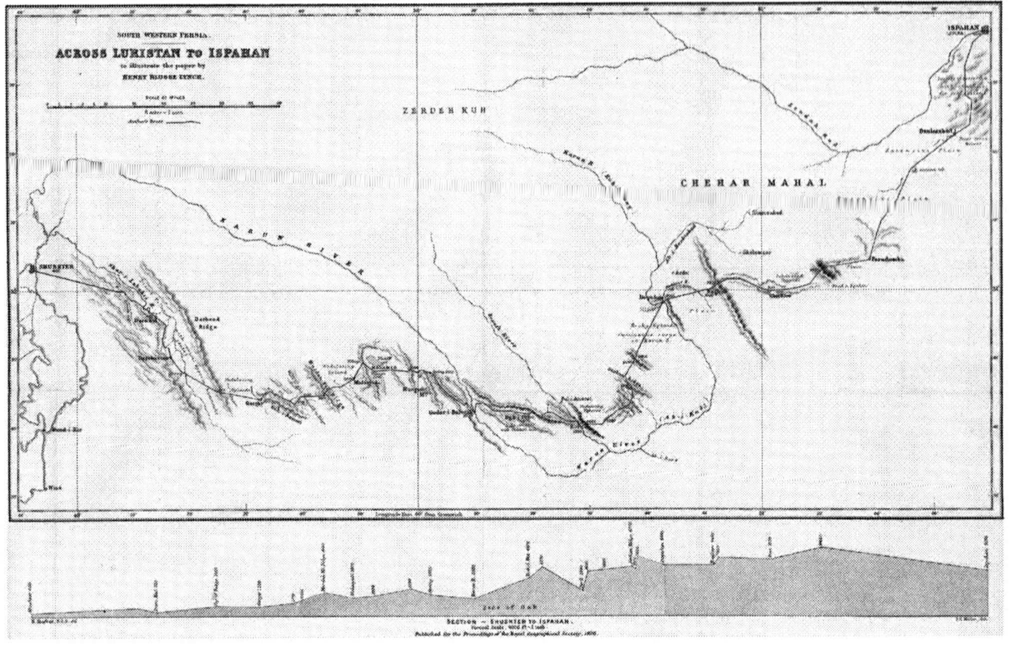

Henry Lynch's map of the stages along the Bakhtiyari Road, 1890. Lynch, "Across Luristan to Ispahan," *PRGS* (London, 1890).

Lynch viewed the building of the road as a project that would revive Iran and bring the Bakhtiyari closer to civilization. It would accelerate processes of settlement already under way in the nineteenth century. In describing the pastoral economy of the Bakhtiyari tribes, he noted that some of the tribes were in the early stages of becoming settled. Although the Bakhtiyari were pastoral-nomadic, relying on their flocks and herds for subsistence and living in black goat-hair tents, they had developed some "fixed settlements" in their winter quarters, and some tribesmen had become *dih nishin*, "those who dwell in villages." The market of Isfahan drew some of the produce from their flocks, but Lynch concluded, "In the absence of communications their trade is insignificant."[64] The building of the road would bring them closer to the market and begin their assimilation.

With the British Empire gravitating toward the Bakhtiyari and southwestern Persia, the government of India ordered Lieutenant Colonel H. A. Sawyer of the intelligence branch of the Indian Army, along with his assistant Imam Sharif, to conduct a reconnaissance mission through the Bakhti-

Bakhtiyari women and girls stand beneath a black goat-hair tent, 1890. Bird Album, UCLA.

yari Mountains.[65] Sawyer's mission was to ascend and traverse the Bakhtiyari Mountains in all directions, survey the land, scale it down to the inch, and visit as many tribes as possible in their encampments.[66] The prolific Scottish traveler Isabella Bird accompanied the Sawyer survey mission. Bird followed Sawyer for part of his journey and the two spent the summer of 1890 in the Bakhtiyari country together.[67] Both Bird and Sawyer published accounts of their travels: Bird in *Journeys in Persia and Kurdistan* (1891) and Sawyer in his *Military Report on the Bakhtiyari Mountains* (1890). Bird also took an unknown number of photographs during her journeys, although these did not appear in her two-volume travelogue published by John Murray.[68] From these photographs we can begin to retrace the road from Isfahan to Luristan as it appeared in the late nineteenth century, shortly before its reconstruction.[69] By the 1890s British contacts with the Bakhtiyari had been re-established and again promised to open the Zagros Mountains to British trade. For the Bakhtiyari the opening of the road represented the lure of British subsidies and leverage against the ruling Qajar state. Yet the Bakhtiyari

A group of Bakhtiyari khans, headmen (*kalantaran*) and "white beards" (*rish safidan*) loyal to Isfandiyar Khan, along with a mendicant (*darvish*), on the Upper Karun, 1890. Bird Album, UCLA.

always retained certain reservations about the road and the threat it posed to Bakhtiyari tribal autonomy.

The Raids of the Bakhtiyari

On December 21, 1895, a band of Bakhtiyari tribesmen robbed the caravan of a European merchant employed by the trading firm Ziegler and Company. The merchant, A. Escherich, and his caravan of four *charvadar* (mule drivers) and two attendants had originated their journey in Isfahan and had reached a caravanserai on the road, near the village of Dihhak. Two of the *charvadar* proceeded ahead of the caravan and, according to Escherich, they

> had not gone very far, hardly half a *farsakh*, when, on the road leading through some small hills we noticed some horsemen coming across

> the hills right upon us at full speed and ere we had time to consider we were confronted with them. The man pointed his gun, a good Martini at my servant in front of the caravan and bid him to get down from the horse, threatening to shoot if he did not comply at once. I hardly had time to watch these proceedings when I was attacked by another man, who, noticing that I made an attempt to extract my revolver from the holsters, struck me repeatedly with a heavy club on my right arm, stunning it for the moment and consequently making me defenseless.[70]

Armed with rifles, revolvers, and swords, the raiders led the caravan away from the high road and deeper into the Zagros Mountains. They assured their captives that "they were not bad people but were greatly in debt and had, in order to raise the wind, to take to robbery."[71] They asked Escherich how much money he had in his possession and became rather disappointed to find that the caravan did not carry a rich cargo, admitting that they were expecting at least 1,000 pounds sterling in cash.

In a crevice at the foot of the mountains, about a mile from the high road, the tribesmen ordered the merchants to stand aside and commenced to plunder the caravan. The total value of the stolen articles was estimated to be approximately 180 pounds sterling. When the tribesmen had taken what they wanted from the caravan, they blindfolded and bound the travelers and left them to their own resources in the mountains. After the tribesmen had departed with their plunder, the members of the caravan freed themselves in the dark to find the remains of their belongings "scattered about—camp bed, tables, chairs, and quilts, as well as books, letters, collars, and cuffs."[72]

The Bakhtiyari raid on the agent of Ziegler and Company, an established trading firm operating out of Sultanabad and often credited with commercializing the Persian rug industry, was an indication of the insecurity merchants and travelers faced on the roads outside Isfahan. British plans for the development of trade through the Zagros Mountains were at times dashed by news of raids and robberies on the roads. Persian and British sources reveal the steady occurrence of the Bakhtiyari *chapu* or raid during the late nineteenth century. Among the tribes the raid was an accepted form of social banditry, combining the ideals of bravery and independence with the skill of good horsemanship. For the tribes raiding was also seen as sanctioned resistance taken against the "oppression and unjust exaction" of the Qajar government.[73] From the perspective of Qajar and British authorities, however, restive and disordered tribal

Bakhtiyari horseman (*savar*) and footmen armed with Martini Henry rifles, 1890. Bird Album, UCLA.

populations carried out the raids. The correspondences of the provincial governor of Luristan, Amir Tuman Hishmat al-Dawla, and the reports of Consul Preece of Isfahan each provide glimpses of Bakhtiyari tribal unrest in the 1890s.

The archives reveal a trail of Bakhtiyari raids. In the 1890s, a tribal strongman by the name of ʿAbdallah Khan Bakhtiyari and his followers were freely raiding the province of Luristan and the hinterland of Burujird. According to villagers and peasants not even the governor's forces at Burujird were a match for the Bakhtiyari insurgents. With just fifty horsemen, ʿAbdallah Khan was plundering (*takht va taz*) the province while also withholding taxes from the Qajar government.[74] In spring 1892, Preece reported incidents of intra-tribal feuding from the Bakhtiyari *yaylaq* and *qishlaq*. About 200 residents of Urujan, a village in Chahar Mahal, had been driven from their homes by the retinues of Riza Quli Khan.[75] There were "considerable disturbances among the Bakhtiyari in their winter quarters" and rumors that anticipated "a great fight."[76]

Consul Preece reported a complex web of intra-tribal feuds, raids, and rivalries that rankled the Bakhtiyari and turned khan against khan.

In the spring of 1893, Preece wrote that Bakhtiyari fighting was spilling over into the surrounding countryside. Shahab al-Saltana was reported to be "busy chapaoing" [raiding] Isfandiyar Khan's villages in Chahar Mahal, a provocation that had led to some fighting among the tribes.[77] In November 1893, Bakhtiyari tribesmen under Khusraw Khan raided Chahar Mahal, where they "held the whole district in terror for some weeks . . . so that no caravans could pass."[78] Isfandiyar Khan had grown bolder since he had "received great marks of consideration from the Shah, who had sent him two very handsome Kellats and separate firmans appointing him Eel Khaneh, Eel Beggi, and Mir-i Zaman."[79] Meanwhile the wife of Riza Quli Khan had taken refuge at the house of the cleric Aqa Najafi in Isfahan, complaining that she was unsafe and prey to Isfandiyar Khan, the current favorite of Amin al-Sultan and the Qajar government.[80] Late in 1893 Preece wrote to the British legation in Tehran that "from Sultanabad to Kashan" there were "stories regarding the looting by the brothers of Isfendiar Khan."[81]

Najaf Quli Khan, a powerful and influential son of the late *ilkhan*, had become a virtual outlaw and brigand. In the summer of 1893, the Qajar government ordered a regiment, along with artillery, to march against him and his band of followers.[82] Najaf Quli Khan was reported to have claimed that "he had no other resource to gain his living, the Prince [Zill al-Sultan] and his people had completely devastated his villages and flocks and compelled him to follow this life; all of the effects of the last few years of good government, which had given peace to and enabled the Bakhtiyaris to recover themselves to a certain extent, were completely obliterated." Preece added that he had heard that Najaf Quli Khan had "sworn to capture the prince and kill him."[83] With the tribal leadership in disarray and amid intense rivalries between the khans, their Bakhtiyari retinues commenced to plunder Isfahan and its hinterland. In the fall of 1894, Preece reported Bakhtiyari raids on the road between Shiraz and Isfahan. "The state of affairs in general," the consul wrote, "is very unsatisfactory. . . . robberies occur frequently both on the road and in the town." A "gang" of Bakhtiyari had robbed the courier at Izadkhast and later attacked a larger "camel caravan carrying tea, sugar, piece goods, etc."[84]

The Qajar government perennially sought to display its command over Iran's peripheries through punitive military campaigns and expeditions against the tribes. In the Zagros Mountains, the Qajar state attempted to assert its dominion over the Bakhtiyari and Lur tribes. In 1892, Amir Tuman

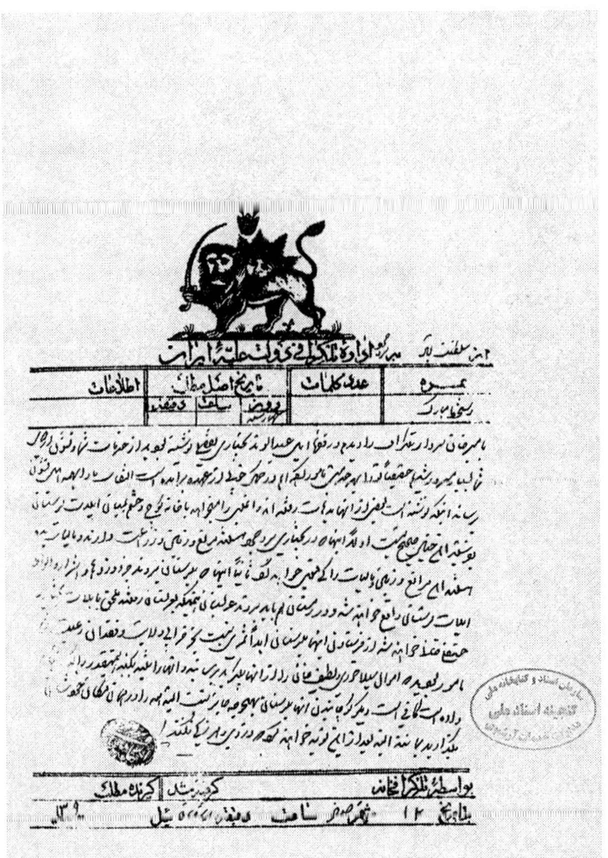

Letter from Sultanabad to Burujird detailing the settlement and agricultural practices of the Bakhtiyari and Lur tribes (1892). INA.

Hishmat al-Dawla, the governor of Luristan and Burujird, made a military expedition against the rebellious ʿAbdalvand tribe, a group of settled Bakhtiyari who practiced agriculture—*martab va zamin va zaraʿat darand.*[85] Similarly, in 1894 Hishmat al-Dawla received telegraphs from Tehran ordering him to establish order (*nazm*) among other Lur tribes loosely attached to the Bakhtiyari, including the Sagvand and Dirakvand.[86] In a separate decree sent the same year, the governor of Luristan was charged with maintaining peace and tranquility (*asayish*) among the peasantry (*raʿiyat*) and preserving the safety of the roads and highways—*intizam-i turuq va shavari.*[87] In addition to limiting these disorders, the Qajar government also had more everyday concerns, such as controlling the seasonal migrations of the Bakhtiyari tribes.[88] In 1898, Isfandiyar Khan was compelled to send several horsemen to accompany the caravan of Jacques de Morgan and the French Scientific Mission in Persia to provide protection on their journey to Isfahan via the Bakhtiyari Road.[89]

Following an attack by "Lurs" on the mission's newly constructed chateau at Susa, Isfandiyar Khan wrote a letter to de Morgan requesting that his party not return by the Bakhtiyari Road on their way back to the sites because "the country was not in a safe condition and some untoward circumstance might occur."[90] The disgruntled Zill al-Sultan, who in 1888 had been stripped of all his provincial governorships in the south except for Isfahan, complained to Consul Preece: "How bad the situation of the country is, how utterly without government it is everywhere."[91] Tribal raids in the Zagros Mountains and on the margins of Isfahan threatened to undermine the prospects of the Bakhtiyari Road and the expansion of British trade into the interior of Iran.

The Bakhtiyari Road

Roadbuilding was a central feature of Anglo-Russian imperial rivalry in *fin de siècle* Iran. The British had adopted a forward policy of building roads in southern Iran through negotiations with subsidiary tribes to offset Russian advances in the north. In the 1890s, a Russian firm called Compagnie pour l'Assurance et le Transport en Perse worked the road from Rasht to Tehran and held the concessions for extensions from Qazvin to Hamadan and Qazvin to Tabriz. Keeping up with Russian advances, in 1893 the British-run Imperial Bank of Persia completed "a good carriage road" southward from Tehran to Qum and "a fair-weather road" from Qum to Sultanabad.[92] British officials showed an interest in increasing their influence in the Zagros Mountains and strengthening the Bakhtiyari tribes, "so as to enable them to hold their own in the event of a collapse of the Central Power, or of trouble in South-Western Persia."[93] Mortimer Durand, who was appointed British minister in Tehran in 1895, just two years after the demarcation of the "Durand Line" separating the Northwest Frontier Province of India from Afghanistan, suggested the British should win the cooperation of tribes in the south through the payment of subsidies and kind treatment.[94]

In April 1895, J. R. Preece, British consul in Isfahan, embarked on a journey through the Bakhtiyari Mountains to the plains of the Karun River. The aim of Preece's expedition was to collect reconnaissance on the local roads and to survey the prospects of opening the mountains to British commercial traffic. On 3 April, Preece's party departed from Isfahan, heading west into "the hills of the Bakhtiari country still well clad in snow." The road, closed four months of the year by snow, made a sharp ascent and wound along the side of the mountain, "up and down, and up and down," bringing them over the pass and into the summer pastures of the Bakhtiyari tribes. On the road Preece found "the Black Tents of the Tribes dotted all over the plain and large numbers of mares with their yearling colts and foals at foot, cows, buffaloes, etc. grazing all about." Describing the Bakhtiyari's migratory way of life, he wrote:

> It is a curious and picturesque scene encountering one of these tribes making their migration. The women and children even the little ones of three or four years old are employed in looking after and driving the mares and foals, donkeys and oxen laden with their tents and household goods. . . . Some of the higher class women ride favorite mares and some of them were like their sisters of the town, anxious to hide their faces from the profane gaze of the Faringhi. The Chiefs ride the horses and go along independently with two or three attendants most of them are heavily armed, generally with Martinis. The other male members of the tribe are distributed all over the hillside driving the numerous flocks, which are grazed as they go along.[95]

The Bakhtiyari hinterland, however, was "beginning to see daylight" in the flow of "traffic" and "goods." Preece noted the local exports of wool, opium, and indigo and imports from Manchester, Bombay, and Marseilles. The consul trusted that "the day is not far distant" when the Bakhtiyari Road would be the main route of trade and communication between the Persian Gulf and Isfahan. Preece saw the rebuilding of the road as a part of Britain's imperial destiny. While traveling though the Zagros he remembered an inscription on an artifact he had seen back in London: "On an obelisk in the British Museum there is depicted an Assyrian King walking with attendants and a horse drawing a chariot which is being lifted by other attendants, he is passing over a series of peaks or sugar-loaved shaped mounds placed close together. It is supposed to represent a mountainous country but I take it that it really represents a made road or Kotal as they are known here."[96] The opening of the road through the Bakhtiyari Mountains seemed destined in Preece's view to become a British imperial project in Persia.

Since 1892, when Preece was appointed consul of Isfahan, Isfandiyar Khan had sent his horsemen to the consul to inform him that the Bakhtiyari tribes were in order and ready to receive him in the *yaylaq*.[97] In April 1895, Preece met with Isfandiyar Khan and his younger brother 'Ali Quli Khan in the Bakhtiyari territory and found them supportive of the plan to construct a road through their mountains. He wrote, "The Bakhtiari Khans are fully alive to the value of

The Bakhtiyari Road at the Shamsabad Bridge with Kuh-i Sukhta in the distance, 1890. Bird Album, UCLA.

good and safe roads."[98] Preece noted the progressiveness of the Bakhtiyari on the subject of the road and reported that the khans "saw how it would open up their country and improve the prospects of the tribes, and generally help to the much wished-for end of taking the tribesmen out of their wild state and civilizing them."[99] The Bakhtiyari seemed willing to guarantee the safety of the road, build caravanserais, and take care of maintenance. And yet the Bakhtiyari, 'Ali Quli Khan in particular, continued to remain cautious due to fears that Britain would use the road to attack the north or annex Khuzistan.

Meanwhile British officials were seeking to establish the Qajar government's precise position on the Bakhtiyari Road project. This was also meant to satisfy Lynch, who did not possess a monopoly on the road and claimed he could not invest money in it without a guarantee from the central government for interest and capital in case of breaches of contract by the tribal khans. In 1897, the Qajar Foreign Minister Mushir al-Dawla suggested that the Bakhtiyari preferred the capital required for the construction of the road to come from a Persian subject and not from a foreign source. Nizam al-Saltana, the governor of Khuzistan and Bakhtiyari who had emerged as a potential Iranian investor, offered to pay the original estimate of 3,000 pounds for the road's construction, with the work still being carried out by the Lynch Brothers.[100]

In 1888 Nizam al-Saltana had traveled through the Bakhtiyari Mountains on a military expedition, traversed the Bakhtiyari roads, and kept a memoir during his tour.[101] During his time as governor of Khuzistan and Bakhtiyari he came into competition with the Lynch Brothers Company, which was running its steamers on the Karun, over the commercial opening of southwestern Iran. During the 1890s he opposed Lynch's efforts to gain control of the trade in Khuzistan and on the Karun.[102] In correspondence with Colonel E. C. Ross, the British resident at Bushire, Nizam al-Saltana had offered to build trading houses to lease to the Lynch Company, allowing the foreign firm to fly the standard of the lion and the sun, the imperial symbols on Iran's flag, on their ships from the time they entered the Shatt al-Arab.[103] Such postures were taken to reassert Persian control, as well as Nizam al-Saltana's authority, over the Karun trade.

Seeking a share of the profits as the governor of Khuzistan, Nizam al-Saltana challenged the Lynch Brothers' attempts to monopolize the trade on the Karun. The British company encountered all sorts of resistance. When Lynch's agent Taylor entered Shushtar in 1888, "he found difficulty even procuring drinking water and the commonest necessities of life, so loth were the people to have any dealing with such 'an unclean thing.'"[104] Nizam al-Saltana was among a group of Qajar officials and notables determined to bring the trade and the concession "under Persian hands" and prevent the Lynch Company from collecting profits from the increased trade in the region. Nizam al-Saltana, who had built up the port at Nasiri, was joined in his stand by his brother Sa'ad al-Mulk, the governor of Bushire, and the wealthy Persian Gulf merchant Mu'in al-Tujjar. Some of Shushtar's *ulama* opposed British trade in the region and many of the locals had been ordered to boycott European products.[105] In the midst of these obstacles, Lynch Brothers was also incurring a "steady loss" financially, although they held on, hoping that the trade in southwestern Iran would become lucrative in the future.[106]

In 1894, local reactions against the presence of the Lynch Brothers firm boiled over in two violent incidents involving company agents. In the first of these, a group of Farahani soldiers under Nizam al-Saltana's command were involved in a melée with Lynch's representatives at Nasiri, during which Taylor was wounded on the head and had his watch stolen.[107] Taylor immediately left for Basra, where he contacted British authorities and blamed the Qajar's lack of authority in the provinces for his misfortunes. Nizam al-Saltana was reprimanded and forced to send his servant Mirza Nasrallah, who had been in command of the Farahani soldiers, to be punished in he presence of Lynch's agents. During the same year, however, Taylor's replacement in Shushtar, Tanfield, was attacked by his servant Sadiq, who chopped off the agent's left hand, reportedly because he had taken free license with local women and prostitutes during the Shi'i holy month of Muharram.[108]

In response to these incidents, Mortimer Durand ordered Percy Sykes, then British consul in Kirman and later to become commander of the South Persia Rifles, to travel with a force to the Karun and back the Lynch Company's position. Nizam al-Saltana and Sykes quickly clashed when the latter ordered that the governor pay an indemnity for the assault on Lynch's agents.[109] An alarmed Sykes referred to "the murderous attack" on Tanfield and complained to Tehran that Nizam al-Saltana had refused to recognize his authority.[110] Sykes prevailed in his appeal to Tehran, and the central government ordered Nizam al-Saltana to pay the equivalent of 300 pounds. Shortly thereafter he was removed from his post as governor of Khuzistan and Bakhtiyari in 1895.[111] It came as little surprise when Nizam al-Saltana, removed from his post, withdrew his offer to invest in the building of the Bakhtiyari Road at the end of 1897.[112]

In October 1897, Charles Hardinge, the secretary of the British legation in Tehran, informed Lynch that he had obtained written assurance from the Qajar government, signed by the prime minister and the minister of foreign affairs, in the following terms: "The Persian Government having taken cognizance of the agreement between the Bakhtiyari and Lynch for the construction of a road from Ahwaz to Isfahan . . . gives an assurance that the above mentioned Bakhtiyari chiefs or any such chiefs as may be appointed by the Persian Government, even if placed at the head of the tribe, will be made to carry out the terms of the agreement and this will be one of the conditions of the Bakhtiyari chieftainship."[113]

The Qajar administration of Bakhtiyari affairs had become officially entwined with British imperial interests in southern Iran. The Qajar state granted the concession for the Bakhtiyari Road to the ruling Bakhtiyari khans, who in turn reached an agreement with Lynch to invest in the development of the road.[114] As the Bakhtiyari khans and Qajar officials were conscious of foreign intervention or control of what was believed to be one of the country's principal trade routes, all mention of the Lynch Brothers was omitted from the concession. However, a clause was inserted establishing the right of the

Bakhtiyari "to call in the aid of capitalists who may lend them money."[115]

On 23 May 1898, a deal was signed between the Lynch Brothers and the Bakhtiyari chiefs Isfandiyar Khan, 'Ali Quli Khan, and Muhammad Husayn Khan. The former undertook construction of the road for a sum not exceeding 5,500 pounds, to be repaid by the Bakhtiyari in twenty-five yearly installments. Lynch's representative and engineer, along with Indian workmen, built the road, as the khans did not allow the Bakhtiyari tribes to have direct contact with Lynch employees. The rather humble goal was to create a clear mule track; rocks obstructing the road were to be blasted and the first steel suspension bridges in Persia were to be built.[116]

The ten-point agreement promised significant changes in the land. Some of the articles are worth mention here. Article 3 of the agreement gave the Lynch Brothers firm the right to develop the land by building roads, bridges, and caravanserais for a payment of 5,500 pounds. In article 4, the Bakhtiyari assumed responsibility for the maintenance and upkeep of the road, requiring frequent consultation with Lynch Company engineers to keep "the roads and bridges in good order." Article 5 established the terms under which the Bakhtiyari rank-and-file would become employed as laborers on the road, bridges, and caravanserais. In article 6, the Bakhtiyari were charged with the task of policing the road and protecting engineers, workmen, and merchants passing through the mountains. The eighth article gave the Bakhtiyari khans permission to collect tolls on the traffic up and down the road.[117] The seals of the Bakhtiyari chiefs and the signature of the British chargé d'affaires made the terms of the agreement official.

The construction of the road lasted twenty-two months, from 24 June 1898 to 5 April 1900. The working party blasted rocks on stages of the road as a preliminary to the work of leveling and extension.[118] The track was completed in 1899. Soon thereafter the two steel bridges, whose materials had been carried through the mountains in small pieces on the backs of mules, were built across the upper waters of the Karun at Gawdar-i Balutak, where a new caravanserai was also built, and across the Karun's tributary Ab-i Bazuft at Pul-i Imarat, thus completing the work. These were the first modern bridges in Iran. The last rivet of the bridge at Gawdar-i Balutak was driven on 14 December 1899 "in the presence of all the khans."[119] The bridge at Pul-i Imarat was completed in March 1900. The finished track, which covered a distance of 270 miles and crossed the width of the Zagros Mountains, was soon opened, leading to an increase in the volume of trade in Bakhtiyari territory and the hinterland of Isfahan.

Trade and Traffic on the Bakhtiyari Road

The first years of traffic on the road opened up the Bakhtiyari Mountains. A smoother commercial road had paved over a rocky track used by nomads during migrations. A stream of caravans from the towns of Shushtar, Dizful, and Isfahan traveled through the Bakhtiyari Mountains. Increasingly the tribesmen sold the products of their flocks and herds in towns, where they purchased the newer necessities of life—matches, sugar, piece-goods, cotton textiles, spades, and ploughs.[120] Describing the Bakhtiyari "highlanders" in 1902 the special correspondent for the *Times* of London wrote, "Though essentially men of the hills, they are also men of the plains. They have ceased to be merely pastoral nomads, and, though they still derive their chief means of livelihood from their herds and flocks, they no longer disdain to till the soil, whether on the upland slopes, where they spend the summer months, or the fertile plains of Arabistan, to which they descend on approach of winter."[121] The khans had built houses and traveled in carriages on paved roads.[122] Writing in July 1902 Preece saw great promise in the Bakhtiyari Road as the route of a railway and a surface for automobiles. He wrote, "The more I see of this road and consider its possibilities the more I am impressed with the idea of its being converted into one capable of carrying vehicular traffic of one sort or another."[123]

The khans profited in several ways from the building of the Bakhtiyari Road. Its construction had forged closer ties between the Bakhtiyari and the British. The Bakhtiyari khans saw the road and their ties to the British as the means to gain greater autonomy from the Qajar government. Mortimer Durand recalled that in a conversation with Isfandiyar Khan just after the road had opened in December 1899, the chieftain assured the British of the Bakhtiyari's loyalties: "The Chiefs breached the question themselves, the Sardar Isfandiar Khan, being very emphatic on the subject. Riding by my side on the day we parted, he said to me, after looking round to see that all Persians were out of hearing, 'Remember, if we are ever wanted, we are ready to join you with 20,000 horsemen, all well-armed, and footmen besides.'"[124] The khans' official relations with the British and the subsidies they collected from their agreement certainly enhanced their power on the Iranian periphery in the short term. For both the khans and the British the Bakhtiyari Road was a precursor for future contacts regarding the strategically important Zagros Mountains and the resource-rich province of Khuzistan. The opening of the Bakhtiyari Road paved the way for the further transformation of environment and society in southwestern Iran.[125]

The road opened the Zagros Mountains to an increased volume of trade as caravan traffic during 1904 nearly doubled that of 1903.[126] This proved lucrative for the khans, as they collected tolls on the trade that passed through the mountains. During those years the Bakhtiyari khans collected nearly 14,000 pounds in tolls. Moreover, the steel suspension bridges served as efficient collection points for the annual flock tax, known as *galladari*, levied on the tribes as they migrated to summer pastures. Between 1900 and 1907, with fewer opportunities to miscount or evade the tax except by taking alternate routes of migration, the amount of revenues paid to the Bakhtiyari chiefs tripled.[127] As a result the distance between the khans' way of life and that of the tribal rank-and-file widened.

In the end, the Bakhtiyari Road did not turn out as Lynch and its British backers had imagined. Although trade up and down the route increased substantially, the traffic did not open southwestern Iran to commerce in the way Lynch had envisioned. It would not become the main thoroughfare between the Persian Gulf and the interior of Iran. Almost from the beginning the road was beset by various obstacles including deterioration, the shortage of pack animals, the lack of caravanserais, and insecurity caused by tribal raids. Lynch complained in 1901 that the muleteers of Isfahan were reluctant to use the new route and preferred the more beaten and known track through Shiraz.[128] The difficulties of travel also caused the *charvadars* to hesitate before taking the Bakhtiyari Road.

Writing shortly after the road's completion Durand claimed, "The road is like marching along the edge of a saw. . . . Naturally the result is not what in England would be called a road at all. It is a mere track, often very rough and stony, sometimes carried across the face of the solid rock above the streams. . . . There are many places where a slip or shy on the part of a horse would almost certainly result in the death of horse and rider."[129] These natural obstacles were gradually compounded by the deterioration of the rebuilt road. By the autumn of 1903 rains had washed away sections of the road, and in some parts the track was entirely gone. A report by a company agent on the condition of the road three years after it had been built made the following assessment:

> The track has been allowed to fall into a ruinous condition simply for the want of regular attention. . . . Any road or track, however well constructed, running through such mountainous country as the Bakhtiyari, is bound to become obstructed by stones falling into the cuttings, and worn away by the traffic and washed away by rain. . . .

> Such is now the condition of the Bakhtiyari track, and it is a matter of great regret that so soon after incurring expenditure for its construction it should be allowed to fall into its original state for the want of a small yearly expenditure.[130]

Two years later in 1905 the same agent noted that the need for more caravanserais had been demonstrated "by the frequent complaints from muleteers and by the condition in which goods arrive in Isfahan."[131] On the eighteen stages of the road there were only four caravanserais "in good condition" and three others "in ruins."[132] Lynch's agent Fraser Parry described places where the road had been "washed away by flood water running down the hill." Some of these "wash-outs" were thirty feet wide. The khans had repaired some of them through temporary measures such as "placing a branch of a tree on the outer edge of the track and lodging smaller branches and twigs between it and rocks on the inner edge, covering the whole with a thin layer of earth."[133] Loose debris brought down by flood water also made it difficult for loaded mules to pass. Parry reported that the road was "rough" and covered with stones, making the passage of mules and camels extremely difficult. He concluded his report on the road and its prospects skeptically:

> It is very difficult to make any sort of road here, which is likely to be permanent. The track is bad and broken away to a dangerously narrow path in many parts. All of these places were in a good condition when the road was first handed over to the Chiefs, and have come to their present condition owing to neglect. . . . I can safely say without exaggeration that as a track for laden animals to travel over, it cannot be considered otherwise than dangerous in parts and extremely difficult for some considerable distances.[134]

The Bakhtiyari and British, it appeared, had different notions and practices of mobility and transit.

For the Bakhtiyari the road remained, above all, a safe path for their spring and fall migrations, and the basis of their pastoral economy. Because of their seasonal migrations the Bakhtiyari could not commit to carrying cargo long-term, nor was the deterioration of roads over time a major concern for them. They were accustomed to and could tolerate the rough surfaces of Iran's mountain roads. As one British official noted, "All over the Bakhtiyari country remains are to be found, bridges and forts and stone causeways, but it is always the same story, 'It is old, very old, now it is ruined—*Qadim ast, khayli qadim, hala kharab shud*.'"[135] In fact, the Bakhtiyari liked rough roads and objected to a smooth track. Some tribesmen found the rebuilt road too smooth (*saf*), with "no stones for your feet to catch hold of" and took to disregarding its "carefully constructed zigzags," climbing instead straight uphill.[136]

The road's disrepair was worsened by the fact that it had become a robbers' haunt and the frequent site of Bakhtiyari raids, an indication of the persistence of tribalism and local power in the Qajar periphery. Since the 1890s the Qajar government's control over the tribes on the margins of the empire had slackened.[137] Raids and "serious robberies" disrupted trade and travel on the Bakhtiyari Road. One observer described the banditry on the road and its effects on the caravan trade:

> On the 15th of May [1901] the first caravan of the season came through from the Bakhtiyari road; it had reached a distance of seventeen miles from Isfahan and was in sight of that city when it was attacked and looted. This was a lamentable occurrence, as it discredited the road at the commencement of the season and trade has been withdrawn from it.[138]

The insecurity of the road and the growing British interest in the natural resources of Khuzistan prompted the appointments in Luristan of new consuls who were to "get into touch with the tribesmen" and raise a body of road guards to police the land.[139] The tolls demanded by the tribal guards, however, intimidated and discouraged merchants from traveling their way. With few caravanserais there was little protection from night robberies, and the tribes along the road had gained a reputation of stopping caravans with aggressive demands for tea, sugar, paper, medicine, and rifles.[140]

Perhaps the most infamous bandits were from the Kuhgilu tribes, Lurs from the mountainous frontier between Fars and Khuzistan provinces. The Kuhgilu had been in rebellion and had not paid taxes since the end of Nasir al-Din Shah's reign in 1896.[141] Technically under the jurisdiction of Fars Province, Kuhgilu bands crossed into Khuzistan, raided caravans on the Lynch Road, and then returned to the safe shelter of Fars, where Bakhtiyari guards could not pursue them.[142] At the turn of the century, with Iran entering a period of anarchy and with the Bakhtiyari Road bringing unprecedented amounts of goods and capital to the edges of their territory, the heavily armed Taiyibi and Dushman Ziyari tribes of Kuhgilu became notorious caravan raiders.[143] The

Tribesmen with Martini Henry rifles under an elm tree on the road, 1890. Bird Album, UCLA.

Bakhtiyari khans were held responsible for the safety of the road but could do little other than threaten to close the road or post notices alerting merchants and travelers about the insecurity of the route.[144]

The Bakhtiyari Road project was also beset by the incessant financial disagreements between Lynch and the khans. To begin there were misunderstandings over the cost of the road. The Lynch Brothers firm agreed to build the road as the agents for the Bakhtiyari chiefs, but the costs of construction had exceeded their original estimates of 5,500 pounds. Partly because of the two suspension bridges, the cost of the road turned out to be nearly 9,000 pounds, and the khans refused to consider anything beyond the original figure decided upon, paying neither capital nor interest. The Lynch Company was also persistent in seeking compensation from the Bakhtiyari for part of the losses they had incurred, which they reported to total over 34,000 pounds for the period between 1888 and 1906.[145] In addition, Lynch's personal relations with the Bakhtiyari khans had broken down considerably since he had traveled through the Zagros and helped renew relations between the Bakhtiyari and the British in 1890. Isfandiyar Khan had died in 1903, and the friendship between his younger brother ʿAli Quli Khan Sardar Asʿad and Lynch had become strained under the pressure of business surrounding the road.[146]

British officials and press often sided with the Bakhtiyari, fearing that Lynch's petty claims would lead the tribes to sympathize with the Russians. As the London *Times*' special correspondent in Persia wrote in 1902:

> It was mainly to secure [British] good will that the Bakhtiyari chiefs agreed to construct and protect a caravan route through their mountains. They are in many respects more open to progressive ideas than the average Persian official, and they value not only the direct profit they themselves derive from the road in the shape of tolls, but also the indirect benefits it has conferred upon their people. For with the growth of traffic cultivation has extended along the road in a very remarkable degree, and the tribesmen are beginning to find a ready market for produce which they had never before dreamt of raising. It is much to be regretted that in these circumstances a misunderstanding should have arisen between the chiefs and Messrs. Lynch as to payment for the construction of the road. . . . But the Bakhtiyari chiefs would probably not have proved so intractable on this point if the primary object for which they agreed to open up the mountains they had hitherto so jealously guarded against all comers had not been disappointed.[147]

With the Constitutional Revolution under way, the Bakhtiyari khans sought to sever their ties with Lynch and assume independent responsibility for the road. The khans offered to pay Lynch's legitimate claims in cash if the firm consented to the cancellation of the 1898 agreement. At a meeting with the British envoy in Tehran, Evelyn Grant Duff, Lynch's agent Malleson, and other Bakhtiyari khans, Sardar As'ad openly declared, "If Lynch removed their business from Persia there would be universal rejoicing and no one would be so delighted as the Bakhtiyaris," while the other chiefs added, "Inshallah! Let him go."[148] To some observers it appeared that although the Lynch Company had regarded itself as "the pioneers of the Karun route," time had proven that "the Khans [were] the masters of the road."[149]

Conclusion

The building of the Bakhtiyari Road in 1899 marked the opening of a tribal hinterland in Iran. By the late nineteenth century the British viewed the mountain road from the Karun River to Isfahan as a means to expand their trade and influence from the Persian Gulf to the interior of Iran, a buffer against the Russian sphere in the north. As the road paved over the mountains it would also smooth over the roughness of tribal Iran. The Bakhtiyari Road was cast as a project of "civilizing" pastoral nomadic tribes, bringing them closer to the market, and gradually settling them down.[150] In the end, the road did not open up the Zagros Mountains and the Bakhtiyari hinterland in the way the British had intended. The story of the Bakhtiyari Road is not one of British imperial mastery, but rather of negotiation. The construction of the road and the opening of tribal territory to international trade were mediated by the Bakhtiyari, who did not easily surrender their autonomy on the periphery of Qajar Iran. The Bakhtiyari Road opened the Zagros Mountains to British commerce and the world economy, but it was an imperial project built upon compromise and accommodation with tribal subjects. The story of the Bakhtiyari Road demonstrates the uncertainties involved in the modernization of nineteenth-century Iran. The road brought the world economy to a distant tribal population and signaled further changes to come without fully diminishing the independence and power of the tribes.

4

IN THE FIELDS OF OIL

THE FIRST OIL WELLS in the Middle East were drilled in the southern Iranian province of Khuzistan, near the Parthian ruins of a stone temple called Masjid-i Sulayman ("Mosque of Solomon"). The exploration for oil began in 1905, when the D'Arcy Oil Syndicate, a British company with the exclusive right to develop petroleum resources in Iran, set its sights on a tract of land in the territory of the Bakhtiyari tribes known as Maydan-i Naftun, "the field of oil." The tribes whose winter pastures lay in the vicinity of the fields were soon forced to adapt to a radically transformed environment. Oil derricks and pipelines appeared on the landscape and roads were paved through the mountains.[1] Where flocks and black goat-hair tents had once quietly dotted the hills, houses with running water, schools, and hospitals were built. The company organized levies of tribal guards to police and discipline the local tribal population, many of whom became employed as workers earning wages in the oil fields, remaining in the lowlands instead of making the seasonal migration to the summer pastures. Unlike the pastoral economy of the migratory Bakhtiyari, the D'Arcy Oil Syndicate, which became the Anglo-Persian Oil Company in 1909, made permanent use of the land, continuously mining its subterranean resources.[2]

This history of the early exploration for oil and the encounter between the British Empire and indigenous peoples on the margins of Iran can be traced through documents found in dusty leather-bound volumes in a London archive. Volumes FO 248/894 and FO 248/923, held at the British National Archives, formerly the Public Record Office, contain an array of company and consular records, reports, and correspondence sent to the D'Arcy Oil Syndicate from the Bakhtiyari Mountains between the years 1905 and 1909. Written by company engineers and staff, British agents and officials, and the ruling khans, these documents detail the impact of British oil exploration on the Bakhtiyari tribal confederation. In addition to these materials, there remain company records in the British Petroleum Archive at the University of Warwick. On the basis of these archival materials, the following pages reconstruct a history of oil and imperialism on the distant margins of Iran.[3]

Some have depicted the early history of oil in Iran as the tale of rough and rugged Europeans developing a primitive land, of pioneering in Persia. The contemporary correspondence of D. L. R. Lorimer, the British vice-consul at Ahvaz, and George B. Reynolds, the managing engineer of the oil fields, exemplify this point of view and have subsequently been echoed by company historians Laurence Lockhart and R. W. Ferrier.[4] According to this romantic narrative British oil exploration initiated "progress in Persia" and its wild hinterlands.[5] Other authors, particularly those writing at the time of the nationalization of the Iranian oil industry, presented a critical view of the advent of the oil economy. Among the first narratives written in this vein were found in the Marxist newspaper *Shafaq-i Surkh* (Red Sunset) and later Abu al-Fazl Lisani's book *Tala-yi Siya ya Bala-yi Iran* (Black Gold or Iran's Curse), published in Tehran in 1950.[6] These were followed by works by Husayn Makki, Kazim Afshin, Nasrollah Saifpour Fatemi, L. P. Elwell-Sutton, and Mustafa Fatih, all of whom wrote critically of the oil industry in Iran after the fall of the nationalist Prime Minister Muhammad Mussadiq in 1953.[7] As one author put it, "The story of the Anglo-Iranian Oil Company in Persia is a dismal one. It is an instructive case-history, a lesson in how not to conduct one's dealings with people of other lands, different backgrounds, strange cultures. . . . It is an admonition to those who would like to patronize the 'natives.'"[8]

None of these critics of British oil exploitation in Iran, however, directly examined the encounters between the Anglo-Persian Oil Company and the Bakhtiyari tribes during the early years of exploration. Until quite recently, most works have focused on nationalist narratives of later periods and the Mussadiq era in particular. These narratives emphasize Mussadiq's aborted attempt to nationalize the Iranian oil industry and his overthrow by a CIA-funded coup in 1953.[9] This emphasis on the politics of oil justifiably highlights how the Western interest in Iranian crude toppled a popular, grassroots government and returned an American- and British-backed shah to the throne.

This chapter, by contrast, explores an earlier and lesser known episode: the exploration for oil in the Bakhtiyari fields of southwestern Iran from 1905 to 1911. Drawing upon company and consular records, it argues that oil exploration at Masjid-i Sulayman transformed environment and society among the

Bakhtiyari. In a radical departure from the customary land rights that prevailed before, fields once held in common by the tribes became the private property of the Anglo-Persian Oil Company. What is more, the British viewed and justified the exploration for oil as an imperial project that would discipline the tribes and induce them to end their pastoral nomadic way of life. As the company developed the natural resources of the land, it also sought to assimilate and settle the Bakhtiyari tribes.[10]

Rich Soil: Jacques de Morgan and the Geological Survey of Persia

The discovery of natural resources in southwestern Iran was fostered by the modern science of geology in the late nineteenth century. Just as travelers and adventurers had described the surface of the Zagros Mountains in the years leading up to the building of the Bakhtiyari Road in 1899, they now began to speculate about the subterranean resources that lay below the ground. None of these geological surveys was as influential as those conducted by Jacques de Morgan and the French Scientific Mission in Iran during the 1890s.

Mining had taken place in Iran long before the nineteenth century. Medieval and early modern geographers had noted the country's mineral riches, particularly in the province of Khuzistan, which comprised the mountains between the Iranian Plateau and the Mesopotamian Plains. According to the tenth-century Persian geographer Istakhri, a resident of nearby Fars province, Khuzistan encompassed the warm alluvial plains lying at the lower course of the River Dujayl ("Little Tigris," known today as the Karun) and the mountain chains near Izaj.[11] The anonymous tenth-century Persian geographical text *Hudud al-'Alam* (Boundaries of the World) defined the frontiers of Khuzistan and listed the resources of the province:

> East of this province lies Pars [Fars] and the borders of Sipahan [Isfahan]; south of it, the sea and some the 'Iraq frontier (*hadd*); west of it, some of the borders (*hudud*) of 'Iraq, and of the countryside (*savad*) of Baghdad and Wasit; north of it, the lands of the province of Jibal. This province is more prosperous than any province adjoining it. Great rivers and running waters are found in it. Its countryside is flourishing and its mountains full of utility.[12]

In Istakhri's "road book," *Masalik va Mamalik* (Book of Routes and Provinces), we hear of vast tracts in the mountains to the north of Khuzistan known as "al-Lur," where "no trace of town or settlement" existed.[13] Muslim geographers noted the mountainous nature of this land, which according to al-Muqaddasi lay on the frontiers of 'Iraq, and named it Jabal, the Arabic word for mountains.[14] The anonymous author of the geography *Hudud al-Alam* described the fire temple of Masjid-i Sulayman in Khuzistan as one of the "wonderful buildings" in a mountainous region where iron and silver mines were found.[15]

The seventeenth-century French travelers Chardin and Tavernier described the efforts of Shah 'Abbas I (1588–1629) to utilize the mineral riches of Iran during the Safavid era (1501–1722). These minerals included iron, steel, copper, and silver mines near Isfahan, Kirman, and Mazandaran, iron mines in Parthia and Bactria, lead mines near Kirman and Yazd, and naphtha springs in Chalddea (Khuzistan). During the eighteenth century Nadir Shah Afshar (r. 1736–1747) also showed an interest in mining, establishing an iron foundry in Mazandaran.[16] Nineteenth-century Western travelers more readily turned their attention to Iran's promising mines near Masjid-i Sulayman. On a march through the Bakhtiyari territory in 1836, Henry Rawlinson observed "naphtha pits . . . on the road from Shuster to Ram Hormuz."[17] In the 1840s, the adventurer Austen Henry Layard observed, "There is no spot in Khuzistan to which so many legends attach as to the Musjedi-Suleiman, and it is looked upon by the Lurs as a place of peculiar sanctity."[18] According to local folklore it was the foot of Solomon's throne (*pa-yi takht*), where "all the monarchs of the earth came to his 'salam'" (to greet him with peace) and where he held court before going to war.[19] This historic site of legends would be the place where the first oil was later discovered. At the time, Layard's archaeological interests raised local suspicions that he was in search of the legendary treasures Solomon had buried in the palace. Although Layard found no buried treasures at Masjid-i Sulayman, he did note having reached some naphtha springs that belonged to the Chahar Lang chieftain Muhammad Taqi Khan.[20]

Foreign concessions would prove to be instrumental in the opening of the Bakhtiyari land and the development of its natural resources. In 1872, Nasir al-Din Shah (r. 1848–1896) granted the rights for the development of Iran's natural resources for a down payment of 40,000 pounds in the infamous Reuter Concession. In this agreement, the shah signed away "the exclusive and definite privilege to work, all over the Empire, the mines of coal, iron, and copper, lead, petroleum" to a British subject, Julius de Reuter. The Concession also granted monopolies in the construction of railways and canals, as well as the rights to exploitation of uncultivated lands. But as European knowledge of and interest in Iran's mines increased, many Iranians themselves came "to think that their native soil concealed an El Dorado of wealth."[21] Western interest awakened the Qajars to the land's vast resources. In 1881, the government dispatched 'Abd al-Ghaffar Najm al-Mulk to report on the province of Khuzistan, and in his travelogue he described fields of oil (*ma'dan-i naft*) in the vicinity of Shushtar at sites such as Naft-i Safid (White Oil Springs).[22]

Met with Russian opposition and widespread protest by the Iranian people, the Reuter Concession was cancelled. In 1889, however, Reuter was given a more limited, amended concession that granted him exclusive mineral rights, including the right to the exploitation of oil, and the authority to found a bank over a term of sixty years.[23] This led to the establishment of the Imperial Bank of Persia and the Persian Bank Mining Rights Corporation, which gained "the exclusive and definite privilege of working throughout the Empire, the iron, copper and lead, mercury, coal, petroleum, manganese, borax, and asbestos mines belonging to the State."[24] The Mining Rights Corporation's operations, mostly in southern Iran near the Persian Gulf, were ineffective, however, resulting in its voluntary liquidation in 1894.[25]

It was not until the research of Jacques de Morgan and the French Scientific Mission, conducted between 1889 and 1897 while Reuter's men worked further south, that the prospect of finding large quantities of oil in Iran was rekindled. In February 1892, de Morgan published a report on oil deposits at Chah Surkh, ninety miles south of Kirmanshah, in the journal *Annales des Mines*. De Morgan, who had a colorful career as an Egyptologist before arriving in Iran and also established the French Archaeological Mission at Susa, later published his findings in a multivolume, encyclopedic work, *Mission Scientifique en Perse*. In the second volume of the work, largely devoted to the geography and geology of the Zagros Mountains, he suggested that western Iran contained rich deposits of petroleum and rested on an oil-bearing stratum the Qajar government could choose to exploit and develop as a considerable source of state revenue. Between Mesopotamia and Luristan, in the hills and among "unknown peoples" (*populations inconnues*), de Morgan discovered a vast oil-rich zone ripe for development.[26] He even mentioned in his report that in the Bakhtiyari hills, on the road from Shushtar to Malamir, were signs of oil near an ancient fire temple called Masjid-i Sulayman.[27] Although his research on oil in the region was not particularly detailed or conclusive, he recommended more thorough geological studies on the Zagros region to determine where oil would be found there.[28]

The D'Arcy Oil Concession of 1901

At the Paris Exhibition in 1900 Reuter's agent Edouard Cotte discussed de Morgan's reports with Antoine Kitabji, the director of Persian customs and acting Persian commissioner-general at the exhibition. Kitabji was an acquaintance of the Iranian Prime Minister Mirza 'Ali Asghar Khan Amin al-Sultan and an early advocate for the development of the oil industry in Iran. In 1901, Kitabji, who had played a leading role in the second Reuter Concession of 1889, joined with Henry Drummond Wolff, the conservative former British minister in Tehran, a leading figure behind opening the Karun River to international traffic in 1888. Together they offered a concession for oil exploration in Iran to William Knox D'Arcy, a capitalist from Devonshire, England, who had already made a fortune from the Mount Morgan gold mines in Queensland, Australia.[29] D'Arcy showed his interest in the venture by dispatching two geologists, H. T. Burls and W. H. Dalton, to conduct geological surveys not only of Chah Surkh but also of the environs of Shushtar and Maydan-i Naftun. Receiving favorable reports from his surveyors, in 1901 D'Arcy sent his secretary A. L. Marriott to Tehran to join Kitabji and Cotte in negotiations with the prime minister, Amin al-Sultan, who presented a copy of the proposed concession to Muzaffar al-Din Shah Qajar (r. 1896–1907).

Although the concession excluded the five northern provinces of Iran, a total of 480,000 out of 628,000 square miles, the Russians opposed it from the beginning. News arrived that Amin al-Sultan had taken the concession to the shah but he had not signed it, having gone hunting instead. D'Arcy closed the deal, however, when he offered the shah 40,000 pounds down and 40,000 pounds upon formation of the company, as well as 16 percent rather than 10 percent of net profits, plus a 10,000-pound advance. [30] Thus, on 28 May 1901, the shah and D'Arcy crafted a concession that presented the latter with "a special and exclusive privilege to search for, obtain, exploit, develop, render suitable for trade, carry away, and sell natural gas petroleum, asphalt and ozokerite throughout the whole extent of the Persian Empire for a term of 60 years."[31] Preceding the Constitutional Revolution and signed when oil was still a novelty and its existence below the soil was uncertain, the concession was a virtual secret agreement. The D'Arcy Concession was not published in either Iran or Britain.[32] According to an apocryphal story the Persian minister, Amin al-Sultan, sent the Russian embassy a description of the concession in the difficult-to-read, "broken" Persian script of *shikasta* at a time when the only person in the embassy who could read this writing was away, causing the draft

Bakhtiyari encampment in the vicinity of the oil fields, 1908. Lorimer Collection, SOAS.

to lay unread in the Russian legation until after the concession was signed.[33]

To lead the exploration for oil D'Arcy hired George B. Reynolds, an experienced engineer who had drilled for oil in Sumatra and had been in the Public Works Department in India. The company began drilling in 1902 at Chah Surkh, south of Kirmanshah, but had very little success in finding commercial quantities of oil there. The difficulties of drilling at Chah Surkh did not justify the high cost of a 300-mile pipeline to the Persian Gulf, and so all operations there ceased by June 1904. Drilling moved further south to the winter pastures of the Bakhtiyari tribes, where the manager of the oil fields, Reynolds, had previously surveyed "oil found in Gypsiferous rocks" near the Parthian ruins at Masjid-i Sulayman.[34] Reynolds had also come to realize that the Bakhtiyari tribes were autonomous from the Qajar state and the D'Arcy Concession was not binding on them. By the terms of the concession the Qajar government permitted operations to take place and promised to establish security for oil exploration. The authority of the central government, however, could

Bakhtiyari encampment in the winter quarters or *qishlaq* near Maydan-i Naftun, 1908. Lorimer Collection, SOAS.

not guarantee the safety of oil exploration in the Zagros Mountains and the Bakhtiyari territory.

The inaccessibility of the Zagros, which loom over western Iran, provided pastoral nomadic groups with political, cultural, and economic refuge from the state. In fact, the Persian government distinguished between crown lands (*khalisa*) and private lands (*milk*), which in this case were in the possession of the tribes. If the company was to pursue operations in the Bakhtiyari Mountains, then it first had to obtain permission from the tribal khans, who were the local authorities on the ground.[35] As one British observer wrote about the company's predicament:

> The position of a Company which is working under a Concession from one Government (Persian) but depends on the goodwill of a provincial administration (Arab and Bakhtiyari) and the military and moral support of a third (British and Indian), with a head office in

Bakhtiyari women rolling bread, making yoghurt or perhaps curd, and churning butter under the shade of a black goat-hair tent, 1908. Lorimer Collection, SOAS.

> Glasgow, dealing with the Foreign Office (in London), and a Foreign Department (Simla) through local offices (in Persia) is not easy."[36]

Although the company had attained a concession from the central government, the land where it was believed oil would be found lay in the territory of the independent Bakhtiyari tribes.

Bakhtiyari Oil Agreement of 1905

In June 1905, D'Arcy and the Foreign Office enlisted J. R. Preece, the consul general of Isfahan who had brokered the Bakhtiyari Road Concession in 1895, to assist in discussions with the khans on plans "to open up their country to exploring." Negotiations took place on 16 and 19 October 1905 in the village of Shalamzar in the foothills of the Zagros, with the ***ilkhan*** Najaf Quli Khan Samsam al-Saltana, the ***ilbayg*** Ghulam Husayn Khan Shahab al-Saltana, Nasir Khan Sarim al-Mulk (later Sardar Jang), and 'Ali Quli Khan Sardar As'ad,

A shallow creek in the Bakhtiyari winter quarters, 1908. Lorimer Collection, SOAS.

whom Reynolds then described as a "masterful" spokesman for the khans, representing the tribes.[37] Sardar As'ad insisted that the tribes would not lease any part of their country and must be partners in the affair, receiving 20 percent of the profits. Preece reported that the Bakhtiyari had "great faith in the capacity of their oil-bearing country; they think that Baku will be nothing to it in comparison. They describe the oil-belt as being about 100 miles long by about 8 miles to 12 miles broad. . . . There is one place known as Maidan-i-Man Naftan (the plain of much naphtha), which is full of oil according to them."[38]

After four days of following the khans from fortress to fortress, Preece succeeded in lowering their asking price to 5 percent, which D'Arcy still rejected. At this point Preece convinced the governing chiefs of the tribes, Samsam al-Saltana and Shahab al-Saltana, to accept 3 percent of the shares out of consideration for their "friendship." Sardar As'ad, however, refused to sign the agreement, warning the other chiefs before a crowd of tribesmen: "If you want to sign this Agreement do so, but you are creating a very dangerous situation for yourselves and the tribes." Two days later, Preece and the other khans con-

Bakhtiyari tribesmen stand behind the boiler they are transporting to the oil fields, 1909. BP.

vinced Sardar As'ad to sign what became known as the Bakhtiyari Agreement. In his report on the negotiations, Preece admitted his own surprise at convincing the Bakhtiyari to settle for "next to nothing," while noting that the khans "have but the very crudest ideas of Companies, shares, and such like things."[39]

In the Bakhtiyari Agreement of November 1905, the ruling khans sold to the D'Arcy Oil Syndicate the permission to survey, drill, build roads, and lay pipelines in the winter quarters. The Bakhtiyari were required to provide the land "at the fair price of the day" if arable, but at no cost if uncultivated. This upheld the precedent of the terms of the D'Arcy Oil Concession of 1901, which had not recognized pastoral rights to the land. Article 3 of the concession stated: "The Imperial Persian Government grants gratuitously to the concessionaire all uncultivated lands belonging to the state which the concessionaire's engineers may deem necessary for the construction of the whole or any part of the works." Article 1 of the Bakhtiyari Agreement promised the same: "The Chiefs of the Bakhtiari tribe will give free of cost all uncultivated ground required for this work." The Bakhtiyari were also to furnish guards to protect the works, assuming responsibility for robberies. In return, the khans accepted a 3 percent share in the profits and a subsidy of 2,000 pounds per year with an additional 1,000 pounds for safeguarding the pipeline when it was built.[40]

The Bakhtiyari Agreement had important repercussions for the tribal confederation. The wealth and political power acquired by the khans fractured tribal solidarity. Since the late nineteenth century three ruling families, the Ilkhani, the Hajji Ilkhani, and the Ilbaygi, had unified the Bakhtiyari tribes.[41] During the same period the ruling Haft Lang khans had become landlords in Chahar Mahal and the foothills of the Zagros. In agreements with British imperial companies such as Lynch Brothers and the D'Arcy Oil Syndicate, they claimed as their property tribal lands previously used collectively on a seasonal basis. While the khans profited immensely from oil revenues, they were delegitimized in the eyes of their tribal subjects, who came to view the chieftaincy as politically and economically co-opted by the British.

The Bakhtiyari agreement also strained tribe and state interactions in Qajar Iran. In January 1906, the Qajars declined "to recognize arrangements made by His Majesty's consul at Isfahan with the Bakhtiyari chiefs, stating that the latter had no right to make it" and adding that D'Arcy should have consulted the central government beforehand.[42] The Qajar government resented a situation in which a British company recognized the Bakhtiyari as the authorities in the Zagros in writing and paid them an annual subsidy for guarding a British enterprise in Iran. In a letter written to the British legation in 1906, the Persian Foreign Minister Mushir al-Dawla stated that the British "cannot, without the knowledge or approval of the Persian Government, make with any person an agreement, which affects the rights of the Government."

Tehran argued that the British exploration for oil in Khuzistan and their independent relations with the Bakhtiyari violated the sovereignty and undermined the authority of the central government. As Fatemi has observed in his study of oil diplomacy in Iran, "The government of Iran vehemently protested against the direct negotiations of the company with the tribal chiefs," a policy that "strengthened feudalism and tribal rule . . . by subsidizing and encouraging the tribes to declare themselves independent of the central government."[43] For the British, material development and capital profits deriving from oil outweighed the territorial integrity of Iran. The waning power of Tehran over the tribes during the reign of Muzaffar al-Din Shah and the subsequent constitutional movement certainly also opened up opportunities for the British to maneuver in the space between the Iranian center and periphery.

While the Bakhtiyari khans expressed their dissatisfaction with the agreement, British authorities dismissed their objections. In the spring of 1906,

Sardar As'ad, Samsam al-Saltana, Shahab al-Saltana, and Sultan Muhammad gained an invitation to the British legation in Tehran, where they complained to Evelyn Grant Duff, the British chargé d'affaires, about the current payments for Bakhtiyari guards. Sardar As'ad claimed that the Bakhtiyari regretted their agreement with Consul Preece, noting that "at the time of the signature of the Agreement, the consul was their guest and out of regard for him they had given way in certain important matters without realizing what they were undertaking." The khans now realized "they were unable to carry out their obligations in regard to certain clauses in the agreement."[44] Sardar As'ad, who acted as the spokesman, requested that "a new agreement be drafted and the existing one cancelled," adding that he would not hesitate to bring matters to the notice of the central government. British officials saw this as an effort by the Bakhtiyari khans to get more money from the company, which had "the reputation of being very rich."[45] Meanwhile Preece held firm that the "agreement was made by the Chiefs with their eyes wide open," dismissing the khans' discontent as an example of the "greed, dishonesty, and cupidity of the Bakhtiari."[46]

Workers in the Fields

The company began by drilling at three locations in Bakhtiyari territory—Mamatain, Shardin, and Maydan-i Naftun. The third of these places, Maydan-i Naftun, was the most promising site.[47] The Oil Syndicate's operations there would be centered near the ruins of the ancient fire temple at Masjid-i Sulayman. At an altitude of 1,200 feet, the "field of oil" was surrounded by limestone rocks known as Kuh-i Asmari or the Asmari Mountains and was the winter quarters for 400 tents, or approximately 2,000 members of the Haft Lang.[48] In addition, 250 ploughs were at work in Maydan-i Naftun, producing barley, wheat, and small amounts of rice, even though the district had limited irrigated cultivation and its nomadic population outnumbered its sedentary population by a ratio of more than eight to one.[49] Most of the lands designated for oil exploration were used by Bakhtiyari pastoralists and cultivators with customary rights at Maydan-i Naftun.[50] According to the *Tarikh-i Bakhtiyari*, the tribes' "winter pastures were in Arabistan-i Ajam" and "during the cold season several thousand black tents were pitched near Dizful, Shushtar, and Ram Hurmuz."[51] Every year in the last month of summer the tribes gathered their crops and followed the grass down to the *qishlaq*, where they found green and lush pastures throughout the winter.[52] Between 1905 and 1911, Masjid-i Sulayman made the transition to a company town.

According to the terms of the 1905 Bakhtiyari agreement, the D'Arcy Oil Syndicate made the claim that uncultivated and fallow lands were wasteland and thus should be ceded free of charge. Throughout the period of exploration the company maintained its position of not paying compensation for lands not under cultivation, including the hills and grazing lands.[53] In 1911, the Anglo-Persian Oil Company purchased nearly 7,000 acres of the Bakhtiyari's winter pastures and fields around Maydan-i Naftun, paying 22,000 to the Haft Lang khans, who acted as the sole owners of the property, thereby displacing numerous tribes from customary grazing lands and arable fields. In what became known as the Bakhtiyari Land Agreement of 1911, the company continued its claim that non-arable lands were "wasteland." Although the khans contested, the company acquired more than 3,000 acres of pastures free of charge.[54] This deal brought the company into conflict with the local nomadic and semi-nomadic tribes, demanding restitution for lost lands and depleted resources in the vicinity of Maydan-i Naftun.

The arrival of the company and the promise of paid work drew pastoralists and peasants from the surrounding countryside. Finding employment in the "fields," Bakhtiyari tribesmen accepted new demands of discipline, orderliness, and punctuality, becoming incorporated into the lower ranks of the world economy.[55] The oil company did not merely transform the terrain but also local societies, "the human material" it sought to mold into modern subjects.[56]

The industrial development of Maydan-i Naftun brought with it the possibility of work for local tribesmen. Many tribesmen with winter pastures in the hills surrounding the oil fields found employment with the company as laborers (*'amalajat*), receiving pay in cash on the fifteenth day of every month. In accordance with paragraph 12 of the D'Arcy Oil Concession, with the exception of technical experts all the workmen had to be Persian subjects. Bakhtiyari peasants and pastoral nomads comprised a main source of the working class in Khuzistan, providing unskilled labor to the British oil industry. They made up the ranks of the approximately 2,000 "Persians" who had become employed in the oil industry by 1911.[57] The engineers of the oil company hired local tribesmen on a seasonal basis to work on building roads, clearing boulders, leveling sites, loading and unloading equipment, and transporting heavy machinery. The tribesmen worked as masons, construction workers, porters, and mule drivers.

After the discovery of commercial quantities of oil, the Bakhtiyari worked in "pipeline gangs," laying the line from Maydan-i Naftun to the refinery at Abadan.[58] A thousand local laborers worked on the pipeline for eighteen

Bakhtiyari khans and their retinues in their winter quarters neighboring the oil fields, 1908. Lorimer Collection, SOAS.

months, laying it across two ranges of hills and along the Karun River. Because of the mountainous terrain, the lack of navigable rivers other than the Karun, and the scarcity of paved roads, laying the pipeline required a great deal of manual labor, including transporting materials and equipment, a burden that fell on the shoulders of the Bakhtiyari. The pipes arrived in the Persian Gulf "stacked into barges going upstream on the Karun River, either dumped along the banks at intervals or carried as far as Ahwaz before being conveyed overland along a tramway for three miles and then by sternwheelers on the upper river beyond the rapids to the company depot." From there the pipes were transported by mule-drawn "jimms" to designated spots along the route of the line. Gangs of fifty men under a European overseer worked on various sections of the pipeline, "cleaning and greasing the pipes before screwing them together using six pairs of tongs with six men on each."[59]

In some reported cases, cultivators were "leaving their fields and working for the company," then hiring men to plough for them.[60] An Afghan visitor to the oil fields offered an overly optimistic description of the Bakhtiyaris' assimilation:

> To mould to the exigencies of modern industry such refractory material as is presented by these gaunt, fierce, undisciplined men, was the task to which the Company set from the first. The process was slow but gained strength from year to year; to begin with, few men would work for more than six months at a time, after which they returned to their flocks. . . . Gradually a community began to settle on the spot. . . . [T]he great majority of the elaborate machinery both at Abadan and at Masjid-i Sulaiman and Ahwaz is worked . . . by tribesmen.[61]

It seemed clear, however, that the Bakhtiyari and other tribesmen performed the company's most difficult work as unskilled laborers earning low wages.[62] The company archives also reveal difficult labor conditions and the poor health of native workers. The type of work done by the tribesmen was both exhausting and dangerous, with company medical logs documenting frequent injuries of all kinds to laborers, as well as the high occurrence of fever among former pastoral nomads unaccustomed to summers in the lowlands, where the average temperature in July 1908 was 117.4 degrees Fahrenheit.[63] There was a new culture of work at Maydan-i Naftun. While the oil company operated despite the seasons, the tribes lived by the seasons. During times of harvest and the migration of the tribes to the upper mountains of the *yaylaq*, workers were difficult to find.[64] Pastoral values of mobility, liberty, and honor also prevented tribesmen from committing themselves permanently to the company's demands for wage labor. In a letter to the Concessions Syndicate, a vexed Reynolds complained of his difficulties in procuring laborers from among the tribes: "It is impossible to get a native whom one can put in charge of a gang of men to do the earth-work or any other work there may be to do."[65]

Bakhtiyari tribesmen saw no long-term security in working for the British company in the early years of exploration, and they still sought to tend to their seasonal obligations. Pastoral nomads often worked on a temporary basis, preferring to eschew the baked mud houses that the company built as shelters for the families of its workers. A large number of employees still drank river water, forgoing the new facilities for obtaining drinking water.[66] In July 1907, for example, the entire gang of men working at Shardin stopped work "to go and cut their crops," returning to find that they were no longer needed, with other laborers "engaged in their places and the work continued."[67] The

A group of Bakhtiyari oil guards, 1908. Lorimer Collection, SOAS.

tribesmen were not accustomed to work in a rigid system of labor that required a month's notice for time off and deducted fifteen days' pay as penalty if such notice was not given. Describing the early years of the oil industry in Iran, one author noted that "men frequently turned up at the gate in the morning to find that their number had been 'stopped.' . . . the fear of unemployment was always present in the company worker's mind."[68] Nasir Khan Sarim al-Mulk, a Bakhtiyari chieftain with land holdings near Mamatain and Shardin, to whom the tribal workers often complained, wrote to Reynolds in defense of the workers' rights:

> From the time you have started working the Ma'dan up to the present I have incurred a great loss in crops, as much as two thousand Tumans. The ryots having abandoned their fields have come to work for you. Seeing this was for the benefit of your work I took no account of my losses. Amir Pir Murad and his people have also complained that they have been working for you for a few months and have not received their full wages. It is better to have a consideration for their

> condition seeing they have no access to their fields and are dependent on the service they expect to render you. . . . As so much loss has been sustained by me, I would request you to pay them their wages in full and allow them to continue working for you.[69]

The company's first priority, however, remained the continuous work of drilling for oil, far outweighing the livelihoods of the Bakhtiyari rank and file. Field manager Reynolds encouraged workers to use a portion of their regular pay every month to hire labor to tend to their crops, adding that "any creature can cut crops or plant rice and plough the fields, whereas men who have been to a certain extent trained cannot well be spared from the work they have been trained to do."[70] The Bakhtiyari were not easily coerced or disciplined by the company in its drive for oil exploitation. As a company engineer later wrote:

> The peculiarity of the problem that faced the Anglo-Persian Oil Company from the start lay in the character of the human labour available. The inhabitants of that part of Persia (Khuzistan) in which the work was to be done were, for the most part, pastoral nomads, consisting mainly of the famous Bakhtiyari tribes. The Bakhtiyari follow the grass. . . . They live in tents or in rude shelters. . . . Their wants are few and the hardships of such a life are to them scarcely irksome. Of money they have little need and such exchange as they require is done largely by barter. . . . It was from this nomadic human material that the company had to enlist the labour it required. The character and habits of these tribesmen presented human and sociological problems as peculiar and as complex, in their own ways, as the physical and chemical problems raised by the nature of the crude oil obtained from below. It was not sufficient to attract the tribesmen to service with the Company by the prospect of regular pay and the additional comforts that pay could bring; measures had to be taken to keep them when enrolled. The nomadic instinct is not easily extinguished.[71]

The Bakhtiyari tribes, like their land, were to be domesticated and made productive. The discovery of oil had begun to discipline and settle the tribes in the vicinity of Maydan-i Naftun. Although tribesmen struggled to maintain their pastoral economy and culture, with some working on a temporary basis and continuing to make the great migrations, gradually "the roar of machinery was inducing the Persian workers into becoming non-nomadic."[72]

The Company, the "Natives," and the Formation of the Bakhtiyari Guards

The fields became the site of often-violent encounters between the Bakhtiyari tribes and the staff of the oil company. Confronted by the demanding presence of the oil company on their land, the tribes resorted to "everyday forms of resistance." The company faced a mountainous environment and a host of natural barriers, some of which seemed at times impossible to overcome. The steep mountains, the long distances, the roads washed away by late rains and floods from melting snows made for difficult work conditions.[73] The localism of the Bakhtiyari tribes, who made it clear that they wanted the company off their land, was arguably the greatest of these obstacles. The British imperial project set out not only to "tame nature" through the exploration for oil but also to reform the "character" of the Bakhtiyari.[74]

With the country in the midst of the Constitutional Revolution of 1906–1911, and with the agreement between the khans and the company in doubt, the tribes naturally became increasingly restive. According to the terms of the Bakhtiyari Oil Agreement of 1905, regiments of guards (*mustahfizan*) were to protect the oil fields. The company was to pay the khans 2,000 pounds per year in quarterly installments for the furnishing of guards. The khans accepted responsibility "for any robbery which may occur in the Bakhtiyari country" to the company's property. Originally two bodies of guards totaling eighty men were to be stationed at the three drilling sites, with guards to be paid between 50 and 100 tumans a year as wages, plus fodder for their horses.[75]

The volumes of documentation in British archives on the recruitment of the Bakhtiyari guards highlight the uncertainties the company faced during the early phase of oil exploration. The imposing presence of the local tribes and the remote and isolated environs in which the company had to work were first described by the field manager Reynolds, who was attacked and then abandoned by his guards on the way to Ahvaz in 1905.[76] Reynolds was "a man of 50, very active in body and mind, accustomed to long journeys on mule or horseback, a competent geologist and a good Civil Engineer."[77] Despite his experience and determination, finding oil in Iran proved elusive, and his correspondence between 1905 and 1908 reveals the uncertainty of exploration in the Bakhtiyari Mountains.[78]

From the beginning of operations the company found it difficult to procure guides and guards. In November 1905, Reynolds wrote to the Bakhtiyari *ilkhan*, Samsam al-Saltana, that all the *savars* sent to protect his crew at Shardin expected him to pay them and feed their horses, as they had no money and had received nothing from their chieftain, Khuda Karim Khan of the Chahar Lang. What is more, they insisted it was the custom of English travelers to pay their guides and escorts. To make matters more difficult, Shahbaz, the horseman ordered by Samsam al-Saltana to guide Reynolds through the routes into Maydan-i Naftun, abandoned the party at Ram Hurmuz.[79] In December 1905, Reynolds reported to the *ilkhan* that as he and his crew entered the Bakhtiyari Mountains via Ahvaz, they were met by angry tribesmen who violently threatened to stop the company's work:

> Dear Friend, I arrived here safely on 2nd December though shot at by the men of Shaikh Rashid at Shake, about ten or fifteen shots were fired at me, they mistaking my caravan for your men coming to attack them. This happened on the 1st December. Fortunately no one was hurt. On reaching this I find a report current that you have died suddenly, which may God forbid! I do not however believe the report. Yesterday I received a letter from my surveyor whom I left at Marmaten to survey the ground. He writes me as follows: that on 1st December for the purposes of his work he went near the village of Mahomet Tahir Khan where he was told that "it is not permitted for you to travel in our country, and if you have not a guard, I will break your head." On 2nd December, two men from Mirza Jowad Sadur ul-Ashraf came to him asking him by what order he had pitched his tent at Marmaten, and on 3rd December they kept troubling him asking him by what order he worked in the land of Sarim ul-Mulk saying "we will not let you work in this country." You will see that it is impossible to work among the wild men of these parts without a proper authority from you, and as the delay in communicating with you is very great, I must beg that you will forthwith send such orders in writing as being respected will absolutely put an end to all behaviour such as I have described in this and my letter to you of 28th November in the future.[80]

There was clearly resentment toward the presence of the oil company in the Bakhtiyari territory.

The guarding arrangements were further complicated by the Qajar's administration of the Bakhtiyari and the complex intra-tribal rivalries between the khans. In January 1906, the shah deposed Samsam al-Saltana as *ilkhan* in favor of his half-brother 'Ali Quli Khan Sardar As'ad, only adding to the

Bakhtiyari tribes in the vicinity of the oil fields, 1908. Lorimer Collection, SOAS.

confusion surrounding the guarding arrangements. Writing from the capital Evelyn Grant Duff, the British chargé d'affaires, shed light on the role of the Qajar government in bringing about the reappointment of the Bakhtiyari *ilkhan*ship. From Tehran Duff claimed, "I strongly suspect that the Persian Government, who are very jealous of our dealings with the Bakhtiyari, are supplanting the Samsam al-Saltana and keeping him here."[81] A correspondence from Samsam al-Saltana and Shahab al-Saltana to Sardar As'ad verified that "the Persian government declined to allow them to leave Tehran until they had revised their agreement with the D'Arcy Oil Syndicate in such a way that it meets with the approval of the shah."[82]

Qajar policies created divisions among the ruling khans and their retinues, with "powerful factions formed and hostilities engaged."[83] Of the signatories to the Bakhtiyari Oil Agreement, Samsam al-Saltana belonged to one faction while his half-brother Sardar As'ad was loyal to another. Having "visions of attaining immediate wealth from the oil," the Bakhtiyari khans were each seeking control of the payments for the guards.[84] In Tehran, Samsam al-Saltana contested his brother's appointment as *ilkhan*. Fearing that "the Naphtha

Company will pay money for guards directly to ʿAli Quli Khan," he requested "that no money should be paid without sealed receipt of all the chiefs party to the agreement."[85] Meanwhile, Sardar Asʿad's younger brother, Khusraw Khan, perhaps emboldened by his brother's appointment as *ilkhan*, jockeyed for control over the guards' subsidies, reportedly driving away the guards sent by Samsam al-Saltana to protect the oil fields at Mamatain.[86] Indeed, Reynolds had trouble even keeping in contact with the ruling khans. It was uncertain whether a letter would reach the *ilkhan* Sardar Asʿad in the mountains.

Meanwhile, the Bakhtiyari khans were attempting to renegotiate the terms of the agreement. When Samsam al-Saltana and Shahab al-Saltana suddenly returned to the posts of *ilkhan* and *ilbayg* in September 1906, they refused to approve the commencement of work at Maydan-i Naftun until the agreement was revised. With all the trouble surrounding oil in their land, the khans recognized that what they had hoped to be a blessing was a curse. Thoroughly disappointed in the oil agreement, the khans recommended that the company drill no new wells until a settlement was reached:

> Mr. Preece and the manager know that when we made the agreement we were very much disturbed and could not go into details and consider the question carefully as to its advantages and disadvantages. We now see that it has great disadvantages and we have no doubt that the British Government, with its well known sense of Justice, will not admit that we should lose in this business and will see that we should not incur any loss on account of the agreement in question. . . . We therefore request you to instruct the manager not to have any new wells made till the agreement is modified and the objections are removed. We will then help in the progress of his intentions.[87]

Moreover, in the summer of 1906, Lutf ʿAli Khan Shuja al-Sultan (later given the title Amir Mufakhkham) complained in a letter to the Qajar Minister Mushir al-Dawla that the Syndicate had never asked his permission to drill for oil on his lands.[88] Anticipating some of the divisions that would arise during the tribes' emergence in the Constitutional Revolution in 1909, Lutf ʿAli Khan claimed that his property had been taken over by the company, which had brought in machinery for the purpose of extracting oil while he was serving Crown Prince Muhammad ʿAli Mirza in Azarbayjan province. Hinting that the new shah had refused to recognize the Bakhtiyari agreement, he ordered the company to halt operations:

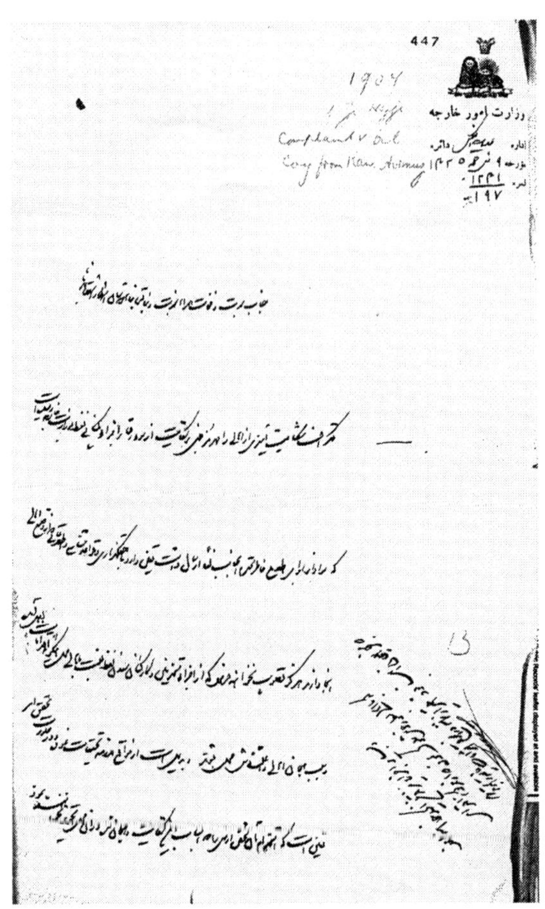

447

1907

وزارت امور خارجه

Letter from the chiefs and inhabitants of Ram Hurmuz to the British legation, January 1907. BNA, Foreign Office 248/923.

Being attached to the crown prince and being sent on duty in different parts of the country, I did not know exactly what was going on back home and used to hear from time to time that an English company intend to work the petroleum wells in the Bakhtiyari district but I did not know when and how. Now I hear from my people that the Company, without my knowledge, is carrying on operations for extracting petroleum and that they are bringing machines for that purpose. It appears from the inquiries I have made that it has been stipulated in the concession that the company must buy or lease any lands required by them. I also understand that the Persian Government has refused to recognize a proposed agreement between some of the Bakhtiyari chiefs and the company. It therefore appears that they have no right to carry on operations in my property without my consent.[89]

۵۰۱

از اصفهان به طهران — اداره تلگرافی دولت علیه ایران — صفحه

نمره	عدد کلمات	تاریخ اصل مطلب	اطلاعات
۱۶۷	۲۸۰	روز — ساعت — دقیقه	

بتاریخ ۲۵ شهر — ساعت — دقیقه — سنه ۱۳۲۵

Letter from Samsam al-Saltana, *ilkhan*, and Shahab al-Saltana, *ilbayg*, to the British legation in 1907, complaining of the policies of the consul of Ahvaz. BNA, Foreign Office 248/923.

Reacting against British imperial expansion on their land and the raised expectations of law and order that accompanied it, the khans asserted their local power and authority.

The khans' opposition to the oil company coincided with the resistance of the tribal rank and file. The archives chronicle the widespread disdain on the part of tribesmen for the foreign oil company. The company and consular archives recount a history of popular resistance and protest against the foreign control and unequal distribution of the oil revenues. One is likely to find it anywhere there is foreign control over a country's natural resources. In this context, the oil fields became the site of violent encounters between the Bakhtiyari and company staff.

In the winter of 1906, the *nayib al-hukuma* or deputy governor of Ram Hurmuz, stopped the work of a company surveyor disdained by many villagers, preventing him from going to Shardin for four or five days because the tribes in the neighborhood of the oil springs were "disturbed and robbers are numerous."[90] When Reynolds complained in writing to the *ilbayg*, Khusraw Khan, the latter sent a sharply defiant response:

> What have you to do with Soldiers and Guards, as to when they came and when they did not come, when they were present and when they were absent? . . . A thousand such men as you employed could not guard you, were it not for the well organized Government of the Bakhtiyari. In such a way have we organized our country and its boundaries that never is it necessary to have any Guard for anything at all.[91]

Reynolds feared "the wild creatures, the Lur . . . over-running the Camp and works and doing as they please."[92] In late March, following the Iranian New Year, Reynolds again complained to the *ilbayg*, claiming "no horsemen have been deputed to accompany my Caravan to Ram Hurmuz where my depot is and it travels quite unprotected and with no watchmen at night."[93] He also sent the following statement of his expectations of the Bakhtiyari:

> To all Kadkhodas and Kalantars who are under the orders of the Bakhtiyari Chiefs, they are hereby informed that George B. Reynolds, Manager of the Oil Company, may come to visit your neighborhood, or he may send some of his men, and if so you will please remain in his or their service. I would wish you to accompany him, giving him every sort of assistance and sending such number of Sowars and Guides with him as may be needed and to take him to any place he may want to visit and you will provide him with night watchmen. Let this order remain in his hands or in the hands of the man who brings it, to enable him to show it to other Kadkhodas and Kalantars. When he leaves you take a certificate from him and note that he is not to pay you for watchmen or guards.[94]

The correspondence between Reynolds and the *ilbayg* seems to have ended there.

But the hostile encounters between the company and tribes continued. In one incident, tribesmen "laid hands on" the theodolite of the company's surveyor, shook it, and told him they would break his head and his instrument.

Another time, a Lur by the name of Jahangir Khan demanded compensation for the land occupied at Maydan-i Naftun and threatened to stop the work. Coming down again to the fields the following year he demanded 500 tumans in compensation for the ground taken up by the company in the district, adding that "the land was all his and the Khans had not a say in the matter."[95] At Ram Hurmuz the guards abandoned their posts and the company's surveyor while "wandering Lurs" scared the company's mules away and took target practice at the boilers.[96] In 1907, tribesmen stole the large bellows and small forge, unnoticed by the guards on duty. The damaged and mangled bellows, needed by the blacksmiths in the oil works, were found early the next morning about a quarter of a mile away.[97]

In the same year, H. E. Bradshaw, the engineer in charge of building the road to Masjid-i Sulayman, complained about the laborers sent by Samsam al-Saltana. He wrote that a gang of tribesmen had attacked the workers and after "severely mauling several of them, persuaded all the rest of them to stop work" and demand higher wages, "ten tomans and twelve tomans per man per month and no limit to the time they stayed, whether one day or three months." The leaders of the event, Rahman of the village of Farsan and Ruz 'Ali and Panj 'Ali, both of Dih Chishma, insulted and used "the most abusive language towards" the company's European employees, threatening their lives and property.[98] The reports of incidents in the oil fields and camps do not end there. A letter received from Masjid-i Sulayman complained of serious insubordination among the workmen and of robberies in which sheep were stolen at Mamatain during the nights of March 18 and 19. When the khans sent *savars* to collect a fine from the villages of Mamatain and Shardin, "all men from Number Two Well [at Shardin] fled to the Hills," shutting down work for the day.[99]

These disorders occurred in large part because the khans were divided and in competition with one another. In April 1907, Shahab al-Saltana was appointed *ilkhan* in place of Samsam al-Saltana, but although he managed to win the favor of the central government and the British, he proved to be ineffective as *ilkhan*.[100] Moreover, his appointment incited opposing factions of the Bakhtiyari to armed clashes. Samsam al-Saltana, the former *ilkhan*, refused the Persian government's order to come to Tehran and allowed his armed retinues to plunder the oil fields. He also incited the neighboring Kuhgilu tribes to rob the oil works at Mamatain, where numerous loaded mules were carried away. And for weeks the Bakhtiyari khan had a party of seventy followers on the Tehran-Isfahan Road, robbing European travelers of all their belongings and raiding the country between the mountains and Isfahan.[101] In such a climate, it came as no surprise that the rank and file of tribesmen became restive as well.

In June 1907, some workers at Batvand assaulted a company driller after a crowd gathered on a hillside a few yards from the company's camp and scuffled with some of Bradshaw's men riding to Masjid-i Sulayman. Rasuk Alias, the Mirza at Batvand, who experienced the attack firsthand, described the incident to Reynolds:

> I was going to Maidan-i Naftun with some of Mr. Bradshaw's men, I was riding by mule, and a few yards from the Camp there was a crowd of Batwand people waiting for us on the hill by the way. As soon as we came near to them, one of the crowd, by the name ʻAli, with a stick in his hand, began beating the men who were with me and the others started throwing stones all round me. Aidi, the brother of Mashdi Muhammad ʻAli, late Kaid of Batwand, told them to kill me as it were thro' me that they were not engaged as laborers.[102]

As a company driller named Harris emerged from his tent, he was "waylaid" with stones by a Lur called Qasim, who shouted in Persian, "Either we will work by force or you must shift your Camp from here, or we will return shortly and tear your tents to pieces."[103]

On another occasion, at Maydan-i Naftun, a Lur named Khurma'i became "violent" and "aggressive" as a result of the drilling on his land. Near the time of completion of the road to Maydan-i Naftun late in the summer of 1907, he had "severely thrashed one of Mr. Crawford's water carriers" to the point "that medical attendance was necessary for the man." The same Lur had "also threatened to beat anyone in the employ of Mr. Crawford who came for water, and to stop Mr. Crawford obtaining the water necessary for the camp."[104] Fears were widespread of tribal violence against company employees.[105] The company came to realize that "no responsible representative of the Ilkhan" was to be found from Batvand to Maydan-i Naftun.[106] Company reports give a sense of the precariousness of oil exploration in the Bakhtiyari hinterland and the sense of panic over the lack of guards:

> The tribes-men are coming down here by the hundreds at this time of year, and as they are all around us, our being practically without Guards does not tend to add to their respect for us, which is at any time, as you know well, nil. . . . They seem to be pretty well occupied just now, fighting among themselves but who knows, they may

seek pastures new in tackling us, seeing our unprotected state. Only a few days ago in a fight just near the Camp, some 7 men were killed and 8 or 9 men, women, and children badly wounded. . . . With this state of affairs continually going on you must be ready prepared for anything."[107]

The intra-tribal feuds of the Bakhtiyari, coupled with the widespread local resentment over the exploration for oil by an intrusive European company, had resulted in a myriad of disturbances. The violent encounters between the company and the tribes also suggested the environmental, economic, and cultural changes occurring at the time.

Oil and Empire

In its efforts to secure the oil fields, the company consulted David Lockhart Robinson Lorimer, the first British vice-consul at Ahvaz in the southwestern province of Khuzistan. Lorimer effectively oversaw British interests in the oil-rich Zagros Mountains between 1904 and 1909.[108] With the Anglo-Russian entente of 1907 and the division of Iran into two spheres of influence on the horizon, Lorimer broke all protocol in his interactions with the khans. By 1906 he had assumed the role of the company's liaison in negotiations with the Bakhtiyari khans; in this position he proved intent on impressing upon the tribes the weight of the British Empire in southern Iran. He viewed the Bakhtiyari as primitive tribes that had to be prevented from hindering progress, by force if necessary. Lorimer led the company's effort to enforce a modern, disciplined industrial order upon the Bakhtiyari tribes.

Stationed in Luristan since 1903, Lorimer had become familiar with the local dialects and geography of the tribal populations. He seemed to understand that the opening of the Bakhtiyari country and the exploration for oil were forever changing a way of life, as reflected by his effort to collect and record Bakhtiyari vernacular folklore. Collecting Bakhtiyari songs about the seasons and the tribal migrations through the mountains, Lorimer set out to write down and record the Bakhtiyari dialect before it was diluted by the Persian of the towns.[109] What is more, Lorimer's experience of violent encounters with the tribes of the Zagros perhaps shaped his outlook toward the Bakhtiyari. In November 1904, while traveling in Luristan with an escort furnished by the chiefs of the Dirakvand tribe, he and a military attaché from Tehran were attacked and injured by a group of tribesmen.[110] Perhaps partly as a result of this incident Lorimer adopted a harsh and brazen attitude toward the Bakhtiyari and other Lur tribes, and his demeanor was evident in his dispatches from Ahvaz.

Lorimer used his authority as an agent of the British government to add urgency to the D'Arcy Syndicate's demands for the security of the oil works. His policies toward the Bakhtiyari gave the D'Arcy Oil Concession an undeniably British imperial stamp. The consul at Ahvaz made it clear that the British government had a firm interest in the D'Arcy Concession, that the exploration for oil in Iran concerned the crown directly. Disregarding the *ilkhan*'s order to drill no new wells until a settlement was reached, Lorimer commanded Reynolds to proceed with work at the promising new site of Maydan-i Naftun and "to engage for himself a few guards," adding that "the Bakhtiaris must not be allowed to think they can stop the work of the Company."[111] Such bold and heavy-handed tactics only fueled the resistance of the tribes around Maydan-i Naftun, who threatened to stop the work unless they received compensation for land taken by the company.[112]

Breaking the native chain of command, Lorimer wrote directly to the appointed head guard, As'adallah Khan, whom he blamed for never being present at the works and for not supplying guards to various camps and caravans that were subsequently robbed of mules and goods. He ordered the head guard to improve security and to come at once to the oil fields.[113] In his reply, As'adallah expressed some of the Bakhtiyari's widely held misgivings about the consul:

> You wrote that it was necessary to send up to 40 guards. The reason of this I have not heard. You wish the right of defence and protection from us, not that of demanding that we supply cooks, butlers, and servants. Should anything ever befall to make it necessary for you to have sowars or riflemen assuredly we will send 200. But no such talk has ever been held with the Khans or with us that 40 men should be sent. You also have no right to make excessive claims, that you should make demands contrary to all laws and regulations. If the Khans give such orders I shall comply with them. We have not such a number of men without employment to send there to endure the cold and rain. You also will not suffer to the extent of 100 *Tumans* by making a place for the Guards to live in. Whatever orders the Khans may give I am ready to obey. Tomorrow we shall send a few men and Azizullah will also visit you. At this time we have not permission to send more

> than ten riflemen. It is also not becoming that you should display such insistence (*sakhtgiri*). We are not serving for a few days that you should take captious objections to things, on the other hand we hope to render greater and better services than these, and we hope to win the approval both of the Khans and yourself. Without doubt it is due from your rank to display love and kindness towards us. It is certain that at the time of writing you were suffering from annoyance over some extraneous matter, otherwise we cannot imagine that we would have been the object of such unkindness.[114]

Lorimer thought little of such objections and continued to make exacting demands on the Bakhtiyari khans.[115]

In spring 1907, Lorimer held negotiations with the Bakhtiyari khans at Kima, near Ram Hurmuz. The Bakhtiyari felt they had tolerated all sorts of illegal actions on the part of the company. As the consul saw the situation, the treatment of the company's officials by various khans and the thefts they permitted had led "the surrounding savages to the natural conclusion that they could insult or interfere with anyone connected with the company." [116] When Lorimer pressured the khans to settle the amount of compensation for thefts, a vexed Samsam al-Saltana responded that they would pay the amount due but only on the condition, put in writing, that the British would not hold them responsible for the security of the works in the future. The khans threatened to abandon the company to its own resources. Lorimer considered such actions as the khan's attempt to mock (*rishkhand*) "the Legation whom they knew could not see the state of things here with their own eyes" and those less familiar with the tribes.[117]He himself was less convinced of the khans' "bluffs," citing current political divisions within the Bakhtiyari tribal leadership during the Constitutional Revolution of 1906–1911. Samsam al-Saltana and Shahab al-Saltana, the *ilkhan* and *ilbayg*, were "isolated and far from secure position," and there were also rumors that the latter's younger brothers, Sultan Muhammad and Sarim al-Mulk, were dissatisfied and had joined Lutf 'Ali Khan in Tehran. Meanwhile Sardar As'ad's faction was anticipating "future causes of friction among themselves and with the Central Government."

Lorimer sought to take advantage of the divisions among the khans. Further, the consul was certain "the Khans would as soon part with their lives as with the two thousand pounds a year and the hope of three percent of shares." Nor would the khans want the tribes, among whom the oil fields were situated, to take general license to rob the company and its staff. As Lorimer put it, "The Khans would be as alive as we are to the risks incurred by opening the way to the tribes, and would quite know that they would in the long run have personally to account for any grave occurrences inspired."[118]

But this was a miscalculation of the Bakhtiyari's genuine dissatisfaction with oil exploration and the company's presence on their land. On visiting the oil works, Samsam al-Saltana and Shahab al-Saltana called on Lorimer's camp, raising three principal points: (1) the agreement should receive the endorsement of the Qajar government; (2) the khans should be relieved of responsibility for losses caused by the Kuhgilu tribes under the jurisdiction of Fars Province; and (3) all land occupied, whether cultivated or not, should be paid for.[119] After receiving another letter from Reynolds that criticized the situation in the fields and made additional claims for thefts, Samsam al-Saltana became enraged during an open tribal assembly. He "at once fell into a fury, declaring his inability to carry on affairs in the face of such inexorable and unconscionable exactingness on [the part of the company], and saying that he would repay all the money received and wash his hands of all responsibility, and that he would forthwith withdraw all the guards."[120] In the end, Lorimer departed from Kima empty-handed after twenty-two days of unsuccessful negotiation with the Bakhtiyari.

The rigid demands and tactics of Lorimer and Reynolds did not always advance the cause of exploration in the Bakhtiyari land. Rather, company agents antagonized the tribes and provoked animosities between the two sides. Company representatives could have secured the cooperation of the Bakhtiyari with a keener, and less imperialistic, understanding of their tribal society and position as a powerful federation on the periphery of Iran. Instead, they viewed the Bakhtiyari, as the more sympathetic Layard had a century before, as primitive and "wild tribes" awaiting progress.

By August 1907, Lorimer had urged the introduction of British Indian troops to protect the oil fields in Iran. He forwarded the reports of insecurity from the fields, along with his own commentary, to Sir Cecil Spring-Rice, the British minister plenipotentiary in Tehran. Lorimer judged the situation in the Bakhtiyari lowlands to be "very serious" and warned of "the complete sense of impunity among the tribesmen" that put the lives of the European employees of the company in constant danger. The khans were divided and punished criminals only "under extreme pressure" and "after long delay," with "no moral effect" on the tribes.[121] In Lorimer's jaded view, this was primarily due to the khans' "total lack of administrative capacity, their want of trustworthy underlings, and their domestic quarrels which make them afraid in many cases of alienating to a rival the support of tribesmen who look on any form of discipline with abhorrence."[122] He portrayed the rank and file of the Bakhtiyari tribesmen as a dangerous class of rebellious characters ready to break out in open revolt:

> The serious element in the situation is the character of the Bakhtiari Tribesmen. Sudden and ungoverned in their passions, they are accustomed to exercise them among themselves with little regard to future consequences. . . . Their relations with Europeans in the past have been almost nil, and they have been guided in them by a vague apprehension that unknown calamities must follow injury to a European. This fear is however gradually disappearing throughout Persia, and during the past year or two the Bakhtiaris have been conducting a series of experiments on their own account. The results of these can only be tending to assure them that Europeans and their property are in no way inviolate, and they have gained the certainty that their Khans are either unable or opposed to securing for Europeans effective protection.[123]

The security of the oil fields, Lorimer claimed, required a British force to discipline tribesmen who threatened to halt the company's work.

For the consul the Bakhtiyari's autonomy mattered little in comparison with British imperial projects. Although the Bakhtiyari were on the verge of becoming icons of the Iranian Constitutional Revolution, they were in Lorimer's judgment "not morally qualified for independence" and required "a prompt check."[124] The consul's campaign to convince his superiors of the necessity of protecting the oil fields with foreign guards was highly successful in the short term. Having convinced Cecil Spring-Rice that the tribesmen were beyond all control, Lorimer wrote to Charles Marling, counselor to the British Embassy in Tehran, requesting seventeen British Indian soldiers, as well as a junior British officer to learn Persian and work under him at Ahvaz.[125] Lorimer sought to secure the employment of detachments of the Bengal Lancers, a British Indian force, as sentries wherever Europeans (or Canadians) were engaged in work, in the hope that this would give company workers more security and confidence in their surroundings. More important, the move was intended to have "a moral effect on the Lurs" by assigning a number of mounted guards to protect the area of drilling and accompany the syndicate's officials on the roads between the fields.[126] The consul made it seem like a desperate situation: With the oil fields under attack by unruly tribes, the introduction of British Indian troops was preferable to the company having to abandon work at Masjid-i-Sulayman.[127]

In late September, an emboldened Lorimer left Isfahan, taking with him a guard from Zill al-Sultan as well as three Bakhtiyari guides, to hold half-hearted and antagonistic discussions with the khans. He announced his impending arrival in advance to Samsam al-Saltana at Shalamzar, intimating his desire to be received with an *istiqbal*, or an official reception on the road, a courtesy the khans had yet to show him. The consul was met and welcomed by Murtaza Quli Khan, the *ilkhan*'s son, and a group of horsemen and escorted to the *ilkhan*'s residence. But Lorimer's negotiation tactics again frustrated the khans to the point that they continued to try to break their commercial ties to British companies by shutting down the oil fields and closing down the Lynch Road as a caravan route. The Bakhtiyari khans complained that the company was disrupting lives and offending the local population while demanding calm so it could conduct its operations with more ease. The vexed khans plainly suggested their desire for the cancellation of the Bakhtiyari Oil Agreement in a letter to the consul of Ahvaz:

> We restrained the people of Mamatain and Shardin who were daily complaining and crying out against the tyranny and oppression of the employees of the Syndicate. At no time may we have failed to serve you, and however much the Bakhtiari tribes complained, we have kept them in order, and up to now have not suffered them to make an outcry, but the time is near when the means of control will pass from our hands and the Bakhtiari will break out and rise up against this contract and agreement which we have made. In view of our having thus always been ready as we are now to serve your interests and commands we have failed to understand the reason for the unkindness which you have displayed towards us. If it is in your mind to break off the agreement we are only too willing and anxious for this, for the reason that the Bakhtiaris have raised their voices in this affair and by one means or other we have reduced everyone to silence, but we are tired and oppressed by the course which things have taken at Mamatain and Maidan Munaftun. The Bakhtiari tribes have broken out into complaints and are appealing against the acts of oppression of the Oil people. If this agreement and what it entails is cancelled it will be better for ourselves and the tribes and we will be at peace.[128]

The khans sincerely seemed prepared to cut their ties to the British company.

Undeterred, Lorimer then left Shalamzar for Batvand, where he intended to personally find and punish the tribesmen who had earlier attacked the company driller "Harris."[129] Reaching the village, Lorimer arrested two suspects and "had them tied to the carts of the Oil Syndicate, and well beaten in public," after which they were "turned out of the village bag and baggage."[130] Lorimer boasted that this action had instilled a "moral effect" on the people of Batvand, although he still feared that with the "Nomads due shortly in the neighbourhood," there was no assurance that the khans could "preserve order and secure the Syndicate against aggression."[131] Lorimer used these reports to full effect, warning that more aggressive behavior by the tribesmen was to come as they moved down to the lowlands for the winter.[132]

The *ilkhan* and *ilbayg* complained in writing of Lorimer's policies in a letter to Spring-Rice at the British legation in Tehran. Lorimer, they wrote, was causing "unprecedented difficulties" with them by withholding sums of money due to be paid for the guarding of the oil fields. The khans concluded that such "proceedings are intolerable" and requested that "the affairs of the Bakhtiyari be referred to the Isfahan Consul" once again.[133] In response, Spring-Rice upheld Lorimer's position, citing the original concession for the Bakhtiyari Road, signed 23 April 1897, as well as article 6 of the Bakhtiyari Agreement, which stipulated that "the Imperial Persian Government grants to the concessionaires the right of protecting the whole road and all caravanserais and the concessionaires engage to hold themselves responsible for the safety of all caravans and all in connection therewith, either as regards cash, animals, merchandise, or persons, over all parts of the road."[134] Spring-Rice further stated that Consul Lorimer was the trustee of the British government in Khuzistan and the work of the oil company was under his authority.

The Bakhtiyari khans, having no doubt heard of the impending arrival of the Indian guards, also hastened to show they were maintaining order in the land. They wrote to Lorimer describing the steps they had taken to protect the oil fields and promised to do "everything to secure the ease and comfort of the company's employees and laborers." These measures included the appointment of headmen to oversee the tribal migrations to the winter pastures that season and the supervision of the tribes in the vicinity of Maydan-i Naftun.[135] The syndicate resumed the payment of the guard installments in full to secure quiet working conditions for the months to come. With Iran in the midst of a revolution, when the shah's orders were "not even running in Tehran," the company had no alternative native force on which it could rely but the Bakhtiyari. In a memorandum, Consul Preece of Isfahan even suggested, "When it was arranged to pay the khans 2,000 pounds per annum, it was done as much for permission to use their ground as for guards."[136] The work being carried out at Maydan-i Naftun was of such promise, he urged, that it was not worth sacrificing over a few pounds. In Lorimer's prevailing view, however, the ineffectiveness of the Bakhtiyari guards and the lack of security in the oil fields had emboldened the surrounding tribes and made the introduction of troops an absolute necessity.

In November 1907, Arnold Talbot Wilson and twenty men from the Eighteenth Bengal Lancers departed from India for Masjid-i Sulayman.[137] The Qajar government scrambled to respond to and address the situation in Khuzistan, hoping to avoid the introduction of foreign troops on Iranian soil. The Persian minister of foreign affairs, Mushir al-Dawla, wrote to the British legation insisting that the Persian government was capable of protecting the employees of the D'Arcy Oil Syndicate independently and providing a secure environment for exploration. Moreover, the minister enclosed a telegram he had received from the Bakhtiyari khans to the effect that the employees of the company were "enjoying peace and harmony," removing any need for the introduction of foreign troops, whose presence would not only make an "unfavorable impression," but also taint the good relations between Iran and the British government. According to Mushir al-Dawla, "The collection of Indian Sawars in the district and their dealings with the inhabitants whose character is to a certain extent known will possibly give trouble both to the Persian Government and the Legation. . . . No doubt the local chiefs can make better arrangements for security and peace for the oil employees."[138] If the detachments of the Bengal Lancers had already landed in Iran, the Persian minister insisted, then they had to be withdrawn. It was all too little too late. On 20 January 1908, Lorimer arrived at Maydan-i Naftun, accompanied by the newly arrived British officers Arnold Talbot Wilson and J. Ranking, as well as the soldiers of the Bengal Lancers.[139]

The First Oil

The guarding of the fields soon would be inconsequential if oil was not discovered—and given the company's poor fortunes since exploration began, that possibility seemed likely. As previously mentioned, by the fall of 1907, Reynolds had closed down work at Mamatain and Shardin, where the two wells reached 2,000 feet without striking oil, and had moved all the company's rigs

The workers at Masjid-i Sulayman, 1910. BP.

to an open ledge near a shallow stream about two miles away from the ancient fire temple of Masjid-i Sulayman. Despite the arrival of the Bengal Lancers and the added British imperial presence, confrontations took place when the tribes reached their winter pastures. The stream of negative reports from Reynolds continued to flow:

> Nomads are now beginning to reach the Maidan Munaftan, and Mr. Bradshaw has already had trouble with them, though as yet it has not gone beyond words. . . . The country generally is in a very disturbed condition, caravans having been looted during the last week or two. . . . Communications with the Khans practically impossible and messengers can't be procured.[140]

Reynolds's sense of anxiety was the result of nearly six years' exploration without finding oil, an outcome that had led D'Arcy and the directors of the syndicate to lose faith in the venture and consider closing it down. The company's difficult financial straits and D'Arcy's limited funds had been revealed in 1905, when he enlisted the aid of the Burma Oil Company, a British firm engaged in oil production in Burma, to continue operations, forming the Concessions Syndicate Limited, based in Glasgow. In the spring of 1908, the syndicate sent word by telegraph to Reynolds that their funds were exhausted and there was no more capital for further exploration under the D'Arcy Concession. D'Arcy had "already spent more than he could afford—about two hundred and fifty thousand pounds," and therefore Reynolds was "to cease work, dismiss the staff, dismantle anything worth the cost for re-shipment, and come home."[141] Reynolds decided to allow work to continue until he received written confirmation of the syndicate's command.

While Reynolds waited, at 4:30 a.m. on 26 May 1908 oil was struck at Well Number 1B, one of the two wells at Masjid-i Sulayman. Wilson, who was sleeping outside his tent near the rig when the discovery was made, recalled, "It rose fifty feet or so above the top of the rig, smothering the drillers and their devoted Persian staff who were nearly suffocated by the accompanying gas."[142] This day saw the birth of the oil industry in the Middle East. The British engineers and workers took off their hats and rubbed the oil on their faces. Even the local workers rejoiced and celebrated. Wilson wired secret messages to Lorimer, delivering the news. Not having a code, Wilson wrote the following words: "See Psalm 104 verse 15 third sentence, and Psalm 114 verse 8 second sentence." Referring to the Old Testament, Lorimer saw that these passages read: "That he may bring out of the earth oil to make him a cheerful countenance" and "The flint stone into a springing well."[143]

The discovery of oil at Maydan-i Naftun changed the stakes of the D'Arcy Oil Concession altogether. As far as the syndicate was concerned their financial dilemmas were resolved. Plans were made for a pipeline to be constructed to carry the oil approximately 100 miles south to the new refinery at Abadan, near the Persian Gulf.[144] For their part the Bakhtiyari khans sought to claim their share of the profits while demanding the withdrawal of the Indian guards from Bakhtiyari territory. In 1908, Sardar As'ad met with Charles Hardinge, then the permanent under-secretary of state for foreign affairs, and Henry Lynch, the financier of the Bakhtiyari Road project, among others in London.[145] Sardar As'ad promised to visit the oil works himself when he returned to Iran and see that workers were not being threatened by the tribes, adding that there was no further need for Indian guards to protect the oil fields. In addition, Sardar As'ad personally reiterated the Bakhtiyari's dislike for Lorimer, claiming that although British consuls had been cordial toward the Bakhtiyari, Lorimer had treated the tribes with open hostility. He appealed to Hardinge to help restore good relations between the British and the Bakhtiyari. Coinciding with the

Discovering oil—a gusher at Masjid-i Sulayman, with a Bakhtiyari tribesman in the foreground, 1908. BP.

newly crowned Muhammad ʿAli Shah's dissolution of the Parliament or Majlis (discussed in the next chapter), the meeting might have included some discussion of the Iranian Constitutional Revolution, although the particulars of this exchange remain unclear.[146] Sardar Asʿad might have gained some understanding of the British reaction to the Bakhtiyari's impending participation in the Constitutional Revolution.

By the summer of 1908, the company was contemplating whether it would retain the Indian guards following the upcoming spring season. Lorimer stressed the absolute necessity of keeping the Indian guards near the fields and predicted "trouble" if they were not retained.[147] Contrary to Lorimer, however, D'Arcy made his opinion known that he considered the retention of the Indian guards during the spring and summer unnecessary, since "the Bakhtiyari tribes have behaved well."[148] The removal of the Indian guards roughly coincided with the emergence of the Bakhtiyari in national politics during the Constitutional Revolution. In January 1909, Samsam al-Saltana and Ibrahim Khan Zargham al-Saltana led hundreds of Bakhtiyari horsemen into the city of Isfahan in support of the constitutional cause. By the summer of 1909 Sardar As'ad had returned to the Bakhtiyari Mountains from Europe and was gathering the tribes to march on Tehran to restore the Parliament or Majlis, which Muhammad 'Ali Shah Qajar (1907–1909) had bombarded. In spring 1909, with the tribes preparing to depart for the north, "there was great confusion and wild rumours of all kinds," including the hint that Sardar As'ad intended to break the new guarding arrangements unless the Bengal Lancers were removed and direct relations were maintained between the company and the Bakhtiyari.[149] In July 1909, the Indian guards were withdrawn, and soon after Lorimer left the Zagros Mountains.

Before dismissing the soldiers from British India, the company ensured the security of the oil fields by gaining more direct control over the Bakhtiyari guards. The departure of the Bengal Lancers and the new arrangements reached between the company and the Bakhtiyari were facilitated by the efforts of Dr. M. Y. Young, the company medic who had arrived from Glasgow in 1907. Young became the leading representative between the company and the Bakhtiyari. Following the departure of Lorimer and Reynolds, he sought to mend the relationship with the Bakhtiyari and proved to be indispensable to the Anglo-Persian Oil Company. Among the Bakhtiyari tribes, Young earned the reputation of a trusted doctor, overcoming "the distrust of the tribesmen and their women and their just fears of surgical operations performed by European doctors, of whom they had little or no experience." Young also became "exceedingly competent in the Persian language and familiar with the local dialects," leading him to become the company's most effective representative to the local tribes.[150]

Earlier in the year, the resourceful Young had secured supplementary guarding arrangements with the Bakhtiyari khans on behalf of the company. In February 1909, Ghulam Husayn Khan Sardar Muhtasham requested that Young travel to Malamir to attend to his ill son, and at that time the Scottish medic met several of the leading Bakhtiyari khans. Staying as their guest until the boy's condition improved days later, he attempted to bring about "an improvement in their relations with us, which, as we all know, and the khans above all, were not altogether what they should be."[151] While in the Bakhtiyari Mountains Young proceeded to sketch the outline of new guarding arrangements with the khans, even having them put their terms in writing.

The letters, sealed by Sardar Muhtasham and Sardar As'ad's son Ja'far Quli Khan Sardar Bahadur, outlined new terms for the guards. Perhaps most important, the guarding arrangements were to be turned over at once to the company and its manager, who was to fix and pay the guards' salaries, the sum of which would be deducted from the 2,000 pounds paid annually to the Bakhtiyari khans.[152] Perhaps with the Bakhtiyari's emergence in the Constitutional Revolution, the khans were seeking to settle their disputes with the oil company. What is more, as the Bakhtiyari joined the constitutionalist cause, it became important for them to protect the territorial integrity of Iran and eliminate the presence of the British Indian guards. Cooperation with the Bakhtiyari certainly also appealed to the British, who were well aware of the Bakhtiyari's rising political fortunes, although they were uncertain of the role the tribes would play in the future government of Iran.

A "Supplementary Agreement" between the Bakhtiyari khans and the company respecting the guarding of the oil fields was signed at Malamir on April 1, 1909, coinciding with the Constitutional Revolution and civil war in Iran. The khans and the syndicate agreed that the manager of the fields would pay all the guards, horsemen and footmen on the fifteenth of every month. The agreement further defined the salaries and the specific numbers of guards to be stationed.[153] The syndicate assumed "full control of all the Guards including the Chief of the Guards"; indeed, without permission from the manager of the fields neither the guards nor their horses could leave the camp.[154]

In the same year, the Anglo-Persian Oil Company formed in London with a capital of 2 million pounds, receiving all rights granted in the D'Arcy Concession. The formation of the company was an indication of the political and economic inroads the British had made in the tribal hinterland of Qajar Persia. The Anglo-Persian Oil Company was an imperialist venture soon linked to the British admiralty. It was common knowledge that before the company's formation the admiralty saw a copy of its charter and then made certain changes in the wording that made possible the inclusion of contracts for the supply of oil to fuel the British navy.[155]

In July 1911, the Anglo-Persian Oil Company completed a pipeline that carried oil from Maydan-i Naftun approximately 138 miles south to the new refinery at Abadan on the Persian Gulf. The completion of the pipeline signaled that the company had penetrated the Bakhtiyari land, mined its subterranean deposits of oil, and carried them away. In 1914, the British navy converted from coal to oil, making Britain profoundly dependent on a natural resource imported from Iran. To supply such a strategic commodity the British government purchased 51 percent of the stock of the Anglo-Persian Oil Company for 2 million pounds on the eve of the First World War. The British justified their action by claiming that oil initiated the development of Iran's economy

Moving pipes on iron-wheeled jimms drawn by mules for the construction of the pipeline from Masjid-i Sulayman to the Persian Gulf, 1909. BP.

and improved its "moral" character.[156] Winston Churchill, the first lord of the admiralty, was instrumental in garnering the government's 51 percent share of the Anglo-Persian Oil Company in 1914, declaring that the development of the oil fields at Maydan-i Naftun "would make the Persian Government strong and the tribesmen tame," while hastening "the gradual civilization of distant provinces" in Persia.[157] This civilizing mission became the pretext and justification for British oil exploration in the Bakhtiyari fields.

The Land Purchase of 1911

With its formation, the Anglo-Persian Oil Company embarked on efforts to officially acquire the oil fields from the Bakhtiyari. In the spring of 1911, land negotiations took place between the Bakhtiyari and the company, represented by Dr. Young. In a memorandum on the "Bakhtiyari Land Problem" written during the cold season of 1911, when the tribes were in the plains and foothills of the *garmsir*, Young outlined the company's predicament: It had an "oil territory" at Maydan-i Naftun, where operations were going on "without any very definite understanding with the owners of the land there."[158] During agreements the company had regarded the khans as the sole owners of the territory, and this policy had denied the rights of pastoralists and peasants to the land. Young wrote:

> The Lurs are resisting all our attempts to make use of any land, whether they actually require it or not. The Khans have done very little to stop such resistance and it seems as if at best they are able only to mitigate it. They now want to be compensated for every piece of ground we wanted to acquire, whether we build on it, drill on it, or travel on it, and before we know where we are we shall have to pay when we walk on it. The Khans are sorry for what they signed and are doing their best to retreat even from those terms agreed upon. The Company have . . . delayed the matter too long and on realizing its gravity only last winter, they very hastily committed themselves by word and deed, thereby exhibiting such weakness that the Khans, and indeed the whole countryside have become possessed of one notion: "Pay or we shall stop your work!"[159]

The tribes expelled from their land were interfering with the company's work during winter seasons. In his memorandum, Dr. Young described the anger of the tribesmen around Masjid-i Sulayman:

> The ordinary Lur, whose life depends on the few acres of land given him to cultivate, knows, as well as we do, that the Khans will pocket every available kran, even if it be for land which he, his father and forefathers have been cultivating. He knows further that once a settlement has been arrived at with the Khans, he will be expelled from the place and told to go find a place elsewhere, no more trouble being taken on his behalf. It is not an easy matter to move these people and as every piece of ground, in any way cultivable, is already taken up, we need not be at all surprised at his reluctance to go. Now such a Lur (he has a good many followers) can be no friend of ours. To his simple mind it appears that we have robbed him of his land, of his crops, of all he possesses, and not only have we not paid him for it, but have actually been the cause of his expulsion from the place altogether. Hence the resistance shown by some; and by others, the refusal to part with land under any consideration whatsoever. We can hardly blame these people since they are left uncompensated and unprovided for in every way. . . . In this way, we are breeding enemies all over the place

who take advantage of the slightest incident to cause a row. . . . The Company retaliates by complaining to the Chiefs who subject these people to harsh treatment and thereby "love" is not lost between our neighbours and ourselves.[160]

Although restricted, the Lurs continued to plough the lands of Maydan-i Naftun; some clans went so far as to plow around machinery laid ready for the construction of a rig, and others ploughed part of the company road to Masjid-i Sulayman. As for the khans, they had been forever delegitimized in the eyes of their subjects, "the people on the Maidan." Their decrees (*hukm*) to the people not to interrupt the company's work further alienated their constituents. The tribes had lost confidence in the chieftaincy. In a district in the north of the Bakhtiyari territory, the tribes would not allow the acting *ilkhan* and *ilbayg* to camp, although the khans had stayed there in the past.[161]

In 1911, as the company made preparations for renewed land negotiations with the Bakhtiyari representatives, G. B. Scott and "four natives" were completing the first detailed survey and map of the oil fields.[162] In mid-April, the figures from Scott's surveys became available. Surveying Maydan-i Naftun and its surroundings, the pipeline, the road, and the pumping station, Scott estimated damages to nearly 2,000 acres of old fallow, new fallow, and land under crop, as well as to 4,500 acres of hills and grazing lands.[163] Meanwhile Young established contact with Chahar Lang chieftains, such as Khuda Karim Khan, seeking to make them responsible for the security of the oil fields, roads, and telephone lines, which had been under attack by the Chahar Lang. He also convinced Sardar Muhtasham of the ruling Haft Lang to warn the tribes of the Maydan not to interfere with the company's work. Sardar Muhtasham gave Young an ominous warning: If the question of land compensation was not settled before the next winter, when the tribes again returned to the lowands, "he would be compelled to resign his leadership here and for his own safety he would get out of the country . . . implying that there would be an outbreak among the Lurs."[164]

With Young and Ranking representing the company and Sardar Muhtasham and Sardar Bahadur representing the Bakhtiyari khans, land negotiations took place at Masjid-i Sulayman on 17–18 April 1911.[165] Upon their arrival Sardar Muhtasham and Sardar Bahadur insisted on seeing the boundaries of the land, and for one-and-a-half days they climbed hills and walked around the oil fields with Young, Scott, and Ranking. According to Young, the khans indicated that ʿAli Quli Khan Sardar Asʿad was "their leading spirit";

"White beard" G. B. Scott and his Bakhtiyari assistants working on the first survey of the fields at Maydan-i Naftun, where the pipeline, the road, and the pumping station damaged nearly 2,000 acres of old fallow, new fallow, and land under crop, as well as 4,500 acres of hills and grazing lands, 1911. BP.

they continuously spoke in his name, "what he would accept, what he would refuse, what he would be pleased or displeased with."[166] When discussions began the main questions under negotiation centered on the compensation the tribe was to receive for arable, fallow, and non-arable land, as well as the price of the oil fields.

There were disagreements over the compensation for the different types of land: cultivated, old fallow, and non-arable. The company claimed that non-arable lands were "wasteland" and sought to acquire them at no charge. The khans contended that no land was free, while the company upheld the terms of the Bakhtiyari Agreement of 1905, which spelled out that the company was required to pay only for cultivated land, defined as land that had been farmed every second or third year. Thus old fallow, land not under cultivation for several years, was left vaguely undefined. The khans claimed that old fallow was cultivated land, as the *ra'iyat* farmed all flat land "at some time or another," making it therefore of equal value.[167] The khans also refused to give up the hills for free, claiming they were the grazing lands of the tribes. Moreover, the khans argued that the original Bakhtiyari Agreement contained no clause that bound them to supply non-arable land free of charge, an act that would entail excluding tribes from tracts of land that were their customary pastures. Furthermore the khans earned revenues when they taxed these grazing lands. The Bakhtiyari could not simply abandon the hills and pastures, as the khans stated to Young and Ranking: "We do not force you to buy them. Buy as many or as few *Jaribs* [approximately three acres] as you like, but let our tribes make use of the rest."[168] With the question of compensation for old fallow and grazing lands still unsettled, discussions shifted to the price of the land. In the end, the Anglo-Persian Oil Company purchased more than 6,000 acres of the Bakhtiyari's winter pastures and fields around Maydan-i Naftun from the khans for 22,000 pounds.

The Bakhtiyari khans began with an asking price of thirty-five pounds per acre for arable and three-and-a-half pounds per acre for non-arable land, based on calculations of the yield of the land. Although Young later admitted that "their rates were fair," he and Ranking countered the khans' offer, leading to the amount being lowered to fifteen pounds per acre of arable and three-and-a-third pounds per acre of non-arable land. When Young and Ranking refused this offer, negotiations broke off altogether. Young's good relations with the Bakhtiyari however, again served the company well. Young and the Bakhtiyari "had some heated discussions," but they maintained "a fairly friendly attitude" throughout the negotiations, a mood that neither Lorimer nor Reynolds had been able to nurture. As Young put it, "We were very careful in that respect and on the very day we broke off, I had them over to lunch at our house as if nothing had happened. I really thought that they would excuse themselves, but they came. Nevertheless, we all knew very well what it might mean to us were these people to leave in a rage and with the land question unsettled."[169] While wiring company superiors in Tehran, the convincing Dr. Young continued to hold "unofficial" negotiations. In a puzzling and naïve move, the khans agreed to a price of approximately twelve pounds per acre of arable and one pound per acre of non-arable land. As a "personal favour" to Young and a sign of their willingness to come to a settlement, they gave Young two-thirds of the total area of non-arable land for free. According to the survey's figures, this equaled 3,054 acres of land free of charge. Young summed up the deal with the claim, "We have bought about nine and half square miles or six thousand one hundred and thirty one acres of oil bearing land for twenty-two thousand pounds."[170]

Sardar Muhtasham, Sardar Bahadur, Young, and Scott then signed and sealed the original Persian text of the agreement, as well as copies of the company maps of the oil fields. The agreement still made no mention of payments for either old fallow or non-arable land. The Maydan-i Naftun became the property of the company and clear boundaries were established to repel local cultivators and nomads. The agreement established that the Bakhtiyari khans had sold all the Maydan-i Naftun to the First Exploitation Company. The defined lands became "the absolute property" of the company, which was free "to drill wells, to erect machinery, to build houses, to cultivate the land, to make gardens, and to utilize any water power of springs or rivers." The agreement also spelled out the cruel reality that the tribes would be expelled from the land:

> Moreover, none of the Bakhtiyari Khans shall have any right to make any further monetary claim in connection with this transaction and should any one of them do so, it shall be disregarded. Further, in the future, any Lurs who have hitherto inhabited and cultivated these lands, shall have no right to do so, or to graze their flocks and cattle within these boundaries. And thus also, any Lurs inhabiting the neighbourhood of the said lands, shall have no right whatever to enter, to cultivate, or to graze their flocks and cattle within these boundaries. Should they come and transgress the boundaries or disregard the rights of the company, or cause any damage, the Khans shall be held liable in compensation for the same.[171]

The immense implications of this sale of the Bakhtiyari fields apparently did not fully dawn upon the negotiating khans until after they had signed the deal. On the evening before the khans left Maydan-i Naftun, they sent a secret message to Young, asking him to come and meet them. In Young's words, "they seemed very cut up over the agreement" and begged him to use his best endeavors with the company's *mirzas* and others to keep the sale of the land secret for six months at least, to prevent word from getting "into the Persian newspapers in Teheran that they have handed over a portion of the Bakhtiari territory to the British."[172]

Conclusion

The following winter season proved an adverse time for the tribes in the area of Maydan-i Naftun. Although the khans had plans to compensate the tribes for the lands the company had acquired, they were so preoccupied with events in Tehran during the Constitutional Revolution that they overlooked the matter of compensation.[173] In September tribesmen began to arrive at the fields, only to find "that the land they have tilled for generations is no longer theirs."[174] Sultan Muhammad Khan, the acting *ilkhan* in the Bakhtiyari territory, informed Young frankly that he had "neither land nor money to offer" the tribes of the *garmsir*, who had been "reduced practically to starvation" and no longer had confidence in the khans.[175] Tribesmen still attempted to plough at Maydan-i Naftun, crossing the boundaries of company property and pitching their tents near the oil fields. On occasions, large crowds gathered for demonstrations and threatened to take back their land by force.

The exploration for oil in the Zagros Mountains had transformed environment and society on the southwestern periphery of Qajar Iran. The khans had relinquished their semi-independent position and tribal autonomy in the Zagros in exchange for British subsidies and a fixed share of the profits from the fields under their control. Although some tribal subjects had found work in the fields as laborers and guards, adapting to the changes brought about by oil exploration, in the end they gave more than they got. Near the fire temple of Masjid-i Sulayman, lands once used collectively for grazing and cultivation by the Bakhtiyari tribes had become the first commercial oil fields in Iran and the Middle East.

5

THE BAKHTIYARI TRIBES IN THE IRANIAN CONSTITUTIONAL REVOLUTION

"The Bakhtiyari tribes have at different times played an important part in the history of Persia. Their chiefs would descend into the plains at the head of large bodies of brave and daring horsemen. Sometimes they threatened Isfahan, the capital; at others they encountered the enemies of their country."

—AUSTEN HENRY LAYARD
Early Adventures in Persia, Susiana, and Babylonia

ON THE ROAD leading west from Isfahan into the Zagros Mountains and the province of Chahar Mahal and Bakhtiyari, past the town of Farsan, is a mountainous spot known as Pir Qar, or the "Old Cave." On the rock face of the mountain, worn away by the elements and the passage of time, is an inscription in Persian *nastaliq* script. Made on the order of ʿAli Quli Khan Sardar Asʿad in 1905, the inscription details the genealogy and history of the Bakhtiyari tribal confederation and memorializes the nineteenth-century chieftain Husayn Quli Khan Ilkhani, who united the tribes and raised them to power. Written in the "hope that the name of the clan will not be lost," the inscription was a sign of the autonomy of the tribes on the mountainous southwestern edge of Iran. Just above it another inscription, made a decade later, recounts the march of a thousand Bakhtiyari horsemen on Tehran in the summer of 1909 to restore the Parliament (Majlis) and constitutionalism (*mashrutiyat*) in Iran.

The Constitutional Revolution of 1906–1911 marked the onset of modern representative politics in Iran. Initiated during the reign of Muzaffar al-Din Shah Qajar (1896–1907), punctuated by a civil war (1908–1909), and finally overturned under pressure from foreign powers, the Constitutional Revolution introduced new social and political ideals in Iran, based on the rule of law (*qanun*) and the principle of individual rights.

Broad sections of the Iranian population participated in the revolution on both sides of the struggle, and the tribes were no exception. During the Constitutional Revolution, the loyalties of the tribes proved to be meaningful and decisive. What is more, the tribes found opportunities in revolutionary political culture. Under the electoral laws the tribes were counted among the inhabitants of their province and given the right to vote, while the Shahsevan, Qashqa'i, Khamsa, Turkmen, and Bakhtiyari were each to send one representative to the national assembly.[1] To these institutional changes were added the revolutionary experiences of ethnic and tribal populations in Iran. Among the tribes in Iran none played a more significant role in the Constitutional Revolution than the Bakhtiyari. As supporters of the constitutional cause the Bakhtiyari tribes were fondly portrayed in the revolutionary press as the tribes of the homeland, appearing prominently in the pages of *Habl al-Matin*, *Kashkul*, and *Zayanda Rud*, among other newsletters and gazetteers. In the revolutionary newsletter *Habl al-Matin* (The Firm Rope), the Bakhtiyari were lauded as "the protectors of the people" (*hami-yi millat*) from despotic rule and European imperialism.[2] An article in the 5 July 1909, edition of *Habl al-Matin* beckoned the tribes to join the revolution and the constitutional movement:

> Oh lucky Bakhtiyari, oh persevering Qashqa'i, oh brave Shahsevan, oh Pushtikuhian, oh Kalhurian—rise up (*barkhizid*). Unite for Islam and the nation. Put aside your differences and drive away the foreigners from the sanctuary. Don't stand content while your country's independence is blown to the wind.[3]

The encounter between tribalism and constitutionalism was narrated in the revolutionary press, which defined the Iranian homeland as encompassing different tribal and ethnic populations.

The place of the Bakhtiyari in the movement has lived on in the historiography of the Constitutional Revolution. Some authors have interpreted their role in the revolution as that of nationalists. Edward G. Browne, author of *The Persian Revolution* (1910), hailed the Bakhtiyari tribes as supporters of the constitutional cause, calling them "the brave and hardy Bakhtiyaris who so often played a part in Persia's endless wars."[4] In contrast, others have pointed out that the Bakhtiyari had tribal, not national, interests in mind when they entered the constitutional movement. 'Ali Akbar Dihkhuda, the writer for the newspaper *Sur-i Israfil* (Trumpet Call of Israfil), feared that the Bakhtiyari were supporting the constitutional cause as a pretext for ascending to the throne and warned that they were "a lot more dangerous than the weakened Muhammad 'Ali Shah."[5] In his articles for the London *Times* and in *Persia and Turkey in Revolt*, David Fraser portrayed the Bakhtiyari as chaotic and still committed to nomadic ideals of liberty. Fraser's reports in the *Times* tended to portray "the Bakhtiyaris as completely indifferent to the Constitution, and as actuated solely by tribal ambitions, innate love of fighting, and hatred of a dynasty at whose hands they had suffered much."[6] According to Fraser the Bakhtiyari tarnished the revolution and in turn the revolution corrupted them—they had been "carried into the vortex of city life, given pay in cash, tempted and seduced by new delights," becoming "a gambler, a tavern haunter, and a convert to crime in the city."[7] Still others have suggested Bakhtiyari collusion with the British as a prelude to their emergence in national politics, citing the simultaneous British exploration in the Bakhtiyari oil fields as their sole evidence.[8]

Surprisingly, the existing scholarship in English has yet to provide a full account, employing the available sources, of the Bakhtiyari's decisive participation in the Constitutional Revolution. The fullest account appears in Gene Garthwaite's *Khans and Shahs: A Documentary Analysis of the Bakhtiyari in Iran* (1983), which explores the subject through the lens of British diplomatic sources and focuses on the political machinations of the elite khans, Sardar As'ad in particular.[9] This chapter, by contrast, examines the social and cultural history of the tribes in the constitutional period through previously unexplored textual sources, including revolutionary print and *Tarikh-i Bakhtiyari*, the tribal narrative of the revolution. Tracing the Bakhtiyari's involvement in the movement from their emergence in revolutionary Isfahan in 1909 to their desertion of the constitutional cause in 1911, this chapter reveals the ways homeland (*vatan*) came to encompass different tribal confederacies and identities.[10] The following pages thus offer an account of the Constitutional Revolution from the perspective of a tribal confederacy on the periphery of Qajar Iran.[11]

The Bakhtiyari Tribal Confederacy on the Eve of the Revolution

The Constitutional Revolution occurred as the tribes in Iran were becoming increasingly subject to state expansion and centralization. Although pastoral nomads remained semi-independent on the peripheries of the "guarded domains" of Iran, the late Qajar period saw the opening of Iran's tribal hinterlands. The Qajar dynasty precipitated this process in the late nineteenth century. Under Nasir al-Din Shah, the state indirectly ruled tribal confederacies through the traditional methods of appointing paramount chiefs (*ilkhan*; *ilbayg*). In the case of the Bakhtiyari, this occurred in 1867 with the appointment of Husayn Quli Khan as the paramount khan. The Qajars also appointed powerful prince governors, such as Mas'ud Mirza Zill al-Sultan of Isfahan, to keep the tribes in check.[12] The state had enhanced its ability to control and tax the edges of the empire. A report from *Tarikh-i Bakhtiyari*, written in 1906 by Mirza 'Abdal-Rahim Kashani, describes how the Bakhtiyari fled from Qajar tax collectors (*zabit*) and agents of the khans.[13] As detailed in the preceding chapters, modern projects also had begun to overcome the geographical limits of southwestern Iran in the years leading up to the constitutional period. The building of the Bakhtiyari Road through the Zagros Mountains and the development of the Anglo-Persian oil fields in the Bakhtiyari winter pastures had hastened the incorporation of the tribes into an expanding world economy, opening the Bakhtiyari hinterland. Likewise, echoes of the constitutional movement also reached the peripheries of Iran.

Following the death of Isfandiyar Khan in 1903 various Bakhtiyari khans vied for control over the tribes. Perhaps the most influential was 'Ali Quli Khan Sardar As'ad. Born around 1856 he was the fourth son of the *ilkhan* by his most noble wife, Bibi Mihrijan.[14] In 1876, he was appointed a colonel (*sarhang*) of the Bakhtiyari horsemen in the service of the governor of Isfahan, and in 1881 he was appointed brigadier (*sartip*) of the 100 Bakhtiyari horsemen who comprised Prime Minister 'Ali Asghar Khan Amin al-Sultan's elite guards in Tehran.[15]

Following his release from Isfahan in 1883, where he was kept after the execution of his father the previous year, 'Ali Quli Khan established himself as the Bakhtiyari's man of letters, translating a seventeenth-century English travelogue into Persian and opening a tribal school in the mountains.[16] He had also made the pilgrimage to Mecca in 1879, becoming Hajji 'Ali Quli Khan. In 1900, he traveled to various European cities via India and Egypt, returning to Iran after residing in Europe for two years, during which time he reportedly became a freemason. During the reign of Muzaffar al-Din Shah (1896–1907) he acquired the title Sardar As'ad (Commander of Lions). According to Mihdi Malikzada he also emerged as an important figure in the semi-clandestine

Isfandiyar Khan Samsam al-Saltana, the *ilbayg*, surrounded by his cousins, Lutf 'Ali Khan (*standing left*) and Ghulam Husayn Khan (*standing center*), 1890. Lutf 'Ali Khan would go on to gain the title of Amir Mufakhkham, becoming a counter-revolutionary and supporter of Muhammad 'Ali Shah Qajar during the Constitutional Revolution. Ghulam Husayn Khan would later receive the titles Shahab al-Saltana and Sardar Muhtasham. Bird Album, UCLA.

Revolutionary Committee.[17] In late 1906, however, with the coronation of Muhammad 'Ali Shah and the selection of Lutf 'Ali Khan Amir Mufakhkham as head of the elite royal guards, Sardar As'ad fell out of favor in Tehran. True to his belief, corresponding to two conceptions of freedom, the constitutional and the pastoral, that "one should live in civilized places or else the mountains" (*dar mamalik-i mutamadduna ya jabal*), he again left for Europe, seeking treatment for his failing eyesight.[18]

Sardar As'ad was one of several Bakhtiyari khans vying for power and prestige. Among them was Najaf Quli Khan Samsam al-Saltana, who in contrast to Sardar As'ad, his younger half-brother, was a more traditional Lur leader with a reputation for bravery in raids and forays. Before he had reached fifteen years of age, his father had dispatched him to lead a thousand horsemen on a raid against Arab tribes in Khuzistan.[19] Samsam al-Saltana became *ilkhan* of the Bakhtiyari after the death of Muhammad Husayn Khan Sipahdar in 1905, but the following year Sardar As'ad replaced him in the post. Subsequent to his removal from office Samsam al-Saltana permitted his followers to raid caravans on the roads to Isfahan, thus discrediting Sardar As'ad's leadership. He also incited the Lurs of Kuhgilu to rob the oil fields and plunder sections of the Bakhtiyari Road, difficulties that led to a reversal of policy and to his reinstatement as *ilkhan* by the central government in 1907.[20] His replacement again the following year, when Muhammad 'Ali Shah appointed Khusraw Khan Sardar Zafar as *ilkhan*, certainly contributed to his decision to declare his support for the constitutionalists of Isfahan.

With the ascension of Muhammad 'Ali Shah to the throne, Lutf 'Ali Khan Amir Mufakhkham (formerly Shuja al-Sultan) of the Hajji Ilkhani Bakhtiyari, who had served Muhammad 'Ali Shah during his days as crown prince and governor of Azarbayjan, was appointed as the head of the royal guard in the capital. Following the coup in 1908 and the subsequent revolt in Tabriz, the shah ordered Amir Mufakhkham to gather a cavalry of Bakhtiyari horsemen to put it down. Soon 500 horsemen were sent from the *yaylaq* to Tehran to receive the shah's orders.[21] Amir Mufakhkham gained support from other members of the Hajji Ilkhani clan and network, including his younger brother and tribal strongman Nasir Khan Sardar Jang (formerly Sarim al-Mulk), commander of the tribal cavalry stationed in Tehran. Although Sardar Jang was "poorer in property" than the other ruling chiefs, he was known as "a man of force and determination."[22] Once committed to the defense of Muhammad 'Ali Shah Qajar, he did not quit the task. In October 1908, it was reported that he had left to quell the uprising in Tabriz at the head of 500 Bakhtiyari horsemen.[23] Sultan Muhammad Khan Sardar Ashja', the commander of the Bakhtiyari Horse in Khuzistan, halfheartedly sided with his brothers Amir Mufakhkham and Sardar Jang, although the headmen loyal to him were hesitant to support the despotic Muhammad 'Ali Shah. Khusraw Khan Sardar Zafar of the Ilkhani family also joined the loyalist khans and was instrumental in gathering horsemen for Tehran. In 1908, Muhammad ʿAli Shah appointed Sardar Zafar *ilkhan* of the Bakhtiyari, replacing his rival half-brother Samsam al-Saltana.[24] In 1909, however, after Bakhtiyari revolutionaries had taken possession of Isfahan, Sardar Asʿad convinced Sardar Zafar to switch sides and withdraw his support from the shah. Intra-tribal rivalries as well as the desire to be on the victorious side thus shaped the Bakhtiyari's participation in the Constitutional Revolution. Moreover, lasting memories of the murder of Husayn Quli Khan Ilkhani in 1882 would remain a source of Bakhtiyari enmity toward the Qajars that they would vent during the revolution.[25]

The Bakhtiyari retinues summoned by the loyalist khans for the defense of Muhammad ʿAli Shah were hosted generously upon their arrival in the capital, being taken to Bagh-i Shah, where they were allowed to set up their tents.[26] However, after it was announced that the tribesmen should prepare to march on Tabriz with Amir Mufakhkham, they refused to go, claiming they could not ride behind a chief who preferred the royal court to his own tribe.[27] The Bakhtiyari horsemen in Tehran simply sought to return to the tribal territory in the Zagros Mountains. Iskandar Khan ʿAkkasha of the Babadi tribe, whose men, along with regiments from the Chahar Lang and the Bakhtiyarvand, were among those loyal to and being paid by Sultan Muhammad Khan, left a rare account in his memoirs of the mood of the Bakhtiyari cavalry in Tehran in late 1908. As the Bakhtiyari cavalries disbanded in Tehran, some detachments drifted toward the constitutionalists. From their sanctuary in Shah ʿAbd al-ʿAzim Mosque the constitutionalists sought to convince the tribesmen to switch sides, luring them with offers of cash and "worldly possessions" (*mal-i dunya*).[28] The news of this possible link worried Muhammad ʿAli Shah. In an effort to avoid the shah's anger, the khans in Tehran scrambled to rein in their independent-minded retinues. Sultan Muhammad Khan, who was personally wavering as to which path to take, visited Iskandar Khan ʿAkkasha's encampment outside Tehran and sought to convince him to back the shah. Iskandar Khan claims to have responded to this request by reminding Sultan Muhammad Khan that "all the people of Iran seek the constitution (*mashruta talab mibashand*), and it will not be long until this is accomplished, so why not make a good name for yourself" by defending it.[29] With great difficulties and despite much reluctance, Sultan Muhammad and the other khans in Tehran had persuaded the Bakhtiyari horsemen to march to Tabriz under Amir Mufakhkham when news arrived that Bakhtiyari retinues led by Samsam al-Saltana and Ibrahim Khan Zargham al-Saltana had taken Isfahan on behalf of the constitutionalists.[30]

The Bakhtiyari and Isfahan

The Bakhtiyari's emergence in the Constitutional Revolution in 1909 was precipitated by several factors, including news of the insurgency in Tabriz and protests in Isfahan against the bombardment of the Parliament and the appointment of the reactionary prince governor, Iqbal al-Dawla. Seeking a military force to withstand the government troops, the Revolutionary Society (*Anjuman*) of Isfahan, led by the town's influential cleric Aqa Najafi, called on the Bakhtiyari tribes, sworn enemies of Zill al-Sultan, to take up arms against the Qajars. Sending a messenger to deliver a Qur'an to Samsam al-Saltana in the village of Shalamzar in Chahar Mahal, the Revolutionary Society of Isfahan invited the Bakhtiyari to enter the city.[31] Taking into consideration the divisions among the tribes and the designs of the loyalist Sardar Zafar on the post of *ilkhan*, Samsam al-Saltana must have seen a glimmer of opportunity in the pleas of the Anjuman. According to Nurallah Danishvar 'Alavi, Samsam al-Saltana called a tribal council (*jalasa*), inviting all the khans and kalantar of the tribes to gather in Shalamzar within one week.[32] Around 250 chiefs and headmen reportedly arrived for the council. When presented with the option of liberating Isfahan, the representatives of the tribes deliberated for a day and decided they were ready to march to the city in support of the constitution. They wanted to be certain that Isfahan was sincerely behind the movement and that Ibrahim Khan Zargham al-Saltana, an influential khan from the Ilbaygi branch of the Duraki Haft Lang and a cousin of Samsam al-Saltana, would support such a move.

Representatives from the Revolutionary Society assured the khans of Isfahan's support, pledged that the tribal cavalry would be welcomed in the city, and promised to pay the stipends of Bakhtiyari horsemen and footmen.[33] Following a consultation with the *darvish* or spiritual guide of Chahar Mahal, Sayyid Ahmad Nurbakhsh Dihkurdi, Zargham al-Saltana decided to join in the march on Isfahan and ordered the headmen and "white beards" of the clans to gather at Paradumba.[34] It is said that Bibi Sahib Jan, Samsam al-Saltana's wife from the Ilbaygi branch of the ruling clan, wrote letters in her own hand to the wives of the uncommitted chiefs, urging them to send their husbands to defend Isfahan.[35] Once the loyalties of Isfahan and Zargham al-Saltana were determined, Samsam al-Saltana ordered the headmen and "white beards" of the tribes to gather armed horsemen and bring them to Shalamzar, recalling the tribe's intent "to end oppression" (*kar-i ma raf'-i zulm ast*).[36] Samsam al-Saltana and Zargham al-Saltana then met in the village of Dizak in Chahar

Mahal, where they displayed signs of solidarity in the view of their tribal retinues.[37] In Isfahan, expectations were that a large contingent of Bakhtiyaris was about to enter town. Fearing for British lives and property when the Bakhtiyari came, Consul Grahame of Isfahan reported the situation as "very grave."[38]

On January 2, 1909, Zargham al-Saltana headed toward Isfahan with 110 *savaran* chanting *"Ali-an Vali Allah."*[39] When the governor heard of the Bakhtiyari's impending arrival, he ordered his soldiers to drive the city's *mujahidin* from the Masjid-i Shah Mosque, where they were gathered. One hour before dawn the following day, trumpets were heard from the buildings of the Talar-i Istable (stables), and the Masjid-i Shah came under a barrage of artillery and bullets. The royal troops entered Maydan-i Naqsh-i Jahan and opened fire on the mosque from positions in the Ali Qapu Palace but discovered that the *mujahidin* were returning fire from fortifications on the roof of the mosque. In the course of battle, the minarets of the Masjid-i Shah were hit and several of the mujahidin were wounded. Reinforcements for the troops entered the Maydan through the coppersmith's bazaar (*bazaar-i misgaran*) but were fended off, retreating to the Mosque of Shaykh Lutf Allah on the opposite side of the Maydan. Many of the government troops turned to looting the bazaar. Malikzada described the artillery and gunfire in the Maydan-i Naqsh-i Jahan as so fierce that it shook Isfahan and covered the blue-domed city square with dust.[40]

On the morning of January 3, 1909, the advance force of Bakhtiyari tribes entered Isfahan from the direction of the neighborhood (*mahala*) of Chahar Suq-i Shirazian. Describing the Bakhtiyari's arrival in the city British Consul Grahame recalled hearing "shots from the street and bullets whistling across the garden." Going outside the consulate he saw "a band of mounted men wheel round and gallop off" and was told they were "Lurs" accompanying Zargham al-Saltana.[41] The Bakhtiyari's capture of Isfahan was described in the local newspapers. The pages of *Jahad-i Akbar* (The Great Striving) detailed the fighting that took place in the city.[42] When the tribesmen reached Naqsh-i Jahan and moved toward the Masjid-i Shah, they were fired on by government troops entrenched all around the square. Near the mosque the Bakhtiyari dismounted their horses and Zargham al-Saltana chose twelve select khans, as there were twelve Shi'i saints, instructing them to begin the fight against about 200 royalist troops stationed in the city. The Bakhtiyari engaged in the battle and soon soldiers could be seen falling from the heights of the Ali Qapu Palace, where the government's guns were perched. According to Bakhtiyari lore Zargham al-Saltana's son Abu al-Qasim fired a legendary shot that struck a soldier in the head, toppling him to the ground from the lofty Ali Qapu Palace. By noon the sound of cannons had ceased and the city was in the control of the Bakhtiyari. The prince governor, Iqbal al-Dawla, sought refuge in the British consulate, while many more of his scattered troops became uncontrollable and turned to pillaging the bazaar.[43] In a telegraph to George Barclay, the British minister in Tehran, Grahame reported from Isfahan "much plundering and firing all night" and "no responsible authority in town: complete anarchy." The consul noted that the Bakhtiyari uprising in Isfahan "calls itself a nationalist movement but private grievances of the Bakhtiari chiefly Samsam and Zargham are probably the real reason," while adding that "there may be a certain sediment of nationalism in the cup." Zargham al-Saltana sent news of the capture of Isfahan to Samsam al-Saltana, and on 5 January 1909 the *ilkhan* entered town at the head of a thousand Bakhtiyari cavalry and was "acclaimed as a national hero."[44]

The Bakhtiyari tribesmen in Isfahan were put to the task of arresting and dispersing the government soldiers who were looting the bazaar. Grahame received a telegram from the British minister in Tehran, directing him to "tell the Ilkhani that we look to him for the maintenance of order and for the security of our nationals."[45] However, Muhammad 'Ali Shah refused to appoint Samsam al-Saltana as provisional governor of Isfahan on the grounds that he had no confidence in him; instead he appointed 'Abd al-Husayn Mirza Farman Farma, the former governor of Kirman and Fars, who refused to proceed to Isfahan. Within days it was reported that Isfahan was in the possession of the Bakhtiyari, who were guarding the city and maintaining satisfactory order.[46] Grahame reported to Tehran that a thousand armed Bakhtiyaris were in possession of the town, citadel, and arsenal and the "Persian Government must be made to realize that all power is now in the hands of the Bakhtiari."[47] The Bakhtiyari were providing guards for foreign firms and collecting merchandise robbed in the sack of the bazaar by the prince governor's disbanded troops. Moreover, the consul of Isfahan related that he had confidential news that "tends to show that all Bakhtiari Khans at this end are in harmony and are in touch with their relatives in Paris and I have reason to believe that they even contemplate an advance upon Tehran."[48] On 8 January Samsam al-Saltana called on the people of Isfahan to elect representatives for a provincial assembly (*anjuman-i vilayat-i*) within three days, or else the tribes would retire to their mountains, leaving Isfahan to its own resources.[49] David Fraser reported in the *Times*, "The mullahs preached to the city's fathers to give their daughters to the Bakhtiyaris as inducement for them to remain."[50] The assembly soon began

Najaf Quli Khan Samsam al-Saltana in Isfahan, 1909. Edward G. Browne, *The Persian Revolution, 1905–1909* (Cambridge, 1910).

to meet three times weekly at Chihil Sutun Palace. The Bakhtiyari arrested wayward government troops, disarmed them, and ousted the soldiers from the city.[51]

Distraught by the news of Isfahan's capture Muhammad 'Ali Shah urged Farman Farma to march to Isfahan at the head of four regiments and artillery to oust the constitutionalist Bakhtiyari.[52] When Farman Farma declined, the shah appealed to the loyalist Bakhtiyari khans (Amir Mufakhkham, Nasir Khan Sardar Jang, Khusraw Khan Sardar Zafar, and Sultan Muhammad Khan Sardar Ashja'), forcing them to swear their allegiance to him on the Qur'an and ordering them to ride against their own tribesmen in Isfahan.[53] A confrontation between the opposing tribal factions seemed imminent, and rumors circulated that government troops were on their way to subdue the revolutionaries in Isfahan. Grahame reported that Isfahan was bracing itself: "Numerous doors have been put up in all quarters of the town to act as barricades," and "notices have been posted threatening all persons who may befriend the enemy and promising to pay men to serve on Samsam's side."[54] In preparation, the Bakhtiyari in Isfahan were constructing trenches and fortifications (*sangar*) outside the city, stockpiling arms, and practicing firing their rifles daily as Samsam al-Saltana gathered more tribesmen from the surrounding districts. In a conversation with the British consul at Isfahan, the *ilkhan* stated that he was ready to retire but added that if the shah sent forces, "He could not abandon the people of Isfahan nor they him." It was his opinion that the Bakhtiyari khans in Tehran "cannot and will not fight with him," as they were cut off from the tribal territory and could not raise a force.[55] Meanwhile Barclay claimed that he had "reason to believe that Sardar Assad from Paris has urged the Bakhtiaris at Tehran and at Ispahan to throw in their lot with the nationalists."[56] There was reason to believe that the Bakhtiyari tribes were seriously contemplating a march on Tehran.

In Praise of Brave Men: The Tribes in the Constitutional Press

Narratives about the tribes and ethnic groups in Qajar Iran did not emerge suddenly during the constitutional period. Nineteenth-century Persian gazetteers, chronicles, and geographical histories provided narratives and depictions of the different ethnicities and cultures in "the guarded domains of Iran" (*mamalik-i mahrusa-yi Iran*). These texts include the mid-nineteenth-century chronicles *Nasikh al-Tavarikh*, by Mirza Muhammad Taqi Lisan al-Mulk Sipihr, and *Rawzat al-Safa-yi Nasiri*, by Riza Quli Khan Hidayat, as well as Muhammad Hasan Khan I'timad al-Saltana's geographical dictionary, *Mir'at al-Buldan*, and official history *Tarikh-i Muntazam-i Nasiri*. Narratives about the tribes appeared in Iran's first official newspaper, *Ruznama-yi Vaqa 'i'-yi Ittifaqiya*, and Mirza Abu al-Hasan Sani' al-Mulk Ghaffari's illustrated gazetteer, *Ruznama-yi Dawlat-i 'Alliya-yi Iran*. These historical and geographical texts set a precedent for Qajar representations of the tribal populations on the margins and the frontiers of the empire.[57]

The significant shift that occurred with the advent of the constitutional press in Iran was that the tribes no longer appeared as subjects of the empire but as people of the homeland. An edition of *Habl al-Matin* from December 1908, just before the Bakhtiyari's entry into Isfahan, appealed to the tribes of

The orderly and the disorderly revolutionaries. Bakhtiyari tribal retinues in camp outside Isfahan, 1909. Edward G. Browne, *The Persian Revolution*.

the Zagros Mountains to support the constitutional movement:

> We ask that the Bakhtiyari and the Qashqa'i should understand that the homeland (*vataniat*) and the constitution are the will of God. So far, the Qashqa'i have remained neutral and have not taken part in oppression. And the Bakhtiyari, who call themselves Iranians, would not act against the nation . . . because anyone with pure Iranian blood

(*khun-i pak-i Irani*) in their body would not take part in the oppression of Iran. . . . One hundred Bakhtiyari and Qashqa'i tribes, if they opposed this movement, would become defeated and filled with regret.[58]

Habl al-Matin appealed to the tribes to become involved in the revolution and to embrace the Iranian homeland. In the revolutionary press, tribal khans and headmen were no longer simply regarded as the chieftains of their respective confederacies and tribes but as the commanders of the people (*sardaran-i milli*).

The values of the Bakhtiyari chimed with those of Sattar Khan, the hero of Tabriz and icon of the revolution, whom they much admired and sought to emulate as folk revolutionaries. The Bakhtiyari found appeal in Sattar Khan's humble origins, his bravery, and his appearance of rustic masculinity. Well armed and accompanied by his retinues, Sattar Khan provided a revolutionary image and myth of brave men palatable to the Bakhtiyari. In *Tarikh-i Bakhtiyari*, Sattar Khan is lauded as the commander of the people (*sardar-i milli*) and is credited with inspiring the Bakhtiyari's entry into Isfahan and the Constitutional Revolution. According to the tribal history, "Due to the example of the resistance of Sattar Khan, the commander of the people in Azarbayjan, and the defeat of the government troops, most of the lands of Iran have become mobilized."[59] This theme was registered in the revolutionary press in newsletters such as *Habl al-Matin*, which counted the Bakhtiyari khans as among the *sardaran-i milli*, lauding the bravery of their men (*mardan*) with slogans following their entry into Isfahan: "Long live Hajji 'Ali Quli Khan Sardar As'ad / Everlasting the endeavors of men / Uplifting the people of Iran."[60] Other slogans linked the Bakhtiyari to Sattar Khan and the insurgents of Azarbayjan: "Long live (*zindabad*) Samsam al-Saltana and Sattar Khan who raised up the great name of Iran."[61] Circa 1909 *Habl al-Matin* and other nationalist newsletters depicted the Bakhtiyari khans as brave men and commanders of warlike revolutionary armies.

Following the capture of Isfahan *Habl al-Matin* and other nationalist newsletters reported the event and depicted the Bakhtiyari *ilkhan* as a national hero. In *Habl al-Matin*, there was speculation that Samsam al-Saltana had 100,000 Bakhtiyari horsemen behind him ready to capture Tehran if they marched on the capital, bringing "woe to the clan of the Qajars."[62] The Bakhtiyari uprising, it was thought and hoped, would lead the Qashqa'i to act in Fars and the Kalhur Kurds to rise up in Kirmanshah.[63] *Chihra Nama*, a Persian newsletter printed in Cairo, published photographs of Bakhtiyari revolutionaries and hailed Samsam al-Saltana as a "unique pioneer of freedom (*huriyat*)" and the preserver of the kingdom and its people (*mulk u millat*).[64] In the pages of the constitutional press, the Bakhtiyari entered the political culture of modern Iran, with Samsam al-Saltana emerging as a grassroots symbol of revolutionary Isfahan. Meanwhile Samsam al-Saltana declared in public that he was "not a governor (*hakim*) and had only come to establish the constitutional government," adding that he had no intention of bringing an entourage of servants and footmen (*farash va shatir*) to Isfahan.[65] Taking control of the telegraph house, Samsam al-Saltana began sending news of the Bakhtiyari victory in Isfahan all over Iran, as well as to constitutionalists taking refuge in the Ottoman Empire.[66] From Isfahan he wrote to *Habl al-Matin*, "The city is in order, the *anjuman* in place, the people safe, awaiting comrades (*muntazir-i hamrahi*)."[67] He sent a telegram to the revolutionary hero of Tabriz, Sattar Khan, referring to him as fellow sufferer (*hamdard*) and brother (*baradar*), recounting the sacrifices made by his tribes for the homeland (including coming to Isfahan when the rest of the tribes were in the *garmsir*, or winter quarters).[68] Telegrams honoring him and applauding the efforts of the Bakhtiyari soon arrived from two of the ranking ulama of Najaf, Mulla Muhammad Kazim Khurasani and Shaykh 'Abdallah Mazandarani, the provincial anjuman of Tabriz, and constitutionalists in Istanbul.[69] The ulama addressed the Bakhtiyari *ilkhan* with the utmost respect as "the greatest and most glorious excellency" (*jinab-i ajal akram*) and praised him for "helping the seekers of Islam (*Islam khahan*) and disposing of the oppressive government." They added that the success of the revolutionary society and the *mujahidin* of Isfahan had caused the ulama the "greatest joy" and acknowledged that the heroism and chivalry (*futuvvat*) of the *ilkhan* and the Bakhtiyari had protected the public (*'umum-i ahali*). The message from Tabriz to the Bakhtiyari *ilkhan* was similar, except that it perhaps stressed *vatan* more than Islam: "Your support for friends is like medicine for our life and soul (*dava-yi dil va ruh*) and sent from saints."[70] After thanking the *ilkhan* for defending the homeland from the "oppressive sultan," the revolutionary society of Tabriz proposed mobilizing other parts of Iran and stirring the uprising (*qiyam*) of Gilan, Mazandaran, and Astarabad.

Ultimately, the constitutional press provided a medium to discuss and narrate the encounter between tribalism and constitutionalism. In an interview that appeared in a February 1909 edition of *Habl al-Matin*, Samsam al-Saltana discussed his plans and provided a laudatory narrative of the history of the Bakhtiyari and Iran:

> I have no other aim apart from answering the call of the oppressed (*dadrisi-yi mazlumin*), putting an end to chaos (*harj u marj*), and preserving this blessed homeland of ours. The purest blood of Iran (*paktarin khun-i Irani*) from the time of the Sasanians until today has been in the bodies of the Bakhtiyari, who have throughout history preserved the homeland and served the state (*saltanat*). The Bakhtiyari have always, without obligation, been there to assist the state of Iran and their dear nation. Even though the Bakhtiyari tribes have always regarded themselves as a partner of the Iranian state (*sharik-i saltanat*), they have offered their services during the reign of every shah. Without thoughts of sensual gains and due to their inborn love of the homeland (*habb-i vatan*), they have worn the shield on their chests and come to the rescue every time the independence of Iran has seemed in harm. . . . This city, which for centuries was the seat of Iran's throne, invited me to participate in the nationalist government. Still my vote is but a single vote. . . . What Isfahan seeks is the same as Azarbayjan, Astarabad, Gilan, Mazandaran, Khurasan, Kirman, and Laristan and that is the proclamation of popular elections (*intikhabat-i milli*), the restoration of the Parliament, and the establishment of the rule of law.[71]

During the course of the interview Samsam al-Saltana obviously highlights the noble intentions of the Bakhtiyari as patriotic and "pure-blooded" tribes of Iran. Still the *ilkhan*'s words undeniably suggest a perceptive understanding of the political language of the times, suggesting the ways that the revolution had reached the provinces and tribes of Iran. Samsam al-Saltana and the Bakhtiyari emerge as brave men and warlike tribes that raised the call of *mashrutiyat* in Isfahan.[72] Through their participation in the constitutional movement the Bakhtiyari had empowered their tribal confederacy. Their bold participation in the Constitutional Revolution served as a reminder of the heterogeneous population of Iran and the different tribal confederacies on the periphery of the country.

The local press of Isfahan was rife with references to and stories about the Bakhtiyari. During the Constitutional Revolution the people of the city could choose from a number of newsletters published there. The flowering of the revolutionary press in Isfahan coincided with the presence of the Bakhtiyari in the city following 1909; consequently the local press published many accounts about the activities of the tribes. The Bakhtiyari khans, moreover, used the

Bakhtiyari tribesmen mustering in the Maydan-i Naqsh-i Jahan, 1909.
Browne, *The Persian Revolution*.

press as a means of communication and a forum to express their commitment to the constitutional cause. The local press is thus a unique and previously unused source on the role of the Bakhtiyari tribes in the revolutionary politics of Isfahan.

The local press in Isfahan may be traced to the publication of the official Qajar gazette *Farhang* (Culture), which ran from 1879 to 1891 and was edited by Mirza Taqi Khan Sartip, the head physician (*hakimbashi*) and attendant of Mas'ud Mirza Zill al-Sultan, the prince governor of the city.[73] This official gazette contained reports and news about the Bakhtiyari tribes and the periphery of Isfahan. By the constitutional period Isfahan could boast of a number of newsletters and papers. The first examples of the constitutional press in the city included *Anjuman-i Isfahan* (The Revolutionary Society of Isfahan), established in 1906 and edited by Siraj al-Din Sadr al-Musavi, and *al-Jinab* (Highness), first printed in 1906 and edited by Hajji Mirza Sayyid 'Ali Jinab. In the following year appeared *Jahad-i Akbar* (Great Striving), edited by Mirza 'Ali Aqa Khurasani; *Anjuman-i Baladih* (Revolutionary Society of the City and Region), edited by Aqa Mirza Nur al-Din Majlisi; and *Isfahan*, edited by Mirza Husayn Khan. By 1909, the year of the Bakhtiyari's arrival in the city, the following weeklies appeared: *Zayanda Rud*, edited by Mirza 'Abd al-Husayn Khvansari; *Naqus* (Bell), edited by Aqa Masih Tukizgani; *'Urvaq al-Vusqa* (Bonding Vessels), edited by Jalal al-Din Muhayni; and *Parvana* (Butterfly), edited by Sayyid Hasan Muminzada. In the same year in Isfahan, Majd al-Islam Kirmani revived the popular satirical newsletter *Kashkul* (Mendicant's Bowl), formerly printed in Tehran before the lesser tyranny of Mohammad ʿAli Shah.[74]

The image of the Bakhtiyari tribes that emerged in the local press of Isfahan, echoing that of *Habl al-Matin*, was characterized by bravery and honor. In the long-running newsletter *Zayanda Rud*, poems lauded the Bakhtiyari and their defense of the homeland, some drawing meaning from Samsam al-Saltana's title, "Sword of the State." "When the sword was raised from its sheath / The people's struggle became complete / Bakhtiyari, essence of zeal (*ghayrat*), long live / Flourishing chief of retinues long live!"[75] Samsam al-Saltana and other Bakhtiyari khans strived to fit the image of tribal chieftains as commanders of the people. Revolutionary publications became a means for the Bakhtiyari khans to project their power, profess their love of the homeland, and enter the political and cultural arena of the times.

Tribes of the Homeland

From Paris, Sardar Asʿad, who had the left the country to seek treatment for his failing eyesight, became increasingly active in directing the Bakhtiyari tribes in the revolution. He sent messages to the royalist Bakhtiyari khans, discouraging them from waging war on fellow tribesmen and recommending that they withdraw their support from the shah.[76] He sent a telegraph from Paris warning the Bakhtiyari khans not to stir intra-tribal discord—*"nefaghe khanevadeghay nakanide taberessem."*[77] By the end of January 1909 he had persuaded his younger brother Sardar Zafar, who had occupied Qum with his retinues, to reach a truce with Samsam al-Saltana.[78] Disagreements arose within the Bakhtiyari camp loyal to Muhammad ʿAli Shah. Soon Sardar Zafar withdrew his support from the shah, following messages from Sardar Asʿad delivered to him by a Lynch Transport Company employee and later by Yusuf Khan Amir Mujahid.[79] When Amir Mufakhkham blamed Sardar Zafar for a scuffle that occurred between men of the Bakhtiyari cavalry and those of the Cossack Brigade in Qum, the latter disbanded his 400-man retinue, letting them return to the Bakhtiyari country, as well as sending word of his support to Samsam al-Saltana. Sultan Muhammad Khan, wavering in his support for his brother Amir Mufakhkham, was compelled to change sides as well.[80] Moreover, it was reported that Bakhtiyaris serving the shah in the north were protesting against the oath they had been made to take and were disturbed by "the idea of being

A group of darvishan and Bakhtiyari tribesmen in camp outside Isfahan, 1909. Browne, *The Persian Revolution*.

led against their own tribesmen," with many having deserted.[81] Amir Mufakhkham and Sardar Jang were the only Bakhtiyari chiefs who remained loyal to Muhammad ʿAli Shah.

Meanwhile Sardar Asʿad was campaigning in Paris in favor of the Constitutional Revolution. He sent a letter to the London *Times* stating that the sole object of the Bakhtiyari's entry into Isfahan was "to put an end to the disorders that had broken out in that city and to preserve the peace," adding that they intended to deny "any pretext for foreign intervention in national affairs."[82] In Paris he made contacts with other Iranian exiles opposed to the Qajars. According to Mukhbir al-Saltana Hidayat, who was also in Paris at the time, Sardar Asʿad's door was always open, and people frequently gathered at his table (*ashkhas sar-i sufra-yi u hazir mishavand*). In the afternoons the Bakhtiyari khan could be found with Persian expatriots gathered around him at the Café de la Paix, next to the Paris Opéra.[83] Following Muhammad ʿAli Shah's bombardment of the Majlis and the onset of the lesser autocracy (*istibdad-i saghir*), Sardar Asʿad received encouragement from various partisans to return to Iran, take charge of the Bakhtiyari tribes and direct them to restore the constitution. In his memoirs, Mukhbir al-Saltana Hidayat recalls urging Sardar Asʿad to act following the pro-constitutional uprising of the Bakhtiyari in Isfahan: "It isn't the time to sit in Paris, go to Isfahan and take charge of this event. . . . if things do not go well you can return. Paris is not going anywhere and you can be in comfort again. But if the plan works you will become a different kind of sardar (*sardar-i digari khahid bud*)."[84] Sardar As'ad decided to return to Iran and guide the Bakhtiyari through the revolution into which they had been drawn.

In 1908, after oil was struck at Masjid-i Sulayman, Sardar As'ad met with Charles Hardinge, the British under-secretary for foreign affairs and Henry Lynch, the financier of the Bakhtiyari or Lynch Road, among others in London.[85] Discussions centered on the Bakhtiyari oil fields but certainly touched on political events in Persia and the Constitutional Revolution as well. Sardar As'ad promised to visit the oil fields when he returned to Iran and to see to it that the tribes did not threaten company workers. He sought the removal of D. L. R. Lorimer, the unpopular and strict British consul at Ahvaz, and the Bengal Lancers that had been brought in to protect the oil company in 1907. There was also "conversation among other matters," perhaps the Constitutional Revolution, but it remains unclear what, if any, assurances the Bakhtiyari received regarding their participation in the revolution. It is likely that in this meeting Sardar As'ad gained some understanding of the British position toward the Bakhtiyari's activities in the constitutional movement. The friction between the Bakhtiyari and the oil company over the question of the guards, however, reveals the complexity of the relations between the Bakhtiyari tribes and the British.

Soon after Sardar As'ad departed from Europe, reaching Iran in the spring, entering through the province of Khuzistan, where he met with Shaykh Khaz'al, the chief of the neighboring Bani Ka'b Arab tribes in the Persian Gulf region of Muhammara. After collecting 10,000 pounds from Shaykh Khaz'al for land near Ram Hurmuz, Sardar As'ad traveled on the Bakhtiyari Road to Isfahan, gathering horsemen for his cavalry along the way. He also sent his son Ja'far Quli Khan Sardar Bahadur to the *garmsir*, where he recruited additional cavalry.[86] The Bakhtiyari remaining under Amir Mufakhkham had begun their march southward and were encamped at Khalidabad, eighty miles from Isfahan, when Samsam al-Saltana telegraphed the diplomatic corps in Tehran on 2 May 1909. He announced that as the shah had not granted the constitution, the tribes intended "to march on the capital and enforce their demands at the point of the sword."[87] Samsam al-Saltana and Sardar As'ad made contact with Muhammad Vali Tunakabuni, the Sipahdar, and the *mujahidin* of Gilan regarding a plan to close in on Tehran from the north and south.[88]

On 6 May, Muhammad 'Ali Shah informed Barclay that the military operations against the Bakhtiyaris in Isfahan had collapsed and been abandoned. The shah then quickly retreated by signing a proclamation announcing measures

"The Victorious National Rifles," a caricature of the Bakhtiyari's march on Tehran, from the newsletter *Kashkul* of Isfahan (1909). University of Isfahan Archives.

for the re-establishment of the constitution, forcing Sardar As'ad to return to Isfahan and disband his horsemen.[89] In June, however, when the shah raised objections during the drafting of the new electoral law, the Bakhtiyari cavalries reassembled. On this occasion Sardar As'ad was determined not to turn back. On 17 June, 800 Bakhtiyari horsemen moved toward Tehran, leading the shah to appeal frantically to the Russian legation for help.[90] The British and Russian consuls at Isfahan were ordered to pursue the Bakhtiyari and encourage them to turn back.[91] Within a week British Consul Grahame had caught up with the Bakhtiyari in Qum and was twice fired upon as he entered the city. Grahame tried to convince Sardar As'ad that there was no need to fight for a constitution that had already been restored. Although he warned him that the Bakhtiyari's march on the capital was displeasing to the powers and "would only complicate matters and delay the restoration of order," the Bakhtiyari would not be diverted from moving on Tehran.[92] Sardar As'ad then "telegraphed jointly all the foreign legations asking that the Powers should now interfere no further" in Iran's internal affairs, as "they and all other Nationalists were about to force on His Majesty the fulfillment of pledges made to his people."[93]

Incendiary letters from Sardar As'ad appeared in the pages of *Kashkul*, *Zayanda Rud* and *Jahad-i Akbar*. In June 1909, the following letter from Sardar As'ad appeared in the Isfahan newspaper *Kashkul* as the Bakhtiyari were on their way to Tehran:

> I would like to remind all that the headmen of the Bakhtiyari are not thinking about *hukumat* and *saltanat* and live content lives. And I was in Europe for diversion and treatment. But upon hearing for ten months about the behavior of the shah and his court and after being advised by the *maraji'-yi Islam* and Europeans that the only way for saving Iran is through *mashruta*, I decided to do what I could for the sake of my religion and homeland. . . . And nothing can scare or stop me. I am not worried at all about the military camp at Kashan. The only way I'll stop and return is when I hear the news of *mashrutiyat*. Send the news to our brothers in Azarbayjan and Gilan, and the people of Tehran, we will all be at Baharistan. Long live the people of Iran. Long live freedom. Martyr of the people of Iran (*Zindabad millat-i Iran. Zindabad azadi. Fada-yi millat-i Iran*), 'Ali Quli Khan Bakhtiyari.[94]

Here Sardar As'ad invokes the Bakhtiyari's love of the homeland and their brave commitment to upholding the constitution. The satirical cartoon parodies the weakness of the shah's troops in the face of the bold and daring horsemen of the Bakhtiyari. They are honored as "The Victorious Rifles of the People" (*Qushun-i Zafarnimun-i Milli*), while the government troops are lampooned as deserters fearful of even the thought of confrontation with the martial tribes. In the caricature, they are seen uttering cowardly remarks as they drop their rifles and flee from the advance of Sardar As'ad's retinues, one of them seeking a mouse hole (*yak surakh-i mush*) in which to hide from the warlike tribes.[95] News arrived to the consuls' dismay that Samsam al-Saltana had gathered reinforcements estimated at "about six hundred Bakhtiyari mounted rifles" for his brother.[96] In a series of dispatches on the "Bakhtiyari Advance," published in the *Times* in late June 1909, Fraser suggested that the Bakhtiyari aimed "to dethrone the Shah."[97] There was widespread panic and fear of looting in Tehran as word spread that the Bakhtiyari tribesmen were on the way.

Meanwhile, on the outskirts of the capital, Nasir Khan Sardar Jang and 400 horsemen returned from Tabriz and joined Amir Mufakhkham's retinues, who had ridden from Khalidabad to Kashan to Qum in pursuit of Sardar As'ad and his men.[98] Seeking to avoid a confrontation with his kinsmen loyal to the shah, Sardar As'ad wrote to Amir Mufakhkham, offering him all of his own wealth and the office of *ilkhan* to avoid a battle between the Bakhtiyari tribes. But, as Amir Mufakhkham had already secured a written promise from the shah entitling him to the Ilkhani family's property, he refused Sardar As'ad's offers.[99] When these attempts at conciliation failed, Sardar As'ad changed his route, leading his cavalry, which had swelled to 1,200 men, to an encampment at Rubat Karim southwest of the capital. From there they planned to meet Sipahdar and the Gilan *mujahidin* at the Karaj River.[100]

On 10 July, the pro-constitutionalist Bakhtiyari, now united with the *mujahidin* from the north, came face to face with fellow tribesmen at the village of Badamak on the Karaj River, fifteen miles west of Tehran. During the evening Amir Mufakhkham attacked the combined revolutionary forces, reporting numerous casualties among his enemies. Iskandar Khan 'Akkasha recalls in his memoirs that some Bakhtiyari tribesmen caught on opposing sides recognized and sought to protect one another.[101] The two days of fighting at Badamak finished inconclusively: About fifteen Bakhtiyari, along with sixty to seventy horses, were killed on Amir Mufakham's side, while Sardar As'ad's forces suffered more than twenty casualties and lost seventy horses. Early in the morning of July 12, the Bakhtiyari and the *mujahidin* moved quietly out of the village of Badamak toward the capital.[102] They approached Tehran from the hills north of the city, entering the capital through the northern Bahjatabad Gate and avoiding the government soldiers stationed to guard the southern gates, their supposed entry point. The Bakhtiyari immediately took control of the quarter that housed the foreign legations, replacing guards and police with tribesmen and organizing tribal patrols to preserve order. They set up their headquarters at Baharistan, the site of the ruined Parliament, which had been bombarded by the forces of Muhammad 'Ali Shah during the coup of 1908. News of the capture of Tehran spread through the surrounding villages and caravanserais. People in the capital cheered the tribes, who wore red badges to show their support for the constitution.[103]

The revolutionary armies faced their most intense clash at Cannon Square (Maydan-i Tupkhana), where they met the shah's Cossack Brigade under Colonel Liakhoff. But as the number of Bakhtiyari tribesmen in the capital had swelled to nearly 2,000, the Russian-led Cossack Brigade was forced to surrender and the shah compelled to seek refuge in the Russian legation.[104] The Revolutionary Committee chose the twelve-year-old Ahmad Shah as his father's successor, and Azad al-Mulk was appointed regent. Despite the coronation of the young Qajar heir, the Bakhtiyari tribes had attained the greatest influence in the country as a revolutionary army. Bakhtiyari prestige extended beyond their military prowess as Sardar As'ad became interior minister (*vazir-i dakhila*), Samsam al-Saltana officially became governor general of Isfahan, and various other khans rose to provincial governorships. Following the Qajar practice of dispersing appointments among princes, the Bakhtiyari had suddenly become the dominant group in the central government.

Mercenaries of the Revolution

From the time of their entry into Tehran the Bakhtiyari cavalry assumed responsibility as a revolutionary army defending the constitutional government in Iran. Under the command of Sardar As'ad's son, Ja'far Quli Khan Sardar Bahadur, Bakhtiyari horsemen were dispatched to put down rebellions all over the country. Throughout Tehran it was popularly believed that in their native mountains the khans possessed vast contingents of horsemen whom they could call upon if necessary.[105] In times when the constitution seemed in peril, the Bakhtiyari served as revolutionary armies. For instance, in the winter of 1909, when the reactionary Shahsevan tribes plundered Ardabil and threatened to march on Tehran and restore Muhammad 'Ali Shah to the throne, a detachment consisting largely of 300 Bakhtiyari horsemen under Sardar Bahadur set off on a punitive campaign in Azarbayjan. Joined by Yeprem Khan, his *mujahidin* from the Caucasus, and their Maxim guns, the Bakhtiyari defeated the Shahsevan insurgents.[106] Again in July 1911, amidst rumors of the return of Muhammad 'Ali Shah at Gumish Tappa near Astarabad in the Turkmen Sahra, a new cabinet was formed with Samsam al-Saltana as minister of war and premier, ensuring the continued services of the Bakhtiyari cavalry. As Morgan Shuster, the American financial adviser appointed treasurer-general by the Majlis, described in *The Strangling of Persia*, the mercurial Bakhtiyari premier offered "to put a pistol to the breast [of Muhammad 'Ali Shah] and kill him," and sought to put lucrative bounties on the head of the shah and his brothers.[107]

After the government declared martial law, Samsam al-Saltana sent Sardar Bahadur and the Bakhtiyari cavalry on a "nationalist expedition" against the royalist troops of Rashid al-Sultan, whom they routed at a narrow pass in the mountains of Firuzkuh, northeast of the capital. Later the Bakhtiyari repelled 2,000 Turkmen tribesmen marching on Tehran from the northeast under the direction of one of the ex-shah's generals.[108] It was reported that at Imamzada-yi Ja'far, the sound and effect of Yeprem Khan's Maxim guns "threw the Turkman into confusion." After the Bakhtiyari charged they fled via the Mashhad Road to the Khurasan frontier, leaving 60 to 70 dead, 300 to 400 wounded and captured.[109] In the late summer and early fall of 1911, the ex-Shah's brother, Salar al-Dawla, gathered thousands of Kurdish tribes in northwestern Iran, marched on Kirmanshah and Hamadan, then advanced on Tehran.[110] To meet this threat the Bakhtiyari cavalry, joined again by Yeprem Khan's volunteers and artillery, marched against Salar al-Dawla's Kurdish troops and defeated them at the village of Bagh-i Shah.[111]

In the summer of 1910, Bakhtiyari tribesmen were dispatched along with the forces of Yeprem Khan to disarm the nearly 1,000 unemployed, gun-toting volunteers from Azarbayjan and Gilan who were scattered throughout the streets of Tehran.[112] These freedom fighters and *mujahidin* gathered and held demonstrations at Atabayg Park near the foreign legations. In August the grassroots hero Sattar Khan and some 300 followers barricaded themselves in Atabayg. They refused to give up their arms, precipitating a shootout with government forces that included the Bakhtiyari. The Bakhtiyari tribes thus clashed with Sattar Khan, a figure who had precipitated their own entry into the struggle for *mashrutiyat*.[113] By August 1910, the Bakhtiyari cavalry and the followers of Sattar Khan had ended up on opposing sides. In the shootout at Atabayg Park, the Bakhtiyari defeated the volunteers. Sattar Khan was wounded in the skirmish and unceremoniously removed from the revolutionary stage. Later in the century, however, it would be Sattar Khan and the volunteers from Tabriz, not the Bakhtiyari, who would be remembered as icons of the Iranian Constitutional Revolution.

The Bakhtiyari also faced resistance from otherwise pro-constitutional tribes that resented their domination of the central government. In the south, the heavily armed Qashqa'i tribes of Fars and their *ilkhan*, Isma'il Khan Sawlat al-Dawla, supported the constitution but challenged the Bakhtiyari when they meddled in the affairs of Fars. Among the most influential figures in Fars during the constitutional period, the Qashqa'i *ilkhan* sought to harness the revolution to gain prestige for the Qashqa'i, as had been the case for the Bakhtiyari. In April 1907, when popular demonstrations broke out in Shiraz against Qavam al-Mulk, the chief of the Khamsa tribes and provincial rivals of the Qashqa'i, Sawlat al-Dawla entered the town at the head of a large group of Qashqa'i tribesmen in support of the constitution and contributed 800 *tumans* to the popular party. In January 1909, rumors circulated in the south that as a result of the Bakhtiyari's success in Isfahan the Qashqa'i chief was being incited to try a similar coup in Fars.[114]

Over time Sawlat al-Dawla Qashqa'i became threatened by the growing power of the Bakhtiyari, whose khans maintained a friendship with Qavam al-Mulk of Shiraz, the *ilkhan* of the Khamsa. Resenting the Bakhtiyari alliance with his provincial rivals, Sawlat al-Dawla allied with Shaykh Khaz'al and Ghulam Riza Khan, the *vali* of the Pusht-i Kuh Lurs, to form the "League of the South," a bloc against growing Bakhtiyari power. In 1910, when Sardar As'ad convinced the government to depose Sawlat al-Dawla as *ilkhan* of the Qashqa'i, the restive chieftain ordered 300 horsemen to Isfahan and threatened to march on Tehran but turned back when 2,000 Bakhtiyari horsemen were sent to confront them.[115]

Tensions between Sawlat al-Dawla Qashqa'i and the Bakhtiyari again resurfaced in 1911, when the rivalry between the Qashqa'i chieftain and Qavam al-Mulk threatened the stability of Fars and its capital, Shiraz. This conflict was precipitated when the new provincial governor Nizam al-Saltana arrested Qavam al-Mulk and his brother Nasir al-Dawla, ostensibly for failing to capture certain brigands.[116] Sardar As'ad and the Bakhtiyaris in the capital "moved heaven and earth with the Government" to arrange the release of the Qavams, but Nizam al-Saltana, who had sided with Sawlat al-Dawla in the feud, refused to release the captives.[117] The governor then released the Qavams, but they were attacked on the way to Tehran by a group of Kashkuli Qashqa'i, who killed Nasir al-Dawla and caused Qavam al-Mulk to flee and take sanctuary in the British consulate.[118] By the summer of 1911 Shiraz was enveloped by chaos as Qashqa'i and Khamsa tribesmen gathered in the city quarters and outside the city gates. In September, the Bakhtiyari-led cabinet dismissed Nizam al-Saltana as governor of Fars, but he refused to abandon his post, instead inviting Sawlat al-Dawla to come to Shiraz with a large Qashqa'i contingent.[119] Although in October the acting British consul at Shiraz reported that the Qashqa'i were retreating from the city in large numbers and migrating with the tribes to the *garmsir*, Nizam al-Saltana and Sawlat al-Dawla both left Shiraz as "fugitives," the latter encamped some six miles outside of town after he "declared publicly that he would raise such disorders on the Bushire Road as had not before been seen."[120]

Tribal Unrest in the Provinces

As the Bakhtiyari khans assumed leadership in Tehran and the provinces, they became distant from their tribal subjects (*ra'iyat*) in the Bakhtiyari Mountains. The khans' estrangement from their tribal contingents had been occurring since the late nineteenth century, as the ruling chiefs of the Haft Lang became landlords in Chahar Mahal as well as partners in British-led development projects such as the Bakhtiyari Road and the Anglo-Persian Oil Company. As British developers and collaborating khans sought control of the Bakhtiyari land and its resources, the rank-and-file of the tribesmen became alienated from the land and disenchanted by the tribal leadership. The increase in banditry and brigandage by the Bakhtiyari during the constitutional period was partly a reflection of how out of touch the khans had become from their subjects.[121] Perhaps the spread of the spirit of *mashruta* among the lower-ranking and younger tribesmen led them to attempt to cast off the authority of the ruling khans. As one observer noted, "The ancient tribal feeling of the Bakhtiyari is being disturbed at present. . . . the wave of unrest and discontent with their rulers which is sweeping over the whole Muhammedan world has reached the tribesmen."[122]

In June 1910, there were reports that the lesser khans and clan heads were showing a "refractory spirit," complaining that for over a year they had supplied men and lost lives with nothing in return, while the Bakhtiyari khans rose to the highest positions in the land. They were prepared to pay their taxes directly to the central government and to elect their own heads of the tribes, throwing off their allegiance to the old khans unless their taxes were lightened.[123] In December 1910, Khuda Karim Khan, the influential chieftain of the Janiki of the Chahar Lang, wrote to Sardar As'ad claiming he had been forced to divide the Janiki between his sons and could no longer maintain his position over the tribes. That winter reports arrived from Isfahan and Ahvaz warning that a rebellion was stirring against the big khans. A number of minor khans from the Chahar Lang, led by the Mahmud Salihi and joined by some of the Haft Lang, were "trying to throw off the yoke of the Ruling Bakhtiari Chiefs, and have telegraphed to Tehran, asking to be given a separate Government. . . . The Bakhtiari Khans are now reaping the first fruits of 'azadi' among their own tribesmen."[124] Bakhtiyari tribesmen returning from military campaigns demonstrated at the Anjuman of Isfahan, complaining that their leaders had broken their promise to pay them and taken all the spoils for themselves. They remained in Isfahan pressing their demands for pay, while in the Bakhtiyari Mountains discontented tribes marauded on the roads with the avowed intention of attacking Isfahan.[125]

Late in 1910 Sardar Bahadur and Sardar Muhtasham led a group of horsemen to put down the growing rebellion against the khans in the Bakhtiyari country and Isfahan.[126] By the end of January it was reported that with the Bakhtiyari cavalry sent to subdue them, the rebelling Lurs had left Isfahan and fled to Chahar Mahal and the Zagros. In the spring, however, Zargham al-Saltana, also disillusioned and feeling uncompensated for the sacrifices he had made for the constitution, made common cause with the discontented young khans in the south.[127] There were continuous reports of raiding and looting by Chahar Lang and Bakhtiyarvand tribes, as well as news that Zargham al-Saltana was collecting horsemen in Paradumba. According to rumors in Isfahan, the young khans and headmen in the area had gathered around Zargham al-Saltana and were about to march on the city. In June 1911, as Chahar Lang and Haft Lang tribes clashed in the region beyond Dih Kurd, Zargham al-Saltana had discussions with Sawlat al-Dawla Qashqa'i, who urged him to move on Isfahan and offered to help when the Qashqa'i tribes reached their summer quarters south of the city. In response, Sardar Muhtasham and Sardar Bahadur marched to Dih Kurd at the head of 600 horsemen and prepared to mount an expedition against the Chahar Lang and Zargham al-Saltana's forces. By the end of the month it was reported that the insurgent tribesmen had largely disbanded and given up their revolt.[128]

The open rebellion of the young khans was subdued, but more anarchic and dispersed forms of resistance persisted among the Bakhtiyari. Robberies and raids were endemic in the provinces when authority was weak, and they increased markedly during the revolution. During Husayn Quli Khan's rule intra-tribal fighting among the Bakhtiyari had ceased, bandits were kept in check, and their plundering raids were brought to an end. Crimes in the provinces had increased, however, following the assassination of Nasir al-Din Shah in 1896 and the ascent of Muzaffar al-Din Shah to the throne. Around Isfahan tribal raids and robberies on the roads certainly also increased following the removal of Zill al-Sultan as governor in 1907. With the weakening of the central government and the breakdown of order during the Constitutional Revolution, the tribes were left virtually independent in the provinces.

British administrative reports, correspondence, and gazetteers described the southern roads as a haven for "highwaymen" and "marauders." An Isfahan agent reported that the Bakhtiyari Road was safe only when the Chahar Lang were away in their winter quarters, and the routes between Shiraz and Isfahan were in the hands of cattle-thieving brigands.[129] Bakhtiyari tribesmen plundered caravans, robbed posts, and stole herds of cattle on the outskirts of Isfahan. The constitutionalist press now condemned the Bakhtiyari as the cause of insecurity (*na amni*) throughout the countryside. Although the Bakhtiyari had given their lives for the constitution, it was increasingly observed that they did not follow its laws (*dar hich qanun-i nimiravand*).[130]

An important factor contributing to the prevalence of tribalism during the revolution was the arming of the tribes. Horseback riding and shooting (*savari va tufang indakhtan*) had long been cherished cultural skills among the Bakhtiyari, and Firdawsi's *Shahnama* (Book of Kings) was like a code of war among them.[131] Going back to the eighteenth century tribes in Iran had used matchlock rifles (*tufangha-yi fitila-yi*) and later flintlock rifles (*tufangha-yi chakhmaq*). These were made in Iran and were long and heavy. In the mid-nineteenth century, A. H. Layard left an Orientalist depiction of the culture surrounding the Bakhtiyari and their weapons, including the recounting of legendary stories and battles from the *Shahnama*.[132] Describing the Bakhtiyari tribesmen's attachment to firearms and accoutrements, Layard wrote:

> A long matchlock is rarely out of their hands. Hanging to a leather belt round their waist, they carry a variety of objects for loading and cleaning their gun—a kind of bottle with a long neck, made of buffalo hide, to contain course gunpowder; a small curved iron flask, opening with a spring, to hold the finer gunpowder for priming; a variety of metal picks and instruments; a mould for casting bullets; pouches of embroidered leather for balls and wadding; and an iron ramrod to load the long pistols always thrust into their girdles.[133]

In the latter half of the nineteenth century, many of these matchlock and flintlock rifles were made into percussion-cap rifles (*tufangha-yi chashni*). Increasingly, mass-produced rifles of European make had become accessible not only to khans and headmen but to the rank-and-file of the tribes as well. Although matchlock and flintlock rifles remained in use throughout the provinces during the constitutional period, they were no longer manufactured and were becoming obsolete. In Isfahan, once an important center for gun making, all the smiths were busy replicating Western makes.[134]

The modern rifle denoted power and prestige. By the late nineteenth century in some parts of Iran, rifle and cartridges were "considered essential possessions for a grown-up man, and no one could hope to marry a wife till he can produce them."[135] Armed men could most easily find employment in the retinues of the khans. In the late nineteenth century, Martini Henrys and modern European rifles of that class could be obtained in Fars and Khuzistan with 100 rounds of ball cartridge at prices varying from forty to fifty *tumans*.[136] Guns were valuable commodities, often paid for in kind by tribesmen ready to part with almost anything to get rifles in return. The Bakhtiyari tribesmen attached to the ruling khans during the Constitutional Revolution were using revolvers and automatics, even though some tribesmen who occupied Isfahan apparently did so equipped with no more than heavy sticks (*chub* or *gurz*). A list of the guns available during the revolution appears along with an estimate of their values in the *Tarikh-i Bakhtiyari*. They included five-shot (*panj tir*) German rifles and revolvers, Browns, Mackenzies, Mausers, and Wrendels.[137] The Constitutional Revolution provided the ultimate occasion to brandish and use these arms.

Deserting the Constitution

In 1911, Morgan Shuster, the American treasurer-general of Iran, attempted to form a tax-collecting corps of national gendarmes, a planned force of 15,000 men, mounted and armed with Mauser pistols and rifles, to collect revenues and maintain order. Shuster sought to modernize Iran's military forces and to halt the government's reliance on the "indefinite number of unorganized Bakhtiyaris spread out in Isfahan, and on the road to Tehran."[138] A regularly paid and provisioned gendarmerie capable of policing the country and its roads developed under the direction of Swedish officers, recruiting men from all places and classes, including the tribes.[139] The national gendarmes posed a threat to the military power of the Bakhtiyari and were among the factors that convinced them to abandon the constitutional cause in the winter of 1911, when the khans decided not to resist the Russian occupation of Qazvin and accepted the Russian ultimatum to close down the Majlis. When Sardar Asʿad, who had been so instrumental in steering the tribes along a nationalist line in the past, returned to Iran from Europe in late 1911, some expected him again to mobilize the tribes behind the constitutional cause. Instead, he urged the acceptance of the Russian ultimatum, seeking to avoid the occupation of Iran.[140]

The Bakhtiyari seemed never to have been firmly united behind the constitutional cause, and some seemed ready to back away from their role as defenders of the revolution. Crimes committed by the Bakhtiyari in the cities and on the roads revealed a tenuous commitment to constitutionalism and the rule of law. Groups of Bakhtiyari militias remained in Tehran, in the area of ʿAla al-Dawla Street, and skirmished with the gendarmes, their gun battles pouring into the streets, alleys, and bazaars.[141] By 1913 all armed Bakhtiyari, apart from small escorts reserved for the khans, had left Tehran and returned to the

Zagros Mountains.[142] Over time the Bakhtiyari fell from grace in the pages of the constitutionalist press. In Isfahan, where the retinues of the various khans had swelled and Bakhtiyari rebels (*ashrar*) had burned and looted the Constitutional Assembly, the people sought to be rid of the Bakhtiyari. They sent the leading members of city's ulama, headed by Aqa Najafi, to ask the tribes to return to their mountains.[143] In the Azeri newsletter *Mulla Nasruddin*, a cartoon portrayed the tribes as devils and condemned the "injustice of the Bakhtiyari in Tehran" (*Tehranda Bakhtiyarilarak zulmi*).[144]

The British minister in Tehran, Walter Townley, aptly summarized the experience of the Bakhtiyari in the Constitutional Revolution:

> One has but to put oneself in their place for a moment to realize what it meant to them. They had played a most prominent part in all the events which had resulted in the expulsion of the ex-Shah from Persia; they had fought against him when he returned; they had defended the country against Salar-ed-Dowleh; and the wheel of political fortune had brought them into high office, several of them having been Cabinet Ministers, whilst one of their number had been the Prime Minister. Then out of an incident, with a force commanded by foreign officers, they were to see themselves humbled, by their tribesmen being disarmed in the face of all Persia, and their numbers at the capital reduced, as if they had been mere malefactors instead of men who had served their country well.[145]

The longstanding balance of power in Iran between the state and the tribes, the center and the periphery, had shifted beneath the Bakhtiyari's feet. The Bakhtiyari tribes returned to the mountains, leaving the capital and the constitutional movement behind. The complexities of the Bakhtiyari's political behavior stemmed from their long history as a tribal confederacy on the empire's edge. In 1911, they returned to the Zagros after having taken part in a constitutional movement that underscored the ethnic difference that marked the population of Qajar Iran while also signalling the emergence of a modern state no longer beholden to tribal power.

Conclusion

The significance of the Constitutional Revolution in Bakhtiyari history is suggested by the completion of *Tarikh-i Bakhtiyari*, which was compiled during the constitutional period under the direction of Sardar As'ad and largely written by 'Abd al-Husayn Lisan al-Saltana Sipihr, who completed the manuscript in 1911. As mentioned above it was the first written history of the Bakhtiyari and the first tribal ethnography in the Persian language. The original manuscript consists of about 600 lithographed pages detailing the history, genealogy, environment, and customs of the Bakhtiyari tribes. In a letter written to Edward G. Browne in 1911, Sardar As'ad mentioned the completion of the draft of *Tarikh-i Bakhtiyari*, despite difficulties involved in "extracting historical information," and promised to send Browne a two volume version of the text.[146] Written partly to memorialize the tribes' role in the Constitutional Revolution, *Tarikh-i Bakhtiyari* presents a narrative of *mashrutiyat* from the margins of Qajar Iran.

The question still remains, however: To what degree did the Constitutional Revolution reach the Bakhtiyari tribes? How did the women, sub-khans, and ordinary tribal people experience the revolution? Some observers attested to the fact that the revolution had initiated important transformations among the tribes. As the Bakhtiyari visited Tehran and other cities, they claimed, their outlook "was proportionately extended as they gained an increased familiarity with ordinary Persian and an enlarged vocabulary."[147] The Bakhtiyari vernacular was growing and incorporating extra-tribal words; culturally the tribes were looking beyond the geographical limits of the Zagros Mountains. Back in the tribal territory women were mobilized and kept informed about the revolution. In Bakhtiyari society women had customarily enjoyed relative freedom and held great influence over their husbands and sons. They were, by some accounts, "never veiled," and until the constitutional period they were used to accompanying the men everywhere, even going into camp with them at the yearly gathering of the tribes at Chaqakhur.[148] After 1909, with many tribesmen away for months at a time in Tehran or in distant provinces, the khans' wives or *bibis* gained greater influence and were often responsible for governing the tribes during the ruling khans' absence.[149] During the revolution they also oversaw the migrations and managed the khans' estates in Chahar Mahal. The British doctor Elizabeth Ross recalled that the Bakhtiyari *bibi*s were politically aware and concerned about the Constitutional Revolution. They wrote letters to the wives of the uncommitted chiefs, urging them to send their husbands to defend the constitution, and listened to phonograph records sent from Samsam al-Saltana in Tehran with his speeches recorded on them. They took an interest in the suffragists and desired "to read history," asking questions about Robespierre, Marat, and Louis XVI.[150] For many of the Bakhtiyari tribal subjects, however, the Constitutional Revolution might have remained inconsequential, irrelevant, and distant.[151] In his memoirs, Hajj Sayyah recounts traveling with Sardar As'ad's Bakhtiyari retinues to Tehran in 1909. On asking one of the Bakhtiyari horsemen if he knew where he was going and what he was taking part in, Hajj Sayyah received the following reply: "*Khayr*! We obey and follow the commands of the Sardar."[152] The elevated status and consciousness attained by the khans during the Constitutional Revolution did not always extend to the retinues they led.

The history of the Bakhtiyari in the Constitutional Revolution shows that despite the persistence of tribalism in Iran, the late Qajar period was a time of social, political, and cultural transformation. The discussion of the assimilation of nomadic tribes in Iran has often centered on Riza Shah Pahlavi's programs of military pacification (*sarkub-i nizami*) and sedentarization (*takht-i qapu*) in the 1920s and 1930s. In the case of the Bakhtiyari, however, the significant changes in tribe and state interactions that occurred in the Qajar period must also be taken into account. The opening of the Bakhtiyari land, culminating in the participation of the tribes in the Constitutional Revolution, anticipated Riza Shah's tribal policies and might explain why "the disintegration of Bakhtiyari power" happened relatively easily in the 1920s and 1930s.[153] The Bakhtiyari's participation in the national representative politics of the Constitutional Revolution represents a strange moment in the narrative of the making of modern Iran, for here were pastoral nomadic tribes that at least for a time were Iran's revolutionary armies. This reality seems difficult to reconcile with a historiography that has privileged the urban classes as the natural carriers of nationalist sentiments and has often dismissed the tribes as the enemies of a unified, independent, and modern Iran. Although violence certainly marked the frontier between the center and the periphery, the tribes had long served as retinues of the "guarded domains of Iran." This duality between autonomy and assimilation may also be seen in the Bakhtiyari's actions in the Constitutional Revolution. During the revolution the Bakhtiyari khans, with their retinues behind them, embraced the homeland—*vatan*—even though they did not entirely relinquish their traditional tribal motives or leave their tribal consciousness behind.

CONCLUSION

WRITING IN THE 1880S, Muhammad Taqi Khan Hakim described the independent status of the Bakhtiyari tribes in the hinterland of Isfahan:

> If a strong state were created, the reprisal of law would spread among the tribes and in the mountains, places that are now far from the manners and culture of the cities. In fact, their condition is completely contrary to that of the city. The Bakhtiyari tribes are spread from the mountains of Isfahan to Shushtar . . . and it can be said that they, and other tribes, have never been fully under the rule of any sultan. In their impenetrable and lofty mountains, they still live according to their own old customs and ways. They pay little heed to the central government and its representatives, only providing some soldiers and paying scant taxes for the portions of land they hold in the foothills. To the point that it has been able, the state has followed a policy of urging these tribes to settle (*sukna*) on the land—mostly because if they settled on the land, perhaps with the passing of time they would become assimilated to adjacent lands that had always been exposed to their gallop and attack.[1]

To govern the tribes was a perennial task for the Qajar state. Migrating between their seasonal quarters in the Zagros Mountains, the Bakhtiyari tribes presented challenges to authorities seeking to identify, tax, and rule them. Yet, by the late Qajar period, as suggested by Muhammad Taqi Khan, the state could at least strive for the incorporation, assimilation, and settlement of tribal populations.

The preceding pages have considered the nature of tribe and state interactions on the periphery of nineteenth-century Iran. It has been suggested here that the Qajar dynasty exhibited a flexibility that allowed for tribal autonomy and a plurality of power on the margins of empire. The state possessed a decentralized structure and the tribes remained effectively beyond its reach. The nomadic and semi-nomadic populations in the hinterlands and on the frontiers of nineteenth-century Iran were incorporated into the state as tribal confederacies. In recognizing different spheres of political authority, the Qajar dynasty was able to maintain the empire with only limited use of force.[2] Such a system in turn allowed tribal subjects to retain political and cultural autonomy while providing nominal allegiance and services to the state, most often by paying light taxes and offering retinues to the royal cavalry. This confederate and decentralized state structure was the hallmark of the early modern state in Iran.

The long-standing balance between the state and the tribes, the center and the periphery, was altered during the late nineteenth century as the British Empire made inroads into the margins of Qajar Iran. Like the early modern Islamic empires of Iran, of which the Qajars were the last examples, the British were forced to bargain with the tribes and accommodate their autonomous position on the imperial periphery. British authority on the edges of Iran was circumscribed and limited by the power and independence of tribal confederacies. Despite this continuity in the interactions between tribes and empire, the nineteenth century saw the development of imperial projects—ethnographic surveys, telegraph lines, roads, and scientific exploration—that permitted the state to enter once-inaccessible places. These projects gradually allowed authorities to overcome obstacles to controlling, taxing, and conscripting nomadic and semi-nomadic tribes that were increasingly settling down during the course of the nineteenth century. This shift in the power relations between the center and periphery was of great consequence for the autonomy of tribes on the edges of Iran. The pervasive order, based on the indirect rule of independent and semi-independent tribes, gave way as imperial projects penetrated the countryside and a more far-reaching, modern state appeared on the horizon. A more assertive state, less tolerant of the political and cultural autonomy of its heterogeneous population, replaced the early modern state and its policies of indirect rule over tribal areas and frontiers. The long nineteenth century saw the waning of the era Marshall Hodgson referred to as the age of nomadic prestige. This process is illustrated by the opening of the Bakhtiyari Mountains in southwestern Iran.[3]

Drawing upon imperial chronicles, geographical gazetteers, tribal histories, and archival materials, this book has presented an account of the assimilation of tribes in nineteenth-century Iran. The narrative spans both ends of the nineteenth century, from the tribal independence and indirect rule that marked the early Qajar era to the imperial projects that transformed the edges of *fin de siècle* Iran. It began by exploring the dynamics of tribe and state interactions on the mountainous periphery of early Qajar Iran, and in the hinterland of Isfahan in particular, when the tribes enjoyed great independence and autonomy in the Zagros Mountains. It then examined late nineteenth century imperial projects in the Bakhtiyari territory, beginning with the building of the Bakhtiyari or Lynch Road, a route that was to open the region to the British global empire and its trade by linking the Persian Gulf to Isfahan via the Karun River and the rugged Zagros Mountains. The road paved the way for the grandest imperial project in the Bakhtiyari territory, the British exploration for oil between 1905 and 1911, as the khans and their retinues emerged in the Iranian Constitutional Revolution. The Bakhtiyari weathered these changes and even found new opportunities in them, although with consequences that forever transformed the nature of tribal autonomy in the mountains.

This study has avoided the association of the modern state with the notion of "progress." Rather, the emphasis has been on the ways the margins of Iran were incorporated into the state and what this development meant for tribal and nomadic societies. Above all this process was part of nineteenth-century imperial expansion. This is not to deny the significance of changes in the early modern period for the tribes in Iran. It remains to be seen in detail how the Safavid age and its aftermath in the eighteenth century reshaped tribalism in the hinterlands and on the frontiers. Such a study of the integration of pastoral nomads into the early modern world would certainly involve other sorts of questions and different archives than those presented here.

Still, the Qajar dynasty had much in common with early modern Islamic empires into the reign of Nasir al-Din Shah. Relations between the state and the nomadic tribes in the nineteenth century reveal the continuities between the Qajar state and preceding early modern Islamic empires in Iran. These tribal states ruled an ethnically heterogeneous population, which enjoyed great autonomy and power on the periphery of empire. Various pastoral nomadic tribes were virtually free from state authority, and the boundaries between the center and the periphery were marked by autonomy, flexibility, and accommodation. The tribes were at once part of the state and also its greatest rivals. Although tribal confederations gave nominal submission to the shah, they managed to maintain their autonomy and power on the distant periphery. Official nineteenth-century chronicles, gazetteers, and histories reveal that the

Qajar state was well aware of the ethnic and tribal differences throughout the "guarded domains of Iran." Knowing the limitations of rule from the center, the state relied on existing tribal structures to integrate pastoral nomadic populations into the empire.

The Qajar dynasty, like its predecessors the Safavids and the Afshars, ruled the tribes through a confederate system that allowed for political and cultural autonomy on the empire's edge. This tribal state exerted a limited and indirect control over the tribes, relying on intermediaries such as tribal khans and headmen. The Qajar government struggled to bring the tribes under imperial control through various means that included punitive military expeditions into tribal territories, detention of tribal chiefs and their families as hostages in the capital, recruitment of tribesmen into the military, collection of light taxes, and forced migration of tribes. During instances of tribal insubordination the state could exert military force, but these measures were costly and temporary, with limited long-term effects on the independence of the nomadic and seminomadic tribes.

The connections between city and hinterland began to change in the second half of the nineteenth century, as seen in the history of the relationship between the provincial capital of Isfahan and its mountainous tribal periphery. The city of Isfahan was vitally linked to the Bakhtiyari Mountains, the waters of the town's famed Zayanda Rud finding their source in the peaks of Zard Kuh. In the mountains behind Isfahan, the Bakhtiyari kept their summer quarters; and every spring, as they reached their upland pastures, they entered into close contact with the city, trading their flocks and herds for the goods of the bazaar. The presence of the nomadic Bakhtiyari on the periphery of Isfahan was also a cause of uncertainty and fear for the people of the city. Archival correspondence, histories, and gazetteers from the 1860s to the 1880s detail the Isfahan provincial government's attempts to control the Bakhtiyari, centering on the political struggle between the tribal *ilkhan*, Husayn Quli Khan, and the Qajar prince governor of Isfahan, Zill al-Sultan. As the Bakhtiyari reached the peak of their tribal power and solidarity on the margins of nineteenth-century Isfahan, entering into independent commercial relations with the British Empire, they became increasingly subject to Qajar state centralization and control.

Road building in the Zagros Mountains during the 1890s signaled the opening of the Bakhtiyari hinterland. In the late nineteenth century, the Bakhtiyari tribes, whose power was based on the impenetrability of their mountains, consented to British plans to restore an ancient highway through their land. The

British viewed the road as a means to expand their trade and influence to the interior of Iran and a buffer against the Russian sphere in the north. Yet the Bakhtiyari Road was also justified as a civilizing measure that would "tame" the tribes, end their migrations, and assimilate them into the British imperial system and global economy. The smooth road was to be a precursor of commerce, communication, and progress in a mountainous hinterland. First and foremost a speedy commercial trade route from the Persian Gulf to Isfahan, the road would also pave over the roughness of tribal Iran. Completed in 1899 and including two steel bridges, it marked the development of the Iranian periphery and could be considered the first modern mountain road in Iran. From the Karun River through the Zagros Mountains to Isfahan, the road overcame the impenetrability of the Bakhtiyari territory, bringing the tribes closer to the market and the culture of the Iranian Plateau.

The road also set the precedent for official Anglo-Bakhtiyari ties and paved the way for what in 1905 would become the British Empire's most important development project, the exploration for oil in the Bakhtiyari's winter quarters at Maydan-i Naftun. The scientific exploration of the Zagros Mountains and the discovery of oil at Masjid-i Sulayman had ecological and economic consequences for the Bakhtiyari hinterland. The Bakhiyari tribes tried to make the most of the British venture for oil on their land. The khans gained British subsidies and a fixed share of the profits from the fields under their control, while tribal subjects found work in the oil fields as laborers and guards receiving regular wages. In the process tribesmen were disciplined and incorporated into an imperialist world economy. With the discovery of oil in 1908, the Bakhtiyari's winter quarters around Masjid-i Sulayman, once held in common by tribes, became a prized possession of the British Empire and the Anglo-Persian Oil Company, compromising the autonomy of the Bakhtiyari as well as the sovereignty of Qajar Iran.

During the Constitutional Revolution the Bakhtiyari tribes were assimilated into the political culture of Iran. Under the electoral laws the tribes were counted among the inhabitants of their province and given the right to vote, while the Bakhtiyari and other tribes were each to send one representative to the National Assembly. During the revolution the homeland came to be defined as composed of different tribal confederacies and identities. None of the tribes in Iran had a more profound (and tangled) role in the Constitutional Revolution than the Bakhtiyari. During the Constitutional Revolution of 1906–1911 the Bakhtiyari tribes backed the *mashruta* movement, marching to Tehran to restore the Majlis in 1909. Under the banner of constitutionalism the Bakhtiyari defended the homeland, which was conceived as encompassing different ethnic populations, but they did so without relinquishing their tribal consciousness and traditional motives. The *Tarikh-i Bakhtiyari*, among other sources, offer views of the Constitutional Revolution from the periphery of Qajar Iran.

Thus, tribal confederation, surveying, road building, and scientific exploration during the Qajar period precipitated the Bakhtiyari's incorporation into the modern state. The case of the Bakhtiyari is certainly unique in terms of the acuteness and contours of their encounter with an encroaching modern world. But they were not the only tribes in Iran to experience such changes during the long nineteenth century. Other tribal groups, such as the Baluch, the Turkmen, the Qashqa'i, and the Kurds, also experienced the expansion of the state during the Qajar era.

The late nineteenth century was a time when the eastern borderlands of Iran in the region of Baluchistan were being explored and demarcated. After the death of Nadir Shah Afshar in 1747 the Baluch ceased to pay tribute to the Iranian state, and Baluchistan became a frontier between Iran and the nascent Afghan Durrani state. This frontier remained porous, permeable, and unmarked until the mid-nineteenth century and the arrival of the British. In 1857, as a result of British imperial interests in India, Herat was separated from Iran and awarded to Afghanistan. In the 1870s, Major General Frederic Goldsmid of the Indian Telegraphic Department led boundary commissions that determined the Makran boundary and established the Helmand River as the border between Iran and Afghanistan in the region of Sistan. After 1876 the autonomous Baluch tribes of Kalat were effectively incorporated into British India.

North of Baluchistan in Khurasan Province the Turkmen underwent similar processes. Following Nadir Shah's death in 1747, with the Persian Zand capital in distant Shiraz, Turkmen nomads, including the Tekke, the Sariq, the Salor, and the Ersari, moved into the eastern borderlands of Iran, settling in Marv, in Sarakhs, and along the banks of the Oxus and Murghab Rivers. Through most of the nineteenth century the Turkmen remained independent of the Qajar dynasty and enjoyed great autonomy on the eastern frontier. By the mid-nineteenth century, however, the Turkmen faced increasing state military campaigns in their territory. In 1861, the Tekke Turkmen defeated thousands of Persian troops that had marched in a campaign on Marv, capturing their guns and chasing the surviving troops across the desert. The disastrous defeat marked Iran's diminishing frontiers in Central Asia, further opening the way for Russian imperial expansion. The pacification and settlement of the Turkmen would become a Russian imperial project, facilitated by the Trans-Caspian Railway, which was fast parting the steppes and annexing the oases of Central Asia.

In the southern province of Fars, the Qashqa'i tribal confederacy, like the Bakhtiyari, saw developments in the Qajar period that hastened their integration into the state structure. This process began perhaps in the 1870s with the assertive tribal policies of the Qajar prince governor of Shiraz, Farhad Mirza Mu'tamad al-Dawla. In addition, strategic and commercial interests in the Persian Gulf and Fars brought the British into contact with the Qashqa'i. In seeking to expand its authority in the Persian Gulf and secure its trade on the Bushire-Shiraz Road, the most heavily traveled commercial route in southern Iran, the British Empire met resistance from the Qashqa'i tribes. The British effort to establish security for their trade and empire in the Persian Gulf and Fars ultimately led to the formation of the South Persia Rifles, a rural gendarmerie created to pacify and police the tribes.

Among the Kurds, various factors during the second half of the nineteenth century made it possible for them to be integrated into the state. In the early Qajar period, the state did not possess the leverage to enforce its rule on the Kurdish populations within Iran. But the expansion of agriculture and the increasing settlement of pastoral nomads in late nineteenth century Kurdistan, as well as the growing military power of the state, rendered the region more governable than ever before.[4] What is more, across the border in the Ottoman realm, following the developments of the Tanzimat period of reforms (c. 1839–1876) Istanbul held more firm control over the tribes. The independence and mobility of the Kurds were also curtailed by the demarcation of the Ottoman-Qajar borderlands by Turco-Persian boundary commissions in the second half of the nineteenth century.

The modernization of the state during the nineteenth century was even more pronounced in neighboring lands, such as the Ottoman Empire and Egypt. In the Ottoman Empire, the building of the Hijaz Railway from Istanbul to the Arabian Peninsula, the opening of the Tigris and Euphrates Rivers to European steamships, the spread of the telegraph, and the establishment of schools for tribes during the Tanzimat era were among the developments that enabled the centralization of state power. In Egypt, the construction of the Suez Canal in 1869, considered the greatest feat of engineering at the time, linked the Mediterranean and the Red Sea and signaled the expansion of the world economy in the region. European empires, which held a dominant position in this global economy, were deeply involved in these projects of development.

In Qajar Iran, the modernization of the state was not as sustained. Despite some of the reform-minded ministers within his court, Nasir al-Din Shah Qajar pursued modernization projects ambivalently and indecisively, seemingly content to farm out such initiatives to foreign firms. Indeed, the Qajar state had long relied on the ruggedness and inaccessibility of its tribal frontiers and hinterlands to preserve the boundaries of the empire. Nevertheless, Qajar Iran still witnessed significant changes in relations between the state and its subjects. By the late nineteenth century it had become possible for the state to extend its authority even into the distant margins of the empire, reaching tribal areas such as the Bakhtiyari Mountains.

These imperial projects were ultimately efforts to tame nature. In the Bakhtiyari territory, the environmental changes of the long nineteenth century were perhaps the most striking. The encroachment of the modern state into the mountains and the changing boundaries between city and hinterland entailed an ecological transformation. The Qajar period proved to be a momentous time for the environmental history of Iran, a subject that is worthy of further scholarly attention.[5] The expansion of empire in nineteenth-century Iran enabled the modern state to attempt to control natural environments and indigenous populations. The ecological impact of imperialism could be observed on the edges of Qajar Iran. With the opening of the Bakhtiyari Mountains the state entered a remote tribal territory and incorporated pastoral nomads into the world economy. These developments, which also occurred elsewhere in the Qajar dynasty, were an outome of the encounter between imperialism and nature in nineteenth-century Iran. The Bakhtiyari Mountains, once off the map and beyond the writ of the state, were opened up and transformed by the inroads of empire.

NOTES

Introduction

1 The population of Iran circa 1800 was around 5 to 6 million. See Charles Issawi, *The Economic History of Iran, 1800–1914* (Chicago, 1971), 20. Also see Nikki Keddie and Mehrdad Amanat, "Iran under the Later Qajars, 1848–1922," *Cambridge History of Iran,* vol. 7: *From Nadir Shah to the Islamic Republic,* ed. Peter Avery, Gavin Hambly, and Charles Melville (Cambridge, 1991), 174.

2 Ann Lambton, *Landlord and Peasant in Persia* (Oxford, 1953), 282–94; Richard Tapper, "The Tribes in Eighteenth- and Nineteenth-Century Iran," *Cambridge History of Iran,* vol. 7, 526.

3 Lambton, *Landlord and Peasant,* 139–42.

4 Abbas Amanat, *Pivot of the Universe: Nasir al-Din Shah Qajar and the Iranian Monarchy, 1831–1896* (Berkeley, 1997), 2; Keddie and Amanat, "Iran under the Later Qajars, 1848–1922," 174. From the reign of the Saljuq Atabaygs in the eleventh century until the effective fall of the Qajar Dynasty in 1921, Iran was ruled by a series of tribal states. These included the Saljuq (1038–1194), the Ilkhanid (1256–1353), the Timurid (1370–1506), the Safavid (1501–1722), the Afshar (1736–1750), the Zand (1750–1795), and the Qajar (1795–1925).

5 By the end of the nineteenth century the number of nomads dropped to one-quarter of the Iranian population. This decrease was caused by the growth of cities and urban populations, which saw the country swell to 10 million people in 1914, while the number of pastoral nomads remained stationary. See Keddie and Amanat, "Iran under the Later Qajars," 174; Issawi, *The Economic History of Iran,* 20. On the state and "people who move around," see James C. Scott, *Seeing like a State: How Certain Schemes to Improve the Human Condition Have Failed* (New Haven, 1998), 1.

6 'Abbas Shawqi, *Dasht-i Gurgan* (Tehran, 1314/1935); Muhammad Bahman-baygi, *'Urf va Adat dar 'Ashayir-i Fars* (Tehran, 1324/1945–46); Mahmud Bavar, *Kuhgiluya va Ilat-i An* (Gachsaran, 1324/1945); Muhandas Muhammad 'Ali Mukhbir, *Baluchistan* (Tehran 1325/1946).

7 Fredrik Barth, *Nomads of South Persia: The Basseri Tribe of the Khamsah Confed-*

eracy (Oslo, 1961); Lois Beck, *The Qashqa'i of Iran* (New Haven, 1986); Jean-Pierre Digard, *Techniques des nomads baxtiyari d'Iran* (Cambridge, 1981); Gene Garthwaite, *Khans and Shahs: A Documentary Analysis of the Bakhtiyari in Iran* (Cambridge, 1983); William Irons, *The Yomut Turkmen* (Ann Arbor, 1975); Richard Tapper, *Pasture and Politics* (London, 1979); Tapper, ed., *The Conflict of Tribe and State in Iran and Afghanistan* (London, 1983); Tapper, *Frontier Nomads of Iran: A Political and Social History of the Shahsevan* (Cambridge, 1997).

8 Barth, *Nomads of South Persia*, Foreword.

9 Digard, *Techniques des nomads baxtiyari*. Also see Digard, "Histoire et anthropologie des societes nomades: Le cas d'une tribu d'Iran," *Annales: Économies, Sociétés, Civilisations* 28, no. 6 (1973), 1423–35. See also S. Caton, "Anthropological Theories of Tribe and State Formation in the Middle East: Ideology and the Semiotics of Power," *Tribes and State Formation in the Middle East*, eds. Philip Khoury and Joseph Kostiner (Berkeley, 1990), 81.

10 Garthwaite, *Khans and Shahs*, 5.

11 See Tapper, *Frontier Nomads of Iran*, 1–33.

12 On the Bakhtiyari, see 'Abd al-'Ali Khusravi Qayid Bakhtiyari, *Tarikh va Farhang-i Bakhtiyari* (Isfahan, 1372/1993); Qayid Bakhtiyari, *Bakhtiyari dar Jilvagah-i Farhang* (Isfahan, 1379/2000); Qayid Bakhtiyari, *Farhang-i Siyasi-yi 'Ashayir-i Junub-i Iran* (Isfahan, 1381/2002); Ghulam Riza Darrashuri, *Bakhtiyariha va Qajariya* (Shahr-i Kurd, 1373/1994); Ghulam 'Abbas Nawruzi Bakhtiyari, *Kitab-i Anzan* (Tehran 1374/1995); Isfandiyar Ahanjida, *Bakhtiyari va Mashruta* (Tehran, 1375/1996); Ahanjida, *Chahar Mahal va Bakhtiyari va Tamaddun-i Dirinaha-yi An* (Tehran, 1378/1999); Hafiz Idivandi, *Nigarishi bar Il-i Bakhtiyari* (Ahvaz, 1377/1998); Bahram Amir Ahmadiyan, *Il-i Bakhtiyari* (Tehran, 1378/1999); Kiyanush Kiyani Haft Lang, *Zarb al-Masalha-yi Bakhtiyari* (Tehran, 1378/1999); 'Ali Salihi, *Il-i Buzurg-i Bakhtiyari: Farhang-i Vazhigan-i Bakhtiyari* (Tehran, 1370/1991); Siyavash I'timadi, *Bakhtiyari dar Guzargah-i Zaman* (Tehran 2002). On the Lurs, see Sekandar Amanallahi, *Qawm-i Lur* (Tehran, 1370/1991); Amanallahi, *Kuch Nishini dar Iran* (Tehran, 1370/1991). On the Buyr Ahmad, see Nadir Afshar Nadiri, Javad Safi Najhad, 'Aziz Rakhsh Khurshid, Hasan Parsa, and Hushang Kishavarz, *Jam'iyat va Shinasnama-yi Ilat-i Kuhgiluya* (Tehran, 1347/1968); Nadir Afshar Nadiri, *Ilat-i Kuhgiluya va Buyr Ahmad* (Tehran, 1365/1986); Safi Najhad, *'Ashayir-i Markazi-yi Iran* (Tehran, 1375/1996); Yaqub Ghaffari, *Tarikh-i Ijtima 'i-yi Kuhgiluya va Buyr Ahmad* (Isfahan, 1379/2000). On the Qashqa'i, see M. Qahramani Abivardi, *Tarikh-i 'Ashayir-i Fars* (Tehran, 1373/1994); Riza Mustawfi al-Mamaliki, *Jughrafiya-yi Kuch Nishini* (Tehran, 1377/1998); Kavih Bayat, *Shurish-i 'Ashayir-i Fars* (Tehran, 1365/1986); Muhammad Nasir Sawlat Qashqa'i, *Salha-yi Buhran: Khatirat-i Ruzana-yi Muhammad Nasir Sawlat Qashqa'i*

(Tehran, 1366/1987); and ʿAbdallah Shahbazi, *Il-i Nashinakhti: Pajhuhishi dar Kuh Nishinan-i Surkhi-yi Fars* (Tehran, 1367/1988). On the Kurds, see Mohammad Hossein Papoli-Yazdi, *Le Nomadism dans le Nord du Khorassan* (Paris, 1991); Masʿud Gulzari, *Kirmanshahan va Kurdistan* (Tehran, 1357/1978); Karim Sanjabi, *Il-i Sanjabi va Mujahidat-i Milli-yi Iran* (Tehran, 1380/2001); Rashid Yasimi, *Kurd va Payvastigi-yi Najhadi va Tarikhi-yi U* (Tehran, 1363/1984). On the Baluch, see Muhandas Muhammad ʿAli Mukhbir, *Baluchistan* (Tehran, 1325/1946); Iraj Afshar Sistani, *Nigahi bi Sistan va Baluchistan* (Tehran, 1363/1984), Iqbal Yaghma'i, *Baluchistan va Sistan* (Tehran, 1355/1976). On the Shahsevan, see Muhammad Riza Baygdili, *Ilsevanha-yi Iran* (Tehran, 1372/1993); Ahad Qasimi, *Mughan Nigin-i Azarbayjan* (Tehran, 1377/1998). On the Turkmen, see Amin Guli, *Tarikh-i Siyasi va Ijtimaʿi-yi Turkmenha* (Tehran, 1366/1987); Baygdili, *Turkmenha-yi Iran* (Tehran, 1369/1991). Also of note is Sistani's useful compendium of the tribes. See Sistani, *Ilha, Chadurnishinan, va Tavayif-i ʿAshayiri-yi Iran* (Tehran, 1366/1987).

13 On tribe and state interactions in early modern Iranian history; see Lambton, "The Tribal Resurgence and the Decline of the Bureaucracy in the Eighteenth Century," *Studies in Eighteenth Century Islamic History*, ed. Thomas Naff and Roger Owen (London, 1977); Lambton, *Landlord and Peasant in Persia* (London, 1953); Lambton, "Ilat," *Encyclopaedia of Islam*; Laurence Lockhart, *Nadir Shah* (London, 1938); Lockhart, *The Fall of the Safavi Dynasty and the Afghan Occupation of Persia* (Cambridge, 1958); Peter Avery, "Nadir Shah and the Afsharid Legacy," *The Cambridge History of Iran,* vol. 7, 3–62; John Perry, *Karim Khan Zand* (Chicago, 1977); Perry, "The Zand Dynasty," in *The Cambridge History of Iran*, vol. 7; Perry, "Forced migration in Iran during the seventeenth and eighteenth centuries," *Iranian Studies*, 8, no. 4 (1971), 199–215; Perry, "The Banu Kaʿb: An amphibious brigand state in Khuzistan," *Le monde iranien et l'Islam* 1 (1971), 131–52; Robert Olson, *The Siege of Mosul and Ottoman-Persian Relations, 1718–1743* (Bloomington, 1975); Kathryn Babayan, *Mystics, Monarchs, and Messiahs: Cultural Landscapes of Early Modern Iran* (Cambridge, MA, 2002).

14 The tribes have often been merely a side note in the existing literature on state building and imperialism in nineteenth-century Iran. Much of the research has been state-centered, emphasizing the world of statesmen, the bureaucratic offices, and the structure of the central government, even when the tribes and the periphery enter in the discussion; see Firuz Kazemzadeh, *Russia and Britain in Persia: 1864–1914* (New Haven, 1968); Shaul Bakhash, *Iran: Monarchy, Bureaucracy, and Reform Under the Qajars, 1858–1896* (London, 1978); Bakhash, "Center-Periphery Relations in Nineteenth-Century Iran," *Iranian Studies* 14 (1981), 29–51; Guity Nashat, *The Origins of Modern Reform in Iran, 1870–1880* (Urbana, 1982). In A. Reza Sheikholeslami's more recent,

The Structure of Central Authority in Qajar Iran, 1871–1896 (Atlanta, 1997), the state-centric, modernist, and top-down approach is again presented uncritically in a theoretically and methodologically outdated structuralist study of the central government in the Nasiri period that silences the places where the shah's authority was scarcely felt. This narrow and bureaucratic perspective needs to be decentered.

15 Elements of the history of the tribes in nineteenth-century Iran have appeared in a number of works. Nikki Keddie has called attention to the role of ethnic and tribal groups in the making and composition of modern Iran. Gavin Hambly's articles on the early Qajar period, although still centered on the reigns of the shahs, are informed by tribe and state interactions. Abbas Amanat has examined the genealogy of the Qajars and their rise "from the tent to the throne." While Afsaneh Najmabadi has provided a fascinating account of gender and the slave raids of the Turkmen tribes during the Constitutional Revolution. See Lambton, *Landlord and Peasant in Persia*; Nikki Keddie, "The Minorities Question in Iran," *Iran and the Muslim World: Resistance and Revolution* (New York, 1995); Gavin Hambly, "Aqa Muhammad Khan and the Establishment of the Qajar Dynasty," *The Cambridge History of Iran,* vol. 7, 104–43; Hambly, "Iran During the Reign of Fath 'Ali Shah and Muhammad Shah," *The Cambridge History of Iran,* vol. 7, 144–73; Amanat, *Pivot of the Universe*; Afsaneh Najmabadi, *The Story of the Daughters of Quchan Gender and National Memory in Iranian History* (Syracuse, 1998).

16 See H. E. Chehabi, "Ardabil Becomes a Province: Center-Periphery Relations in Iran," *International Journal of Middle East Studies*, 29, 2 (May 1997), 235–53; Tapper, *Frontier Nomads of Iran*; Mohammad Kazembeyki, *Society, Politics, and Economics in Mazandaran, Iran, 1848–1914* (London, 2003); Vanessa Martin, *The Qajar Pact: Bargaining, Protest and the State in Nineteenth-Century Persia* (London, 2005); Heidi Walcher, *In the Shadow of the King: Zill al-Sultan and Isfahan under the Qajars* (London, 2008).

17 See Halil Inalcik, *An Economic and Social History of the Ottoman Empire*, vol. 1: *1300–1600* (Cambridge, 1994); Inalcik, "The Yuruks: Their Origins, Expansion, and Economic Role," *Medieval Carpets and Textiles: Mediterranean Carpets, 1400–1600*, vol. 1 (London, 1986); Suraiya Faroqhi, *Peasants, Dervishes, and Traders in the Ottoman Empire* (London, 1986); Suraiya Faroqhi, Bruce McGowan, Donald Quataert, and Sevket Pamuk, *An Economic and Social History of the Ottoman Empire*, vol. 2: *1600–1914* (Cambridge, 1994); Rudi Paul Lindner, *Nomads and Ottomans in Medieval Anatolia* (Bloomington, 1983); Eugene Rogan, "Asiret Mektebi: Abdulhamid II's School for Tribes (1892–1907)," *International Journal of Middle East Studies*, 28, no. 1 (February 1996), 83–107; Reşat Kasaba, *A Moveable Empire: Ottoman Nomads, Migrants, and Refugees* (Seattle, 2009).

18 For examples of the literature on the Ottoman provinces and periphery, see Metin Kunt, *The Sultan's Servants: The Transformation of Ottoman Provincial Government* (New York, 1983); Beshara Doumani, *Rediscovering Palestine: Merchants and Peasants in Jabal Nablus, 1700–1900* (Berkeley, 1995); Dina Rizk Khoury, *State and Provincial Society in the Ottoman Empire: Mosul, 1530–1834* (Cambridge, 1997); Eugene Rogan, *Frontiers of the Ottoman Empire: Transjordan* (Cambridge, 1999); Karen Barkey, *Bandits and Bureaucrats: The Ottoman Route to State Centralization* (Ithaca, 1994); Julia Clancy-Smith, *Rebel and Saint: Muslim Notables, Populist Protest, Colonial Encounters—Algeria and Tunisia, 1800–1904* (Berkeley, 1994).

19 On "history from below," see E. P. Thompson, "The Moral Economy of the English Crowd in the Eighteenth Century," *Past and Present* 50 (1971), 76–136; Thompson, "The Crime of Anonymity," *Albion's Fatal Tree: Crime and Society in Eighteenth Century England*, ed. Douglas Hay (New York, 1975); Richard Cobb, *The Police and the People: French Popular Protest, 1789–1820* (London, 1970); Cobb, *Paris and Its Provinces, 1792–1802* (London, 1975). For more recent examples of European social history, see Alain Corbin, *Village Bells: Sound and Meaning in the Nineteenth-Century French Countryside* (New York, 1998 [1994]); Corbin, *The Village of Cannibals: Rage and Murder in France, 1870* (Cambridge, 1992 [1990]). For some examples of the literature on Middle Eastern social history, see Andre Raymond, *Cairo* (Cambridge, Mass., 2001); Ehud Toledano, *State and Society in Mid-Nineteenth-Century Egypt* (Cambridge, 1990); Kenneth M. Cuno, *The Pasha's Peasants: Land, Society, and Economy in Lower Egypt, 1740–1858* (Cambridge, 1992); Khaled Fahmy, *All the Pasha's Men: Mehmed Ali, His Army and the Making of Modern Egypt* (Cambridge, 1997); Joel Beinin, *Workers and Peasants in the Modern Middle East* (Cambridge, 2001). For some recent works on the social history of Iran, see Martin, *The Qajar Pact*; Stephanie Cronin, *Tribal Politics in Iran: Rural Conflict and the New State, 1921–1941* (London, 2007); Touraj Atabaygi, *The State and the Subaltern* (London, 2007). For edited collections of essays on the social history of the Middle East, see Edmund Burke, ed., *Struggle and Survival in the Modern Middle East* (California, 1993); Eugene Rogan, ed., *Outside In: On the Margins of the Modern Middle East* (London, 2002).

20 Suraiya Faroqhi has made this observation in regard to Ottoman historiography; see Faroqhi, *Approaching Ottoman History* (Cambridge, 1999), 21–22.

21 Rudolph Matthee, *The Politics of Trade in Safavid Iran: Silk for Silver 1600–1730* (Cambridge, 1999), 62. On this theme, also see Martin, *The Qajar Pact.*

22 John Richards, *The Unending Frontier: An Environmental History of the Early Modern World* (Berkeley, 2003), 22.

23 Timothy Mitchell, *Rule of Experts: Egypt, Techno-Politics, Modernity* (Berkeley, 2002), 52.

24 Ibid., 36.

25 Ibid., 35.

26 Karl Marx and Friedrich Engels, *The Communist Manifesto* (New York, 2002), 223.

27 Mirza Muhammad Taqi Lisan al-Mulk Sipihr, *Nasikh al-Tavarikh*, ed. Jamshid Kiyanfar, 3 vols. (Tehran, 1377/1998); Riza Quli Khan Hidayat Lalabashi, *Rawzat al-Safa-yi Nasiri*, ed. Jamshid Kiyanfar, vols. 9–10 (Tehran, 1338–39/1959–60); Muhammad Hasan Khan I'timad al-Saltana, *Mir'at al-Buldan*, ed. 'Abd al-Husayn Nava'i, 3 vols. (Tehran, 1367/1988); I'timad al-Saltana, *Tarikh-i Muntazam-i Nasiri*, ed. Muhammad Isma'il Rizvani, 3 vols. (Tehran, 1363/1984); Hajj Mirza Hasan Fasa'i, *Farsnama-yi Nasiri,* 2 vols., ed. Mansur Rastigar Fasa'i, 2 vols. (Tehran, 1367/1988).

28 Fourteen authors and translators collaborated on this history of the Bakhtiyari. See 'Ali Quli Khan Sardar As'ad and 'Abd al-Husayn Lisan al Mulk Sipihr, *Tarikh-i Bakhtiyari*, ed. Jamshid Kiyanfar (Tehran, 1376/1997), 30–33, 45.

29 Edward Said, *Orientalism* (New York, 1978).

1 *On the Periphery of Nineteenth-Century Iran*

1 Lisan al-Mulk Sipihr, *Nasikh al-Tavarikh*, vol. 1, 277.

2 On the different tribal populations of Iran in the Qajar period, see Muhammad Hasan Khan I'timad al-Saltana, *Tarikh-i Muntazam-i Nasiri*, vol. 1, 539–60. Lady Mary Sheil guessed that if all the clans were counted their population would equal the number of townspeople. Mary Sheil, *Glimpses of Life and Manners in Persia, with notes on Russia, Koords, Toorkomans, Nestorians, Khiva, and Persia* (London, 1856), 393. The population of Iran has been estimated at 5 to 6 million around 1800. See Charles Issawi, *The Economic History of Iran, 1800–1914* (Chicago, 1971), 20.

3 Ibn Khaldun, *Muqaddimah*, trans. Franz Rosenthal (Princeton, 1958), vol. 1, 332.

4 Far from strangers, tribes and the state in nineteenth-century Iran were in many ways symbiotic. Contemporary observers noted that the Qajars never lost their attachment to their nomadic background. William Ouseley wrote that Fath 'Ali Shah Qajar preferred "an erratick to a settled life; a village to a city, and a tent to a palace." See William Ouseley, *Travels in Various Countries of the East*, vol. 3 (London, 1819), 151. The later Qajar ruler Nasir al-Din Shah also remained true to his nomadic roots, as indicated by his lifelong love of the outdoors and of riding and hunting. See Amanat, *Pivot of the Universe*, 69; Darrashuri, *Bakhtiyariha va Qajariya*, 135–36; Lambton, "Ilat," 1103.

5 Riza Quli Khan Hidayat, *Rawzat al-Safa-yi Nasiri*; *Nasikh al-Tavarikh*.

6 Muhammad Hasan Khan I'timad al-Saltana, *Mir'at al-Buldan-i Nasiri* (hereafter MB); *Tarikh-i Muntazam-i Nasiri*; Mirza Abu al-Hasan Sani' al-Mulk Ghaffari, *Ruznama-yi Dawlat-i 'Alliya-yi Iran* (Tehran, 1370/1991); Government of Iran, *Ruznama-yi Vaqa 'i'-yi Ittifaqiya* (Tehran, 1373/1994).

7 Henry Rawlinson, "Notes on a March from Zohab, at the foot of the Zagros, along the mountains to Khuzistan (Susiana), and from thence through the province of Luristan to Kirmanshah, in the year 1836," *Journal of the Royal Geographical Society of London* (hereafter JRGS) 9 (1839), 102–3; Austen Henry Layard, "A Description of the Province of Khuzistan," JRGS 16 (1846), 101–5. Rawlinson's estimate of 28,000 tents equals approximately 140,000 people. Layard's figure of 51,200 tents equals roughly 256,000 individuals. Rawlinson's and Layard's estimates most likely provide more reliable figures than the one given by James Morier, who speculated in 1809 that the Bakhtiyari consisted of 100,000 families. See Morier, *A Journey Through Persia, Armenia, and Asia Minor, to Constantinople, in the Years 1808 and 1809; in Which is Included, Some Account of the Proceedings of His Majesty's Mission, Under Sir Harford Jones to the Court of Persia* (London, 1812), 242.

8 See, for instance, the reports of Bakhtiyari looting in Isfahan during Fath 'Ali Shah's rule in Hidayat, *Rawzat al-Safa-yi Nasiri*, vol. 9, 631–32.

9 Richard Tapper, "The Tribes in 18th and 19th Century Iran," *Cambridge History of Iran,* vol. 7, ed. Peter Avery, Gavin Hambly, and Charles Melville (Cambridge, 1991), 506. In his more recent and extensive study of the Shahsevan, *Frontier Nomads of Iran*, Tapper examines nineteenth-century Persian chronicles to reconstruct tribal history. See Tapper, *Frontier Nomads of Iran*.

10 See Pamela Kyle Crossley, Helen Siu, Donald Sutton, eds., *At the Margins of Empire: Culture, Ethnicity, and Frontier in Early Modern China* (Berkeley, CA, 2006).

11 Brent D. Shaw, "Bandit Highlands and Lowland Peace: The Mountains of Isauria-Cicilia (Continued)," *Journal of the Economic and Social History of the Orient* 33 (3) (1990): 269.

12 Sardar As'ad and Lisan al-Mulk Sipihr, *Tarikh-i Bakhtiyari* (hereafter TB), 192.

13 TB, 496. Also see A.H. Layard, "Ancient Sites among the Bakhtiari Mountains," JRGS, 12 (1842), 102–9.

14 Ibn Hawqal, *Kitab Surat al-Ard* (Configuration de la Terre), vol. 2, trans. J. H. Kramers and G. Wiet (Paris, 1964), 255.

15 See Minorsky, "Lur," 41.

16 Amir Sharaf Khan Bidlisi, *Sharafnama-yi Tarikh-i Mufassal-i Kurdistan* (Tehran, 1343/1964), 47. Also see Minorsky, "Lur," 42.

17 Hamdallah Mustawfi, *Nuzhat al-Qulub*, ed. G. Le Strange (Leiden, 1919), 185, 207. Also see Le Strange, *The Lands of the Eastern Caliphate* (London, 1905),

207, 233.

18 Tapper suggests that during the seventeenth century the tribes of the Zagros numbered "up to one million people." Tapper, "The Tribes," 512. On the history of the Safavids see Roger Savory, *Iran under the Safavids* (Cambridge, 1980); Rudolph Matthee, *The Politics of Trade in Safavid Iran: Silk for Silver, 1600–1730*; Kathryn Babayan, *Mystics, Monarchs, and Messiahs: Cultural Landscapes of Early Modern Iran* (Cambridge, MA, 2002). On the tribes in Safavid Iran, see Tapper, "Shahsevan in Safavid Persia," *Bulletin of the School of Oriental and African Studies*, 37, 2 (1974), 321–54; Tapper, "Black Sheep, White Sheep and Red Heads, A Historical Sketch of the Shahsevan of Azarbaijan," *Iran*, 4, 61–84; James J. Reid, *Tribalism and Society in Islamic Iran 1500–1629* (Malibu, 1983).

19 For instance, see Iskandar Bayg Munshi, *Tarikh-i 'Alamara-yi 'Abbasi*, trans. Roger Savory, *The History of Shah 'Abbas the Great* (Boulder, 1978); Iskandar Bayg Munshi, *Tarikh-i 'Alamara-yi 'Abbasi*, ed. Iraj Afshar, 2 vols. (Tehran, 1382/2003); *Tadhkirat al-Muluk*, trans. V. Minorsky (London, 1943).

20 Ahanjida, *Il-i Bakhtiyari va Mashrutiyat*, 23–24.

21 Minorsky, "Lur," 45; *Sharafnama*, vol. 1, 48; Ahanjida, *Il-i Bakhtiyari*, 25.

22 For complete lists of the Bakhtiyari tribes and subtribes, see TB, 617–19.

23 TB, 154; Sardar Zafar, *Yaddashtha va Khatirat*, 150–51.

24 Munshi, *Tarikh-i 'Alamara*, vol. 2, 677, 1312.

25 Lambton, "Ilat," 1101.

26 See the list of *amiran* and their tribal retinues in the Safavid administrative manual *Tadhkirat al-Muluk*, 100–105.

27 *Tadhkirat al-Muluk*, 43–44, 104.

28 John Malcolm, *The History of Persia, from the Most Early Period to the Present Time: Containing an Account of the Religion, Government, Usages, and Character of the Inhabitants of that Kingdom*, vol. 2 (London, 1815), 457–58. On the Safavids and tribal religion, see Kathryn Babayan, *Mystics, Monarchs, and Messiahs: Cultural Landscapes of Early Modern Iran* (Cambridge, MA), 2003.

29 David Brooks, "The Enemy Within: Limitations on Leadership in the Bakhtiari," in *The Conflict of Tribe and State in Afghanistan*, 347. For a contemporary description of Safavid building projects in Isfahan, see Munshi, *Tarikh-i 'Alamara*, vol. 2, 724–25, 1038–39.

30 Munshi, *Tarikh-i 'Alamara*, vol. 2, 1170–71, 1180. Also see Sarhang Abu al-Fath Uzhan Bakhtiyari, *Tarikh-i Bakhtiyari* (Tehran, 1345/1966), 8–12, 330–31.

31 Munshi, *Tarikh-i 'Alamara*, 1170–71, 1180. For references to the unfinished Kuh Rang dam in seventeenth-century European travelogues, also see Jan Janszoon Struys, *The voyages and travels of John Struys through Italy, Greece, Muscovy, Tartary, Medea, Persia, East India, Japan and other countries in Europe, Africa, and Asia* (London, 1684), 314–16; N. Sanson, *The Present State of Persia,*

With a Faithful Account of the Manners, Religion, and Government of That People (London, 1695), 55–56.

32 Munshi, *Tarikh-i ʿAlamara*, vol. 2, 1170; Uzhan, *Tarikh-i Bakhtiyari*, 8.

33 Munshi, *Tarikh-i ʿAlamara*, vol. 2, 1170–71; Uzhan, *Tarikh-i Bakhtiyari*, 9.

34 Ibid., vol. 2, 1180.

35 Adam Olearius, *The voiyages and travels of the ambassadors sent by Fredrick, Duke of Holstein, to the Great Duke of Muscovy and the King of Persia* (London, 1669), 218.

36 John Chardin, *The Travels of Sir John Chardin into Persia and the East Indies; The Coronation of Solyman III, King of Persia* (London, 1686), 147.

37 John Fryer, *A new account of East-India and Persia, in eight letters* (London, 1698), 391–92.

38 Here Ogilby is describing the southwestern Iranian province of Khuzistan. See John Ogilby, *Asia, The First Part Being an Accurate Description of Persia and Several Provinces Thereof* (London, 1673), 34.

39 Fryer, *A new account of East-India and Persia*, 328

40 Thomas Herbert, *Some yeares travels into divers parts of Asia and Afrique* (London, 1638), 130.

41 Sanson, *The Present State of Persia*, 30.

42 Ibid., 31.

43 Jean de Thévenot, *The Travels of Monsieur de Thévenot in the Levant* (London, 1687), 71.

44 Ogilby, *Asia*, 103.

45 Lambton, "Ilat," 1102; Tapper, "Tribes," 513.

46 Mirza Muhammad Mihdi Khan Astarabadi, *Jahangusha-yi Nadiri*, ed. Saʿid ʿAbdallah Anvar (Tehran, 1341/1962), 2–3. For partial translations of Astarabadi's text in French and English, see William Jones, *Histoire de Nader-Chah, connu sous le nom de Thahmas Kuli Khan, Empereur de Perse* (Paris, 1770); Jones, *The History of the Life of Nadir Shah, King of Persia: Extracted from an Eastern Manuscript, which was translated into French by order of His Majesty the King of Denmark* (London, 1773).

47 On the waning of the Qizilbash, see Babayan, *Mystics, Monarchs, and Messiahs*, 295–482.

48 See Lambton, "The Tribal Resurgence and the Decline of the Bureaucracy in the Eighteenth Century," *Studies in Eighteenth Century Islamic History*, eds. Thomas Naff and Roger Owen (London, 1977); Lambton, *Landlord and Peasant in Persia* (London, 1953); Lambton, "Ilat," *Encyclopaedia of Islam*; Laurence Lockhart, *Nadir Shah* (London, 1938); *The Fall of the Safavi Dynasty and the Afghan Occupation of Persia* (Cambridge, 1958); Peter Avery, "Nadir Shah and the Afsharid Legacy," *The Cambridge History of Iran*, vol. 7, 3–62. John Perry, *Karim Khan Zand: A History of Iran* (Chicago, 1979); Perry, "Forced migra-

tion in Iran during the seventeenth and eighteenth centuries," *Iranian Studies*, 8, 4 (1971), 199–215; Perry, "The Zand Dynasty," in *The Cambridge History of Iran,* vol. 7; Perry, "The Banu Ka'b: an amphibious brigand state in Khuzistan," *Le monde iranien et l'Islam* 1 (1971), 131–52; Robert Olson, *The Siege of Mosul and Ottoman-Persian Relations, 1718–1743* (Bloomington, 1975). Michael Axworthy and Ernest Tucker have recently published monographs on Nadir Shah Afshar. See Axworthy, *The Sword of Persia: Nadir Shah, from Tribal Warrior to Conquering Tyrant* (London, 2006), and Tucker, *Nadir Shah's Quest for Legitimacy in Post-Safavid Iran* (Gainesville, 2006). For a social history of the Afshar years in Persian see Riza Sha'bani, *Tarikh-i Ijtima'i-yi Iran dar 'Asr-i Afshariya*, 2 vols. (Tehran, 1377/1998).

49 For contemporary accounts of the Afshar period in European languages, see Pere Louis Bazin, *Mémoires sur les dernières anées du règne de Thamas Kouli-Kan et sa mort tragique, contenus dans une lettre du Frère Bazin* (Paris, 1780), 277–364; James Fraser, *The History of Nadir Shah, formerly called Thamas Kuli Khan, the Present Emperor of Persia* (London, 1742); Jean Otter, *Voyage en Turquie et en Perse, avec une Relation des expéditions de Tahmas Koulikhan* (Paris, 1748); Jonas Hanway, *An Historical Account of the British Trade over the Caspian Sea: With a Journal of Travels through Russia into Persia*, 4 vols. (London, 1753).

50 Muhammad Kazim Marvi, *'Alamara-yi Nadiri*, ed. Muhammad Amin Riyahi, vol. 1 (Tehran, 1364/1985), 49.

51 Retinues numbering 7,000 Bakhtiyari tribesmen were collected by 'Ali Salih Haft Lang in 1733; 10,000 to 12,000 more were collected by 'Ali Mardan Chahar Lang in the same year, and 4,000 more Bakhtiyari were recruited following the tribes' rebellion in 1736. See Marvi, *'Alamara*, vol. 1, 223, 245; Astarabadi, *Jahangusha*, 300. The Afshar army did not attack Qandahar until January 1738. After cannons had partially damaged Qandahar's fortifications, Nadir Shah allowed 900 tribal volunteers from the Bakhtiyari, Kurd, and Abdali tribes to lead an assault on the city. When this charge was repulsed, amidst rumors that Qandahar still possessed enough provisions to endure four more years of the siege, the shah planned another assault. Seeking to inspire the mercenary instincts of his army he promised a reward of 1,000 *nadiris* to each volunteer who would storm the city, not to mention the spoils of the citadel in the event of conquest. See Marvi, *'Alamara*, vol. 2, 544; also see Malcolm, *History of Persia*, vol. 2, 68.

52 Lockhart, *Nadir Shah*, 268–69.

53 Likewise, pastoral nomadism was encouraged among the men of the army, as the tribes that made up Nadir's military dwelled in tents, subsisted on their flocks, and changed their quarters with the season. Nadir envisioned his army as a fast-moving cavalry, largely composed of pastoral nomadic groups. It appears that he generally discouraged his military men from acquiring

property, preferring them to remain "always on the move" (*khana bi dush*). Lambton, *Landlord and Peasant*, 130. It could even be suggested that when Nadir resettled the Bakhtiyari on the northeastern frontier, giving them land grants over the districts of Jam and Bakhgarz and ordering their cultivation, he was not necessarily seeking the permanent settlement of the Bakhtiyari, but rather to establish administrative control over them and ensure that they protected the agrarian sources of revenue—the crops produced by the local peasantry. See the *raqam* issued by Nadir Shah to 'Ali Salih Haft Lang in 1745–46, Garthwaite, *Khans and Shahs*, appendix 1, documents 2–4, 13.

54 See Astarabadi, *Jahangusha*, passim; Marvi, *'Alamara*, passim. The theme of empire and ethnicity has been brilliantly explored in some recent works on Chinese history. See Pamela Kyle Crossley, *Orphan Warriors: Three Manchu Generations and the End of the Qing World* (Princeton, 1990); Crossley, et al., *Empire at the Margins*; Crossley, "Thinking About Ethnicity in Late Imperial China," *Late Imperial China*, 11, 1 (June 1990), 1–35; Mark Elliot, *The Manchu Way: The Eight Banners and Ethnic Identity in Late Imperial China* (Stanford, 2001). These studies of Manchu ethnicity in late imperial China contrast with South Asian historiography, which has tended to focus on the nineteenth century, the colonial rule of the British Raj, and the imposition of modern western forms of knowledge on the construction of ethnic identities.

55 TB, 154.

56 Ibid., 391.

57 These events are reported in Astarabadi, *Jahangusha*, 188–89; Marvi, *'Alamara*, vol. 1, 234–35; TB, 392.

58 Astarabadi, *Jahangusha*, 189.

59 Astarabadi, *Jahangusha*, 223, 245; TB, 392–93.

60 Marvi, *'Alamara*, vol. 1, 223, 234–35; Astarabadi, *Jahangusha*, 188–89; TB, 392; Lockhart, *Nadir Shah*, 65.

61 Marvi, *'Alamara*, vol. 2, 471. According to Marvi, 'Ali Murad's displeasure had been aroused earlier when he was passed over and not given the title of *bashi* (head or chief) that other Bakhtiyari headmen had received. Nevertheless, he used his reputation as a fierce warrior and "the weight of his sword," as Marvi described, to raise retinues for 'Ali Salih Khan in 1733. The rebellion of the Bakhtiyari and 'Ali Murad is also reported in Astarabadi, *Jahangusha*, 280–84; TB, 393–97.

62 Marvi, *'Alamara*, vol. 2, 471–72.

63 In his chronicle Marvi wrote verses on the flight of the Bakhtiyari from Nadir Shah's army; the following is an excerpt: *Az har su daliran dar anjuman/big-ashtan dar kuh va sahn-i chaman/nadidand asar az an dalir-i dujham/shudand jumla bas khashmgin va dujham/biguftand magar Bakhtiyari tamam/paridand chun murgh az ru-yi dam*. Marvi, *'Alamara*, vol. 2, 474.

64 Astarabadi, *Jahangusha*, 280–84; Marvi, *'Alamara*, 471–77; TB, 114–15, 393–95; Lockhart, *Nadir Shah*, 109–10.

65 Malcolm, *History of Persia*, vol. 2, 67.

66 'Ali Mardan Khan sought to cement his authority over the Bakhtiyari tribes and all of western Iran by making alliances with surrounding tribal potentates, including Karim Khan Zand. A pact was reached between 'Ali Mardan Khan, who assumed the title "Deputy of the Sultan" (*Nayib al-Saltana*); Abu al-Fath Khan Haft Lang, who remained governor of Isfahan; and Karim Khan Zand, who gained the title "Regent of the State" (*Vakil al-Dawla*) and also became commander of the cavalry (*Sardar Sipah*). The seventeen-year old Safavid prince, Abu Turab, was enthroned as Adil Shah. The alliance among these Lur chiefs was short-lived, however. After blinding and killing Abu al-Fath Khan, 'Ali Mardan Khan marched on the southern province of Fars and plundered Shiraz. In 1751, tribal levies from the Zand entered Bakhtiyari territory and defeated the retinues of 'Ali Mardan Khan. In 1754, as the aging 'Ali Mardan tried to rebuild his forces and regain control of the Safavid throne, he was killed by Zand tribesmen near Kirmanshah. See Sardar As'ad and Sipihr, TB, 24, 399, 402–3, 611. The accounts given in the *Tarikh-i Bakhtiyari* differ from Perry's claim, based on Zand sources, that 'Ali Mardan Khan acquired the title *Vakil al-Dawla* at this point; see Perry, "The Zand Dynasty," 66. Garthwaite has noted that on coins struck during this period, 'Ali Mardan is referred to as *banda-yi Isma'il* or the slave of Isma'il; see Garthwaite, *Khans and Shahs*, 54. For vernacular songs and folklore on 'Ali Mardan Khan see *Ash'ar va Taranaha-yi Mardumi-yi Bakhtiyari bi Inzimam-i Sharh-i Jangha va Hamasaha*, (ed.) Bijhan Husayni (Isfahan, 1376/1997), 72–75.

67 Amanat, *Pivot of the Universe*, 2. The Qajar dynasty (1785–1925) became the last nomad state to rule Iran, a history traceable to the arrival of the Saljuq Turks in West Asia during the tenth century.

68 Hidayat's text offered a revised edition of Mirkhvand's chronicle from Timurid Herat, *Rawzat al-Safa*, with the last three volumes providing an original account of Qajar history. It has been noted that Hidayat's historical writings were a part of the *bazgasht-i adabi*, a literary movement that sought to revive the Persian literary style of pre-Timurid times. On Hidayat see Paul Losensky, "Reza Qoli Khan Hedayat," *Encyclopaedia Iranica*, 12, 2 (2003), 119–21; Edward G. Browne, *The Literary History of Persia*, vol. 4 (Cambridge, 1930), 413, 455.

69 *Rawzat al-Safa-yi Nasiri*, vol. 9, 7075.

70 Morier, *A Journey Through Persia, Armenia, and Asia Minor, to Constantinople, in the Years 1808 and 1809; in Which is Included, Some Account of the Proceedings of His Majesty's Mission, Under Sir Harford Jones to the Court of Persia* (London, 1812), 240.

71 Amanat, *Pivot of the Universe*, 433.

72 On I'timad al-Saltana, see Amanat, "Mohammad Hasan Khan Etemad al-Saltana," *Encyclopaedia Iranica*, 8, 6 (1998); Peter Avery, "Printing, the Press, and Literature in Iran," *Cambridge History of Iran, Vol. 7*, 824–25; Browne, *The Literary History of Persia*, vol. 4, 453–55.

73 See the passages on the Bakhtiyari chieftains Asad Khan, Ja'far Quli Khan, Muhammad 'Ali Khan, and Muhammad Taqi Khan in TB.

74 See MB, vol. 1, 122–25 and vol. 2, 1031, 1113, 1120; Muhammad Taqi Khan, *Ganj-i Danish*, 72, 985.

75 *Nasikh al-Tavarikh*, vol. 1, 355.

76 See for example, *Nasikh al-Tavarikh,* vol. 1, 24, 45; TB, 405; Gavin Hambly, "Agha Muhammad Khan Qajar and the Establishment of the Qajar Dynasty," *Cambridge History of Iran,* vol. 7, 114.

77 Iranian National Archives (INA), Asnad-i Milki, 1004/91, Farman from Karim Khan Zand, 1183/1769.

78 INA, Asnad-i Milki, 1004/88, Farman from Karim Khan Zand, 1182/1768.

79 Fasa'i, *Farsnama-yi Nasiri*, vol. 1, 634.

80 *Rawzat al-Safa-yi Nasiri,* 195–96.

81 Tribal histories note the divide-and-conquer tactics Aqa Muhammad Khan employed against the Bakhtiyari, a policy that set the precedent for subsequent Qajar rulers. In *Tarikh-i Bakhtiyari* it is written that Aqa Muhammad Khan fought two wars against the Bakhtiyari. During the first of these the Haft Lang and Chahar Lang were united and routed the enemy. Aqa Muhammad Khan then made promises to various khans, dividing the Bakhtiyari ranks before his campaign into the Zagros in 1786. The Qajar commander realized he could manipulate the existing tribal subdivisions within the Bakhtiyari to his advantage and did not hesitate to bribe rival khans and clans to weaken the Bakhtiyari confederacy. Through this policy Aqa Muhammad Khan managed to avoid full-scale Bakhtiyari resistance. See TB, 166–67. This account is corroborated in Sardar Zafar, *Yaddashtha va Khatirat*, 141.

82 Muhammad Fathallah ibn Muhammad Taqi Saravi, *Tarikh-i Muhammadi ("Ahsan al-Tavarikh"),* ed. Ghulam Riza Tabataba'i Majd (Tehran, 1371/1992), 147.

83 Saravi, *Tarikh-i Muhammadi*, 148.

84 Ibid., 149–50.

85 Ibid., 150–51. Some aspects of the plunder of the Bakhtiyari at the hands of the Qajar regiments are also noted in chronicles of the Nasir al-Din Shah period, see *Nasikh al-Tavarikh*, vol. 1, 48–49; *Rawzat al-Safa-yi Nasiri,* vol. 9, 196.

86 TB, 167.

87 Morier, "Account," 234–35. During the 1840s Austen Henry Layard recorded the tax assessments in mules and tumans for various Bakhtiyari subtribes in a

reconnaissance report written for the *Journal of the Royal Geographical Society of London*, estimating that the sedentary Chahar Lang paid more revenues than the nomadic Haft Lang. See Austen Henry Layard, "A Description of the Province of Khuzistan," *JRGS* 16 (1846), 101–5.

88 Curzon noted in the 1880s that Bakhtiyari revenues were assessed at 22,000 tumans to the governor of Isfahan and 15,000 tumans to the governor of Khuzistan. George Nathaniel Curzon, *Persia and the Persian Question*, vol. 2 (London, 1892), 298. For contemporary references to the Bakhtiyari's taxation in the first half of the nineteenth century, see Rawlinson, "Notes on a March from Zohab," 102–3; C. A. deBode, *Travels in Luristan and Arabistan*, vol. 2 (London, 1845), 88. Also see Garthwaite, *Khans and Shahs*, 65.

89 Morier, "Account," 238.

90 Malcolm, *History of Persia*, vol. 2, 465.

91 M. Louis Dubeux, *La Perse* (Paris, 1841), 407–8.

92 Robert Ker Porter, *Travels in Georgia, Persia, Armenia, Ancient Babylonia, During the Years 1817, 1818, 1819, and 1820*, vol. 2 (London, 1822), 9.

93 Ker Porter, *Travels*, vol. 2, 34.

94 Ibid., vol. 1, 473–75.

95 According to James Morier, who traveled to Iran in the first decades of the nineteenth century, a "white beard" was an "emblem of power and superiority" among tribal communities. See Morier, "Some Account of the I'lyats, or Wandering Tribes of Persia, obtained in the Years 1814 and 1815," *JRGS* 7 (1837), 238.

96 Malcolm, *History of Persia* (London, 1815), vol. 2, 605.

97 Malcolm, *Sketches of Persia* (London, 1849), 158–59.

98 *TB*, 410.

99 Morier, "Account," 234–35.

100 *Nasikh al-Tavarikh*, vol. 1, 372–73; *TB*, 169–70, 413–14. For further accounts of the Bakhtiyari exploits in Iran's wars against Russia in the early nineteenth century, see Mirza Fazlallah Shirazi, *Tarikh-i Zu al-Qarnayn*, vol. 2, ed. by Nasir Afsharfar (Tehran, 1380/2001), 648–51.

101 Shirazi, *Tarikh-i Zu al-Qarnayn*, 911.

102 Also in the service of Hisam al-Saltana were the Bajalan and Biranvand tribes. See *Nasikh al-Tavarikh*, vol. 1, 389; *TB*, 169–70, 413–14; Shirazi, *Tarikh-i Zu al-Qarnayn*, vol. 2, 761.

103 *Nasikh al-Tavarikh,* vol. 2, 595.

104 Ibid., vol. 1, 408–9, 433; *Rawzat al-Safa-yi Nasiri*, vol. 9, 732–34.

105 Ibid., vol. 1, 443–45; *TB*, 414–15; Shirazi, *Tarikh-i Zu al-Qarnayn*, vol. 2, 810–13.

106 See Owen Lattimore, *Inner Asian Frontiers of China* (New York, 1940), 170.

107 Riza Quli Mirza Nayib al-Ayala, *Safarnama-yi Riza Quli Mirza*, ed. Asghar Farman Farmayi Qajar (Tehran 1361/1982), 23.

108 Ibid., 24.

109 Ibid., 25.

110 Recent work in Ottoman and Qajar history that explores this theme includes Leslie Peirce, *Morality Tales: Law and Gender in the Ottoman Court of Aintab* (Berkeley, 2003); Vanessa Martin, *The Qajar Pact: Bargaining, Protest, and the State in Nineteenth-Century Persia* (London, 2004).

111 *Nasikh al-Tavarikh*, vol. 1, 277.

112 TB, 168.

113 Morier, *A Second Journey Through Persia, Armenia, and Asia Minor, to Constantinople Between the Years 1810 and 1816* (London, 1818), 80, 126.

114 See Uzhan, *Tarikh-i Bakhtiyari*, 33.

115 On the Gardane mission see A. Gardane, *Journal d'un voyage dans la Turquie d'Asie et la Perse, fait en 1807 et 1808* (Paris, 1809); J. M. Tancoigne, *Lettres sur la Perse et la Turquie d'Asie*, 2 vols. (Paris, 1819); Harford Jones Brydges, *An Account of the Transactions of the His Majesty's Mission to Persia in the Years 1807–1811* (London, 1834); G. Drouville, *Voyage en Perse*, 2 vols. (Paris, 1825).

116 Sardar Zafar, *Yaddashtha va Khatirat*, 9–17; Uzhan, *Tarikh-i Bakhtiyari*, 34.

117 TB, 168; Uzhan, *Tarikh-i Bakhtiyari*, 35–36.

118 Sardar Zafar, *Yaddashtha va Khatirat*, 9–10. On Diz-i Malikan and other Bakhtiyari fortresses, see Curzon, *Persia and the Persian Question*, vol. 2, 301–3.

119 Sardar Zafar, *Yaddashtha va Khatirat*, 12. There exist a number of studies on Bakhtiyari folkore. In 1884–85, the Russian scholar V. A. Zhukovsky collected nearly 2,000 lines of verse, which were published in the 1920s as *Materiali dlya Izucheniya Persidskikh Marechii. Narechie Bakhtiarov Chekharleng i Kheftleng* (Petrograd, 1922). D. L. R. Lorimer (1876–1962), British vice-consul at Ahvaz, 1904–9, provided the first English-language studies of the Bakhtiyari dialect. Before World War I, Lorimer managed to record 2,800 lines of verse and a large number of Bakhtiyari prose texts totaling 75,000 words. The most comprehensive collection of these materials can be found in the D. L. R. Lorimer Papers at the archives of the University of London–School of Oriental and African Studies (PP MS 66). These materials also became the basis of a collection of Bakhtiyari stories and several anthropological articles published by Lorimer on the Bakhtiyari tribes. They included *Persian Tales* (London, 1919); "The Popular Verse of the Bakhtiari of S.W. Persia—Part 1," *Bulletin of the School of Oriental and African Studies*, 16; "The Popular Verse of the Bakhtiari of S.W. Persia—Part 2," *Bulletin of the School of Oriental and African Studies*, 17; *The Phonology of the Bakhtiyari, Badakhshani, and Madaglashti Dialects of Modern Persian* (London, 1922); "A Bakhtiyari Prose Text," *Journal of the Royal Asiatic Society*, 1930. For more recent studies of Bakhtiyari folklore and dialect, see F. Vahman, *West Iranian Dialect Materials from the Collection of D. L. Lorimer* (Copenhagen, 1987).

120 The study of ethnic folklore has intrigued Western observers of tribal societies since the nineteenth century. Explorers and orientalists who came into contact with the tribes were struck by their poetry and emphasized the importance of the oral tradition in Islamic civilization, with roots in the Bedouin *qasida*. This interest persists, and over the past twenty years several interesting studies of tribal poetry in the Islamic world have been published. This research has primarily been the work of anthropologists; see, for instance, Lila Abu-Lughod, *Veiled Sentiments: Honor and Poetry in a Bedouin Society* (Berkeley, 1986), and Steven Caton, *"Peaks of Yemen I Summon": Poetry as Cultural Practice in a North Yemeni Tribe* (Berkeley, 1990).

121 *Ash'ar va Taranaha-yi Mardumi-yi Bakhtiyari bi Inzimam-i Sharh-i Jangha va Hamasaha*, 25–29. This poem is also recorded in Qayid Bakhtiyari, *Tarikh-i Farhang va Adabiyat-i Bakhtiyari* (Isfahan, 1375/1996), 171–72.

122 Apart from Qajar and Bakhtiyari sources there are scattered references to Asad Khan in European travelogues including Morier, who describes the meeting between Asad Khan and Prince Muhammad 'Ali Mirza in 1813. See Morier, "Account," 235. On Muhammad 'Ali Mirza, see Amanat, "Dawlatshah, Mohammad 'Ali Mirza," *Encyclopaedia Iranica* 7, 2 (1994).

123 *Nasikh al-Tavarikh,* vol. 1, 277–78.

124 Ibid.; 'Akkasha, *Tarikh-i Il-i Bakhtiyari*, 287–89; TB, 169, 409–11.

125 Sardar Zafar, *Yaddashtha va Khatirat*, 150–51.

126 MB, vol. 1, 909. Also see *Nasikh al-Tavarikh*, vol. 1, 515–17; *Rawzat al-Safa-yi Nasiri,* vol. 10, 183–86. Sipihr and Hidayat's accounts were clearly the sources of the version of events given in TB, 416–30.

127 MB, vol. 1, 910; *Nasikh al-Tavarikh,* vol. 1, 517.

128 MB, vol. 1, 924.

129 *Nasikh al-Tavarikh*, vol. 2, 653–54, 661.

130 According to the *Tarikh-i Bakhtiyari* Muhammad Taqi Khan opted for peace to save the Chahar Lang from the hardships of war. In contrast court chronicles claim that it was the fear of Qajar troops that made the Bakhtiyari chieftain "fearfully obedient." TB, 420–21. Also see MB, vol. 1, 924–25; *Rawzat al-Safa-yi Nasiri,* vol. 10, 224–31.

131 Hasan 'Ali Afshar, *Safarnama-yi Luristan va Khuzistan*, ed. Hamid Riza Dilvand (Tehran, 1382/2003), 105.

132 MB, vol. 2, 11; *Nasikh al-Tavarikh*, vol. 31073–75.

133 *Nasikh al-Tavarikh*, vol. 3, 1087.

134 *Khuzistan va Luristan dar 'Asr-i Nasiri: Bi Ravayat-i Farmanha-yi Nasir al-Din Shah, Mukatibat-i Amir Kabir va Mirza Aqa Khan Nuri ba Ihtisham al-Dawla* (hereafter KL), ed. Manuchihr Ihtishami (Tehran, 1383/2004), Order of Mirza Taqi Khan Amir Kabir to Khanlar Mirza Ihtisham al-Dawla, 1267/1851, doc. 5, 28–29.

135 For instance see Afshar, *Safarnama-yi Luristan va Khuzistan*, 164.

136 KL, Mirza Aqa Khan Nuri to Chiraq 'Ali Khan, nayib al-hukuma of Isfahan, 1268/1852, doc. 33, 57.

137 KL, Mirza Aqa Khan Nuri to Khanlar Mirza Ihtisham al-Dawla, 1268/1852, doc. 39, 63–65.

2 *The City of Isfahan and Its Hinterland*

1 Mirza Husayn Tahvildar, *Jughrafiya-yi Isfahan*, ed. Manuchihr Sutuda (Tehran, 1342/1963), 14.

2 Ibid., 37.

3 For some studies of the architectural history of Isfahan, see Husayn Nur Sadiqi, *Isfahan* (Tehran 1316/1937); Lutfallah Hunarfar, *Ganjina-yi Asar-i Tarikhi-yi Isfahan* (Tehran, 1344/1965); 'Aziz Hatami, *Isfahan* (Tehran, 1341/1962); W. Blunt, *Isfahan: Pearl of Persia* (London, 1966); Anthony Welch, *Shah Abbas and the Arts of Isfahan* (New York, 1973); E. Wirth, *Der Bazar von Isfahan* (Wiesbaden, 1978); Oleg Grabar, *The Great Mosque of Isfahan* (New York, 1990); Stephen Blake, *Half the World: The Social Architecture of Safavid Isfahan, 1590–1722* (Costa Mesa, 1999).

4 See Muhammad 'Ali Jamalzada, *Isfahan is Half the World: Memories of a Persian Boyhood* (Princeton, 1983); Mirza Hasan Jabiri Ansari, *Tarikh-i Isfahan* (Isfahan, 1378/1999); Muhammad 'Ali Musavi Faridani, *Isfahan az Nigah-i Digar* (Isfahan, 1379/2000); Hurmuz Ansari and Ahmad Javahiri, *Muqaddamah-i bar Jam'iyashinasi-yi Isfahan* (Tehran, 2000); Heidi Walcher, *In the Shadow of the King* (London, 2008).

5 For studies of Isfahan's geography, see Ann K. S. Lambton, "The Regulation of the Waters of the Zayande Rud," *Bulletin of the School of Oriental and African Studies* 9 (1938), 663–673; 'Ali Javahir Kalam, *Zinda Rud* (Tehran, 1969); Muhammad Mahmudiyan, *Zayanda Rud-i Isfahan* (Isfahan, 1969); Brian Spooner, "City and River in Iran: Urbanization and Irrigation of the Iranian Plateau," *Studies on Isfahan: Proceeding of the Isfahan Colloquium, Journal of Iranian Studies* 7, nos. 3–4 (1974), part 2, 681–712. For some recent studies of the navigation of the Karun River and its trade, see Shahbaz Shahnavaz, *Britain and the Opening Up of South-West Persia, 1880–1914: A Study in Imperialism and Economic Dependence* (London, 2005); Walcher, *In the Shadow of the King*.

6 Robert McC. Adams, "Concluding Commentary," *Studies on Isfahan*, 715–19.

7 On hinterlands, see Robert McC. Adams, *Land behind Baghdad: A History of Settlement on the Diyala Plains* (Chicago, 1965); Kenneth Pomeranz, *The Making of a Hinterland: State, Society, and Economy in Inland North China, 1853–1937* (Berkeley, 1993).

8 See Walcher, "Face of the Seven Spheres: Urban Morphology and Architecture in Nineteenth-Century Isfahan," *Iranian Studies* 33, 3–4 (2000), 337; W. B. Fisher, "Physical Geography," *The Cambridge History of Iran,* vol. 1: *The Land of Iran* (Cambridge, 1968), 106; George N. Curzon, *Persia and the Persian Question*, vol. 2 (London, 1892), 24. Under the Safavids Isfahan reached its height, becoming known as "half the world" (*nisf-i jahan*). The city's population during the sixteenth century was estimated to be at least 600,000 people. See John Chardin, *Les Voyages du Chevalier Chardin en Perse*, edited by L. Langlès, 10 vols. (Paris, 1811); Jean-Baptiste Tavernier, *The Six Voyages of Jean-Baptiste Tavernier* (London, 1678).

9 MB, vol. 1, 94.

10 MB, vol. 1, 123. Also see Shirazi, *Tarikh-i Zu al-Qarnayn*, vol. 2, 787.

11 Muhammad Mihdi ibn Muhammad Riza al-Isfahani, *Nisf-i Jahan,fi taʿrif al-Isfahan*, ed. Manuchihr Sutuda (Tehran, 1340/1961), 94–96.

12 Mirza Ghulam Husayn Afzal al-Mulk, *Safarnama-yi Isfahan*, ed. Nasir Afsharfar (Tehran, 1380/2001), 42.

13 Rawlinson, "Notes on a March from Zohab," 103.

14 Mirza Ghulam Husayn Afzal al-Mulk, *Safarnama-yi Isfahan*, 104.

15 Isfahani, *Nisf-i Jahan,fi taʿrif al-Isfahan*, 96, 333.

16 ICHO, *Hazar Jilva-yi Zindagi: Tasvirha-yi Ernst Hoeltzer az ʿAhd-i Nasiri* (Tehran, 1382/2004), 165. Also see Ernst Hoeltzer, "Beschreibung der Stadt Isfahan" [Description of the City of Isfahan], Papers of Ernst Hoeltzer, Harvard University, Special Collections and Manuscripts.

17 These were the tribes of Lur-i Buzurg or Greater Luristan, a mountainous country that fell under the name Bakhtiyari, extending from the frontiers of Fars in the east to the river of Dizful in the west. Rawlinson's estimate of 28,000 tents equals approximately 140,000 people. The figure of 51,200 tents, given by Layard, equals roughly 256,000 individuals. See Rawlinson, "Notes on a March from Zohab," 102–3; Austen Henry Layard, "A Description of the Province of Khuzistan," 101–5.

18 Ernst Hoeltzer, "Reise in die Gebirge der Persischen Nomadenvolker der Kaschgais und Bachtiaren" [Travels to the Mountains of the Persian Nomadic Tribes, the Qashqa'is and the Bakhtiyari], Papers of Ernst Hoeltzer, Harvard University, Special Collections and Manuscripts.

19 Henry Blosse Lynch, "Across Luristan to Ispahan," *PRGS* (1890), 542. The Bakhtiyari were reported to have hardy horses of Arabian blood adapted to high altitudes, described as "exceedingly fleet, sure-footed, and . . . capable of climbing up mountains with the agility and fearlessness of mountain goats." See de Bode, *Travels in Luristan*, vol. 2, 92.

20 Rawlinson, "Notes on a March from Zohab," 105.

21 de Bode, *Travels in Luristan*, vol. 2, 89–90; Rawlinson, "Notes on a March

from Zohab," 105.

22 *TB*, 57.

23 Rawlinson, "Notes on a March from Zohab," 104.

24 Ernst Hoeltzer, "Reise in die Gebirge der Persischen Nomadenvolker der Kaschgais und Bachtiaren" [Travels to the Mountains of the Persian Nomadic Tribes, the Qashqa'is and the Bakhtiyari], Papers of Ernst Hoeltzer, Harvard University, Special Collections and Manuscripts.

25 Rawlinson, "Notes on a March from Zohab," 103.

26 In addition, during the winter when the tribes were in the *qishlaq*, the Bakhtiyari *ilkhan* was to pay 15,000 tumans in annual revenues to the governor of Khuzistan; see Curzon, *Persia and the Persian Question,* vol. 2, 298.

27 Rawlinson, "Notes on a March from Zohab," 103; de Bode, *Travels in Luristan*, vol. 2, 76–77. As mentioned in the previous chapter, the great divisions of the Haft Lang and the Chahar Lang were based originally on rates of taxation.

28 *TB*, 192.

29 The papers of D. L. R. Lorimer (1876–1962), held at the University of London–School of Oriental and African Studies (SOAS), contain numerous examples of Bakhtiyari vernacular songs and folklore. For the quoted poem, see Lorimer Papers, SOAS, PPMS 66, Box 28, "Popular Verse of the Bakhtiyari."

30 INA, Asnad-i Milki, Series 1004/92–98.

31 INA, Asnad-i Milki, 1004/92, Land Deed from the Village of Junaqan, 1251/1835. See other nineteenth-century land deeds, INA, Asnad-i Milki, 1004/93–98.

32 *MB*, vol. 4, 2048–52; *TB*, 65–68.

33 *MB*, vol. 4, 2049.

34 'Abd al-Ghaffar Najm al-Mulk, *Safarnama-yi Khuzistan* (Tehran, 1342/1963), 131–38.

35 Sani' al-Mulk, *Ruznama-yi Dawlat-i 'Alliya-yi Iran* (Tehran, 1370/1992 [1861–67], 642–43.

36 *MB*, vol. 2, 1062, 1076, 1180, 1203; *NT*, vol. 3, 1000, 1003, 1087, 1073–75; Layard, "A Description," 15–18.

37 The *ilkhan* was the eldest son of Ja'far Quli Khan Duraki, a famed warrior who died in the War of Munar in 1834, and Bibi Shahpasand of the Bakhtiyarvand. His noble lineage from two of the most influential Haft Lang tribes would help him as he rose to power. According to tribal history he was 15 years old during the War of Nine Thousand in 1835 at Chaqakhur, where the retinues of his grandfather, Habiballah Khan Duraki, defeated a coalition of 9,000 horsemen from the Bakhtiyarvand, the Raki, the Chahar Lang, and several other Bakhtiyari tribes headed by Farajallah Khan Duraki. Following

this war Husayn Quli Khan's uncle, Kalb 'Ali Khan Duraki, gained control over the Haft Lang. But by the 1840s Husayn Quli Khan and the other sons of Ja'far Quli Khan challenged their uncle. The two sides fought several wars in the pastures of Zard Kuh. In the War of Bazuft, Husayn Quli Khan and his brothers prevailed over their uncle and assumed leadership of the Haft Lang. On the life of the *ilkhan* see Garthwaite, *Khans and Shahs*, 72–95. Also see TB, 170–71; Sardar Zafar, *Yaddashtha va Khatirat*, 35–36.

38 Bibi Maryam Bakhtiyari, *Khatirat-i Sardar Maryam*, ed. Ghulam 'Abbas Nawruzi Bakhtiyari (Tehran, 1382/2003), 25–26.

39 MB, vol. 2, 1180; Lisan al-Mulk Sipihr, NT, vol. 3, 1073–75, 1087.

40 Sardar Zafar, *Khatirat va Yaddashtha*, 61. On the life and career of Amir Kabir see Amanat, *Pivot of the Universe*, 118–68; 'A. Iqbal, *Mirza Taqi Khan Amir Kabir*, ed. Iraj Afshar (Tehran, 1340/1961); Husayn Makki, *Zindagani-yi Mirza Taqi Khan Amir Kabir* (Tehran, 1360/1981); F. Adamiyat, *Amir Kabir va Iran* (Tehran, 1348/1969). On the Babadi tribes of the Haft Lang see 'Akkasha, *Tarikh-i Il-i Bakhtiyari*.

41 NT, vol. 3, 1175.

42 Sani' al-Mulk, *Ruznama-yi Dawlat-i 'Alliya-yi Iran*, 274, 516.

43 In a royal decree (*farman*) Nasir al-Din Shah recognized Husayn Quli Khan as "the *ilkhan*i of the Bakhtiyari," mandating his authority over the whole tribal confederation: "The khans and leaders of military contingents, the headmen and white beards of the tribes, and the sections of the Bakhtiyari are to consider him to be endowed with this rank and status and recognize respect toward him, to be in keeping with this rank and appropriate to this status, to be incumbent on them." See Garthwaite, *Khans and Shahs*, 82.

44 TB, 171.

45 Zill al-Sultan, *Sarguzasht-i Mas'udi*, vol. 2, 523–24.

46 Amanat, *Pivot of the Universe*, 403. For a recent study of Zill al-Sultan and the provincial capital Isfahan see Walcher, *In the Shadow of the King*.

47 TM, vol. 1, 557.

48 'Akkasha, *Tarikh-i Il-i Bakhtiyari*, 183; TB, 172; Sardar Zafar, *Yaddashtha va Khatirat*, 106; Bibi Maryam, *Khatirat*, 31; Zill al-Sultan, *Sarguzasht-i Mas'udi*, vol. 2, 525.

49 TM, vol. 3, 2143.

50 Fernand Braudel, *The Mediterranean and the Mediterranean World in the Age of Philip II*, vol. 2 (Berkeley, 1995[1949]), 770.

51 Zill al-Sultan, *Tarikh-i Sarguzasht-i Mas'udi*, vol. 2, 523.

52 *Farhang*, Isfahan, 6 January 1881. On *Farhang* of Isfahan, see Sayyid Farid Qasimi, *Avvalinha-yi Matbu'at-i Iran* (Tehran, 1383/2004), 423–87.

53 INA, 295/6, 1073, 1, Report of a robbery on the road from Isfahan to Yazd, n.d.

54 For instance see INA 296/2, 539, 1.

55 INA 295/3, 912, 1–2, Zill al-Sultan to Mustawfi al-Mamalik, Isfahan, Sha'ban, 1296 [1879]. Also see INA 295/3, 912, 1, Mustawfi al-Mamalik to Zill al-Sultan, Tehran, Sha'ban, 1296 [1879].

56 INA 295/3, 822, 1, Mustawfi al-Mamalik to Zill al-Sultan, Tehran, Rabi' al-Sani, 1296 [1879]. Also see INA 295/3, 822, 2–3, Zill al-Sultan to Mustawfi al-Mamalik, Isfahan, Rabi' al-Sani, 1296 [1879].

57 See *Farhang*, Isfahan, 21 August and 28 August 1879.

58 In 1877 Zill al-Sultan spent twenty days at Chaqakhur hunting as the guest of the *ilkhan*. Although in his journal Zill al-Sultan attempts to highlight the friendship between the *ilkhan* and himself, the governor's trips into the Zagros were also meant to size up and survey the Bakhtiyari tribes. The prince also recalls playing chess with the *ilkhan* and records a poem in the "Lur dialect" that the *ilkhan* once recited for him; see Zill al-Sultan, *Sarguzasht-i Mas'udi*, vol. 2, 521–29. In his own "Notebook," Husayn Quli Khan recalls the taxing nature of the unannounced visit by the governor and his entourage in 1877. See Husayn Quli Khan, "Kitabchih," 264.

59 In 1876, when "everywhere in the province of Fars criminals began to rob the highways and wide stretches of the province were alarmed about stealing, raping, and plundering," Nasir al-Din Shah appointed his uncle Farhad Mirza Mu'tamad al-Dawla as governor of Fars and "ordered him to put an end to the depravity and to punish the criminals of the districts and tribes of that province." The prince, a British protégé, soon became known for his strictness. For instance, he summoned the night watchmen of Shiraz and announced that the compensation for all unsolved thefts would be taken out of their own pockets. According to Fasa'i's *Farsnama-yi Nasiri*, he turned "danger into safety" and "chaos into order." Referring to Mu'tamad al-Dawla the people of the province were less enthusiastic and were known to say, "*Fars tamam shud*," "Fars is finished." Fasa'i, *Farsnama-yi Nasiri*, vol. 1, tr. Heribert Busse, as *History of Persia under Qajar Rule* (New York, 1972), 385–87. For the Persian edition see Fasa'i, *Farsnama-yi Nasiri*, vol. 1. On Farhad Mirza Mu'tamad al-Dawla, see Isma'il Navab Safa, *Sharh-i Hal-i Farhad Mirza Mu'tamad al-Dawla* (Tehran, 1366/1987).

60 *TB*, 172.

61 According to Zill al-Sultan the pastoralists (*badish*) of Khana Mirza and Falard paid taxes to the Bakhtiyari, while the agricultural lands (*khakish*) were part of Fars. See Zill al-Sultan, *Sarguzasht-i Mas'udi*, vol. 2, 525. Other sources suggested, however, that during the 1870s, as the jurisdiction of the Bakhtiyari was expanding, Husayn Quli Khan took possession of Falard. See, for example, the collection of eyewitness accounts and rumors from South Persia collected by the British agents in Shiraz during the late nineteenth century

and published in Persian as *Vaqa'i'-yi Ittifaqiya*. The British agent in Shiraz from 1869 to 1879 was Mirza Hasan 'Ali Khan Navab, followed by Haydar 'Ali Khan Navab (FO 60/592, Biographical Dictionary: Fars, 1896). The agents' reports were gathered from local informants cognizant of the activities of ordinary people throughout the province. *Vaqa'i'-yi Ittifaqiya*, ed. Sa'idi Sirjani (Tehran, 1376/1997), 126. Also see Navab Safa, *Sharh-i Hal-i Farhad Mirza*, 154.

62 INA 295/3, 1023, 1, Husayn Qara to Mu'tamad al-Dawla, Sha'ban 1296 [1879]; INA 295/3, 1023, 1–2, Mu'tamad al-Dawla to Husayn Qarra, Shiraz, Sha'ban 1296 [1879].

63 Husayn Quli Khan, "Kitabchih," 269.

64 INA 295/3, 901, 1, Mustawfi al-Mamalik to Zill al-Sultan, Rajab 1296 [1879].

65 INA 295/3, 1079, 1, Mustawfi al-Mamalik to Zill al-Sultan, Tehran, Safar 1296 [1879].

66 INA 295/3, 1033, 1–2, Mustawfi al-Mamalik to Mu'tamad al-Dawla, Tehran, Shavval 1296 [1879]; INA 295/3, 1033, 3, Mu'tamad al-Dawla to Mustawfi al-Mamalik, Shiraz, Shavval 1296 [1879].

67 INA 295/3, 1043, 1–2, Mustawfi al-Mamalik to Mu'tamad al-Dawla, Tehran, Zu al-Qa'da 1296 [1879]; INA 295/3, 1043, 2–3, Mu'tamad al-Dawla to Mustawfi al-Mamalik, Shiraz, Zu al-Qa'da 1296 [1879].

68 Zill al-Sultan, *Sarguzasht-i Mas'udi*, vol. 2, 526.

69 INA 295/3, 1027, 1–2, Mu'tamad al-Dawla to Mustawfi al-Mamalik, Shiraz, Ramazan 1296 [1879].

70 Bibi Maryam, *Khatirat-i Sardar Maryam*, 25.

71 INA 295/3, 901, 2–3, Zill al-Sultan to Mustawfi al-Mamalik, Isfahan, Rajab 1296 [1879].

72 INA 296/1, 298, 1–2, Zill al-Sultan to Nasir al-Din Shah, Isfahan, n.d.

73 'Abd al-Ghaffar Najm al-Mulk, *Safarnama-yi Khuzistan* (Tehran, 1342/1963), 18.

74 *Safarnama-yi Khuzistan* (hereafter SK), 76.

75 SK, 56, 169–70.

76 SK, 145.

77 SK, 55.

78 SK, 154, 155.

79 SK, 155, 169.

80 SK, 77, 160.

81 SK, 53.

82 SK, 159–61.

83 SK, 165.

84 Seeking further reconnaissance the shah also sent Hajji Muhammad Quli, known as Hajji Nayib, a trusted descendant of one of Muhammad Shah's

Turkmen *ghulam*, to report on the Bakhtiyari under the pretext of buying horses. This text by Hajji Nayib is referred to in Zill al-Sultan's memoirs. See Zill al-Sultan, *Sarguzasht-i Mas'udi*, vol. 2, 526–27.

85 C. J. Wills, *In the Land of the Lion and Sun, or Modern Persia: Being Experiences of Life in Persia from 1866 to 1881* (London, 1893), 262.

86 See, for example, the *ilkhan*'s effort to rebuld the ruined *qanats* of Janiki and Malamir as detailed in MB, vol. 1, 2049.

87 George Mackenzie, "Route from Ispahan to Shooster," *A Narrative of a Journey through the Province of Khorassan and on the N.W. Frontier of Afghanistan in 1875*, vol. 2 (London, 1879), 235.

88 According to Mackenzie, Husayn Quli Khan made an agreement with him and the written record was kept on file at the Bushire residency. See George Herbert Sawyer, "The Bakhtiyari Mountains and Upper Elam," *The Geographical Journal* 4 (1894), 504.

89 Government of India, Foreign Department, Proceeding 379, 25 January 1882, Number 18, Report by Walter Baring, 4–5, quoted in Garthwaite, *Khans and Shahs*, 94. For further British reconnaissance on the Bakhtiyari *ilkhan* see H. L. Wells, "Surveying Tours in Southern Persia," PRGS 5, no. 3 (1883), 138–63. Also see Foreign Office, MPK 1/247/5, Plane-Table Sketch of a track between Ispahan and Shuster, by Captain Henry L. Wells, Royal Engineers.

90 Wells, "Surveying Tours in Southern Persia."

91 Edward Stack, *Six Months in Persia*, vol. 2 (London, 1882), 65.

92 Curzon, "The Karun River," 514–15. On the death of the *ilkhan*, see TB, 172–73; Sardar Zafar, *Yaddashtha va Khatirat*, 194–209; 'Akkasha, *Tarikh-i Il-i Bakhtiyari*, 183–90; Bibi Maryam, *Khatirat*, 29–35; Zill al-Sultan, *Sarguzasht-i Mas'udi*, vol. 2, 656. For secondary studies see Garthwaite, *Khans and Shahs*, 89–95.

93 TB, 172–73. On the death of Husayn Quli Khan Ilkhan, also see Sardar Zafar, *Yaddashtha va Khatirat*, 194–209; 'Akkasha, *Tarikh-i Il-i Bakhtiyari*, 183–90; Bibi Maryam, *Khatirat*, 29–35. For secondary studies see Garthwaite, *Khans and Shahs*, 89–95; Ghaffarpur Bakhtiyari, "Qatl-i Husayn Quli Khan Ilkhani Bakhtiyari va Naqsh-i Mu'tamad al-Dawla Hakim-i Fars dar An," *Ganjina-yi Asnad*, vol. 3–4, 51–52 (2003–4), 73–80.

94 Bibi Maryam, *Khatirat*, 33.

95 Ibid., 33.

96 Sardar Zafar, *Yaddashtha wa Khatirat*, 194–271.

97 Isfandiyar Khan was the *ilkhan*'s eldest son, born c. 1851 to Bibi Khanum of the Khadir Surkh of the Zarasvand of the Duraki. 'Ali Quli was the fourth of the *ilkhan*'s six sons, born c. 1856 to Hajjiya Bibi Mihrijan, daughter of Ilyas Khan of the the Zarasvand. See TB, 120.

98 Bakhtiyari tribal solidarity under the *ilkhan* had been showing signs of

rupture since c. 1880. Intra-tribal rivalries between the *ilkhan*'s sons and nephews had appeared just before the *ilkhan*'s death. Husayn Quli Khan and his eldest son, Isfandiyar, the charismatic khan regarded as the rising leader of the Bakhtiyari, were envied by the *ilkhan*'s nephew Muhammad Husayn Khan, who had become commander of the crown prince Muzaffar al-Din Mirza's guard in Azarbayjan, thus coming into the service of Zill al-Sultan's sibling rival for the throne. See 'Akkasha, *Tarikh-i Il-i Bakhtiyari*, 183; Sardar Zafar, *Yaddashtha va Khatirat*, 195–97; Bibi Maryam, *Khatirat*, 29. Garthwaite has written that according to tribal tradition, on one occasion Muhammad Husayn Khan "dared to ride in front of the Ilkhani mounted on a white horse, accompanied by his *bastagan*" while Husayn Quli Khan "shrugged off this breach of manners." See Garthwaite, *Khans and Shahs*, 91.

99 Amanat, *Pivot of the Universe*, 409.

100 Bibi Maryam, *Khatirat*, 34.

101 Ibid., 35.

3 *A Road through the Mountains*

1 On the Reuter Concession, see Nikki Keddie, *Modern Iran: Roots and Results of the Revolution* (New Haven, 2004); Amanat, *Pivot of the Universe*; Issawi, *Economic History of Iran*; Firuz Kazemzadeh, *Russia and Britain in Persia* (New Haven, 1968); Abu al-Fazl Lisani, *Tala-yi Siya ya Bala-yi Iran* (Tehran, 1329/1950); Ibrahim Taymuri, *'Asr-i Bi-Khabari* (Tehran, 1332/1953); Bradford Martin, *German-Persian Diplomatic Relations 1873–1912* (Oslo, 1959); L. E. Frechtling, "The Reuter Concession in Persia," *Asiatic Review* (1938), 518–33. For Foreign Office correspondence regarding the Reuter Concession, see FO 881/2393, Persia: Correspondence Relating to the Reuter Concession (1872–73); FO 539/10, Persia: Correspondence Respecting the Reuter and Falkenhagen Concession (1872–75).

2 Curzon, *Persia and the Persian Question*, vol. 1, 480.

3 For recent works on the commercial opening of the Karun, see Shahnavaz, *Britain and the Opening Up of South-West Persia;* Heidi Walcher, *In the Shadow of the King* (London, 2008). For further literature on the opening of the Karun River, Issawi, *Economic History of Iran*; Kazemzadeh, *Russia and Britain in Persia*; Lisani, *Tala-yi Siya Bala-yi Iran*; Muhammad 'Ali Jamalzada, *Ganj-i Shaygan* (Berlin, 1335/1956); W. F. Ainsworth, *The River Karun: An Opening to British Commerce* (London, 1890); Curzon, *Persia and the Persian Question*; Curzon, "The Karun River." The correspondence of the Foreign Office on the opening of the Karun includes the series FO 60/549, The Navigation of the Karun River (1889); FO 60/550 (1890–93); FO 60/571 (1894–95); FO 60/593

(1896–97); FO 881/4733, Opening of Karun River—Summary of Report of Engineer (1882).

4 Since 1871 the Bushire trading firm Grey, Paul, and Company had tried to obtain a concession to launch a steamer on the Karun River between Muhammara and Shushtar but had been denied because of Nasir al-Din Shah's fears that opening the river could lead to British domination or annexation of Khuzistan. But in 1876 and 1878 the shah twice granted his French physician, Dr. Tolozan, concessions that carried exclusive rights for the navigation of the Karun River and "the development of the surrounding lands." The French proposed to build the dam at Ahvaz, irrigate the surrounding country, and work the mines and forests. After French engineers were sent to survey the region and a line of French steamers was established between Marseilles and Basra, the French concessions were suspended. See Curzon, *Persia and the Persian Question*, vol. 2, 333.

5 Curzon, *Persia and the Persian Question*, vol. 2, 333–34; Issawi, *Economic History of Iran*, 156–57.

6 On roads and railways in Iran, see A. Melamid, "Communications, Transport, Retail Trade, and Services," *Cambridge History of Iran*, vol. 1. *The Land of Iran* (Cambridge, 1968), 552–64; Patrick Clawson, "Knitting Iran Together: The Land Transport Revolution, 1920–1940," *Iranian Studies* 26, nos. 3–4 (1993), 235–50. On roads, nationalism, and ethnicity, see David Yaghoubian, "Hagop Hagopian: An Armenian Truck Driver in Iran," *Struggle and Survival in the Modern Middle East*, ed. Edmund Burke III (Berkeley, 1993); David Yaghoubian, "Shifting Gears in the Desert: Trucks, Guilds, and National Development, 1921–1941," *Jusur: UCLA Journal of Middle East Studies* 13 (1997). For a recent reference to the effects of modern transportation on the Iranian "mind" and "body" in the twentieth century, see Cyrus Schayegh, "'A Sound Mind Lives in a Healthy Body': Texts and Contexts in the Iranian Modernists' Scientific Discourse of Health, 1910s-1940s," *International Journal of Middle East Studies* 37, no. 2 (2005), 173–74.

7 Curzon, "The Karun River and the Commercial Geography of South-west Persia," *PRGS* 12 (1890), 528.

8 W. B. Fisher, "Physical Geography," *Cambridge History of Iran*, vol. 1, 7; Also see Xavier de Planhol, "Caractèrs généraux de la vie montagnard," *Annales Géographique*, 1962, 113–30.

9 Fernand Braudel, *The Mediterranean and the Mediterranean World in the Age of Phillip II, The Mediterranean*, vol. 1(Berkeley, 1995[1972]), 34; James Scott, "Hill and Valley in Southeast Asia." On rough and non-wheeled transit in the Middle East, see Richard Bulliet, *The Camel and the Wheel* (New York, 1990[1975]).

10 Mirza Mihdi Khan is here describing a military expedition carried out against

the Haft Lang by Nadir Shah, then Tahmasp Quli Khan. See Astarabadi, *Jahangusha*, 189.

11 Malcolm, *The History of Persia*, vol. 2, 525.

12 *Sir Austen Henry Layard, Autobiography and Letters*, vol. 2 (London, 1903), 7. The Middle East Centre Archive at St. Antony's College, Oxford, holds copies of six letters (23 sheets) written by Layard to Edward Mitford in the 1840s on his travels though Persia and Mesopotamia (St. Antony's, Layard, GB 165–0178).

13 "Les Persans n'ont guère d'idée de ce que nous appelons des grandes routes; la raison en est que ces voies de communication ne seraient pas fort utiles dans un pays où l'on ne fait pas usage des voitures à roués. Ils connaissent bien les avantages qu'ils pourraient retirer de quelques bonnes routes; mais ils ne sont pas disposés à accepter une amélioration qui pourait faciliter les invasions de l'étranger (M. Louis Dubeaux, *La Perse* [Paris, 1841], 418).

14 Il Rah-i Dizpart, known also as the Atabayg Road, connected the Karun to the mountains west of Isfahan. This was the road rebuilt as Lynch or Bakhtiyari Road in 1899. Various Bakhtiyari tribes—including the Raki, Sadat, Zarasvand, Chahrazi, Chaharbari, Mashayikh, Urak, 'Ali Mahmudi, Sarquli, Nawruzi, Galladaran, and Baladaji—used it on migrations. Il Rah-i Bazuft extends from the *yaylaq* near Bazuft to the *qishlaq* at Masjid-i Sulayman. It was the migratory route of the Mawri, Suhuni, 'Ali Anvar, Bakhtiyarvand, and Babadi tribes. Il Rah-i Hazarcha or Kuh Rang is an extremely difficult road that reaches the *yaylaq* on the slopes of Zard Kuh. It was the migratory path of the 'Ali Anvar, Suhuni, Bakhtiyarvand, Galla, Mawri, Asivand, Babadi, and Zarasvand tribes. For Bakhtiyari migration routes, see Qayid Bakhtiyari, *Tarikh va Farhang-i Bakhtiyari*, vol. 2, 29–33; Sistani, *Ilha, Chadurnishinan, va Tavayif-i 'Ashayiri*, vol. 1, 462–64.

15 The classic silent film *Grass* depicts the spring migration of the Babadi tribes on the difficult Hazarcha route in 1924. See Merrian Cooper, *Grass* (New York, 1925).

16 Denis Wright, the former British ambassador to Iran (1963–71), presents an overall summary of British travelers in nineteenth-century Iran; see Wright, *The English amongst the Persians* (London, 1977). On Orientalism and Iranian history, see Mohamad Tavakoli-Targhi, *Refashioning Iran: Orientalism, Occidentalism, and Historiography* (New York, 2001).

17 An array of nineteenth-century ethnographic writing exists on other tribes in Iran. On the Turkmen, see James Baillie Fraser, *Narrative of a Journey into Khorasan in 1821 and 1822* (London 1825); Alexander Burnes, *Travels into Bokhara: Being the Account of a Journey from India to Cabool, Tartary, and Persia*, 3 vols. (London, 1834); Arthur Conolly, *Journey to the North of India, Overland from England, through Russia, Persia, and Affghaunistaun*, 2 vols.

(London, 1834); Arminius Vambery, *Travels in Central Asia: being the account of a journey from Teheran across the Turkoman Desert on the eastern shore of the Caspian to Khiva, Bokhara, and Samarcand performed in the year 1863* (London, 1864); Charles Metcalfe MacGregor, *Narrative of a Journey through the Province of Khorassan and on the N. W. Frontier of Afghanistan in 1875*, 2 vols. (London, 1879); G. C. Napier, "Extracts from a Diary of a Tour in Khorassan," JRGS 46 (1876), 62–171; Val Baker, *Clouds in the East: Travels and Adventures on the Perso-Turkoman Frontier* (London, 1876); Charles Marvin, *Merv, the Queen of the World; and the Scourge of the Man-stealing Turkomans* (London, 1881); Henri Moser, *A Travers L'Asie Centrale* (Paris, 1885); Edmumd O'Donovan, *The Merv Oasis* (London, 1883); C. E. Yate, *Northern Afghanistan* (Edinburgh, 1888); Curzon, *Russia in Central Asia* (London, 1889). On the Baluch, see Frederic Goldsmid, *Eastern Persia: An Account of the Journeys of the Persian Boundary Commission*, 2 vols. (London, 1876); G. P. Tate, *The Frontiers of Baluchistan* (London, 1909); T. H. Holdich, *The Indian Borderland, 1880–1900* (London, 1901); Charles Yate, *Khurasan and Sistan* (Edinburgh, 1900); H. Bellew, *The Races of Afghanistan* (London, 1880); Charles Masson, *Narrative of Various Journeys in Baloochistan, Afghanistan, and the Punjab*, 3 vols. (London, 1842); H. Pottinger, *Travels in Beloochistan and Sind* (London, 1816); Charles Metcalfe MacGregor, *Wanderings in Balochistan* (London, 1882); H. Raverty, *Notes on Afghanistan and Part of Baluchistan* (London, 1888). On the Kurds, see James Baillie Fraser, *Travels in Koordistan, Mesopotamia* (London, 1840); George Fowler, *Three Years in Persia with Traveling Adventures in Koordistan* (London, 1841); A. H. Layard, *Discoveries in the Ruins of Nineveh and Babylon; with Travels in Armenia, Kurdistan, and the Desert* (London, 1853); Lady Mary Sheil, *Glimpses of Life and Manners in Persia* (London, 1856); F. Millingen, *Wild Life Among the Kurds* (London, 1870); Henry Binder, *Au Kurdistan, en Mésopotamie et en Perse* (Paris, 1887); Isabella Bird, *Journeys in Persia and Kurdistan* (London, 1891); Jacques de Morgan, *Mission Scientifique en Perse*, vol. 2 (Paris, 1895). On the Qashqa'i, see Edward Scott Waring, *A Tour to Sheeraz by the Route of Kazroon and Feerozabad* (London, 1807); Keith Edward Abbott, "Notes Taken on a Journey Eastwards from Shiraz to Fessa and Darab Thence Westwards by Jehrum to Kazerun, in 1850," JRGS 27 (1857), 149–84; Wills, *In the Land of the Lion and Sun*; Edward Stack, *Six Months in Persia*, 2 vols. (New York, 1882).

18 For references to the Atabayg Road, see Henry Creswicke Rawlinson, "Notes on a March from Zohab, at the foot of the Zagros," 79–83; de Bode, *Travels in Luristan*, vol. 2, 5–10; Layard, *Early Adventures in Persia*, 178; Henry Blosse Lynch, "Across Luristan to Ispahan," PRGS 12 (1890), 523–53; Curzon, *Persia and the Persian Question*, vol. 2, 285, 288; Aurel Stein, *Old Routes of Western Iran: Narrative of an Archaeological Journey Carried Out and Recorded*

(London, 1940). For a Persian translation of de Bode's travelogue, including references to the Atabayg's Road, see *TB*, 535–46. For further Persian sources on the road, see Husayn Quli Khan Nizam al-Saltana, *Khatirat va Asnad*, eds. Ma'suma Nizam Mafi and Mansura Ittihadiya (Tehran 1361/1982), 102; *SN*, 153–56. Also see references in the reports of Nizam al-Saltana's chief military agent in the province of Khuzistan in the early 1890s, 'Abdallah Qaraguzlu Hamadani, *Majmu'a-yi Asar*, ed. 'Inayatallah Majidi (Tehran, 1382/2003).

19 Qayid Bakhtiyari, *Tarikh va Farhang-i Bakhtiyari*, vol. 2 (Isfahan, 1372/1993), 29–30.

20 In Khuzistan, Rawlinson's primary scholarly interest was in searching for the ruins of ancient Susa, site of the Palace of Sushan in the Book of Daniel. See Rawlinson, "Notes on a March from Zohab."

21 Due to Rawlinson's knowledge of the Persian language, he was selected in 1833 to be among a small body of officers from the Indian Army deputed to reorganize and discipline the shah's troops. An account of the march against the Chahar Lang Bakhtiyari and Rawlinson's role in it can be found in Lisan al Mulk Sipihr's chronicle of the mid-nineteenth century. The expedition included 5,000 horsemen and footmen as well as six cannons, but the Chahar Lang tribes fled into the mountains. According to the Qajar historian Sipihr, after a truce was reached Rawlinson was allowed to select a thousand Bakhtiyari tribesmen for the Qajar's elite modern army, the New Order (*Nizam-i Jadid*). Bahram Mirza, accompanied by Rawlinson and several thousand horsemen, marched to Mungasht, whereupon the prince honored Muhammad Taqi Khan with a jeweled sword and a robe of honor (*khil'at*). Muhammad Taqi Khan gave his word that the Chahar Lang would be prepared to fight for the shah and would submit their annual taxes. He further sent his brother 'Ali Naqi Khan to be settled in Kirmanshah as a pledge of obedience. See *NT*, vol. 2, 653–54, 661–63. See also *TB*, 418–19; George Rawlinson, *A Memoir of Major-General Sir Henry Creswicke Rawlinson* (London, 1898), xiv.

22 Accompanying the governor of Isfahan, de Bode entered the plain of Malamir, the winter quarters of the Bakhtiyari chieftain Muhammad Taqi Khan, accompanying the governor of Isfahan, to a great, though forced, reception (*istiqbal*) from the Bakhtiyari tribes. De Bode, *Travels in Luristan*, vol. 2, 25. Portions of de Bode's text, like Layard's, were translated and included in *TB*, 525–67.

23 Austen Henry Layard, *Nineveh and Its Remains*, 2 vols. (London, 1849).

24 *TB*, 217–328.

25 Rawlinson, "Notes on a March from Zohab."

26 De Bode, *Travels in Luristan*, vol. 2, 62–63.

27 Ibid., vol. 2, 93.

28 De Bode found these shoes "very useful in climbing up the mountains" and

more convenient than European boots (Ibid., vol. 2, 94).

29 Rawlinson, "Notes on a March from Zohab," 67.

30 Ibid., 79, 83.

31 Ibid., 83.

32 De Bode described the pavement in its present state in detail and provided the first list of the stations along the road between Malamir and Isfahan, information he obtained from the Bakhtiyari ʿAli Naghi Khan. See de Bode, *Travels in Luristan*, vol. 2, 7.

33 By Layard's description, "Mehemet Taki Khan was a man of about fifty years of age, of middle height, somewhat corpulent, and of a very commanding presence. His otherwise handsome countenance was disfigured by a wound received in war from an iron mace, which had broken the bridge of his nose. He had a sympathetic, pleasing voice, a most winning smile, and a merry laugh. He was in the dress which the Bakhtiyari chiefs usually wore on a journey, or when on a raid or warlike expedition—a tight fitting cloth tunic reaching to about the knees, over a long silk robe, the skirts of which were thrust into capacious trousers, fastened round the ankles in by broad embroidered bands. Round his Lur skull cap of felt was twisted the 'lung,' or striped shawl. His arms consisted of a gun, with a barrel of the rarest Damascene work, and a stock beautifully inlaid with ivory and gold; a curved sword, or scimtar, of the finest Khorassan steel—its handle and sheath of silver and gold; a jeweled dagger of great price, and a long, highly ornamental pistol thrust in the 'keshkemer,' or belt, round his waist, to which were hung his powder-flasks, leather pouches for holding bullets, and various objects for priming and loading his gun. . . . The head and neck of his beautiful Arab mare were adorned with tassels of red silk and silver knobs. His saddle was also richly decorated, and under the girths was passed, on one side, a second sword, and on the other an iron inlaid mace, such as Persian horsemen use in battle" (Layard, *Early Adventures*, 149).

34 Ibid., 151.

35 Ibid., 160–61

36 Ibid., 178.

37 Ibid., 193.

38 Ibid., 197.

39 For instance, see Shahnavaz, *Britain and the Opening Up of South-West Persia*, 9.

40 For the governor of Isfahan's campaign in the Bakhtiyari territory, see RSN, vol. 10, 183–86, 226–31. According to Layard, Manuchihr Khan Muʿtamad al-Dawla was a eunuch of Georgian descent, a slave converted to Islam and employed in public service. His jurisdiction as governor of Isfahan extended over the tribal hinterland to the west of the city, including the often rebellious

and semi-independent tribal populations between the mountains of Luristan and the plains of the Euphrates. Layard, *Early Adventures*, 116–22.

41 RSN, vol. 10, 230.

42 The chronicles give ample coverage to the capture of Muhammad Taqi Khan. See MB, vol. 1, 946; NT, vol. 2, 768–77; RSN, vol. 10, 312, 318; TB, 422–30.

43 Layard, *Early Adventures*, 256–58. Also see MB, vol. 1, 946; NT, vol. 2, 768–77; RSN, vol. 10, 312, 318; TB, 422–30.

44 The most long-lived chief minister in the Qajar period, Amin al-Sultan, held office from 1883 until his assassination in 1907 during the Constitutional Revolution. See Nizam al-Saltana Mafi, *Khatirat va Asnad*, vol. 1, 93–95; Amanat, ed., *Crowning Anguish* (Washington, D.C., 1993), 318–20; Keddie and Amanat, "Iran Under the Later Qajars, 1848–1922," 174–212.

45 Nizam al-Saltana, *Khatirat va Asnad*, vol. 1, 92–94. According to tribal histories Isfandiyar Khan, who had reportedly become addicted to opium during his time in Isfahan, set out to claim the leadership of the tribes but never could recreate the tribal solidarity that had existed during his father's lifetime. See Sardar Zafar, *Yaddashtha va Khatirat*, 212.

46 In 1889, Isfandiyar Khan, Riza Quli Khan, and 300 Bakhtiyari horsemen joined Nizam al-Saltana's forces, which included a Shahsevan cavalry as well as mountain guns and artillery, on an expedition against Imam Quli Khan at his stronghold in Chaqakhur. An interesting account of this expedition and a description of Atabayg Road from Isfahan to the Karun appeared in the published memoirs of Nizam al-Saltana. According to his account, his guns and cannons blasted the tops off the Bakhtiyari's tents at Chaqakhur, forcing Imam Quli Khan and his sons to take flight to the fortress of Diz-i Malikan; see Nizam al-Saltana, *Khatirat va Asnad*, vol. 1, 93–136.

47 For an excellent biography of Curzon, see David Gilmour, *Curzon: Imperial Statesman* (London, 1994).

48 Curzon, *Persia and the Persian Question*, vol. 2, 268.

49 Ibid., 300–301.

50 Ibid., 268.

51 Ibid., 299.

52 Ibid., 620.

53 Curzon found the Bakhtiyari Mountains to be "bounded by two lines, which following the prevailing trend of the mountain chains from north-west to south-east, may be said to extend from Burujird to the outskirts of Isfahan on the north, and from Dizful and Shuster to Ram Hormuz and the Behbehan district on the south." Ibid., 283–84.

54 Ibid., 298.

55 Ibid., 271.

56 In addition, the shah claimed the right to levy a horseman and two foot

soldiers for his military from every ten families of the Bakhtiyari. In practice, however, there were merely two mobilized groups of 100 Bakhtiyari horsemen stationed at Isfahan and Tehran. Both groups were selected, armed, and commanded by Bakhtiyari khans from the Haft Lang. This was a mere fraction of the Bakhtiyari tribal cavalry that could be assembled. Curzon estimated the total fighting numbers of the Bakhtiyari tribes to be between 8,000 to 10,000 irregulars in the field, adding that they controlled a number of key forts in the Zagros. See Curzon, *Persia and the Persian Question,* vol. 2, 298; TB, 173.

57 Curzon, *Persia and the Persian Question,* vol. 2, 272.

58 For a contemporary Persian account of the Lynch Company, see Nizam al-Saltana, *Khatirat va Asnad*, vol. 1, 134.

59 Henry Blosse Lynch, "Across Luristan to Ispahan," 533.

60 Lynch divided the journey from Shushtar to Isfahan into four sections and 11 marching days or stages. The four stages of travel and their distances were given as: from Shushtar to Gargir, 52 miles; from Gargir to Malamir, 26 miles; from Malamir to Dupulan, 76 miles; from Dupulan to Isfahan, 95 miles. Lynch divided the daily stages of the journey as follows: first day: Shushtar to Darra Kul, 23 miles; second day: Darra Kul to Gargir, 30 miles; third day: Gargir to Malamir, 26 miles; fourth day: Malamir to Gawdar-i Balutak , 23 miles; fifth day: Gawdar-i Balutak to Dih-i Diz, 12 miles; sixth day: Dih-i Diz to Sarhun, 25 miles; seventh day: Sarhun to Dupulan, 17 miles; eighth day: Dupulan to Chagakhur, 22 miles; ninth day: Chagakhur to Paradumba, 19 miles; tenth day: Parabumba to Dawlatabad, 32 miles; eleventh Day: Dawlatabad to Isfahan, 23 miles (Ibid., 546).

61 Lynch, "Across Luristan to Ispahan," 546–47.

62 TB, 546.

63 Lynch, "Across Luristan to Ispahan," 541.

64 Ibid., 542.

65 H. A. Sawyer, "The Bakhtiyari Mountains and Upper Elam," *The Geographical Journal*, 4 (December 1894), 505.

66 Ibid., 482.

67 Bird and Sawyer made an odd pair. Sawyer was tall and commanding while Bird was short and plain, and each reportedly gained a different reputation among the local tribes. Although Isabella Bird was far from sympathetic toward the Bakhtiyari, word of her Burroughs and Wellcome medicine chest spread through the mountains, and she became known as a European doctor or *hakim*. On the other hand, Sawyer was reportedly heavy-handed and known among the tribes as the "Agha."

68 An album of roughly 100 of these photographs, with paragraph-long captions describing their location, came into the possession of the pro-British Aqanoor family of Julfa in the Armenian quarter of Isfahan. In August 1953, Leon Aqa-

noor and family presented the album to Caro Owen Minasian in Isfahan, and the latter donated it to the archives of the University of California, Los Angeles. Additional archival photographs of the Bakhtiyari tribes may be found in the vast photograph collection of the Gulistan Place in Tehran (Albumkhana-yi Kakh-i Gulistan), at the School of Oriental and African Studies in London, and at the British Petroleum Archives at the University of Warwick, UK. For studies of nineteenth-century photography in Iran, see Antoine Sevruguin, *Sevruguin and the Persian Image: Photographs of Iran, 1870–1930* (Seattle, 1999); Iraj Afshar, "Some Remarks on the Early History of Photography in Iran," *Qajar Iran: Political, Social, and Cultural Change, 1800–1925*, 261–90; Donna Stein, "Three Photographic Traditions in Nineteenth-Century Iran," *Muqarnas: An Annual on Islamic Art and Architecture* (Leiden, 1989); Stein, "Early Photography in Iran," *History of Photography* 7, no. 4 (1983), 257–91; Jennifer Scarce, "Isfahan in Camera: Nineteenth-Century Persia through the Photographs of Ernst Hoeltzer," *Art and Archaeology Research Papers* (1976), 1–22; Ernst Holtzer, *Persien Vor 113 Jahren* (Tehran, 1354/1975); ICHO, *Hazar Jilva-yi Zindagi*. For Persian-language sources on the history of photography in Iran, see Yahya Zuka, *Tarikh-i ʿAkasi va ʿAkasan-i Pishgam dar Iran* (Tehran, 1376/1997); Muhammad Riza Tahmasbpur, *Nasir al-Din, Shah-i ʿAkas* (Tehran, 1381/2002).

69 Recent studies of nineteenth-century photography have discussed the camera in colonialism and how some natives believed that the camera stole one's soul. In contrast, Bird's photographs suggest the ways that Bakhtiyari subjects, the people being photographed, appropriated the imperial camera and turned "photography to their own use." See Terence Ranger, "Colonialism, Consciousness, and the Camera," *Past and Present*, 171 (May 2001), 203–6.

70 FO 248/634, Report concerning robbery taken place Dec. 21 '95 in Dehhak territory, A. Eschrerich, Agence Ziegler and Co., Tehran, 16 January 1896.

71 Ibid.

72 The stolen articles included a winter overcoat, a winter covert coat, a mackintosh, an evening dress suit and jacket, a frock coat, three suits of clothes, three summer linen suits, a shooting suit, socks, boots, linen, flannel, and woolen shirts, underclothing, two plaids, two bed linen, a three- barreled gun, jewelry, sundries, servant's clothing, a pack horse, 500 krans (ten pounds) in cash, a parcel of silver things sent by Consul Preece of Isfahan for Sultanabad. Ibid.

73 FO 248/572, J. R. Preece to Sir Frank Lascelles, Ispahan, 25 July 1893.

74 INA 296/4, 154, 5, Telegraph from ʿIraq to Burujird, Rajab 1308 [1891]. Also see INA 296/1, 497, 2, Sadr Azam to Hishmat al-Dawla, Rajab 1311 [1894]; INA 296/1, 508, 5, Sadr Azam to Hishmat al-Dawla, Rajab 1311 [1894].

75 FO 248/548, J. R. Preece to Sir Frank Lascelles, Ispahan, 10 March 1892.

76 Ibid., 2 May 1892.

77 FO 248/572, J. R. Preece to Sir Frank Lascelles, Ispahan, 15 March 1893.

78 FO 248/572, J. R. Preece to Sir Frank Lascelles, Sultanabad, 28 November 1893.

79 FO 248/548, J. R. Preece to Sir Frank Lascelles, Ispahan, 24 August 1892.

80 Ibid., 6 August 1892.

81 FO 248/572, J. R. Preece to Sir Frank Lascelles, Ispahan, 20 December 1893.

82 Ibid., 25 July 1893.

83 Ibid., 20 December 1893.

84 FO 248/596, Robberies on the Shiraz-Ispahan Road, J. R. Preece, Ispahan, 21 October 1894.

85 INA 296/3, 78, 3, Telegraph from Sultanabad to Burujird, 12 Safar 1309 [1892]. Also see INA 296/3, 78, 2, Telegraph from Tehran to Burujird, 9 Safar 1309 [1892].

86 INA 296/1, 498, 1–6, Telegraphs from Tehran to Burujird, 18 Rabiʿ al-Avval 1311 [1894].

87 INA 296/1, 508, 2, Decree to Amir Tuman Hishmat al-Dawla, Governor of Burujird and Luristan, Rajab 1311 [1894].

88 For instance, see INA 296/1, 509, 5, Sadr Azam to Hishmat al-Dawla, Muharram 1311 [1894].

89 FO 248/676, Minas Stephen Peter Aganoor to Mortimer Durand, Ispahan, 27 August 1898.

90 Ibid., 28 September 1898.

91 FO 248/699, Report of a Conversation with H. R. H. Zil es Sultan on January 23rd 1899, J.R. Preece, Ispahan.

92 In December 1889, the Qajar government had granted a concession to Foreign Minister Mushir al-Dawla for the construction of a road for wheeled traffic between Tehran and Ahvaz. The following month an agent of Mushir al-Dawla approached M. Rabino, manager of the Imperial Bank of Persia, to secure foreign capital for the building of the road. A similar pattern would occur with the Bakhtiyari Road Concession in 1898. See FO 60/661, Roads in Persia, R. V. Harcourt, January 1902.

93 FO 60/690, Memorandum embodying the results of a discussion which took place between the Viceroy and Sir A. Hardinge, on the subject of roads and road guards in the Lur and Bakhtiyari Country, 1904.

94 FO 60/661, Roads in Persia. On the making of the Durand Line, see Louis Dupree, *Afghanistan* (Princeton, 1980); David Edwards, *Heroes of the Age: Moral Fault Lines on the Afghan Frontier* (Berkeley, 1996).

95 FO 60/573, Report of a Journey through the Bakhtiari Country to Shuster, by Consul J. R. Preece, Ispahan, 24 October 1895.

96 Ibid.

97 FO 248/548, J. R. Preece to Sir Frank Lascelles, Ispahan, 24 August 1892.

98 FO 60/573, Report on a Journey through the Bakhtiari Country to Shuster.

99 FO 60/573, Report on a Journey through the Bakhtiari Country to Shuster, quoted in Garthwaite, *Khans and Shahs*, 104.

100 FO 60/631, Charles Hardinge to the Marquis of Salisbury, Tehran, 14 March 1897.

101 Nizam al-Saltana, *Khatirat va Asnad*, vol. 1, 93–136.

102 Due to Nizam al-Saltana's resistance, three years after the opening of the Karun the company still did not have a trading house in Iran, its agent Taylor residing in a mat hut that Lynch rented from the Nizam for 600 tumans or 170 pounds per year. See Nizam al-Saltana, *Khatirat va Asnad*, vol. 1, 135; Curzon, *Persia and the Persian Question*, vol. 2, 353.

103 The post of British resident in Bushire was so influential that its holder was often referred to as the "uncrowned king of the south." E. C. Ross held the post for more than twenty years in the late nineteenth century. Nizam al-Saltana noted that he closed their agreement by sending Ross a Kashmiri robe, which the colonel supposedly donned from Shushtar to Basra. Nizam al-Saltana, *Khatirat va Asnad*, vol. 1, 134.

104 Curzon, *Persia and the Persian Question*, vol. 2, 369.

105 Ibid., 381–85.

106 Ibid., 334.

107 Nizam al-Saltana, *Khatirat va Asnad*, vol. 1, 185.

108 Ibid., 185.

109 Ibid., 186–88.

110 Sir Percy Sykes, *Ten Thousand Miles in Persia or Eight Years in Iran* (London, 1902), 247, 252; also see Sykes, "Recent Journeys in Persia," *The Geographical Journal* 10, 6 (1897), 593.

111 Sykes also managed to bring about the arrest of Tanfield's assailant Sadiq, although Sadiq's brother threatened to take revenge on Sykes, leading him to take such precautions as always keeping his revolver handy and placing a table across the opening of his door when he slept at night. He wrote that "every night bullet after bullet flew across us as a gentle hint to quit." See Sykes, *Ten Thousand Miles*, 254.

112 FO 60/631, T. Sanderson to Charles Hardinge, 15 December 1897.

113 FO 60/631, Charles Hardinge to Henry Lynch, Tehran, 20 October 1897.

114 *TB*, 57.

115 FO 60/631, Charles Hardinge to the Marquess of Salisbury, Tehran, 7 May 1897.

116 FO 416/6, Messrs. Lynch to the Bakhtiyari Chiefs, London, 12 October 1900.

117 See copies of the concession in FO 60/631 and FO 60/661.

118 FO 248/676, J. R. Preece to Mortimer Durand, Ispahan, 8 December 1898.

119 FO 60/631, Secretary of Persian Transport Company to the Under Secretary of

State for Foreign Affairs, London, 30 May 1900.

120 Lorimer, *The Phonology of the Bakhtiyari, Badakhshani, and Madaglashti Dialects of Modern Persian* (London, 1922), 4–5.

121 "Through the Bakhtiyari Country," Ahwaz on the Karun, *Times*, 15 December 1902.

122 British Petroleum Archives (BP) 69813, Consul-General Preece to Sir Arthur Hardinge, Ispahan, 31 December 1904.

123 FO 60/661, Report by Consul-General Preece on the Bakhtiari Road, 1 July 1902. Despite Preece's hopes the British did not pave the Bakhtiyari Road, although in 1905 they briefly considered the feat before concluding that it would be "an extremely expensive process." FO 60/715, Arthur Hardinge to the Government of India, Gulahek, 12 August 1905. For roads and the introduction of paved roads and motor cars in Iran after the turn of the century, see FO 60/715, The Bakhtiyari Road and Other Roads, (1905).

124 India Office Library, Curzon Papers, MSS F 111/351, Mortimer Durand, Report on Western Tour in Persia.

125 J. P. Digard, "Histoire et anthropologie d'une tribu d'Iran," 1431.

126 FO 60/715, The Persian Transport Company Limited to the Under Secretary of State for Foreign Affairs, London, 7 March 1905.

127 Revenues paid to the chiefs increased from approximately 1,090 pounds in 1900 to 3,100 pounds in 1907. FO 248/895, H. N. MacLean, Secretary, Persian Transport Company to the Under Secretary of State for Foreign Affairs, Isfahan, 8 May 1907.

128 FO 416/8, H. F. B. Lynch to Consul-General Preece, London, 17 February 1902; FO 416/9, Consul-General Preece to Lynch, Ispahan, 18 March 1902.

129 India Office Library, Curzon Papers, MSS F 111/351, Mortimer Durand, Report on Western Tour in Persia.

130 FO 60/690, Report on the Condition of Caravan Track between Ahwaz and Isfahan, September 1903, Fred W. Parry, Isfahan, 30 September 1903.

131 FO 60/715, Fraser Parry to Arthur Hardinge, Tehran, 17 April 1905.

132 FO 60/715, Fraser Parry to Evelyn Grant Duff, Ahwaz, 21 August 1905.

133 FO 60/715, Condition of the Bakhtiyari Road by Fred Parry, Ahwaz, 21 August 1905.

134 Ibid.

135 India Office Library, Curzon Papers, MSS F 111/351, Mortimer Durand, Report on Western Tour in Persia. See E. R. Durand, *An Autumn Tour in Western Persia* (London, 1902), 132.

136 Durand, *An Autumn Tour in Western Persia*, 143–44.

137 Tapper, "Tribes in 18th and 19th Century Iran," 523.

138 FO 248/895, Extract of a letter from Messrs. Lynch Brothers, 20 January 1906; C. Alban Young to Arthur Hardinge, Gulhek, 29 May 1901, *Iran Political*

Diaries, 1881–1965, vol. 2: *1901–1905* (Archive Editions, 1997), 17.

139 Memorandum on Persia, R. Grahame, 10 March 1905, *Iran Political Diaries*, 454.

140 FO 248/895, Notes on the Condition of the Bakhtiyari Road, D. L. R. Lorimer, Ispahan, 21 July 1906.

141 India Office Records, L/MIL/17/15/20, Lieutenant J. Ranking, *Report on the Kuhgalu Tribes* (Simla, 1911), 1, 5–6, 19. Frequently the brigands were from the Tayibi and Dushman Ziyari Lurs of Kuhgilu. On the tribes of Kuhgilu in the Qajar period, see Hajji Mirza Hasan Fasa'i, *Farsnamah Nasiri*, vol. 2, 1573–85; Mahmud Bavar, *Kuhgiluya va Ilat-i An*.

142 India Office Records, *Report on the Kuhgalu Tribes*, 5.

143 Ibid., 1, 5–6, 19.

144 FO 60/715, Consul Preece to Evelyn Grant Duff, Junagun, 22 October 1905.

145 FO 248/895, H. N. MacLean, Secretary, Persian Transport Company to the Under Secretary of State for Foreign Affairs, Isfahan, 8 May 1907.

146 Sardar As'ad and Lynch perhaps became estranged after a meeting in London in 1902, when Lynch refused Sardar As'ad's personal request for cash, noting later that "it was evident that physically and morally he was not at all the same man as at the time when [Lynch] had known him in Persia" (FO 248/895, Note on the Subject of the proposed Visit of Haji Ali Kuli Khan Bakhtiari and Haji Khosru Khan Bakhtiari to Europe, H. N. MacLean, Secretary, Persian Transport Company, London, 30 January 1907).

147 "Through the Bakhtiyari Country," Ahwaz on the Karun, *Times*, 15 December 1902.

148 FO 248/895, Bakhtiari Road, Confidential, Evelyn Grant Duff, Tehran, 20 May 1906.

149 Ibid.

150 For the classic argument on this theme, see Eugen Weber's *Peasants into Frenchmen: The Modernization of Rural France, 1870–1914* (Stanford, 1976). Weber viewed late nineteenth- and early-twentieth-century state projects of road building, as well as education and conscription, as the means by which the countryside was transformed from isolated regions of different peoples with different beliefs, speaking different tongues or *patois* into a nation.

4 *In the Fields of Oil*

1 Mustafa Fatih, *Panjah Sal-i Naft-i Iran* (Tehran, 1336/1957), 259–60; Ahmad Kasravi, *Tarikh-i Pansad Sal-i Khuzistan* (Tehran, 1368/1989), 216–18.

2 On the sedentarization of nomads, see Anatoly M. Khazanov and Andre Wink, *Nomads in a Sedentary World* (London, 2001). For some accounts of

the social, political, and cultural effects of the oil economy in Iran and the Middle East, see Danish ʿAbbasi Shahuni, *Tarikh-i Masjid-i Sulayman* (Tehran 1372/1993); Madawi al-Rasheed, *A History of Saudi Arabia* (Cambridge, 2002); ʿAli Riza Abtahi, *Naft va Bakhtiyariha* (Tehran, 1384/2005); Robert Vitalis, *America's Kingdom: Mythmaking on the Saudi Oil Frontier* (Stanford, 2006); Stephanie Cronin, *Tribal Politics in Iran: Rural conflict and the new state, 1921–1941* (London, 2006). For a fictional account of the discovery of oil in an unnamed Arab kingdom, see ʿAbd al-Rahman Munif, *Cities of Salt*, trans. Peter Theroux (New York, 1989). For a recent social history of miners and mining in the Ottoman Empire, see Donald Quataert, *Miners and the State in the Ottoman Empire: The Zonguldak Coalfield, 1822–1920* (New York, 2006).

3 For some studies on imperialism and colonialism in the Middle East, see Timothy Mitchell, *Colonising Egypt* (Berkeley, 1988); Mitchell, *Rule of Experts: Egypt, Techno-Politics, Modernity* (Berkeley 2002); Clancy-Smith, *Rebel and Saint: Muslim Notables, Populist Protest, Colonial Encounters—Algeria and Tunisia, 1800–1904*; Ussama Makdisi, *The Culture of Sectarianism: Community, History, and Violence in Nineteenth-Century Ottoman Lebanon* (Berkeley, 2000). On the development of "inaccessible places," see Anna Lowenhaupt Tsing, *In the Realm of the Diamond Queen: Marginality in an Out-of-the-Way Place* (Princeton, 1993). On the transformation of subsistence societies and economies, see E. P. Thompson, "The Crime of Anonymity," *Albion's Fatal Tree: Crime and Society in Eighteenth-Century England* (New York, 1975); James C. Scott, *The Moral Economy of the Peasant: Rebellion and Subsistence in Southeast Asia* (New Haven, 1976); Ann Stoler, *Capitalism and Confrontation in Sumatra's Plantation Belt, 1870–1979* (New Haven, 1985).

4 For some other examples of this point of view, see Arnold Talbot Wilson, *S.W. Persia: Letters and Diary of a Young Political Officer, 1907–1914* (London, 1942); J. W. Williamson, *In a Persian Oil Field: A Study in Scientific and Industrial Development* (London, 1927); Laurence Lockhart, *The Record of the Anglo Iranian Oil Company*, unpublished BP company record; Lockhart, "Histoire du pétrole en Perse jusq'au début du XX siècle," *La Revue Pétrolifere* (Paris, 1938); Lockhart, "The Emergence of the Anglo Persian Oil Company, 1901–1914," in *Economic History of Iran*, 316–22; Henry Longhurst, *Adventures in Oil* (London, 1959); R. W. Ferrier, *The History of the British Petroleum Company*, vol. 1: *The Developing Years, 1901–1932* (Cambridge, 1982).

5 Ferrier, *History of the British Petroleum Company*, 115.

6 Abu al-Fazl Lisani, *Naft: Tala-yi Siya ya Bala-yi Iran* (Tehran, 1329/1950). Lisani was a politician and an outspoken critic of the Anglo-Iranian Oil Company. For earlier works written by Iranian authors on oil, see A. Zangueneh, *Le Pétrole en Perse* (Paris, 1933); M. Nakhai, *Le Pétrole en Iran* (Brussels, 1938).

7 Husayn Makki, *Kitab-i Siya* (Tehran, 1329/1950). Makki, also known as "the

hero of Abadan," was a leading figure in the oil nationalization campaign. He later became known for his conspiratorial, almost paranoid, style of historiography. Also see Husayn Pirnia, *Dah Sal-i Kushish dar Rah-i Hifz va Bast-i Huquq-i Iran dar Naft* (Tehran, 1331/1952); Kazim Afshin, *Naft va Khuzistan* (Tehran 1333/1954); Nasrollah Saifpour Fatemi, *Oil Diplomacy: Powder Keg in Iran* (New York, 1954); L. Elwell-Sutton, *Persian Oil: A Study in Power Politics* (London, 1955); Mustafa Fatih, *Panjah Sal-i Naft-i Iran.*

8 Elwell-Sutton, *Persian Oil*, 8–9.

9 For the nationalist perspective on Mussadiq and the oil crisis, see Makki, *Kitab-i Siya*; Pirnia, *Dah Sal-i Kushish*; Fatemi, *Oil Diplomacy*; Elwell-Sutton, *Persian Oil*; Fatih, *Panjah Sal-i Naft-i Iran.* For more recent studies, see R. W. Cottam, *Nationalism in Iran* (Pittsburgh, 1979); Ervand Abrahamian, *Iran between Two Revolutions* (Princeton, 1982); James Bill and William Roger Lewis, eds., *Mussadiq, Iranian Nationalism and Oil* (Austin, 1988); Homa Katouzian, *The Political Economy of Modern Iran* (London, 1981); Katouzian, *Mussadiq and the Struggle for Power in Iran* (London, 1991); Mostafa Elm, *Oil, Power, and Principle: Iran's Oil Nationalization and Its Aftermath* (Syracuse, 1992); Nikki Keddie, *Modern Iran: Roots and Results of the Revolution* (New Haven, 2003). For an English translation of Mussadiq's memoirs, see *Mussadiq's Memoirs*, ed. Katouzian (London, 1988). For some recent studies of tribes and the development of the Anglo-Persian Oil Company, see Abtahi, *Naft va Bakhtiyariha;* Cronin, *Tribal Politics in Iran.*

10 Imperial science is a subject explored in a number of recent studies. In *Engineers of Happy Land: Technology and Nationalism in a Colony*, Rudolf Mrazek examines the language underlying different types of technology: "hard and clean" roads, fast trains, urban planning. According to Mrazek, in the late-colonial Dutch East Indies, as "the people handled, or were handled by, the new technologies, their time, space, culture, identity, and nation came to feel awry." See Mrazek, *Engineers of Happy Land: Technology and Nationalism in a Colony* (Princeton, 2002), xvi. On science and empire, also see Khaled Fahmy, *All the Pasha's Men: Mehmed 'Ali, His Army, and the Making of Modern Egypt* (Cambridge, 1997); David Gilmartin, "Scientific Empire and Imperial Science: Colonialism and Irrigation Technology in the Indus Basin," *The Journal of Asian Studies* 53, no. 4 (1994), 1127–49; Timothy Mitchell, *Colonizing Egypt* (Berkeley, 1991); Michael Adas, *Machines as the Measure of Men: Science Technology and Ideologies of Western Dominance* (Ithaca, 1989); Daniel Headrick, *The Tentacles of Progress: Technology Transfer in the Age of Imperialism* (New York, 1988); David Worster, *Rivers of Empire: Water, Aridity, and the Growth of the American West* (New York, 1985). On modern state projects of "legibility," see James C. Scott, *Seeing like a State: How Certain Schemes to Improve the Human Condition Have Failed* (New Haven, 1998).

11 W. Barthold, *An Historical Geography of Iran*, trans. Svat Soucek (Princeton, 1984) 184. On Izaj, see TB, 58–59.

12 *Hudud al-ʿAlam*, trans. V. Minorsky (London, 1937), 129–30.

13 Barthold, *Historical Geography*, 180.

14 Muhammad ibn Ahmad al-Muqaddasi, *Ahsan al-Taqasim fi maʿrifat al-aqalim* (The Best of Divisions on the Knowledge of the Provinces), ed. De Goeje (Leiden, 1877), 138. Le Strange notes that the appellation Jabal fell out of use in favor of "ʿIraq-i Ajam." Le Strange, *The Lands of the Eastern Caliphate*, 185.

15 *Hudud al-Alam*, 126, 130.

16 Hanway, *An Account of the British Trade over the Caspian*, vol. 1, 166.

17 Rawlinson, "Notes on a March from Zohab," 79.

18 Layard, *Adventures in Persia*, 342.

19 Ibid., 341.

20 Ibid., 228. On mining in nineteenth-century Iran, see Curzon, *Persia and the Persian Question*, vol. 2, 510–22.

21 Curzon, *Persia and the Persian Question*, vol. 2, 512.

22 Naft-i Safid got its name ("white oil") because the oil there passed through a natural filter bed, making it suitable for burning in lanterns without refining. Locals had long exploited this oil, for which there was a high demand in Iran. See SK, 25, 139. Also see Lockhart, "The Emergence of the Anglo-Persian Oil Company," 317.

23 On the Reuter Concession, see chapter 3, note 1.

24 Curzon, *Persia and the Persian Question*, vol. 2, 513; Ferrier, *History of the British Petroleum Company*, 24–25. Since the 1870s the Russians had exploited the oil fields of Baku, which they had annexed in 1806. But before the operations of the D'Arcy Oil Syndicate in southwestern Iran, oil had not been found in commercial quantities.

25 Lockhart, "The Emergence of the Anglo-Persian Oil Company," 316.

26 Jacques de Morgan, *Mission Scientifique en Perse*, vol. 2 (Paris, 1895), 80–87.

27 De Morgan, "Note sur les gites de Naphte de Kend-e Chirin," *Annales des Mines* (February 1892), 1–16.

28 Ibid., 182.

29 Elwell-Sutton, *Persian Oil*, 12–13; Lockhart, "The Emergence of the Anglo-Persian Oil Company," 317.

30 Ferrier, *History of the British Petroleum Company*, 38–39.

31 Ibid., 640. Also see Fatih, *Panjah Sal Naft-i Iran*, 255–92.

32 The D'Arcy Concession first appeared in print in the *Official Journal* of the League of Nations in December 1932. George Lenczowski, *Oil and State in the Middle East* (Ithaca, 1960), 205.

33 Lockhart cites the memoirs of Arthur Hardinge as the source of this allegation; see Lockhart, "The Emergence of the Anglo-Persian Oil Company," 317.

Also see Arthur Hardinge, *A Diplomatist in the East* (London, 1928), 278–79.

34 Ferrier, *History of the British Petroleum Company*, 67; Fatih, *Panjah Sal-i Naft-i Iran*, 257.

35 BP 78723, Reynolds to Jenkin, 2 April 1904.

36 Arnold Talbot Wilson, *S.W. Persia, Letters and Diary of a Young Political Officer, 1907–1914* (London, 1942), 84. Wilson's memoirs provide a record of the early exploration for oil among the Bakhtiyari and leave accounts of personalities such as George Reynolds, D. L. R. Lorimer, and Dr. M. Y. Young.

37 Ferrier, *History of the British Petroleum Company*, 74–76; Fatih, *Panjah Sal-i Naft-i Iran*, 257.

38 J. R. Preece, "Report on the Negotiations with the Chiefs of the Bakhtiari Tribes for the Exploitation of Naphtha in their Country," November 27, 1905. *Iran and the Persian Gulf, 1820–1966*, vol. 2 (London, 2000), 429–30.

39 Preece, "Report on the Negotiations with the Chiefs of the Bakhtiari Tribes for the Exploitation of Naphtha in their Country," 429–30.

40 Ferrier, *History of the British Petroleum Company*, 76–77.

41 Only representatives of the Ilkhani and Haji Ilkhani had signed the Bakhtiyari Agreement. The omission of the Ilbaygi from the deal had consequences for the structure of the tribal leadership, as it intensified intra-tribal feuds during the turbulent Constitutional Revolution.

42 Ferrier, *History of the British Petroleum Company*, 77. In keeping with article 11 of the D'Arcy Concession the Qajars appointed Sadiq al-Saltana as commissioner of mines for the central government. But although the commissioner visited the oil fields, inspected the work, and met with company officials, even pressing certain terms of the concession, the company regarded him as more of a nuisance than a representative of the central government. See FO 248/923, Sadiq al-Saltana to George Reynolds, 27 April 1907.

43 Fatemi, *Oil Diplomacy*, 42.

44 Evelyn Grant Duff to Sir Edward Grey, Tehran, 18 May 1906. *Iran in the Persian Gulf*, 433–34.

45 FO 248/894, Evelyn Grant Duff to Sir Edward Grey, Tehran, 18 May 1906.

46 J. R. Preece to Sir Edward Grey, St. James's Palace, 3 June 1907. *Iran in the Persian Gulf*, 446–50.

47 At the time Mamatain was a village north of Ahvaz inhabited by Chahar Lang and other Lur tribes, while nearby Shardin was a small village of about fifteen huts. Both sites were drilled to a depth of 2,500 feet without result. Wilson, *Military Report on Southwest Persia, I: Bakhtyari Garmsir* (Simla, 1909), 117.

48 Masjid-i Sulayman was the part of the winter quarters of the Mawri, Bakhtiyarvand, 'Ali Anvar, and Babadi tribes of the Haft Lang. See Qayid Bakhtiyari, *Tarikh va Farhang-i Bakhtiyari*, vol. 2, 29–33; Wilson, *Military Report on Southwest Persia, I*, 117.

49 Wilson, *Military Report on Southwest Persia, I*, 117. In his time as Lorimer's assistant in Ahvaz, as discussed in the section on the Indian guards below, Wilson grew a beard, dressed as a tribesman, and surveyed the Bakhtiyari Mountains. This source was the first in a five-part military survey on southwestern Iran that Wilson, a prolific writer, compiled for the Indian government. For a biography of Wilson, who would go on become acting civil commissioner of Mandatory Iraq in the 1920s, see John Marlow, *Late Victorian* (London, 1976).

50 Fatih, *Panjah Sal-i Naft-i Iran*, Tehran, 259–60.

51 *TB*, 60.

52 *TB*, 439–40.

53 See, for example, FO 248/894, Lorimer to Political Resident in the Persian Gulf, Camp Ram Hurmuz, 6 March 1907.

54 BP 70335, Report on Bakhtiari Negotiatons, by Dr. M. Y. Young, Maydan-i Naftun, 8 May 1911.

55 For an overview on oil workers in the Middle East, see Lenczowski, *Oil and State in the Middle East*, 253–80.

56 Williamson, *In a Persian Oil Field*, 125.

57 Ferrier, *The History of the British Petroleum Company*, 154.

58 BP 78723, Reynolds to Concessions Syndicate, Ahwaz, 26 March 1906; BP 70335, Dr. M. Y. Young to W. S. Lamb, Representing Agent for Anglo-Persian Oil Company, Maydan-i Naftun, 24 July 1911. On work on the pipeline, see the other correspondence between Young and Lamb, as well as the reports and letters of Charles Ritchie, the field manager following the departure of Reynolds, at the British Petroleum Archives. Also see Ferrier, *The History of the Anglo-Persian Oil Company*, vol. 1, 132–33.

59 Ferrier, *History of the British Petroleum Company*, vol. 1, 132–33.

60 FO 248/923, Sarum al-Mulk to Reynolds, Shardin, 1907.

61 Iqbal 'Ali Shah, *Westward to Mecca* (London, 1928), quoted in Wilson, *Persia*, 97.

62 Elwell-Sutton, *Persian Oil*, 88.

63 The company medic, M. Y. Young, treated hundreds of patients monthly, and his records provide us with a sketch of work conditions during the early years of the oil industry in Iran. Young reported that "the native staff and employees unfortunately suffered much, and the number of patients amongst them increased." This was partially the result of work involving the transport of iron pipes, hot under the sun, through narrow passes and over gypsum hills. Because they did this at first without wearing gloves, workers suffered boils and burns on their hands and arms. Also of concern was the possibility that in the process of drilling for oil, gas could be tapped, with the potential of gas poisoning for all those working on the rig. At night there was the added

risk of the gas igniting. Cases of gas poisoning occurred repeatedly among the workers of Maydan-i Naftun as well. In March 1908, Young reported that "among natives, disease was pretty rife," with "an unusual number of infectious cases," measles, smallpox, and several cases of typhoid fever brought to him, adding that "all these belong to the tribes who spend their winter in this part of the country, and are outside our camp" BP 78737, Young to Bradshaw, Camp Maydan-i Naftun, 3 August 1908; BP 78737, Young to Bradshaw, Camp Maydan-i Naftun, 4 September 1908; BP 78722, Young to Reynolds, Camp Maydan-i Naftun, 19 March 1908.

64 BP 78723, Reynolds to Samsam al-Saltana, Ahwaz, 27 June 1906.

65 BP 78723 Reynolds to Concessions Syndicate Ltd. Garthwaite has noted this problem in regard to the Lynch Road: "Regarding Lynch's complaints on the lack of transport animals . . . tribesmen and their animals were following a pastoral nomadic life which did not free them for any length of time to participate regularly in carrying cargo; nor did such a task fit into their value system"; see Garthwaite, *Khans and Shahs*, 182, n. 23.

66 BP 78737, Young to Bradshaw, Camp Maydan-i Naftun, 3 August 1908.

67 FO 248/923, Reynolds to Lorimer, Mamatain, 23 July 1907.

68 Elwell-Sutton, *Persian Oil*, 90.

69 FO 248/923, Nasir Khan Sarum al-Mulk to Reynolds, received 21 July 1907.

70 FO 248/923, Note by Reynolds on the letter of Sarum al-Mulk, Camp Mamatain, 23 July 1907.

71 Williamson, *In a Persian Oil Field*, 126–27.

72 BP, Mrs. Talbot Clifton, "Maidan-i Naftun," *Naft*, 1, 6, October 1925.

73 BP 78723, Reynolds to Samsam al-Saltana, Ahwaz, 27 June 1906.

74 Williamson, *In a Persian Oil Field*, 125.

75 FO 248/894, British Charge d'Affaires, Evelyn Grant Duff to Sir Edward Grey, Secretary of State for Foreign Affairs, Tehran, 18 May 1906.

76 Fatih, *Panjah Sal-i Naft-i Iran*, 257–58; FO 248/894, Reynolds to Samsam al-Saltana, Shardin, 28 November 1905.

77 Wilson, *S.W. Persia: Letters and Diary of a Young Political Officer*, 27.

78 Ibid., 27.

79 FO 248/894, Reynolds to Samsam al-Saltana, Shardin, 28 November 1905.

80 FO 248/894, Reynolds to Samsam al-Santana, Ilkhani of Bakhtiyari tribes at Shalamzar, Ahwaz, 7 December 1905.

81 FO 248/894, Evelyn Grant Duff to Edward Grey, Tehran, 31 January 1906.

82 FO 248/894, Bakhtiyari chiefs to 'Ali Quli Khan, 14 July 1906.

83 FO 248/894, Lorimer, Vice-Consul for Arabistan, to the Political Resident at Bushire, Ahwaz, 17 January 1906.

84 FO 248/894, Evelyn Grant Duff, Note on the Oil Syndicate, Gulhek, 23 July 1906.

85 FO 248/894, Evelyn Grant Duff to Edward Grey, Tehran, 31 January 1906.

86 FO 248/894, Evelyn Grant Duff to Amin al-Sultan Atabayg Azam, Tehran, 18 February 1906.

87 FO 248/894, Samsam al-Saltana and Shahab al-Saltana to Evelyn Grant Duff, 17 September 1906.

88 FO 248/894, Shuja al-Sultan to Mushir al-Dawla, n.d.; also see Nizam al-Saltana, *Khatirat va Asnad*, vol. 2–3, 397.

89 FO 248/894, From Shuja al-Sultan to Mushir al-Dawla, 1906.

90 BP 78739, Azizullah Khan to Reynolds, Ram Hurmuz, 5 February 1906.

91 BP 78739, Khusraw Khan to Reynolds, Malamir, 13 February 1906; BP 78739, Reynolds to Khusraw Khan, Ahwaz, 8 February 1906.

92 BP 78739, Reynolds to Concessions Syndicate Ltd., 19 February 1906.

93 BP 78739, Reynolds to Salar Arfa, 25 March 1906.

94 BP 78739, Reynolds to Khusraw Khan, 25 March 1906.

95 FO 248/923, Bakhtiyari Khans to Lorimer (Lorimer's notes), 13 November 1907.

96 BP 77/49/3/2, Reynolds to Concessions Syndicate Ltd., Ahwaz, 26 December 1906.

97 FO 248/923, Bradshaw to Reynolds, Maydan-i Naftun, 12 November 1907.

98 BP 78726, Bradshaw to Reynolds, Masjid-i Sulaiman, 19 March 1907; BP 78726, Bradshaw to Reynolds, Masjid-i Sulaiman, 22 March 1907.

99 BP 78726, Bertie to Reynolds, Shardin, 25 March 1907.

100 Garthwaite, *Khans and Shahs*, 111.

101 FO 248/923, Decypher by Barnham, Ardal, June 1907.

102 FO 248/923, Rasuk Alias, Mirza at Batwand, to Reynolds, 1 August 1907, in Extracts and Enclosures from Reynolds to Lorimer, 27 August 1907.

103 FO 248/923, Rasuk Alias, Mirza at Batwand, to Reynolds, 1 August 1907, in Extracts and Enclosures from Reynolds to Lorimer, 27 August 1907.

104 FO 248/923, Bradshaw to Reynolds, Masjid-i Sulaiman, no date, in Extracts and Enclosures from Reynolds to Lorimer, 27 August 1907.

105 FO 248/923, R. Bertie Esq. to Reynolds, Mamatain, 17 July 1907.

106 FO 248/923, Holland to Reynolds, Batwand, 7 August 1907.

107 FO 248/923, Bradshaw to Reynolds, Maydan-i Naftun, 12 November 1907.

108 FO 248/894, Reynolds to D. L. R. Lorimer, Ahwaz, 17 January 1906.

109 Lorimer's papers of vernacular songs and folklore are held at the University of London–School of Oriental and African Studies.

110 Hyacinth Rabino, *Tribus du Louristan* (Paris, 1916), 3.

111 FO 248/894, Lorimer, Notes on discussions between H. B. M. Vice-Consul for Arabistan and the Khans of the Bakhtiari, Junaqun, 24 October 1906.

112 FO 248/923, Bakhtiyari Khans to Lorimer (Lorimer's notes), 13 November 1907.

113 FO 248/894, Lorimer to Hajji Asadullah Khan, Ram Hurmuz, 15 January

1907. See also FO 248/894, Samsam al-Saltana and Shahab al-Saltana to Lorimer, 12 January 1907; FO 248/894, Lorimer to Samsam al-Saltana and Shahab al-Saltana, Ahwaz, 17 January 1907; FO 248/894, Lorimer to Samsam al-Saltana and Shahab al-Saltana, Mamatain, 18 January 1907.

114 FO 248/894, Asadullah to Lorimer, Ram Hurmuz, 17 January 1907.

115 FO 248/894, Samsam al-Saltana and Shahab al-Saltana to Lorimer, 27 January 1907; Lorimer's Memorandum of Instructions handed to Azizullah Khan, Deputy Governor of Ram Hurmuz, 27 January 1907.

116 FO 238/923, Lorimer to Political Resident in the Persian Gulf, Camp Ramuz, 6 March 1907.

117 FO 238/923, Lorimer to Political Resident in the Persian Gulf, Camp Kima, 19 March 1907.

118 Ibid.

119 FO 248/923, Lorimer Confidential to Political Resident in the Persian Gulf, Ahwaz, 27 March 1907.

120 Ibid.

121 FO 248/923, Samsam al-Saltana and Sarum al-Mulk to Reynolds, 23 August 1907.

122 FO 248/923, Lorimer to Cecil Spring-Rice, H. B. M.'s Minister Plenipotentiary at Tehran, Ahwaz, 29 August 1907.

123 Ibid.

124 FO 248/923, Lorimer to Marling, Shalamzar, 29 September 1907.

125 FO 248/923, Lorimer to Marling, Isfahan, 13 September 1907.

126 FO 248/923, Lorimer to H. B. M.'s Political Resident at Bushire, Ahwaz, 29 October 1907.

127 Consul Preece suggested that had Isfandiyar Khan (d. 1903) been alive, the situation would not have reached such an impasse. "The Bakhtiyaris united and strong," he wrote, "could laugh at anything outside their country, and, they maintaining their agreement, we could go on with our work in perfect peace and security." BP 69833, J.R. Preece to Foreign Office, 30 September 1907.

128 FO 248/923, Samsam al-Saltana and Shahab al-Saltana to Lorimer, 23 December 1907; FO 248/923, Samsam al-Saltana and Shahab al-Saltana to Mushir al-Dawla, Ram Hurmuz, 29 December 1907.

129 FO 248/923, Ahwaz Vice-Consulate, Confidential Diary No. 54, Dizful, 18 October 1907. Lorimer wrote that he had the khans' sanction: "They agreed however to recover or pay compensation for a case of opium robbed on the roads and to pay a yearly installment and interest due for the construction of the Bakhtiyari Road, though they insisted that nothing was due from them. They also propose to send two commissioners with me to carry out at Batwand whatever measures I required for the settlement of the Harris case."

130 FO 248/923, Ahwaz Vice-Consulate, Confidential Diary No. 54, Dizful, 18 October 1907.

131 Ibid.

132 FO 248/923, Lorimer to H. B. M.'s Political Resident at Bushire, Ahwaz, 29 October 1907.

133 The khans also complained that Lorimer had overcharged them for the painting of two bridges on the Lynch Road and that the consul had demanded compensation from the Bakhtiyari for robberies committed by tribes not under the Bakhtiyari's authority. See FO 248/923, Samsam al-Saltana and Shahab al-Saltana to Cecil Spring-Rice, 4 October 1907.

134 FO 248/923, Cecil Spring-Rice to Samsam al-Saltana and Shahab al-Saltana, Tehran, 8 October 1907.

135 FO 248/923, Bakhtiyari Khans to Lorimer, 13 November 1907.

136 FO 248/923, Memorandum to Reynolds.

137 Wilson, *S.W. Persia*, 17.

138 FO 248/923, Mushir al-Dawla to British Legation.

139 Arnold Talbot Wilson, who would become the acting civil commissioner of the newly formed mandate state of Iraq in 1920, was at this time a young officer who devoted a good part of his time in Persia to reconnaissance work, publishing a five-volume gazetteer on "Southwest Persia" between 1909 and 1912. See Wilson, *Military Report on S.W. Persia*. Wilson's memoirs paint a vivid picture of his work surveying the Zagros Mountains (see Wilson, *S.W. Persia*).

140 FO 248/923, Lorimer to H. B. M.'s Political Resident at Bushire, Ahwaz, 29 October 1907.

141 Wilson, *S.W. Persia*, 39.

142 Wilson, *S.W. Persia*, 42.

143 Wilson, *S.W. Persia*, 42.

144 FO 248/923, Wilson to Cox, H.B.M.'s Consul, Muhammarah, Camp Maydan-i Naftun, 6 August 1908.

145 See FO 248/923, Visit of the Bakhtiyari Khans to London and Conversation with Sir C. Hardinge, Louis Mallet to C. M. Marling, July 6. 1908.

146 Ibid.

147 FO 248/923, Lorimer to Cox, Ispahan, 21 September 1908.

148 FO 248/923, Grey to Lorimer, 4 November 1908.

149 BP 78749, M. Y. Young, Confidential Special Report, Maydan-i Naftun, 1 May 1909.

150 Wilson, *S.W. Persia*, 28.

151 BP 69830, M.Y. Young, The Bakhtiari Khans at Malamir, Maydan-i Naftun, 28 February 1909.

152 The khans recommended that part of the guards' money be paid to their

families in the north to ensure their staying at the oil fields of the "warm country" during the summer. BP 69830, M. Y. Young, The Bakhtiari Khans at Malamir.

153 BP 69830, Supplementary Agreement between the Bakhtiyari Khans and The Concessions Syndicate Ltd., Malamir, 1 April 1909.

154 BP 69830, Supplementary Agreement between the Bakhtiyari Khans and The Concessions Syndicate Ltd., Malamir, 1 April 1909. Moreover, the syndicate was "authorized to punish them by fines or dismissal for neglect of duty or misbehaviour." The value of stolen articles was to be deducted from the pay of the guard under whose watch theft occurred, up to half his monthly salary, which varied from seven to twelve tumans, could be deducted, depending on whether he was a footman or a horseman. A register of all punishments levied on the guards was to be kept and submitted monthly to the Bakhtiyari khans.

155 Lockhart, "The Emergence of the Anglo-Persian Oil Company," 319.

156 For a reference to the "moral" mission fulfilled by oil exploitation in Iran, see Wilson, *Persia* (London, 1932), 96–100.

157 Quoted in Wilson, *Persia*, 92–93.

158 BP 70335, Bakhtiyari Affairs. The Land Problem, Dr. Young, Maydan-i Naftun, 12 January 1911.

159 Ibid.

160 Ibid.

161 Ibid.

162 BP 70335, Young to Lamb, Maydan-i Naftun, 26 February 1911.

163 BP 70335, Area Figures Supplied by G. B. Scott, Maydan-i Naftun, 15 April 1911.

164 BP 70335, Young to Lamb, Maydan-i Naftun, 26 February 1911.

165 Ferrier, *The History of the British Petroleum Company*, 146.

166 BP 70335, Young to A. Grey, Consul at Ahwaz, Maydan-i Naftun, 9 September 1911.

167 BP 70335, Young's Report on Bakhtiari Negotiatons, Maydan-i Naftun, 8 May 1911.

168 Ibid.

169 Ibid.

170 Ibid.

171 BP 70335, Confidential on the Land Agreement from Young to Lamb, Maydan-i Naftun, 10 May 1911.

172 Ibid.

173 Ibid.

174 Ibid.

175 Ibid.

5 *The Bakhtiyari Tribes in the Iranian Constitutional Revolution*

1 Lambton, "Ilat," 1109–10.

2 *Habl al-Matin* (The Firm Rope), Calcutta, 13 September 1909, number 10, year 7. *"Millat-i azad kard junbish-i khish ashkar/hami-yi millat risid ba sipah-i Bakhtiyar."* Translation: "The people rebelled/the protectors of the people arrived with the cavalries of Bakhtiyar."

3 *Habl al-Matin*, Calcutta, 5 July 1909, number 1, year 7.

4 See Edward G. Browne, *The Persian Revolution, 1905–1909* (Cambridge, 1910), 266. This emphasis on the Bakhtiyari's devotion to the nationalist cause can also be found in the tribal history *Tarikh-i Bakhtiyari*, as well as the following works: Nurallah Danishvar 'Alavi, *Tarikh-i Iran va Junbish-i Vatan Parastan-i Isfahan va Bakhtiyari* (Tehran, 1377/1998); Mihdi Malikzada, *Tarikh-i Inqilab-i Mashrutiyat-i Iran*, 7 vols. (Tehran, 1363/1984); Isfandiyar Ahanjida, *Bakhtiyari va Mashruta* (Arak, 1374/1995). For first-person accounts by Bakhtiyaris on the Constitutional Revolution, see Iskandar Khan 'Akkasha, *Tarikh-i Il-i Bakhtiyari*, ed. Farid Muradi (Tehran, 1365/1986); Bibi Maryam Bakhtiyari, *Khatirat-i Sardar Maryam*.

5 Iraj Afshar, *Mubariza ba Muhammad 'Ali Shah* (Tehran, 1359/1980), doc. 31, 74.

6 See Fraser's articles for the *Times* and his *Persia and Turkey in Revolt* (Edinburgh, 1910), 88. This alarmist perspective on the Bakhtiyari's emergence in the revolution can be read in the correspondence of Grahame, the British consul of Isfahan; see FO 248/965. In similar language Morgan Shuster noted that the Bakhtiyari tribesmen in Tehran aimed to plunder the treasury, wreaked havoc, and were among the forces that brought about the demise of the constitutional movement in Iran. See Shuster, *The Strangling of Persia* (New York, 1912). This view of the Bakhtiyari tribes as a source of "chaos," disorder, and warlordism in national politics during the constitutional period is prevalent in more recent accounts of the revolution as well. In *The Turban for the Crown: The Islamic Revolution in Iran* (Oxford, 1988), Said Arjomand highlights "the rebellion of the tribes *against* the constitution" and attributes the Bakhtiyaris' support for *mashrutiyat* to the convictions of Sardar As'ad; see Arjomand, *The Turban for the Crown*, 48–57. A similarly alarmist outlook on the involvement of tribes in the Constitutional Revolution is presented in Walcher, *In the Shadow of the King*.

7 Fraser, *Turkey and Persia in Revolt*, 200.

8 Noting that the Constitutional Revolution coincided with the exploration for oil at Masjid-i Sulayman, Abu al-Fath Uzhan, a Bakhtiyari historian, speculates that the ruling khans' acceptance of a 3 percent instead of a 10 percent

share of the D'Arcy Oil Company was based on the British promise that they would back the tribe in the Revolution. But this seems improbable, as Uzhan does not provide a source, instead basing his interpretation on the coincidence of the discovery of oil at Masjid-i Sulayman in April 1908 and the Bakhtiyari's emergence in the Revolution in January 1909. See Uzhan, *Tarikh-i Bakhtiyari*, 176. For a similarly unfounded view of the Bakhtiyari as the proxies of the British in the Constitutional Revolution, see Mihdi Bamdad, *Sharh-i Hal-i Rijal-i Iran dar Qarn-i Davazdah, Sizdah, Chahardah Hijri*, vol. 2 (Tehran, 1357/1978), 451. For literature in English on the British influence on the Bakhtiyari during the constitutional period, see Firuz Kazemzadeh, *Russia and Britain in Persia* (New Haven, 1968); Ira Klein, "British intervention in the Persian Revolution, 1905–1909," *The Historical Journal* 15, no. 4 (December 1972), 731–52. For a study of Bakhtiyari connections to the liberal Persia Committee in London, see Mansour Bonakdarian, "Iranian Constitutional Exiles and British Foreign-policy Dissenters, 1908–1909," *International Journal of Middle East Studies* 27, no. 2 (May 1995), 175–91.

9 Garthwaite, *Khans and Shahs*, 112–25.

10 On a similar theme see Peter Sahlins, *Boundaries: The Making of France and Spain in the Pyrenees* (Berkeley, 1989), 197.

11 There have been few studies of the Iranian Constitutional Revolution "from below," apart from Janet Afary's *The Iranian Constitutional Revolution: Grassroots Democracy, Social Democracy, and the Origins of Feminism* (New York, 1996). In contrast, the place of ordinary people in revolutions has been thoroughly examined in French historiography. For France, see Richard Cobb, *Les armées révolutionnaires* (Paris, 1961–63), *The Police and the People: French Popular Protest, 1789–1820* (Oxford, 1970), *Reactions to the French Revolution* (London, 1972), and *Paris and Its Provinces, 1792–1802* (Oxford, 1975); Peter Sahlins, *Boundaries*; Alain Corbin, *Village Bells: Sound and Meaning in the Nineteenth-Century French Countryside* (New York, 1998 [1994]). In other fields of Asian history the struggles of peripheral social groups or "subalterns" in nationalist movements have been more thoroughly explored. See Ranajit Guha, *Elementary Aspects of Peasant Insurgency in Colonial India* (Durham, NC, 1999 [1983]); Guha (ed.), *Select Subaltern Studies* (Oxford, 1988).

12 On the Bakhtiyari in the Qajar period, see Darrashuri, *Bakhtiyariha va Qajariya*; Garthwaite, *Khans and Shahs*; Tapper, "The Tribes in Eighteenth and Nineteenth Century Iran," 506–41.

13 TB, 82.

14 Garthwaite, *Khans and Shahs*, 186. For a brief biography of Sardar As'ad, see Sa'idi Sirjani, "Haji Ali-qoli Khan Sardar Asad Baktiari," *Encyclopaedia Iranica*, vol. 3, 543–48.

15 TB, 472–74; Sa'idi Sirjani, "Haji Ali-qoli Khan Sardar Asad Baktiari," 543.

16 The tribal school, which may have played a role in inculcating modern values and literacy among the tribal youth, employed Shaykh 'Ali Tazi and brought in several teachers from Tehran to educate the children of the khans. Malikzada, *Tarikh-i Inqilab-i Mashrutiyat-i Iran*, vol. 1, 121, and vol. 6, 1079.

17 Ervand Abrahamian, *Iran Between Two Revolutions*, 76–79.

18 TB, 177.

19 TB, 464.

20 FO 248/923, D'Arcy Oil Syndicate, D. L. R. Lorimer to Consul at Isfahan, Ardal, 5 June 1907.

21 FO 248/937, Dr. M. S. Aganoor to Charles M. Marling, Isfahan, 3 July 1908.

22 Wilson, *Military Report on S.W. Persia,* 16.

23 FO 248/937, Dr. Aganoor to George Barclay, Isfahan, 24 October 1908.

24 'Alavi, *Tarikh-i Inqilab-i Mashruta va Junbish-i Vatan Parastan*, 34. On the animosity between Sardar Zafar and Samsam al-Saltana, sons of Husyan Quli Khan by different mothers, see Sardar Zafar, "Vaqa'i'-yi Nagufti az Mashrutiyat," *Khatirat va Asnad* (Tehran, 1369/1990), 192–208.

25 On the death of Husayn Quli Khan Ilkhani see Sardar Zafar, *Yaddashtha va Khatirat*, 190–209; 'Akkasha, *Tarikh-i Il-i Bakhtiyari*, 183–90; Garthwaite, *Khans and Shahs*, 89–95.

26 Malikzada, *Tarikh-i Inqilab-i Mashrutiyat-i Iran*, vol. 6, 1082.

27 'Akkasha, *Tarikh-i Il-I Bakhtiyari, 587.*

28 Ibid., 588.

29 Ibid., 589.

30 'Alavi, *Tarikh-i Inqilab-i Mashruta va Junbish-i Vatan Parastan-i Isfahan va Bakhtiyari*, 35; Ahanjida, *Bakhtiyari va Mashruta*, 117–18; Malikzada, *Tarikh-i Inqilab-i Mashrutiyat-i Iran*, vol. 6, 1083.

31 Hajj Sayyah, *Khatirat-i Hajj Sayyah ya Dura-yi Khuf va Vahshat* (Tehran, 1346/1967), 212.

32 'Alavi, *Tarikh-i Inqilab-i Mashruta va Junbish-i Vatan Parastan*, 35; Ahanjida, *Bakhtiyari va Mashruta*, 117–18.

33 Ahanjida, *Bakhtiyari va Mashruta*, 120.

34 Uzhan, *Tarikh-i Bakhtiyari*, 201–2.

35 Elizabeth MacBean Ross, *A Lady Doctor in Bakhtiari Land* (London, 1921), 42–43.

36 Hajj Sayyah, *Khatirat*, 612.

37 'Alavi, *Tarikh-i Inqilab-i Mashruta va Junbish-i Vatan Parastan-i Isfahan va Bakhtiyari*, 43–44; Ahanjida, *Bakhtiyari va Mashruta*, 120.

38 FO 248/965, Grahame to Barclay, Isfahan, 2 January 1909.

39 Nikzad, *Shinakht-i Sarzamin-i Bakhtiyari*, 211.

40 Malikzada, *Tarikh-i Inqilab-i Mashrutiyat-i Iran*, vol. 6, 1088.

41 FO 248/965, Isfahan News, 4 January 1909.

42 *Jahad-i Akbar*, Isfahan, Muharram 1327/1909. On Zargham al-Saltana and the Bakhtiyari's entry into Isfahan, also see 'Alavi, *Tarikh-i Inqilabi-i Mashruta va Junbish-i Vatan Parastan-i Isfahan va Bakhtiyari*, 39–46.

43 FO 248/965, Grahame to Sir. G. Barclay, Isfahan, January 1909; *TB*, 451–52.

44 Ibid.

45 FO 248/965, Barclay to Mr. Grahame, Tehran, 5 January 1909.

46 Browne, *The Persian Revolution, 1905–1909*, 266.

47 FO 248/965, Grahame to Barclay, Isfahan, January 1909.

48 Ibid.

49 *TB*, 454; Browne, *The Persian Revolution, 1905–1909*, 266; FO 248/965, Grahame to Barclay, Isfahan, 8 January 1909.

50 Fraser, *Turkey and Persia in Revolt*, 199.

51 *TB*, 455–56; FO 248/965, Grahame to Barclay, Isfahan, 23 January 1909.

52 FO 248/965, Grahame to Barclay, Tehran, 7 January 1909.

53 'Akkasha, *Tarikh-i Il-i Bakhtiyari*, 587–93; Khusraw Khan Sardar Zafar, "Vaqa'i'-yi Nagufti az Mashrutiyat," 205.

54 FO 248/965, Grahame to Barclay, Isfahan News, 23 January 1909.

55 FO 248/965, Grahame to Barclay, Tehran, 9 January 1909.

56 FO 248/965, Barclay to Grahame, Tehran, 7 January 1909.

57 See *NT*; *RSN*; *MB*; Mirza Abu al-Hasan Sani' al-Mulk Ghaffari, *Ruznama-yi Dawlat-i 'Alliya-yi Iran* (Tehran, 1370/1991); Government of Iran, *Ruznama-yi Vaqa'i'-yi Ittifaqiya*.

58 *Habl al-Matin*, Tehran, 28 December 1908, year 16, number 24.

59 *TB*, 448.

60 *Habl al-Matin*, Tehran, 7 June 1909, year 16, no. 45. *Zindabad Hajji 'Ali Quli Khan / Payanda bad himat-i mardan / Sar afraz bad millat-i Iran*.

61 *Habl al-Matin*, Calcutta, 26 July 1909, year 7, no. 4. *Zindabad Samsam-i Saltana va Sattar Khan, buland kunanda-yi nam-i nik-i Iran*.

62 See *Habl al-Matin*, Tehran, 11 January 1909, year 16, no. 25.

63 See *Habl al-Matin*, Tehran, 11 January 1909, year 16, number 25; *Habl al-Matin*, Tehran, 15 February 1909, year 16, no. 29.

64 *Chihra Nama*, Cairo, 14 October 1909, year 6, no. 17.

65 *Habl al-Matin*, Calcutta, 8 February 1909, year 16, no. 28. Also see *TB*, 456.

66 *TB*, 456–57.

67 *Habl al-Matin*, Calcutta, 8 February 1909, year 16, no. 28.

68 Malikzada, *Tarikh-i Inqilab-i Mashrutiyat-i Iran*, vol. 6, 1090.

69 *Habl al-Matin*, Tehran, 8 February 1909, year 16, no. 28.

70 Ibid.

71 *Habl al-Matin*, Tehran, 22 February 1909, year 16, no. 30.

72 See, for instance, the August 1909 edition of *Habl al-Matin*, in which an armed Samsam al-Saltana appears on the cover: *Habl al-Matin*, Calcutta, 23

August 1909, year 7, no. 7.

73 On *Farhang* of Isfahan, see Sayyid Farid Qasimi, *Avvalinha-yi Matbu'at-i Iran* (Tehran, 1383/2004), 423–87.

74 These local newsletters can be found at the University of Isfahan Library and Archives. I would like to thank 'Abd al-Mihdi Raja'i, the gifted young scholar of Qajar Isfahan, for generously introducing me to this collection.

75 *Zayanda Rud*, Isfahan, 1327/1909, year 1, no. 5. In Persian the poem reads: *Sar bararad chun ki Samsam az niyam / Kar-i millat mishavad tamam. Bakhtiyari asl-i ghayrat zindabad / Ta abad salar-i hishmat zindabad!*

76 TB, 592.

77 Afshar, *Mubariza ba Muhammad 'Ali Shah*, doc. 198, 364.

78 FO 248/965, Grahame to Barclay, Isfahan News, 30 January 1909.

79 Malikzada, *Tarikh-i Inqilab-i Mashrutiyat-i Iran*, vol. 6, 1093–94.

80 Ibid.

81 FO 248/965, Grahame to Barclay, Isfahan News, 30 February 1909.

82 *Times*, 29 January 1909.

83 Mukhbir al-Saltana Hidayat, *Khatirat va Khatarat* (Tehran, 1363/1984), 181.

84 Ibid.

85 See FO 248/923, Visit of the Bakhtiyari Khans to London and Conversation with Sir C. Hardinge, Louis Mallet to C. M. Marling, July 6, 1908.

86 TB, 179–80.

87 'Akkasha, *Tarikh-i Bakhtiyari*, 596; Browne, *The Persian Revolution*, 298.

88 Browne, *The Persian Revolution*, 293; FO 248/965, Barclay to Grahame, Tehran, 5 May 1909.

89 FO 248/965, Barclay to Grahame, Tehran, 6 and 9 May 1909.

90 Browne, *The Persian Revolution*, 305.

91 Ibid. Bakhtiyari tradition holds, however, that the tribes "were secretly encouraged by the British to continue." See Garthwaite, *Khans and Shahs*, 118.

92 FO 248/965, Barclay to Grahame, Tehran, 17 June 1909; Browne, *The Persian Revolution*, 306.

93 Browne, *The Persian Revolution*, 293.

94 *Kashkul*, Isfahan, Rabi' al-Sani, 1327/1909, year 2, no. 8.

95 Ibid.

96 Browne, *The Persian Revolution*, 312–13.

97 *Times*, 30 June 1909.

98 'Akkasha, *Tarikh-i Il-i Bakhtiyari*, 596–97; TB, 178–79.

99 Hajj Sayyah, *Khatirat*, 624; Malikzada, *Tarikh-i Inqilab-i Mashrutiyat-i Iran*, vol. 6, 1093.

100 *Times*, 5 July 1909; *Times*, 18 August 1909.

101 'Akkasha, *Tarikh-i Il-i Bakhtiyari*, 599–600.

102 TB, 181–82; 'Akkasha, *Tarikh-i Il-i Bakhtiyari*, 599–601.

103 TB, 182; Browne, *The Persian Revolution*, 315–17; *Times*, 14 July 1909.

104 Browne, *The Persian Revolution*, 319–21; *Times*, 15 July 1909.

105 Peter Avery, *Modern Iran* (New York, 1965), 144–46.

106 For an account of the rebellion by the Shahsevan against the constitutional movement, see Tapper, "Raiding, Reaction, and Rivalry: The Shahsevan Tribes in the Constitutional Period," *Bulletin of the School of Oriental and African Studies, University of London* 49, no. 3 (1986), 508–31. On Bakhtiyari involvement in subduing the rebellion, see TB, 184–86.

107 Shuster, *Strangling of Persia*, 90–93.

108 Ibid., 116–17, 127.

109 Ibid., 127–28.

110 TB, 601–8; Shuster, *Strangling of Persia*, 86, 115, 117, 121.

111 Uzhan, *Tarikh-i Bakhtiyari*, 235–53; Shuster, *Strangling of Persia*, 135; TB, 603–4.

112 Uzhan, *Tarikh-i Bakhtiyari*, 232–34; TB, 190, 595; Afary, *Iranian Constitutional Revolution*, 299–300.

113 Afary, *Iranian Constitutional Revolution*, 302.

114 FO 248/965, Telegraph from Grahame to Foreign Office, Isfahan, 4 January 1909.

115 Lois Beck, *The Qashqa'i*, 107–8.

116 *Further Correspondence Respecting the Affairs of Persia*, Persia No. 3 (1912), cd. 6104, 43.

117 Consul Smart to Sir G. Barclay, Shiraz, April 20, 1911, *Further Correspondence Respecting the Affairs of Persia*, Persia No. 3 (1912), cd. 6104, 45; Sir George Barclay, Annual Report on Persia for the Year 1911, *British Documents on Foreign Affairs*, part 1, series B, vol. 14, 219.

118 Acting Consul Knox to Sir G. Barclay, Shiraz, May 18, 1911, *Further Correspondence Respecting the Affairs of Persia*, Persia No. 3 (1912), cd. 6104, 90.

119 Sir George Barclay, Annual Report on Persia for the year 1911, *British Documents on Foreign Affairs*, part 1, series B, vol. 14, 220.

120 Acting Consul Knox to Sir G. Barclay, Shiraz, October 20, 1911, *Further Correspondence Respecting the Affairs of Persia*, Persia No. 4 (1912), cd. 6105, 147.

121 See "The Crime of Anonymity," E. P. Thompson's classic article on arson in the forests of eighteenth-century England in *Albion's Fatal Tree*, 255–308. Also see Thompson, "The Moral Economy of the English Crowd in the Eighteenth Century"; Scott, *The Moral Economy of the Peasant*.

122 Ross, *A Lady Doctor*, 123–24.

123 *Political Diaries of the Persian Gulf*, vol. 4: *1910–1912* (London, 1990), 163–64, 294.

124 Ibid., 327.

125 Ibid., 328.

126 Ja'far Quli Khan Sardar Bahadur, *Khatirat-i Sardar As'ad Bakhtiyari*, ed. Iraj Afshar (Tehran, 1378/1999), 13–14.

127 *Political Diaries*, 351, 364.

128 Ibid., 378–79, 406, 419.

129 FO 248/937, Isfahan News, Dr. M. S. Aganoor to George Barclay, Isfahan 24 October 1908.

130 *Habl al-Matin*, Calcutta, 9 September 1912, no. 9, year 21; also see *Habl al-Matin*, Calcutta, 2 June 1913, no. 2, year 21.

131 ʿAkkasha, *Tarikh-i Bakhtiyari*, 11; Malikzada, *Tarikh-i Inqilab-i Mashrutiyat-i Iran*, vol. 5, 1083.

132 According to Layard, the Bakhtiyari listened "with the utmost eagerness to . . . . episodes from the 'Shahnameh,' describing the deeds of Rustem, the mythical Persian hero." He added that when the remarkable exploits of legendary warriors were repeated, the tribesmen "would shout and yell, draw their swords, and challenge imaginary foes." See Layard, *Early Adventures*, 212.

133 Ibid., 119. Attracted to the Bakhtiyari's martial character, British policymakers in Persia saw the tribes as a potential counterforce in the south to the Russian-led Cossack Brigade in the north. During the 1890s Mortimer Durand proposed the arming of the Bakhtiyari tribes; see *Political Diaries, 1881–1965*, vol. 2: *1901–1905*, 454.

134 Henri Renée Allmagne, *Az Khurasan ta Bakhtiyari*, vol. 1 (Tehran, 1378/1999), 570–76. Originally published as *Du Khorassan au pays de Backhtiyaris* (Paris, 1911).

135 FO 60/604, Report on the Traffic in Arms and the steps taken for its suppression, 21 March 1898, Bushire.

136 FO 60/603, Memorandum from Lieutenant Colonel H. Picot, Tehran, 5 January 1898.

137 TB, 187.

138 Shuster, *Strangling of Persia*, 115–16.

139 Sir George Barclay, Annual Report on Persia for 1911, 236; Sir George Barclay, Annual Report on Persia for 1910, *British Documents on Foreign Affairs*, part 1, series B, vol. 14, 90.

140 TB, 596; Garthwaite, *Khans and Shahs*, 123; Afary, *Iranian Constitutional Revolution*, 333–34.

141 *Habl al-Matin*, Calcutta, 11 August 1913, no. 9, year 21. For an account of the battles between the Bakhtiyari and the gendarmes in Tehran c. 1913, see ʿAbdallah Bahrami, *Khatirat-i ʿAbdallah Bahrami: Az Akhar-i Saltanat-i Nasir al-Din Shah ta Avval-i Kudita* (Tehran, 1963/1984), 151–59.

142 Garthwaite, *Khans and Shahs*, 125.

143 *Habl al-Matin*, Tehran, 3 May 1914, year 21, no. 40.

144 *Mulla Nasruddin*, 12 Rabiʿ al-Avval 1330/1912, no. 8. Janet Afary generously guided me to the image of the Bakhtiyari in this issue of *Mulla Nasruddin* and translated the caption.

145 *Political Diaries, 1881–1965*, vol. 5: *1910–1920*, 576.

146 Cambridge University, Edward G. Browne Papers: Pembroke Box 1/9/29–30, Sardar As'ad to E. G. Browne, Paris 19 October 1911. I thank Farzin Vejdani for providing me with a copy of this letter. Sardar As'ad later sent a copy of the *Tarikh-i Bakhtiyari* to Browne. See Browne Papers: Pembroke Box 2/4/36–37, Sardar As'ad to E. G. Browne, Tehran 23 Safar 1330 [23 February 1912].

147 D. L. R. Lorimer, *The Phonology of the Bakhtiyari, Badakhshani, and Madaglashti Dialects of Modern Persian* (London, 1922), 6–7.

148 Ross, *A Lady Doctor*, 99–121. Ross notes that many of the younger generation of *bibi*s could "read, write, and do accounts"; they reported to the khans and sent letters to them by means of armed messengers. She recalls an occasion when Bibi Sanna, the wife of Sardar As'ad, acted as a judge and tried a thief at Junaqan.

149 For a rare account of the years leading up to the revolution, written by a sister of Sardar As'ad and Samsam al-Saltana, see Bibi Maryam, *Khatirat-i Sardar Maryam*. Elizabeth MacBean Ross, a British doctor who lived among the Bakhtiyari and was the physician of the tribe in Dih Kurd, left a unique Western account of the women of the Bakhtiyari during the constitutional period in her travelogue. See Elizabeth MacBean Ross, *A Lady Doctor in Bakhtiari Land*.

150 Ross, *A Lady Doctor in Bakhtiari Land*, 42–43, 91, 106.

151 On this theme see the classic social histories written by Richard Cobb on revolutionary armies, *sans-culottes*, and ordinary people in the French Revolution, most notably *Les armées revolutionnaires*, *The Police and the People*, and *Reactions to the French Revolution*.

152 Hajj Sayyah, *Khatirat-i Hajj Sayyah ya Dura-yi Khuf va Vahshat*, 625–26.

153 Stephanie Cronin, "Riza Shah and the Disintegration of Bakhtiyari Power in Iran, 1921–1934," *The Making of Modern Iran: State and Society under Riza Shah, 1921–1941*, ed. Cronin (London, 2003), 241–68; Cronin, *Tribal Politics in Iran: Rural Conflict and the New State, 1921–1941* (London, 2006). For other studies of Riza Shah's tribal policies, see Kavih Bayat, "Riza Shah and the Tribes: An Overview," *The Making of Modern Iran*, 213–19; Tapper, "The Case of the Shahsevan," *The Making of Modern Iran*, 220–40.

Conclusion

1 Muhammad Taqi Khan Hakim, *Ganj-i Danish, Jughrafiya-yi Tarikhi-yi Shahrha-yi Iran*, ed. Muhammad 'Ali Suti and Jamshid Kiyanfar (Tehran, 1366/1987), 828.

2 Faroqhi, *Approaching Ottoman History*, 214.

3 Hodgson referred to the period following the Turko-Mongol migrations of the eleventh through the fourteenth centuries as "the age of Mongol Prestige." See Marshall Hodgson, *The Venture of Islam: Conscience and History in a World Civilization*, vol. 2: *The Expansion of Islam in the Middle Periods*, 369–73.

4 David McDowell, *A Modern History of the Kurds* (London, 1996), 66–69.

5 For studies on the environmental history of Iran, see W. B. Fisher, ed., *Cambridge History of Iran*, vol. 1: *The Land of Iran* (Cambridge, 1968); Richard Bulliet, *The Camel and the Wheel* (New York, 1990); Peter Christensen, *The Decline of Iranshahr: Irrigation and Environment in the History of the Middle East, 500 BC to AD 1500* (Copenhagen, 1993). A rich tradition and literature on environmental history has emerged from studies of Native Americans and the American West. For some examples, see William Cronon, *Changes in the Land: Indians, Colonists, and the Ecology of New England* (New York, 1983); Cronon, *Nature's Metropolis: Chicago and the Great West* (New York, 1991); Donald Worster, *Dust Bowl: The Southern Plains in the 1930s* (New York, 1979); Worster, *Rivers of Empire: Water, Aridity, and the Growth of the American West* (New York, 1985); Worster, *A River Running West: The Life of John Wesley Powell* (Oxford, 2001); Richard White, *The Middle Ground: Indians, Empires, and Republics in the Great Lakes Region, 1650–1815* (Cambridge, 1991).

GLOSSARY

abadi	Cultivation
amir	Prince, general
anjuman	Constitutional assembly
'ashayir	Tribes
bayglarbayg	Lord governor
charvadar	Mule drivers
chapu	Raid
dih nishin	Dwellers in villages
diz	Fortress
farman	Royal decree
galla	Flocks
galladari	Flock tax
garmsir	Lowland, winter quarters
gharat	Plunder
ghazi	Frontier warriors
hakim	Provincial prince governor
il	Tribal confederacy
il rah	Tribal migration route
ilbayg	Tribal lord
ilkhan	Paramount tribal chieftain
istiqbal	Reception given a traveling envoy
jabal	Mountains
jadda	Road
jalasa	Tribal council
jalga	Pasture

kadkhuda	Tribal or village headman
kar kunan	Workers
khak	Land
kalantar	Tribal or village headman
khan	Chieftain
khil'at	Robes of honor
kuh	Mountains
lashkar	Armies, soldiers, tribal armies
Majlis	Parliament
maliyat	Taxation
ma'dan	Field
mashruta	Constitution
millat	People
mulaziman-i rikabi	Mounted attendants
muluk al-tavayif	"Kings of the tribes"
munshi	Secretary
mustahfizan	Guards
naft	Oil
nazm	Order
qabila	Tribe, clan
qafila	Caravan
qal'a	Fortress
qanat	Irrigation canal
qanun	Rule of law
qishlaq	Lowland winter quarters
rahzan	Robbers, bandits
ra'iyat	Peasantry
rama	Herd, flocks
rish safid	"White beard," tribal elder
sa'b al-'abur	An arduous road
safarnama	Travel book
sahra nishin	"Dwellers in the desert," nomads
sardar	Commander

sardsir Upland, summer quarters
sarhadd Frontier
savaran Horsemen
shararat Disturbances, uprisings
shuʿba Branches
sipah Cavalry
takht va taz Raid, plunder
tavarikh History, chronicles
tavayif Tribes
tayafa Tribe, clan
tira Subtribes
tujjar Merchants
tumans Persian unit of currency
tuyul Land grant
ulama Islamic cleric
vahshi Wild, untamed
vilayat Province
vali Prince, governor
vatan Homeland
vazir Minister
yaghi In rebellion
yaylaq Upland summer quarters

BIBLIOGRAPHY

Archival Sources

BRITISH LIBRARY, INDIA OFFICE RECORDS

George Nathaniel Curzon Papers

BRITISH NATIONAL ARCHIVES, PUBLIC RECORD OFFICE, KEW, RICHMOND, SURREY, UK

Isfahan, Foreign Office Records

Series FO 60/528 (1891); 60/535 (1892); 60/546 (1893); 60/562 (1894); 60/569 (1895); 60/580 (1896); 60/588 (1897); 60/598 (1898); 60/613 (1899); 60/621 (1900); 60/641 (1901); 60/655 (1902); 60/672 (1903); 60/686 (1904); 60/704 (1905)

Series FO 248/548 (1892); 248/572 (1893); 248/596 (1894); 248/616 (1895); 248/634 (1896); 248/655 (1897); 248/676 (1898); 248/699 (1899); 248/700 (1899); 248/723 (1900); 248/845 (1905); 248/877 (1906); 248/905 (1907); 248/937 (1908); 248/965 (1909); 248/996 (1910)

Bakhtiyari Road, Foreign Office Records

Series FO 60/573 (1895); 60/631 (1897–1900); 60/661 (1901–1902); 60/678 (1903); 60/690 (1904); 60/715 (1905)

Series FO 248/895 (1906–1908)

D'Arcy Oil Syndicate, Foreign Office Records

Series FO 248/894 (1906); 248/923 (1907–1908)

BRITISH PETROLEUM ARCHIVES, UNIVERSITY OF WARWICK, COVENTRY, UK

Company Records, D'arcy Oil Syndicate and the Anglo-Persian Oil Company, 1905–1911

CAMBRIDGE UNIVERSITY LIBRARY

Edward G. Browne Papers

HARVARD UNIVERSITY, WIDENER LIBRARY, MANUSCRIPTS AND ARCHIVES

Ernst Hoeltzer Papers

IRANIAN NATIONAL ARCHIVES, TEHRAN

The Bakhtiyari Khans, Series 1002
Correspondences and Records of Qajar Ministry of the Interior, Series 295
Land Tenure Records, Bakhtiyari and Chahar Mahal, Series 1004
Political and Administrative Records, Bakhtiyari, Series 1003
Printed Editions of Qajar Chronicles, Geographical Gazetteers, and Variants
Provincial Correspondences and Records, Series 296

IRANIAN NATIONAL LIBRARY (KITABKHANA-YI MILLI), TEHRAN

Printed Editions of Qajar Chronicles, Geographical Gazetteers, and Variants

PRINCETON UNIVERSITY, FIRESTONE LIBRARY, NEAR EAST COLLECTION

Persian Histories and Newsletters

UNIVERSITY OF CALIFORNIA, LOS ANGELES, YOUNG RESEARCH LIBRARY, SPECIAL COLLECTIONS

Isabella Bird Photograph Album and Papers

UNIVERSITY OF CHICAGO, REGENSTEIN LIBRARY, MIDDLE EAST COLLECTION

Persian Histories and Newsletters

UNIVERSITY OF ISFAHAN ARCHIVES, ISFAHAN

Printed Editions of Qajar era Gazetteers and Local Newsletters

UNIVERSITY OF LONDON, SCHOOL OF ORIENTAL AND AFRICAN STUDIES (SOAS) ARCHIVES

D. L. R. Lorimer Papers

Persian Newsletters and Gazetteers

Akhtar
Al-Jinab
Anjuman Muqaddas-i Isfahan
Chihra Nama
Farhang
Habl al-Matin
Hikmat
Isfahan
Jahad-i Akbar
Kashkul
Mulla Nasr al-Din
Naghur
Parvana
Ruznama-yi Dawlat-i 'Alliya-yi Iran
Ruznama-yi Vaqa'i'-yi Ittifaqiya
Sipahan
Surayya
Zayanda Rud

Chronicles, Histories, and Printed Editions

'Abd al-Ghaffar Najm al-Mulk. *Safarnama-yi Khuzistan*. Tehran, 1342/1963 [1881].

'Abdallah Qaraguzlu Hamadani. *Majmu'a-yi Asar*. Edited by 'Inayatallah Majidi. Tehran, 1382/2003 [1890].

Ainsworth, W. F. *The River Karun*. London, 1890.

'Ali Quli Khan Mirza I'tizad al-Saltana. *Iksir al-Tavarikh*. Edited by Jamshid Kiyanfar. Tehran, 1370/1991 [1842].

'Ali Quli Khan Sardar As'ad and 'Abd al-Husayn Lisan al-Saltana Sipihr. *Tarikh-i Bakhtiyari*. Edited by Jamshid Kiyanfar. Tehran, 1376/1997 [1911].

Allmagne, Henri Renée. *Du Khorassan au pays de Bakhtiyaris*. Paris, 1911.

Amir Sharaf Khan Bidlisi. *Sharafnama-yi Tarikh-i Mufassal-i Kurdistan*. Tehran, 1343/1964 [1597].

Bazin, Père Louis. *Mémoires sur les dernières anées du règne de Thamas Kouli-Kan et sa mort tragique, contenus dans une letter du Frere Bazin*. Paris, 1780.

Bell, Mark. "A Visit to the Karun River and Kum." *Blackwood's Magazine* (1889): 453–81.

Bishop, Isabella Bird. *Journeys in Persia and Kurdistan*. London, 1891.

———. "The Upper Karun Region and the Bakhtiyari Lurs." *The Scottish Geographical Magazine* 8 (1891): 1–14.

Bode, C. A. de. *Travels in Luristan and Arabistan*. 2 vols. London, 1845.

Browne, Edward G. *The Literary History of Persia*. 4 vols. Cambridge, 1930.

———. *The Persian Revolution, 1905–1909*. Cambridge, 1910.

Bruyn, Cornelis de. *Travels into Muscovy, Persia, and part of the East Indies: Containing an accurate description of whatever is most remarkable in those Countries*. London, 1737 [1711].

Brydges, Harford Jones. *An Account of the Transactions of the His Majesty's Mission to Persia in the Years 1807–1811*. London, 1834.

Burn, R. "The Bakhtiyari Hills: An Itinerary of the Road from Isfahan to Shuster." *Journal of the Asiatic Society of Bengal* 65, no. 2 (1897): 170–79.

Champain, J. Bateman. "On the Various Means of Communication between Central Persia and the Sea." *Proceedings of the Royal Geographical Society* 5, 3 (1883): 121–38.

Chardin, John. *Les voyages du Chevalier Chardin en Perse*, edited by L. Langlès. 10 vols. Paris, 1811.

———. *The Travels of Sir John Chardin into Persia and the East Indies*. London, 1686.

Curzon, George Nathaniel. "The Karun River and the Commercial Geography of South-west Persia." *Proceedings of the Royal Geographical Society* 12 (1890): 509–32.

———. *Persia and the Persian Question*. 2 vols. London, 1892.

D'Allemagne, Henri Rene. *Du Khurasan au Pays de Bakhtiyari*. Paris, 1909.

Drouville, G. *Voyage en Perse*. 2 vols. Paris, 1825.

Dubeaux, M. Louis. *La Perse*. Paris, 1841.

Durand, E. R. *An Autumn Tour in Western Persia*. London, 1902.

Fazlallah Shirazi. *Tarikh-i Zu al-Qarnayn*. Edited by Nasir Afsharfar. 2 vols. Tehran, 1380/2001 [1837].

Fraser, James. *The History of Nadir Shah, formerly called Thamas Kuli Khan, the Present Emperor of Persia*. London, 1742.

Fraser, James Baillie. *Allee Neemroo, The Buchtiaree Adventurer: A Tale of Louristan*. 3 vols. London, 1842.

Fryer, John. *A new account of East-India and Persia, in eight letters*. London, 1698.

Gardane, P. A. *Journal d'un voyage dans la Turquie d'Asie et la Perse, fait en 1807 et 1808*. Paris, 1809.

Government of Iran. *Ruznama-yi Vaqa'i'-yi Ittifaqiya*. 4 vols. Tehran, 1373/1994 [c.1850–1860].

Hajj Mirza Hasan Fasa'i. *Farsnama Nasiri*. Edited by Mansur Rastigar Fasa'i. 2 vols. Tehran, 1367/1988 [1895].

Hajj Sayyah. *Khatirat-i Hajj Sayyah ya Dura-yi Khuf va Vahshat*. Tehran, 1346/1967.

Hamdallah Mustawfi. *Nuzhat al-Qulub*. Edited by G. Le Strange. Leiden, 1919.

Hanway, Jonas. *An Historical Account of the British Trade over the Caspian Sea: With a Journal of Travels through Russia into Persia; and back again through Russia, Germany, and Holland. To which are added, The Revolutions of Persia during the present century, with the particular history of the great usurper Nadir Kuli*. 4 vols. London, 1753.

Hasan 'Ali Khan Afshar. *Safarnama-yi Luristan va Khuzistan*. Edited by Hamid Riza Dilvand. Tehran, 1382/2003 [1848].

Herbert, Thomas. *A Relation of Some Yeares Travel into Divers Parts of Africa and Greater Asia*. London, 1638 [1634].

Husayn Quli Khan Nizam al-Saltana Mafi. *Khatirat va Asnad*. Edited by Ma'suma Nizam Mafi and Mansura Ittihadiya Nizam Mafi. 2 vols. Tehran, 1361/1982.

Ibn Hawqal. *Kitab Surat al-Ard* (Configuation de la Terre). Translated by J. H. Kramers and G. Wiet. 2 vols. Paris, 1964.

Ibn Khaldun. *Muqaddimah*. Translated by Franz Rosenthal. 3 vols. Princeton, 1958.

Iskandar Bayg Munshi. *Tarikh-i 'Alamara-yi 'Abbasi*. Edited by Iraj Afshar. 2 vols. Tehran, 1382/2003.

———. *Tarikh-i 'Alamara-yi 'Abbasi*. Translated by Roger Savory as *The History of Shah Abbas the Great*. Boulder, CO, 1978 [1629].

Iskandar Khan 'Akkasha. *Tarikh-i Il-i Bakhtiyari*. Edited by Farid Muradi. Tehran, 1365/1986.

Jones, William. *Histoire de Nader-Chah, connu sous le nom de Thahmas Kuli Khan, Empereur de Perse*. Paris, 1770.

———. *The History of the Life of Nadir Shah, King of Persia. Extracted from an Eastern Manuscript, which was translated into French by order of His Majesty the King of Denmark*. London, 1773.

Ker Porter, Robert. *Travels in Georgia, Persia, Armenia, Ancient Babylonia, During the Years 1817, 1818, 1819, and 1820*. 2 vols. London, 1822.

Khusraw Khan Sardar Zafar. "Jang-i 'Ashayir-i Qashqa'i va Bakhtiyari dar sal-i 1328 h. q. [1910]," V*ahid* 1.

———. "Vaqa'i'-yi Nagufti az Mashrutiyat," *Khatirat va Asnad*. Tehran, 1369/1990.

———. *Yaddashtha va Khatirat*. Tehran, 1362/1983.

Khuzistan va Luristan dar 'Asr-i Nasiri: Bi Ravayat-i Farmanha-yi Nasir al-Din Shah, Makatibat-i Amir Kabir va Mirza Aqa Khan Nuri ba Ihtisham al-Dawla (*KHL*). Edited by Manuchihr Ihtishami. Tehran, 1383/2004.

Layard, A. H. "Ancient Sites among the Bakhtiari Mountains." *Journal of the Royal Geographical Society* 12 (1842): 102–9.

——. "Description of the Province of Khuzistan." Journal of the Royal Geographical Society 16 (1846): 1–105.

——. *Early Adventures in Persia, Susiana, and Babylonia*. London, 1887.

——. *Nineveh and Its Remains*. 2 vols. London, 1849.

Lorimer, D. L. R. *Persian Tales*. London, 1919.

——. *The Phonology of the Bakhtiyari, Badakhshani, and Madaglashti Dialects of Modern Persian*. London, 1922.

——. *A Report on Pusht-i Kuh*. Simla, 1908.

Lynch, Henry Blosse. "Across Luristan to Ispahan." *Proceedings of the Royal Geographical Society* 12 (1890): 523–53.

Mackenzie, George. "The Bakhtiari Mountains and Upper Elam." *Proceedings of the Royal Geographical Society* 4, 6 (1894): 501–5.

——. "Route from Ispahan to Shooster," *A Narrative of a Journey through the Province of Khorassan and on the N. W. Frontier of Afghanistan in 1875*, vol. 2. London, 1879.

Malcolm, John. *History of Persia, from the Most Early Period to the Present Time: Containing an Account of the Religion, Government, Usages, and Character of the Inhabitants of that Kingdom*. 2 vols. London, 1815.

——. *Sketches of Persia*. London, 1849.

Mas'ud Mirza Zill al-Sultan. *Tarikh-i Sarguzasht-i Mas'udi*. Edited by Husayn Khadivjam. 3 vols. Tehran, 1362/1983.

Mirza Abu al-Hasan Sani' al-Mulk Ghaffari. *Ruznama-yi Dawlat-i 'Alliya-yi Iran*. 2 vols. Tehran 1371/1992 [1860–1870].

Mirza Husayn Tahvildar. *Jughrafiya-yi Isfahan*. Edited by Manuchihr Sutuda. Tehran, 1342/1963 [1877].

Mirza Muhammad Mihdi Khan Astarabadi. *Durra-yi Nadira*. Edited by Sa'id Ja'far Shahidi. Tehran, 1366/1987.

——. *Jahangusha-yi Nadiri*. Edited by Sa'id 'Abdallah Anvar. Tehran, 1341/1962 [1749].

Mirza Muhammad Taqi Lisan al-Mulk Sipihr. *Nasikh al-Tavarikh*. Edited by Jamshid Kiyanfar. Tehran, 1377/1998 [1857–1859].

Morgan, Jacques de. *Mission Scientifique en Perse*, vol. 2. Paris, 1895.

——. "Note sur les gites de Naphte de Kend-e Chirin." *Annales des Mines* (February 1892): 1–16.

Morier, James. *The Adventures of Hajji Baba of Ispahan*. 3 vols. London, 1828.

——. *A Journey Through Persia, Armenia, and Asia Minor, to Constantinople, in the Years 1808 and 1809; in Which is Included, Some Account of the Proceedings of His Majesty's Mission, under Sir Harford Jones to the Court of Persia*. London, 1812.

——. *A Second Journey Through Persia, Armenia, and Asia Minor, to Constantinople Between the Years 1810 and 1816*. London, 1818.

——. "Some Account of the I'lyats, or Wandering Tribes of Persia, obtained in the Years 1814 and 1815." *Journal of the Royal Geographical Society* 7 (1837): 230–42.

Muhammad Fathallah bin Muhammad Taqi Saravi. *Tarikh-i Muhammadi [Ahsan al-Tavarikh].* Edited by Ghulam Riza Tabataba'i Majd. Tehran, 1371/1992 [1797].

Muhammad Hasan Khan I'timad al-Saltana. *Mir'at al-Buldan.* Edited by. 'Abd al-Husayn Nava'i. 3 vols. Tehran, 1367/1988 [1877–1880].

———. *Tarikh-i Muntazam-i Nasiri.* Edited by Muhammad Isma'il Rizvani. 3 vols. Tehran, 1363/1984[1880–1882].

Muhammad Kazim Marvi. *'Alamara-yi Nadiri.* Edited by Muhammad Amin Riyahi. 3 vols. Tehran, 1364/1985 [1753].

Muhammad Mihdi ibn Muhammad Riza al-Isfahani. *Nisf-i Jahan, fi ta'rif al-Isfahan.* Edited by Manuchihr Sutuda. Tehran, 1340/1961 [1870].

Muhammad Taqi Khan Hakim. *Ganj-i Danish, Jughrafiya-yi Tarikhi-yi Shahrha-yi Iran.* Edited by Muhammad 'Ali Suti and Jamshid Kiyanfar. Tehran, 1366/1987.

Ogilby, John. *Asia, the First Part Being an Accurate Description of Persia and Several Provinces Thereof.* London, 1673.

Olearius, Adam. *The Voiyages and Travels of the Ambassadors sent by Fredrick, Duke of Holstein, to the Great Duke of Muscovy and the King of Persia.* London, 1669.

Otter, Jean. *Voyage en Turquie et en Perse, avec une Relation des expeditions de Tahmas Koulikhan.* Paris, 1748.

Ouseley, William. *Travels in Various Countries of the East.* 3 vols. London, 1819.

Rawlinson, H. C. "A March from Zohab, at the Foot of the Zagros." *Journal of the Royal Geographical Society* 9 (1839): 26–116.

Riza Quli Khan Hidayat Lalabashi. *Rawzat al-Safa-yi Nasiri*, vols. 9–10. Edited by Jamshid Kiyanfar. Tehran, 1338–1339/1959–1960 [1854–1857].

Riza Quli Mirza Nayib al-Ayala. *Safarnama-yi Riza Quli Mirza.* Edited by Asghar Farman Farma Qajar. Tehran 1361/1982 [1835–1836].

Sanson, N. *The Present State of Persia, With a Faithful Account of the Manners, Religion, and Government of That People.* London, 1695.

Sardar Maryam Bakhtiyari. *Khatirat-i Sardar Maryam: Az Kudaki to Aqaz-i Inqilab-i Mashruta.* Edited by Ghulam 'Abbas Nawruzi. Tehran, 1382/2003.

Sawyer, H. A. "The Bakhtiyari Mountains and Upper Elam." *Geographical Journal* 4 (1894): 481–505.

———. *Report: A Reconaissance in the Bakhtiyari Country, Southwest Persia.* Simla, 1891.

Schindler, General A. H. "Travels in S.W. Persia in 1877–1878." *Zeitschrift der Gesellschaft fur Erdkunde zu Berlin* xiv (1879): 38–67, 81–124.

Sheil, Mary. *Glimpses of Life and Manners in Persia, with notes on Russia, Koords, Toorkomans, Nestorians, Khiva, and Persia.* London, 1856.

Shuster, Morgan. *The Strangling of Persia.* New York, 1912.

Smith, Murdoch. "Address on the Karun River as a Trade Route." *Journal of the Society of Arts* (1889).

Stack, Edward. *Six Months in Persia.* London, 1882.

Struys, Jan Janszoon. *The voyages and travels of John Struys through Italy, Greece,*

Muscovy, Tartary, Medea, Persia, East India, Japan and other countries in Europe, Africa, and Asia. London, 1684.

Sykes, Sir Percy. "Recent Journeys in Persia," The Geographical Journal 10, 6 (1897).

——. *Ten Thousand Miles in Persia or Eight Years in Iran*. London, 1902.

Tadhkirat al-Muluk. Translated by V. Minorsky. London, 1943 [1726].

Tancoigne, J. M. *Lettres sur la Perse et la Turqie d'Asie*. 2 vols. Paris, 1819.

Tavernier, Jean-Baptiste. *The Six Voyages of Jean-Baptiste Tavernier*. London, 1678.

Thévenot, Jean de. *The Travels of Monsieur de Thévenot in the Levant*. London, 1687.

Wells, H. L. "Surveying Tours in South Persia." *Proceedings of the Royal Geographical Society* 3, 5 (1883): 138–63.

Wills, C. J. *In the Lands of the Lion and Sun, or Modern Persia: Being Experiences of Life in Persia from 1866 to 1881*. London, 1893.

Secondary Literature

Abivardi, M. Qahramani. *Tarikh-i 'Ashayir-i Fars*. Tehran, 1373/1994.

Abrahamian, Ervand. *Iran Between Two Revolutions*. Princeton, 1982.

Abtahi, 'Ali Riza. *Naft va Bakhtiyariha*. Tehran, 1384/2005.

Abu-Lughod, Lila. *Veiled Sentiments: Honor and Poetry in a Bedouin Society*. Berkeley, 1986.

Adamiyat, F. *Amir Kabir va Iran*. Tehran, 1348/1969.

Adams, Robert McC. "Commentary." Studies on Isfahan: Proceedings of the Isfahan Colloquium. *Journal of Iranian Studies* 7, 3–4 (1974).

——. *Land behind Baghdad: A History of Settlement on the Diyala Plains*. Chicago, 1965.

Adas, Michael. *Machines as the Measure of Men: Science Technology and Ideologies of Western Dominance*. Ithaca, 1989.

Afary, Janet. *The Iranian Constitutional Revolution: Grassroots Democracy, Social Democracy, and the Origins of Feminism*. New York, 1996.

Afshar, Iraj. *Mubariza ba Muhammad 'Ali Shah*. Tehran, 1359/1980.

——. "Some Remarks on the Early History of Photography in Iran." In *Qajar Iran: Political, Social, and Cultural Change, 1800–1925*, 261–90.

Afshar Nadiri, Nadir. *Ilat-i Kuhgiluya va Buyr Ahmad*. Tehran, 1365/1986.

Afshar Nadiri, Nadir, Javad Safi Najhad, 'Aziz Rakhsh Khurshid, Hasan Parsa, and Hushang Kishavarz. *Jam'iyat va Shinasnama-yi Ilat-i Kuhgiluya*. Tehran, 1347/1968.

Afshin, Kazim. *Naft va Khuzistan*. Tehran, 1333/1954.

Ahanjida, Isfandiar. *Bakhtiyari va Mashruta*. Tehran, 1375/1996.

——. *Chahar Mahal va Bakhtiyari va Tamaddun-i Dirinaha-yi An*. Tehran, 1378/1999.

Ahmadiyan, Bahram Amir. *Il-i Bakhtiyari*. Tehran, 1378/1999.

Amanallahi, Sekandar. *Kuch Nishini dar Iran*. Tehran, 1370/1991.

——. *Qawm-i Lur*. Tehran, 1370/1991.

Amanat, Abbas. "Dawlatshah Mohammad 'Ali Mirza." *Encyclopaedia Iranica* 7, 2 (1994).

——. "Hajji Baba of Ispahan." *Encylopaedia Iranica* 11, 6 (2003).

——. "Mohammad Hasan Khan E'temad al-Saltana." *Encyclopaedia Iranica* 8, 6 (1998).

——. *Pivot of the Universe: Nasir al-Din Shah Qajar and the Iranian Monarchy, 1831–1896*. Berkeley, 1997.

——, ed. *Crowning Anguish*. Washington, D.C., 1993.

Amir Ahmadiyan, Bahram. *Il-i Bakhtiyari*. Tehran, 1378/1999.

Ansari, Hurmuz, and Ahmad Javahiri. *Muqaddamah-i bar Jam'iyashinasi-yi Isfahan*. Tehran, 2000.

Ansari, Mirza Hasan Jabiri. *Tarikh-i Isfahan*. Isfahan, 1378/1999.

Atabaygi, Touraj. *The State and the Subaltern*. London, 2007.

Avery, Peter. *Modern Iran*. New York, 1965.

Avery, Peter. "Nadir Shah and the Afsharid Legacy." In *Cambridge History of Iran*, vol. 7: *From Nadir Shah to the Islamic Republic*. Cambridge, 1991, 3–62.

Axworthy, Michael. *The Sword of Persia: Nadir Shah, from Tribal Warrior to Conquering Tyrant*. London, 2006.

Babayan, Kathryn. *Mystics, Monarchs, and Messiahs: Cultural Landscapes of Early Modern Iran*. Cambridge, MA, 2002.

Bahmanbaygi, Muhammad. *'Urf va Adat dar 'Ashayir-i Fars*. Tehran, 1324/1945–46.

Bahrami, 'Abdallah. *Khatirat-i 'Abdallah Bahrami: Az Akhar-i Saltanat-i Nasir al-Din Shah ta Avval-i Kudita*. Tehran, 1963/1984.

Bakhash, Shaul. "Center-Periphery Relations in Nineteenth-Century Iran," *Iranian Studies* 14 (1981): 29–51.

——. *Iran: Monarchy, Bureaucracy, and Reform under the Qajars, 1858–1896*. London, 1978.

Bakhtiyari, Ghaffarpur."Qatl-i Husayn Quli Khan Ilkhani Bakhtiyari va Naqsh-i Mu'tamad al-Dawla Hakim-i Fars dar An." *Ganjina-yi Asnad*, vols. 3–4, 51–52 (2003–04): 73–80.

Bakhtiyari, Ghulam. *'Abbas Nawruzi. Kitab-i Anzan*. Tehran, 1374/1995.

Bakhtiyari, Pejhman. "Bakhtiyari dar Guzashta-yi Dur." *Vahid* 3, 1, 25, 1344/1965.

Barkey, Karen. *Bandits and Bureaucrats: The Ottoman Route to State Centralization*. Ithaca, 1994.

Barth, Fredrik. *Nomads of South Persia: The Basseri Tribe of the Khamsah Confederacy*. Oslo, 1964.

Barthold, W. *An Historical Geography of Iran*. Translated by Svat Soucek. Princeton, 1984.

Batatu, Hanna. *The Old Social Classes and the Revolutionary Movements of Iraq*. Princeton, 1978.

Bavar, Mahmud. *Kuhgiluya va Ilat-i An*. Gachsaran, 1324/1945.
Bayat, Kavih. "Riza Shah and the Tribes: An Overview." In *The Making of Modern Iran: State and Society under Riza Shah,* 213–19. London, 2003.
———. *Shurish-i 'Ashayir-i Fars*. Tehran, 1365/1986.
Baygdili, Muhammad Riza. *Ilsevanha-yi Iran*. Tehran, 1372/1993.
———. *Turkmenha-yi Iran*. Tehran, 1369/1991.
Beck, Lois. *The Qashqa'i of Iran*. New Haven, 1986.
Beinin, Joel. *Workers and Peasants in the Modern Middle East*. Cambridge, 2001.
Blunt, W. Isfahan: *Pearl of Persia*. London, 1966.
Bonakdarian, Mansour. "Iranian Constitutional Exiles and British Foreign-policy Dissenters, 1908–1909." *International Journal of Middle East Studies* 27, no. 2 (May 1995): 175–91.
Braudel, Fernand. *The Mediterranean and the Mediterranean World in the Age of Phillip II*, translated by Sian Reynolds. 2 vols. Berkeley, 1995 [1949].
Brooks, David. "Bakhtiyari: Iran." In *Peoples of the Earth: Western and Central Asia*. Edited by Andre Singer. New York, 1973.
———. "The Enemy Within: Limitations on Leadership in the Bakhtiari." In *The Conflict of Tribe and State in Iran and Afghanistan*. London, 1983.
Bulliet, Richard. *The Camel and the Wheel*. New York, 1990 [1975].
Burke, Edmund, ed. *Struggle and Survival in the Modern Middle East*. Berkeley, 1993.
Caton, Steven. *"Peaks of Yemen I Summon": Poetry as Cultural Practice in a North Yemeni Tribe*. Berkeley, 1990.
Chehabi, H. E. "Ardabil Becomes a Province: Center-Periphery Relations in Iran." *International Journal of Middle East Studies* 29, no. 2 (May 1997): 235–53.
Christensen, Peter. *The Decline of Iranshahr: Irrigation and Environment in the History of the Middle East, 500 BC to 1500 AD*. Copenhagen, 1993.
Clancy-Smith, Julia. *Rebel and Saint: Muslim Notables, Populist Protest, Colonial Encounters—Algeria and Tunisia, 1800–1904*. Berkeley, 1994.
Cobb, Richard. *Les armées révolutionnaires*. Paris, 1961–63.
———. *Paris and Its Provinces, 1792–1802*. London, 1975.
———. *The Police and the People: French Popular Protest, 1789–1820*. London, 1970.
———. *Reactions to the French Revolution*. London, 1972.
Cohn, Bernard. *Colonialism and Its Forms of Knowledge: The British in India*. Princeton, 1996.
Cooper, Merrian. *Grass*. New York and London, 1925.
Corbin, Alain. *Village Bells: Sound and Meaning in the Nineteenth Century French Countryside*. New York, 1998 [1994].
———. *The Village of Cannibals: Rage and Murder in France, 1870*. Cambridge, 1992 [1990].
Cronin, Stephanie, ed. *The Making of Modern Iran: State and Society under Riza Shah, 1921–1941*. London, 2003.

——. *Tribal Politics in Iran: Rural Conflict and the New State, 1921–1941*. London, 2007.

Cronon, William. *Changes in the Land: Indians, Colonists, and the Ecology of New England*. New York, 1983.

——. *Nature's Metropolis: Chicago and the Great West*. New York, 1991.

Crossley, Pamela Kyle, Helen Siu, and Donald Sutton, eds. *Empire at the Margins: Culture, Ethnicity, and Frontier in Early Modern China*. Berkeley, 2006.

Crossley, Pamela Kyle. *Orphan Warriors: Three Manchu Generations and the End of the Qing World*. Princeton, 1990.

——. "Thinking about Ethnicity in Late Imperial China." *Late Imperial China* 11, 1 (June 1990): 1–35.

Cuno, Kenneth. *The Pasha's Peasants: Land, Society, and Economy in Lower Egypt, 1740–1858*. Cambridge, 1992.

Danishvar 'Alavi, Nurallah. *Tarikh-i Iran va Junbish-i Vatan Parastan-i Isfahan va Bakhtiyari*. Tehran, 1335/1956.

Darrashuri, Ghulam Riza. *Bakhtiyariha va Qajariya*. Shahr-i Kurd, 1994.

De Planhol, Xavier. "Caractères generaux de la vie montagnard." *Annales Geographique* (1962): 113–30.

——. "Geography of Settlement." In *Cambridge History of Iran*, vol. 1: *The Land of Iran*, 409–67. Cambridge, 1968.

Digard, Jean-Pierre. "Campements Baxtiyari: Observations d'un Ethnologue sur des Materiaux Interessant l'Archeologue." *Studia Iranica* 4 (1975): 117–29.

——. "De la necessité et des inconvenients, pour un Baxtiyari, d'être Baxtiyari. Communaute, territoire et inegalité chez des pasteurs nomades d'Iran." In *Production pastorale et société*. Cambridge and Paris, 1979.

——. "Histoire et Anthropologie des Societies Nomades: Le Cas d'une Tribu d'Iran." *Annales: Economies, Societes, et Civilisations* 28, no. 6 (1973): 1423–35.

——. "Les Nomades et l'Etat central en Iran." *Peuples mediterranéens* 7 (1979): 37–53.

——. "Jeux de structure. Segmentarité et pouvoir chez les nomades Baxtiyari d'Iran." *L'homme* 27, no. 2 (1987).

——. *Techniques des nomades Baxtiyari d'Iran*. Cambridge and Paris, 1981.

Doumani, Beshara. *Rediscovering Palestine: Merchants and Peasants in Jabal Nablus, 1700–1900*. Berkeley, 1995.

Edwards, David. *Heroes of the Age: Moral Fault Lines on the Afghan Frontier*. Berkeley, 1996.

Elliot, Mark. *The Manchu Way: The Eight Banners and Ethnic Identity in Late Imperial China*. Stanford, 2001.

Elwell-Sutton, L. P. *Persian Oil: A Study in Power Politics*. London, 1955.

Fahmy, Khaled. *All the Pasha's Men: Mehmed Ali, His Army and the Making of Modern Egypt*. Cambridge, 1997.

Falcon, N. L. "The Bakhtiyari Mountains of S.W. Persia." *The Alpine Journal* 46 (1943): 351–59.

Faridani, Muhammad 'Ali Musavi, *Isfahan az Nigah-i Digar*. Isfahan, 1379/2000.
Faroqhi, Suraiya. *Approaching Ottoman History: An Introduction to the Sources*. Cambridge, 1999.
——. *Peasants, Dervishes and Traders in the Ottoman Empire*. London, 1986.
Faroqhi, Suraiya, Bruce McGowan, Donald Quataert, and Sevket Pamuk. *An Economic and Social History of the Ottoman Empire*, vol. 2: *1600–1914*. Cambridge, 1994.
Fatemi, Nasrollah Saifpour. *Oil Diplomacy: Powder Keg in Iran*. New York, 1954.
Fatih, Mustafa. *Panjah Sal-i Naft-i Iran*. Tehran, 1956.
Ferrier, R. W. *The History of the British Petroleum Company,* vol. 1: *The Developing Years 1901–1932*. Cambridge, 1982.
Fisher, W. B., ed. *Cambridge History of Iran,* vol. 1*: The Land of Iran,* 3–110, 717–40. Cambridge, 1968.
Fraser, David. *Persia and Turkey in Revolt*. Edinburgh, 1910.
Frechtling, L. E. "The Reuter Concession in Persia." Asiatic Review (1938): 518–33.
Garthwaite, Gene. "The Bakhtiyari Ilkhani: An Illusion of Unity." *International Journal of Middle East Studies* 8 (1977): 145–60.
——."The Bakhtiyari Khans, the Government of Iran, and the British, 1846–1915." *International Journal of Middle East Studies* 3 (1972): 24–44.
——. *Khans and Shahs: A documentary analysis of the Bakhtiyari in Iran*. Cambridge, 1983.
——. "Two Persian Wills of Hajj 'Ali Quli Khan Sardar As'ad." *Journal of the American Oriental Society* (1975): 645–50.
Gellner, Ernest. *Muslim Society*. Cambridge, 1981.
Ghaffari, Yaqub. *Tarikh-i Ijtima'i-yi Kuhgiluya va Buyr Ahmad*. Isfahan, 1379/2000.
Gilmartin, David. "Scientific Empire and Imperial Science: Colonialism and Irrigation Technology in the Indus Basin." *The Journal of Asian Studies* 53, no. 4 (1994): 1127–49.
Gilmour, David. *Curzon: Imperial Statesman*. London, 1994.
Guha, Ranajit. *Elementary Aspects of Peasant Insurgency in Colonial India*. Durham, NC, 1999 [1983].
——. *Select Subaltern Studies*. Oxford, 1988.
Guli, Amin. *Tarikh-i Siyasi va Ijtima'i-yi Turkmenha*. Tehran, 1366/1987.
Gulzari, Mas'ud. *Kirmanshahan va Kurdistan*. Tehran, 1357/1978.
Hambly, Gavin. "Agha Muhammad Khun Qajar and the Establishment of the Qajar Dynasty." In *Cambridge History of Iran,* vol. 7: *From Nadir Shah to the Islamic Republic*. Cambridge, 1991.
——. "Iran during the Reign of Fath 'Ali Shah and Muhammad Shah," *The Cambridge History of Iran*, vol. 7: *From Nadir Shah to the Islamic Republic*. Cambridge, 1991, 144–73.
Hardinge, Arthur. *A Diplomatist in the East*. London, 1928.

Harrison, J. V. "The Bakhtiyari Country, South-Western Persia." *Geographical Journal* 80 (1932): 193–210.

Hartley, A. C. "The Anglo-Persian Oil Company's Pipelines in Persia," *Transactions of the Institution of Shipbuilders and Engineers in Scotland 1934*, no. 921: 85–128.

Hatami, 'Aziz. *Isfahan*. Tehran, 1341/1962.

Headrick, Daniel. *The Tentacles of Progress: Technology Transfer in the Age of Imperialism*. New York, 1988.

Hidayat, Mukhbir al-Saltana. *Khatirat va Khatarat*. Tehran, 1344/1965.

Hodgson, Marshall. *The Venture of Islam: Conscience and History in a World Civilization*, vols. 1 and 2. Chicago, 1961.

Holtzer, Ernst. *Persien Vor 113 Jahren*. Tehran, 1354/1975.

Hunarfar, Lutfallah. *Ganjina-yi Asar-i Tarikhi-yi Isfahan*. Tehran, 1344/1965.

Husayni, Bijhan. *Ash'ar va Taranaha-yi Mardumi-yi Bakhtiyari bi Inzimam-i Sharh-i Jangha va Hamasaha*. Isfahan, 1376/1997.

Idivandi, Hafiz. *Nigarishi bar Il-i Bakhtiyari*. Ahvaz, 1377/1998.

Imam Shushtari, Sayyid Muhammad 'Ali. *Tarikh-i Jughrafiya-yi Khuzistan*. Tehran, 1321/1952.

Inalcik, Halil. *An Economic and Social History of the Ottoman Empire*, vol. 1: *1300–1600*. Cambridge, 1994.

——. The Yuruks: Their Origins, Expansion, and Economic Role." In *Medieval Carpets and Textiles: Mediterranean Carpets, 1400–1600*, vol. 1. London, 1986.

Iqbal, 'Abbas. *Mirza Taqi Khan Amir Kabir*. Edited by Iraj Afshar. Tehran, 1340/1961.

Iranian Cultural Heritage Organization, *Hazar Jilva-yi Zindagi: Tasvirha-yi Ernst Hoeltzer dar Ahd-i Nasiri*. Tehran, 1382/2004.

Irons, William. *The Yomut Turkmen*. Ann Arbor, Mich., 1354/1975.

Issawi, Charles. *The Economic History of Iran, 1800–1914*. Chicago, 1971.

I'timadi, Siyavash. *Bakhtiyari dar Guzargah-i Zaman*. Tehran, 1381/2002.

Ja'far Quli Khan Sardar Bahadur. *Khatirat-i Sardar As'ad Bakhtiyari*. Edited by Iraj Afshar. Tehran, 1378/1999.

Jamalzada, Muhammad 'Ali. *Ganji-i Shaygan*. Berlin, 1335/1956.

——. *Isfahan is Half the World: Memories of a Persian Boyhood*. Princeton, 1983.

Kalam, 'Ali Javahir. *Zinda Rud*. Tehran, 1969.

Karshenas, Massoud. *Oil, State and Industrialization in Iran*. Cambridge, 1990.

Kasaba, Reşat. *A Moveable Empire: Ottoman Nomads, Migrants, and Refugees*. Seattle, 2009.

Kasravi, Ahmad. *Tarikh-i Pansad Sal-i Khuzistan*. Tehran, 1331/1952.

Katouzian, Homa. *The Political Economy of Modern Iran*. London, 1981.

Kayhan, Mas'ud. *Jughrafiya-yi Mufassal-i Iran*. Tehran, 1312/1932–33.

Kazembeyki, Mohammad. *Society, Politics, and Economics in Mazandaran, Iran, 1848–1914*. London, 2003.

Kazemzadeh, Firuz. *Russia and Britain in Persia*. New Haven, 1968.

Keddie, Nikki. "The Minorities Question in Iran." In *Iran and the Muslim World: Resistance and Revolution*. New York, 1995.

———. *Modern Iran: Roots and Results of the Revolution*. New Haven, 2004.

Keddie, Nikki, and Mehrdad Amanat. "Iran under the Later Qajars, 1848–1922." In *Cambridge History of Iran*, vol. 7: *From Nadir Shah to the Islamic Republic*, 174–212. Cambridge, 1991.

Khazanov, Anatoly M., and Andre Wink. *Nomads in a Sedentary World*. London, 2001.

Khoury, Dina Rizk. *State and Provincial Society in the Ottoman Empire: Mosul, 1530–1834*. Cambridge, 1997.

Kirmani, Nazim al-Islam. *Tarikh-i Bidari-yi Iranian*. Tehran, 1984.

Kunt, Metin. *The Sultan's Servants: The Transformation of Ottoman Provincial Government*. New York, 1983.

Lambton, Ann K. S. "Ilat," *Encyclopaedia of Islam*. 2d ed., 3, 1103–9. Leiden, 1986.

———. *Landlord and Peasant in Persia*. London, 1953.

———. "Tribal Resurgence and the Decline of the Bureaucracy in the Eighteenth Century." In *Studies in Eighteenth-Century Islamic History*. Edited by Thomas Naff and Roger Owen. London, 1977.

Lattimore, Owen. *Inner Asian Frontiers of China*. New York, 1940.

Lenczowski, George. *Oil and State in the Middle East*. Ithaca, 1960.

Le Strange, G. *The Lands of the Eastern Caliphate*. London, 1905.

Lindner, Rudi Paul. *Nomads and Ottomans in Medieval Anatolia*. Bloomington, IN, 1983.

Lisani, Abu al-Fazl. *Tala-yi Siya ya Bala-yi Iran*. Tehran, 1329/1950.

Lockhart, Laurence. "The Emergence of the Anglo-Persian Oil Company, 1901–1914." In *Economic History of Iran, 1800–1914*. Chicago, 1971.

———. "Histoire du petrole en Perse jusq'au début du XX siècle." *La Revue Petrolifère* Paris (1938).

———. *Nadir Shah*. London, 1938.

———. *The Record of the Anglo Iranian Oil Company*. Unpublished company record.

Longhurst, Henry. *Adventures in Oil*. London, 1959.

Losensky, Paul. "Reza Qoli Khan Hedayat." In *Encyclopaedia Iranica* 12, 2 (2003).

Mahmudiyan, Muhammad. *Zayanda Rud-i Isfahan*. Isfahan, 1348/1969.

Makdisi, Ussama. *The Culture of Sectarianism: Community, History, and Violence in Nineteenth-Century Ottoman Lebanon*. Berkeley, 2000.

Makki, Husayn. *Kitab-i Siya*. Tehran, 1329/1950.

———. *Zindagani-yi Mirza Taqi Khan Amir Kabir*. Tehran, 1360/1981.

Malikzada, Mihdi. *Tarikh-i Inqilab-i Mashrutiyat-i Iran*. 7 vols. Tehran, 1363/1984.

Marashi, Afshin. *Nationalizing Iran: Culture, Power, and the State, 1870–1940*. Seattle, 2008.

Martin, Bradford. *German-Persian Diplomatic Relations 1873–1912*. Oslo, 1959.

Martin, Vanessa. *The Qajar Pact: Bargaining, Protest and the State in Nineteenth-Century Persia.* London, 2005.

Marx, Karl, and Friedrich Engels. *The Communist Manifesto.* New York, 2002.

Matthee, Rudolph. *The Politics of Trade in Safavid Iran: Silk for Silver, 1600–1730.* Cambridge, 1999.

——. *The Pursuit of Pleasure: Drugs and Stimulants in Iranian History, 1500–1900.* Princeton, 2005.

——. "Unwalled Cities and Restless Nomads: Firearms and Artillery in Safavid Iran." In *Safavid Persia: The History and Politics of an Islamic Society.* London, 1996.

Melamid, A. "Communications, Transport, Retail Trade and Services." In *Cambridge History of Iran,* vol. 1: *The Land of Iran,* 552–64. Cambridge, 1968.

Melville, Charles, ed. *Safavid Persia: The History and Politics of an Islamic Society.* London, 1996.

Metcalf, Charles. *Ideologies of the Raj.* Cambridge, 1995.

Minorsky, V. *Equisse d'une Histoire de Nader-Chah.* Paris, 1934.

——. "Lur." In *Encyclopaedia of Islam.* 2d ed., 5, 821–26. Leiden, 1986.

——. *Tadhkirat al-Muluk.* London, 1943.

Mitchell, Timothy. *Colonising Egypt.* Berkeley, 1988.

——. *Rule of Experts: Egypt, Technopolitics, Modernity.* Berkeley, 2002.

Mrazek, Rudolf. *Engineers of Happy Land: Technology and Nationalism in a Colony.* Princeton, 2002.

Mukhbir, Muhandas Muhammad 'Ali. *Baluchistan.* Tehran, 1325/1946.

Munif, 'Abd al-Rahman. *Cities of Salt.* Translated by Peter Theroux. New York, 1989.

Mustawfi al-Mamaliki, Riza. *Jughrafiya-yi Kuch Nishini.* Tehran, 1377/1998.

Najmabadi, Afsaneh. *The Story of the Daughters of Quchan: Gender and National Memory in Iranian History.* Syracuse, 1998.

——. *Women with Mustaches and Men without Beards: Gender and the Anxieties of Iranian Modernity.* Berkeley, 2005.

Nakhai, M. *Le Petrole en Iran.* Brussels, 1938.

Nashat, Guity. *The Origins of Modern Reform in Iran, 1870–1880.* Urbana, IL, 1982.

Nikzad, Karim Amir Husayni. *Shinakht-i Sarzamin-i Bakhtiyari.* Isfahan, 1354/1975.

Oberling, Pierre. *The Qashqa'i Nomads of Fars.* The Hague, 1974.

Olson, Robert. *The Siege of Mosul and Ottoman-Persian Relations, 1718–1743.* Bloomington, IN, 1975.

Papoli-Yazdi, Mohammad Hossein. *Le Nomadism dans le Nord du Khorassan.* Paris, 1991.

Peirce, Leslie. *Morality Tales: Law and Gender in the Ottoman Court of Aintab.* Berkeley, 2003.

Perry, John. "The Banu Ka'b: An amphibious brigand state in Khuzistan." *Le monde Iranien et l'Islam* 1 (1971): 131–52.

——. "Forced migration in Iran during the seventeenth and eighteenth centuries."

Iranian Studies 8, no. 4 (1971): 199–215.
———. *Karim Khan Zand: A History of Iran, 1747–1779*. Chicago, 1979.
———. "The Zand Dynasty." In *Cambridge History of Iran*, vol. 7: *From Nadir Shah to the Islamic Republic*, 63–103. Cambridge, 1991.
Pirnia, Husayn. *Dah Sal-i Kushish dar Rah-i Hifz va Bast-i Huquq-i Iran dar Naft*. Tehran, 1331/1952.
Pomeranz, Kenneth. *The Making of a Hinterland: State, Society, and Economy in Inland North China, 1853–1937*. Berkeley, 1993.
Qashqa'i, Muhammad Nasir Sawlat. *Salha-yi Buhran: Khatirat-i Ruzana-yi Muhammad Nasir Sawlat Qashqa'i*. Tehran, 1366/1987.
Qasimi, Ahad. *Mughan Nigin-i Azarbayjan*. Tehran, 1377/1998.
Qasimi, Sayyid Farid. *Avvalinha-yi Matbu'at-i Iran*. Tehran, 1383/2004.
Qayid Bakhtiyari, 'Abd al-'Ali Khusravi. *Bakhtiyari dar Jilvagah-i Farhang*. Isfahan, 1379/2000.
———. *Farhang-i Siyasi-yi 'Ashayir-i Junub-i Iran*. Isfahan, 1381/2002.
———. *Tarikh va Farhang-i Bakhtiyari*. Isfahan, 1372/1993.
Quataert, Donald. *Miners and the State in the Ottoman Empire: The Zonguldak Coalfield*. New York, 2006.
Rabino, Hyacinth. *Tribus du Louristan*. Paris, 1916.
Ranger, Terence. "Colonialism, Consciousness, and the Camera." *Past and Present* 171 (May 2001): 203–6.
Rasheed, Madawi al-. *A History of Saudi Arabia*. Cambridge, 2002.
Raymond, Andre. *Cairo*. Cambridge, MA, 2001.
Richards, John. *The Unending Frontier: An Environmental History of the Early Modern World*. Berkeley, 2003.
Rogan, Eugene. "Asiret Mektebi: Abdulhamid II's School for Tribes (1892–1907)." *International Journal of Middle East Studies* 28, no. 1 (February 1996): 83–107.
———. *Frontiers of the Ottoman Empire: Transjordan*. Cambridge, 1999.
———, ed. *Outside In: On the Margins of the Modern Middle East*. London, 2002.
Ross, Elizabeth. *A Lady Doctor in Bakhtiyari Land*. London, 1921.
Sadiqi, Husayn Nur. *Isfahan*. Tehran, 1316/1937.
Safi-Najhad, Javad. *'Ashayir-i Markazi-yi Iran*. Tehran, 1375/1996.
Sahlins, Peter. *Boundaries: The Making of France and Spain in the Pyrenees*. Berkeley, 1989.
Said, Edward. *Orientalism*. New York, 1978.
Sa'idi Sirjani, 'Ali Akbar. "Haji Aliqoli Khan Sardar Asad Bakhtiyari." *Encyclopaedia Iranica* 3, 5 (1988).
Salihi, 'Ali. *Il-i Buzurg-i Bakhtiyari: Farhang-i Vazhigan-i Bakhtiyari*. Tehran, 1370/1991.
Sanjabi, Karim. *Il-i Sanjabi va Mujahidat-i Milli-yi Iran*. Tehran, 1380/2001.
Scarce, Jennifer. "Isfahan in Camera: Nineteenth-Century Persia through the Photo-

graphs of Ernst Hoeltzer." *Art and Archaeology Research Papers* (1976): 1–22.
Schayegh, Cyrus. "'A Sound Mind Lives in a Healthy Body': Texts and Contexts in the Iranian Modernists' Scientific Discourse of Health, 1910s-1940s." *International Journal of Middle East Studies* 37, 2 (2005): 167–88.
Scott, James C. *The Moral Economy of the Peasant: Rebellion and Subsistence in Southeast Asia*. New Haven, 1976.
———. *Seeing like a State: How Certain Schemes to Improve the Human Condition Have Failed*. New Haven, 1998.
Sevruguin, Antoine. *Sevruguin and the Persian Image: Photographs of Iran, 1870–1930*. Seattle, 1999.
Sha'bani, Riza. *Tarikh-i Ijtima'i-yi Iran dar 'Asr-i Afshariya*. 2 vols. Tehran, 1377/1998.
Shahbazi, 'Abdallah. *Il-i Nashinakhti, Pajhuhishi dar Kuh Nishinan-i Surkhi-yi Fars*. Tehran, 1367/1988.
Shahnavaz, Shahbaz. *Britain and the Opening Up of South-West Persia, 1880–1914: A Study in Imperialism and Economic Dependence*. London, 2005.
Shahuni, Danish 'Abbas. *Tarikh-i Masjid-i Sulayman*. Tehran, 1372/1993.
Shaw, Brent D. "Bandit Highlands and Lowland Peace: The Mountains of Isauria-Cicilia." *Journal of the Economic and Social History of the Orient* 33, no. 2 (1990): 199–233.
———. "Bandit Highlands and Lowland Peace: The Mountains of Isauria-Cicilia." *Journal of the Economic and Social History of the Orient* 33, no. 3 (1990): 237–70.
Shawqi, 'Abbas. *Dasht-i Gurgan*. Tehran, 1314/1935.
Sheikholeslami, A. Reza. *The Structure of Central Authority in Qajar Iran, 1871–1896*. Atlanta, GA, 1997.
Sistani, Iraj Afshar. *Muqaddima-yi bar Shinakht-i Ilha, Chadurnishinan va Tavayif-i 'Ashayiri-yi Iran*. Tehran, 1366/1987.
———. *Nigahi bi Sistan va Baluchistan*. Tehran, 1363/1984.
Spooner, Brian. "City and River in Iran: Urbanization and Irrigation of the Iranian Plateau." *Studies on Isfahan: Proceeding of the Isfahan Colloquium, Journal of Iranian Studies* 7, nos. 3–4 (1974), part 2: 681–712.
Stein, Aurel. *Old Routes of Western Iran: Narrative of an Archaeological Journey Carried Out and Recorded*. London, 1940.
Stein, Donna. "Early Photography in Iran." *History of Photography* 7, no. 4 (1983): 257–91.
———. "Three Photographic Traditions in Nineteenth-Century Iran." In *Muqarnas: An Annual on Islamic Art and Architecture*. Leiden, 1989.
Stoler, Ann. *Capitalism and Confrontation in Sumatra's Plantation Belt, 1870–1979*. New Haven, 1985.
Studies on Isfahan: Proceedings of the Isfahan Colloquium. Iranian Studies 7 (1974).
Tahmasbpur, Muhammad Riza. *Nasir al-Din, Shah-i 'Akas*. Tehran, 1381/2002.
Tapper, Richard. "The Case of Shahsevan," *The Making of Modern Iran: State and*

Society under Riza Shah, 1921–1941, 220–40. London, 2003.
———. *The Conflict of Tribe and State in Iran and Afghanistan*. London, 1983.
———. *Frontier Nomads of Iran: A Political and Social History of the Shahsevan*. Cambridge, 1997.
———. *Pasture and Politics*. London, 1979.
———. "The Tribes in 18th and 19th Century Iran." In *Cambridge History of Iran*, vol. 7: *From Nadir Shah to the Islamic Republic*. Cambridge, 1991.
Tavakoli-Targhi, Mohamad. *Refashioning Iran: Orientalism, Occidentalism, and Historiography*. New York, 2001.
Taymuri, Ibrahim. *ʿAsr-i Bi-Khabari*. Tehran, 1332/1953.
Thompson, E. P. "The Crime of Anonymity." In *Albion's Fatal Tree: Crime and Society in Eighteenth Century England*. New York, 1975.
———. "The Moral Economy of the Crowd." *Past and Present* 50 (1971): 76–136.
Toledano, Ehud. *State and Society in Mid-Nineteenth-Century Egypt*. Cambridge, 1990.
Tsing, Anna Lowenhaupt. *In the Realm of the Diamond Queen*. Princeton, 1993.
Tucker, Ernest. *Nadir Shah's Quest for Legitimacy in Post-Safavid Iran*. Gainesville, Fla., 2006.
Uzhan, Sarhang Abu al-Fath. *Tarikh-i Bakhtiyari*. Tehran, 1345/1966.
Vahman, F. *West Iranian Dialect Materials from the Collection of D. L. Lorimer*. Copenhagen, 1987.
Valensi, Lucette. *Fellahs tunisiens*. Paris, 1977.
Vitalis, Robert. *America's Kingdom: Mythmaking on the Saudi Oil Frontier*. Stanford, 2006.
Walcher, Heidi. *In the Shadow of the King: Zill al-Sultan and Isfahan under the Qarjars*. London, 2008.
———. "Face of the Seven Spheres: Urban Morphology and Architecture in Nineteenth-Century Isfahan," *Iranian Studies* 33, 3–4 (2000).
Weber, Eugen. *Peasants into Frenchmen: The Modernization of Rural France, 1870–1914*. Stanford, 1976.
White, Richard. *The Middle Ground: Indians, Empires, and Republics in the Great Lakes Region, 1650–1815*. Cambridge, 1991.
Williamson, J. W. *In a Persian Oil Field: A Study in Scientific and Industrial Development*. London, 1927.
Wilson, Arnold. "The Bakhtiaris." *Journal of the Royal Central Asian Society* 13 (1926): 205–25.
———. *Military Report on S.W. Persia I: Bakhtiyari Garmsir*. Simla, 1909.
———. *Military Report on S.W. Persia II: Arabistan*. Simla, 1912.
———. *Military Report on S.W. Persia III: Bakhtiyari Country North of the Karun River*. Simla, 1910.
———. *SW Persia: Letters and Diary of a Young Political Officer 1907–1914*. London, 1942.

Windfuhr, Gernot. "The Bakhtiyari Dialect." *Encyclopaedia Iranica* 3, 5 (1988).

Worster, Donald. *Dust Bowl: The Southern Plains in the 1930s*. New York, 1979.

——. *A River Running West: The Life of John Wesley Powell*. New York, 2001.

——. *Rivers of Empire: Water, Aridity, and the Growth of the American West*. New York, 1985.

Wright, Denis. *The British amongst the Persians*. London, 1977.

Yaghma'i, Iqbal. *Baluchistan va Sistan*. Tehran, 1355/1976.

Yaghoubian, David. "Hagop Hagopian: An Armenian Truck Driver in Iran." *Struggle and Survival in the Modern Middle East*. Berkeley, 1993.

Yasimi, Rashid. *Kurd va Payvastigi-yi Najhadi va Tarikhi–yi U*. Tehran, 1363/1984.

Zagarell, A. "Nomad and Settled in the Bakhtiyari Mountains." *Sociologus* 25 (1975): 127–38.

——. *The Prehistory of the Northeast Bakhtiyari Mountains, Iran: The Rise of a Highland Way of Life*. Weisbaden, 1982.

Zangueneh, A. *Le Petrole en Perse*. Paris, 1933.

Zhukovsky, V. A. *Materiali dlya Izucheniya Persidskikh Marechii. Narechie Bakhtiarov Chekharlengi Kheftleng*. Petrograd, 1922.

Zuka, Yahya. *Tarikh-i 'Akasi va 'Akasan-i Pishgam dar Iran*. Tehran, 1376/1997.

INDEX

A

B

C

D

E

F

G

K

L

M

N

P

Q

R

S